Zen Ritual

D1674170

Zen Ritual

Studies of Zen Buddhist Theory in Practice

EDITED BY STEVEN HEINE
AND DALE S. WRIGHT

OXFORD

UNIVERSITY PRESS

2008

OXFORD
UNIVERSITY PRESS

Oxford University Press, Inc., publishes works that further
Oxford University's objective of excellence
in research, scholarship, and education.

Oxford   New York
Auckland   Cape Town   Dar es Salaam   Hong Kong   Karachi
Kuala Lumpur   Madrid   Melbourne   Mexico City   Nairobi
New Delhi   Shanghai   Taipei   Toronto

With offices in
Argentina   Austria   Brazil   Chile   Czech Republic   France   Greece
Guatemala   Hungary   Italy   Japan   Poland   Portugal   Singapore
South Korea   Switzerland   Thailand   Turkey   Ukraine   Vietnam

Copyright © 2008 by Oxford University Press, Inc.

Published by Oxford University Press, Inc.
198 Madison Avenue, New York, New York 10016

www.oup.com

Oxford is a registered trademark of Oxford University Press

Library of Congress Cataloging-in-Publication Data
Zen ritual : studies of Zen Buddhist theory in practice / edited by Steven Heine and Dale S. Wright.
    p. cm.
Includes bibliographical references and index.
ISBN 978-0-19-530467-1; 978-0-19-530468-8 (pbk.)
1. Zen Buddhism—Rituals.   2. Spiritual life—Zen Buddhism.   I. Heine, Steven, 1950–
II. Wright, Dale Stuart.
BQ9270.2.Z46   2007
294.3'438—dc22   2006103400

9 8 7 6 5 4 3 2 1

Printed in the United States of America
on acid-free paper

Acknowledgments

We extend our sincere thanks to Cynthia Read for her continuing support for our series of edited volumes on Zen theory and practice, and her remarkably efficient staff at Oxford University Press including Daniel Gonzalez for their professional work on this volume. In addition, we would like to thank Aviva Menashe for her excellent editorial assistance.

Contents

Abbreviations

*D   Ōkubo Dōshū, ed., *Dōgen Zenji zenshū* (Tokyo: Chikuma shobō, 1969–1970).

*DZZ   *Dōgen zenji zenshū*, ed. Kagamishima Genryū, Kawamura Kōdō, Suzuki Kakuzen, Kosaka Kiyū, et. al., 7 vols. (Tokyo: Shunjūsha, 1988–1993).

T   *Taishō shinshū daizōkyō* [Japanese Edition of the Buddhist Canon] (Tokyo: Daizōkyōkai, 1924–1935).

S   Sōtōshū zensho kankōkai, ed., *Sōtōshū zensho*, rev. and enlarged, 18 vols. (Tokyo: Sōtōshū shūmuchō, 1970–1973).

ZZ   *Zoku zōkyō* [Dai Nihon zokuzōkyō] (Kyoto: Zōkyō shoin, 1905–1912).

*These are two different versions of Dōgen's collected works.

Notes on Terminology

First, aware that there are two acceptable systems of scholarly transliteration for Chinese (Pinyin and Wade-Giles), each at this point rather well known, the editors of this volume have allowed authors to work in the system of transliteration that they feel most suitable. Please see the appendix for Pinyin–Wade-Giles conversion table.

Also, there are a number of terms in this volume, both English and foreign words that are common in Buddhist studies, being used in various ways by the contributors, either italicized or romanized, with caps or in lowercase, as one word or separated, or with or without hyphens. Rather than enforcing uniformity in style, we have left these as the author intended. Examples include: abbot, Buddha, Buddha-dharma, Buddha Hall, Buddha nature, Dharma, Dharma Hall, *Fukanzazengi*, Mikkyō, Monks (Monks') Hall, rōshi, Sangha, Tripitaka, Vinaya, zazen, and *Zazenshin*, among others. In addition, please note that some authors have chosen to use diacritical marks for Sanskrit terms but others have not.

Contributors

PAULA K. R. ARAI received her Ph.D. from Harvard University. In addition to several articles and chapters in edited volumes, she has written *Women Living Zen: Japanese Sōtō Buddhist Nuns*. She is also currently completing a book manuscript, *Healing Zen: Japanese Buddhist Women's Rituals of Transformation*. Her research has been funded by two Fulbright grants, American Council of Learned Societies, Reischauer Institute, and Mellon Faculty Fellowship.

WILLIAM M. BODIFORD is professor of Asian Languages and Cultures at the University of California, Los Angeles. He is the author of *Sōtō Zen in Medieval Japan*, editor of *Going Forth: Visions of Buddhist Vinaya*, and associate editor of *Encyclopedia of Buddhism*. He also has authored many essays, articles, and translations concerning Zen Buddhism in particular and Japanese religions in general.

T. GRIFFITH FOULK is professor of religion at Sarah Lawrence College and co-editor-in-chief of the Sōtō Zen Translation Project based in Tokyo. He has trained in both Rinzai and Sōtō Zen monasteries in Japan and has published extensively on the institutional and intellectual history of Chan/Zen Buddhism.

STEVEN HEINE is professor of religious studies and history and director of the Institute for Asian Studies at Florida International University. Heine has published numerous books and articles dealing with the life and thought of Dōgen and the history and philosophy of Zen Buddhism, including *Dōgen and the Kōan Tradition: A Tale of Two Shōbōgenzō Texts*; *Shifting Shape, Shaping Text: Philosophy and Folklore in the Fox Kōan*; *Opening a Mountain: Kōans of the Zen Masters*; and *Did Dōgen Go to China? What He Wrote and When He Wrote It*.

TAIGEN DAN LEIGHTON has taught at the Institute of Buddhist Studies of the Graduate Theological Union, Berkeley. He is author of *Faces of Compassion: Classic Bodhisattva Archetypes and Their Modern Expression* and the forthcoming *Visions of Awakening Space and Time: The Worldview of Dōgen and the Lotus Sutra*. He is editor and co-translator of *Dōgen's Extensive Record: A Translation of the Eihei Kōroku* and *Dōgen's Pure Standards for the Zen Community: A Translation of Eihei Shingi*.

MICHEL MOHR is an assistant professor of religious studies at the University of Hawaii. His research focuses on Japanese religions, with a special emphasis on the Tokugawa and Meiji periods. His publications include *Traité sur l'Inépuisable Lampe du Zen: Tōrei (1721–1792) et sa vision de l'éveil* [Treatise on the Inexhaustible Lamp of Zen: Tōrei and His Vision of Awakening], 2 vols. (1997). Mohr's recent works include the article "Chan and Zen" for the *Encyclopedia of Philosophy, Second Edition* (2005) and chapters in *The Kōan* (2000) and *Zen Classics* (2006).

MARIO POCESKI is an assistant professor of Buddhist studies and Chinese religions at the University of Florida. His research focuses on the history of Buddhism in late medieval China. His latest publication is *The Hongzhou School and the Development of Tang Dynasty Chan*. His other publications include two books and a number of articles on various aspects of Buddhism.

DAVID E. RIGGS is currently a researcher at the International Center for Japanese Studies in Kyoto. He has taught at the University of California Santa Barbara and the University of Illinois. He received his Ph.D. from the University of California, Los Angeles, where his dissertation was entitled, "The Rekindling of a Tradition: Menzan Zuihō and the Reform of Japanese Sōtō Zen in the Tokugawa Era."

ALBERT WELTER is professor of religious studies at the University of Winnipeg, specializing in Chinese and Japanese Buddhism. His previous publications include articles on Chinese Chan, including the recent book, *Monks, Rulers, and Literati: The Political Ascendancy of Chan Buddhism*. He is currently researching the Chan scholiast Yongming Yanshou's Chan-based Buddhist syncretism and preparing a translation of the *Kōzen gokokuron*.

DALE S. WRIGHT is David B. and Mary H. Gamble Professor of Religious Studies and Asian Studies at Occidental College. His area of specialization is Buddhist philosophy, particularly Huayan Buddhism and Chan/Zen Buddhism. His publications include *Philosophical Meditations on Zen Buddhism*, and co-edited with Steven Heine, *The Kōan: Texts and Contexts in Zen Buddhism*; *Zen Canon: Understanding the Classic Texts*; and *Zen Classics: Formative Texts in the History of Zen Buddhism*.

Zen Ritual

Introduction: Rethinking Ritual Practice in Zen Buddhism

Dale S. Wright

Role of Ritual in Zen

Approaching the grand entrance to Eiheiji, one of Japan's premier Zen Buddhist temples, I am both excited and intimidated. I understand that once I enter this gate, every moment of my life for the next three days will be subsumed under the disciplinary structures of Zen ritual. Although I have already trained in the ritual procedures of the Sōtō school, this is the head temple of its founder, the renowned master Dōgen, and I realize how exacting and demanding their adherence to proper ritual will be. Upon entrance, along with a handful of other lay people who have accepted the challenge of this brief meditation retreat, I am given specific instructions on how to conduct myself through virtually every moment of my stay. The details seem endless and excruciatingly difficult to master—how, exactly, to enter the meditation hall, to address the teacher, to bow, to hold one's bowl while engaging in mealtime rituals, and on and on. Where best to draw the mental line between actual Zen ritual and other procedural routines of the Zen monastery baffles me. But virtually all life in a Zen monastery is predetermined, scripted, and taken out of the domain of human choice. Some of these routinized life activities stand out from others as explicit religious ritual by virtue of their obvious sanctity, by their relation to the founding myths or stories of the Zen tradition, and more. But all the routines of the Zen setting appear to be treated as essential to the life of Zen, and all life appears to be ritualized in some sense. Now instructed in proper ritual procedure, my brief immersion in Zen monastic life begins.

That Zen life is overwhelmingly a life of ritual would not always have been so obvious to Westerners interested in Zen. Indeed, early attraction to this tradition focused on the many ways in which irreverent *antiritual* gestures are characteristic of Zen. This side of Zen is not a misrepresentation, exactly, since classical literature from the Ch'an/Zen tradition in China includes some powerful stories and sayings that debunk ritualized forms of reverence. Huang-po's *Dharma Record of Mind Transmission*, for example, dismisses all remnants of Buddhism that focus on "outer form." It says: "When you are attached to outer form, to meritorious practices and performances, this is a deluded understanding that is out of accord with the Way."[1] Following the lead provided by that image, the *Lin-chi lu* directs its strongest condemnation to what it calls "running around seeking outside."[2] Such seeking is deluded and irrelevant because, from Lin-chi's radical Zen point of view, "from the beginning there is nothing to do."[3] "Simply don't strive—just be ordinary."[4] "What are you seeking? Everywhere you're saying, 'There's something to practice, something to prove' . . . As I see it, all this is just making karma."[5] Other now famous stories in classical Zen drive the point home, from Bodhidharma's provocative line to the Emperor that all his pious observances warrant "no merit" to Tan-hsia's sacrilegious act of burning the sacred image of the Buddha.

This critique of ritual piety in early Chinese Ch'an was later understood to be part of a larger criticism of any aspect of Buddhist thought and practice that failed to focus in a single-minded way on the event of awakening. Encompassing formal ritual, textual study, and magical religious practices, a full range of traditional Buddhist practices appear to have been submitted to ridicule—what do any of these have to do with an enlightened life, some Zen masters asked? In this antinomian stream of Zen discourse, ritual was simply one more way that mindful attention could be deflected from the central point of Zen. What the essays in this volume make clear, however, is that although slogans disdainful of ritual can be found in classical texts, the traditions of Chinese Buddhism appear to have proceeded in the same well-established ritual patterns as they had before the critique, even, so far as we can see, in monasteries overseen by these radical Zen masters. Ritual continued to be the guiding norm of everyday monastic life, the standard pattern against which an occasional act of ritual defiance or critique would stand out as remarkable.

The Korean Buddhist film *Mandala* provides a graphic image of this contrast.[6] In it a Zen master "ascends the platform" (see chapter 2 for an analysis of this ritual) in ritual fashion to present a distinctively Zen sermon.

Near the end he challenges the monks to respond to the paradox he has presented—a traditional Zen kōan. At a crucial moment in the ritual, however, filmmaker Im Kwon Taek has a defiant monk charge up to the master, snatch the ritual staff out of his hand, and break it in two. The monk appears to be scornful of this staid ritual pattern in Zen and demonstrates his desire to break out of it. But even this outrageous antiritual gesture is encompassed by the ritual occasion as a whole. Although perhaps shocked by the audacity of the young monk, all in attendance understand how defiance of ritual is almost as traditional a gesture in Zen as the ritual itself—an "anti-ritual ritual" that had been modeled for them in the classic texts of Zen.[7] The image we have of the great Zen masters is that they sought to deepen all Buddhist ritual practices by reminding practitioners that the point of any practice is the transformative effect that it has in awakening mindful presence. While Zen would ideally be about what goes on inside mental space, as a practice that takes place in the "outside" world of coordinated actions and human institutions, ritual is subject to certain risks, such as the danger that preoccupation with "outer form" fails to evoke inner realization.

This kind of critique of ritual struck a chord of appreciation with the first generation of Westerners interested in Zen. What American Beat poets and others began to see in Zen Buddhism was an antidote to the rigidity of postwar Western culture, and their response was to embrace the antinomian character of Zen with passion. For them, Zen stood for a form of spontaneous life that could not be contained within the regularity of ritual. Moreover, a forceful critique of "ritualized religion" had already been firmly established in the Protestant and romantic dimensions of Anglo-American culture that sought to stress inner feeling over outer form. Grounded in this legacy, the Beat poets could see in Zen a spiritual tradition that took enormous pleasure in mocking ritual. From this perspective, they would find most American lives to be "ritualistic" and their religion a dry "going through the motions" without ever encountering the inner soul of its vision. They saw religious ritual as inauthentic, formulaic, repetitive, and incapable of the intense, creative fever of true spiritual experience. At that time, the word "ritualistic" had many of the same dismissive connotations that the word "mantra" does today. To say that what someone has said is "just his mantra" is to say that it is essentially unthoughtful, repetitive, and formulaic, not something that ought to be taken seriously. Similarly, throughout the twentieth century, the Protestant critique of ritual held sway, implying that anything "ritualistic" is shallow, rote, and unconscious.

So, in 1991, when Zen scholar Bernard Faure wrote that "there has been a conspicuous absence of work on Zen ritual,"[8] what he was responding to was the fact that even three to four decades after the fascination with Zen began in the West, few scholars had gotten beyond the early attraction to Zen antiritualism to take seriously all of the ways that ritual pervades Zen life and experience. By the time Faure's book was published, however, Western intellectual culture was in the midst of a fundamental change of perspective, one that would cast new light on ritual and render it much more interesting than it had been for several centuries. Ritual was once again in an intellectual position to be taken seriously. This book—*Zen Ritual*—constitutes one stage in this resurgence of interest in ritual and attempts to focus the work of contemporary historians of Zen Buddhism on this previously neglected, but now obviously important, dimension of East Asian Zen Buddhism. Its guiding intention is to submit important elements in the history of Zen ritual to contemporary analysis.

The ritual dimension of the Zen tradition in East Asia took the particular shape that it did primarily by means of thorough absorption of two different cultural legacies in China, one—the Confucian—indigenous to China and one entering East Asia from India and Central Asia in the form of the Buddhist tradition. Long before Buddhism arrived in China, ritual practices and theory of ritual were well developed in the native Confucian tradition. The Confucian moral, political, and social orders were grounded in a sophisticated conception of ritual as the basis of civilization. The early Chinese character *li*, often translated as ritual, or ceremonial propriety, stood at the very center of the Confucian conception of a harmonious and civilized society. From this point of view, what regulates the desires, habits, and actions of the members of a social order is ritual activity in the sense of the patterns of proper interaction between all participants in a social hierarchy.[9]

In the Confucian worldview, the Way (Dao/Tao) was a ritual order, constructed by the ancient Sage Kings and modeled after the patterns of Heaven. This order was based on a naturalistic conception of the cosmos and was largely nontheistic. Ritual practice was not primarily intended to praise or influence the gods. Instead, it was understood as the model for both collective political organizing and individual self-fashioning. For Hsün-tzu, the most theoretically sophisticated early Confucian on this issue, ritual was the most effective way for human beings to understand and correct their uncultivated "original nature." Although Hsün-tzu argued for an innately evil tendency in human nature, he also recognized that human beings are inherently social and that natural human intelligence allowed for self-correction through the processes of ritual self-cultivation. Confucian ritualists took the behavior and movements of the sages as the model for ritual practice and sought to encourage all members of the society to shape themselves to some extent in their image.

No dimension of human activity and culture was thought to be exempt from the impact of ritual; ritual was understood to inform the human mind in every activity from social engagements to private reflection. For the Confucian ritualists, as for later Zen Buddhists, ritual practice ranged in quality and depth from introductory levels to the most profound, and these differences were thought to be evident in the difference between an ordinary human being and the great sages. At the outset, they assumed that ritual practice would entail discipline. It would restrain the wayward inclinations of ordinary, undisciplined minds. In this sense, ritual acted as an external constraint or pressure on the natural desires and uncultivated habits of those who had not yet been shaped by this order. Confucians realized, however, that as ritual practitioners matured, they would internalize these constraints, altering the ways they understood themselves and the ways they lived in the world. For the sages dwelling at the most humane level, Mencius claimed, ritual practice effects a profound joy, one that accords with the deepest nature of human beings. In this sense, ritual was the Confucian means for transformation and enlightenment, both of individuals in a culture and the culture as a whole.

The second cultural source of Zen ritual comes from the broader Buddhist tradition that arrived from India and Central Asia and spread throughout East Asia in the first six centuries of the Common Era. Here we find another tradition of exacting ritual practice, one focused somewhat less on communal interaction and somewhat more on the cultivation of individual interiority. Different schools of Chinese Buddhism inherited traditional Buddhist ritual practices and adapted them to fit the unique social structures of Chinese Buddhist monasticism. By the Sung dynasty when some Buddhist institutions began to be identified as "Ch'an" monasteries, numerous streams of ritual development had already coalesced from such sources as T'ien-t'ai, Hua-yen, Vajrayana, and Pure Land. As several of the essays in this volume will claim, the ritual practices of the Zen tradition are in full continuity with these other forms of East Asian Buddhism, and in many respects their ritual procedures are surprisingly similar, especially in China where "schools" of Buddhism inhabit the same monasteries and practice ritual together.

If we ask, "what kinds of ritual are characteristic of Zen Buddhism?" we must face two qualifications that preface an answer to this question. First, ritual traditions in Zen Buddhism have changed over historical time and differ from sect to sect and from region to region throughout East Asia. There are no overarching structures of orthodoxy that determine for all Zen Buddhists what ritual procedures are to be followed in a temple or monastery, and that has always been the case. Descriptions of Zen ritual, therefore, are either specific to one region or historical era or text, etc., or generalizations that address tendencies over historical time and geographical space. Second, there are difficult questions about what counts as a ritual. Should any regularly repeated practice performed in a standardized manner be understood as a ritual? If so, then virtually everything done in a Zen monastery is a ritual, including walking, bathing, manual labor, and on and on. Or does a repetitious practice need to make specific allusion to the most basic beliefs or vision of a religion before it becomes a ritual, or is there some other criterion that defines the concept "ritual"?[10]

In her state-of-the-art work on ritual, Catherine Bell cautions us against drawing too firm a line between "authentic ritual" and other "ritual-like" activities.[11] She advises against adherence to a set definition of ritual since this would shape our minds to see what we are studying in one particular light, shutting out other possibly illuminating perspectives. Instead, her approach, which we acknowledge in this book, is to focus on the specific contours of the practice itself and not be concerned about whether the phenomenon should be defined as ritual by adhering to one or another predetermined definition. Bell's approach is to identify "ritual-like" activities—characterized by "formalism, traditionalism, invariance, rule-governance, sacred symbolism, and performance"—and to attempt to understand these activities in their own context of meaning. For the study of Zen Buddhism, this opens many options, and each author in this book adopts his or her own approach. Previewing the phenomenon of Zen ritual, then, what kinds of ritualized activity will we find in Zen monasteries?

The ritual most frequently associated with Zen monastic practice is *zazen*, seated meditation. Indeed, it is from this longstanding Buddhist ritual that Zen (Ch'an/Sŏn) gets its name. Although variations in Zen meditation rituals are substantial, most Zen monks engage in this practice at least two times each day, once in the morning and once in the evening.[12] During my brief stay at Eiheiji, we engaged in *zazen* ritual for approximately six hours each day divided into sitting periods of roughly forty-five minutes each, but this was an unusual amount of time at the temple in which lay people were invited for introductory training. At the Japanese monastery Zuiōji, as described by T. Griffith Foulk, monks meditate between two and three hours per day when they are not in a time of more intense practice.[13] At the Zen Center of Los Angeles, *zazen* is offered twice each day for an hour and a half whenever the community is not engaged in more rigorous *sesshin* practice. In the monastic retreats described by Robert Buswell in Korean Zen monasteries, on the other hand, "upwards of fourteen hours of sitting daily... with between four and six hours of sleep" is typical.[14] Variations between monasteries, sects, and different periods of the calendar year are significant, but no variation undercuts the fact that *zazen* ritual is at the center of contemporary Zen monastic life as it has been for many centuries.

Among the rituals regularly performed in Zen monasteries, we can distinguish between two kinds: those practiced on a daily basis and other periodic rites that are less frequent and in some ways therefore more momentous. *Zazen*, as we have seen, is practiced at least twice each day, always at the same time and in the same carefully prescribed way. What other rituals occur with this frequency? Sutra chanting is one, often performed just prior to *zazen* or immediately thereafter and before both the morning and midday meals. Standing in order based on hierarchical rank, monks or nuns chant sutra passages collectively and from memory, and younger monastics are given specific instructions on how to do this upon entering the monastery. Following the chanting of sutras in the morning and just before noon, all participants engage in a very exacting meal ritual. A simple vegetarian meal is served to monks or nuns in the meditation hall, and at various stages, different dimensions of the ritual are observed, for example, the synchronized bowing, the setting aside of several grains of rice for hungry ghosts, the silence practiced throughout all meals, and the meaningful procedures for cleaning ritual bowls. Also daily, typically early in the morning, it is a widespread ritual custom for the abbot to make incense offerings in several of the halls of the monastery as a way to sanctify the space and the practices of mindfulness and awakening that will occur there. Finally, in some monasteries, the abbot's "ascending the platform" to present a Zen sermon is a daily practice, although in smaller and less prominent monasteries, this may be a less frequent practice.

There are also rituals that have accrued around kōan practices in Zen. No doubt the most significant of these, and the one most frequently discussed, is the ritual of *dokusan* or *sanzen* in which monks go to the abbot for private interviews. These ritual meetings between master and disciple are fraught with anticipation and foreboding and include all the anxiety of face-to-face interviews or examinations. Monks line up outside of the master's room, and one at a time enter the room with strict formality, beginning with a series of prostrations before the master. Instruction, typically on kōans but in principle on any topic at the heart of Zen practice, varies from individual to individual based upon each monk's practice and capacity.[15] During meditation retreats, this ritual may be required of each monk every day or possibly more than once each day, while during other periods of the monastic calendar they may be practiced much less frequently.

A long list of other rituals are practiced at greater intervals, and many of these are determined in accordance either with the calendrical cycle or with the cycles of a human life span (see chapter 1). Annual rituals fall into the first group. They include a New Year's celebration, often associated with rituals of purity, ritual celebration and remembrance of the Buddha's birthday and his enlightenment, rituals commemorating the founder(s) of the particular sect of Zen and/or the founder of that particular monastery, and rituals of prayer and support for the emperor or the nation (see chapter 3 and chapter 7). Still other rituals function as "rites of passage," rites timed to accord with particular phases of the monks' lives. Initiation ceremonies such as traditional Buddhist tonsure fall into this group, when monks are accepted into the order or the monastery, as do pilgrimage rituals, rites installing a new abbot in a monastery, and funerary rites, including those performed periodically for ancestors.

Participatory and Performative Functions

Instructions provided by the tradition on how to enact ritual movement and procedure often fail to communicate any sense of how these rituals function internally for practitioners. That, clearly, is one reason that the ritual practice of others is so easy to belittle. From an outsider's perspective, the rites performed by others will always seem hollow and devoid of meaning just by virtue of one's distance from them. No doubt, the best way to come to understand the point or power of a ritual is to engage in it oneself, even if only empathically.[16] At least, that is all I could really say to anyone following my few days of engagement at Eiheiji. In the act of participation, we sense and understand something that we will otherwise miss altogether. In order to appreciate the ritual dimension of Zen practice, therefore, we must move beyond describing these ceremonies in order to consider what they are and why Zen Buddhists might engage in them. This requires that in addition to asking ourselves what Zen Buddhists do, we also consider what effect their ritual actions might have in creating the kind of life that they envision. In thinking seriously about Zen ritual, we need to reflect on both the goal or the point of these continual ceremonies and how it might be possible that such a goal could be achieved through these particular ritual activities.

An ideal that runs all the way through the Zen tradition is that the goal of Zen ritual is enlightenment—the goal of awakening for individuals and for human beings collectively—however enlightenment is understood to occur in a given time and place. But it doesn't take much study to see that this ideal is not always or everywhere affirmed. Some practitioners, including even monastery abbots, do not demonstrate in their actions or speech that this is the case. And even where the goal of enlightenment is affirmed, conceptions of it vary in many ways, including the variation between mature and immature or enlightened and unenlightened conceptions. Ambiguities abound in both institutions and individual minds, and there is no such thing as a perfectly pure form of either one. Nevertheless, in the midst of all the complexities of human life and behind all of its failures, buried back behind other pressing motives, in its ideal form the overarching goal of the life of Zen—its very reason for being—is enlightenment.

So how does anything as mundane as ritual give rise to anything as exalted as enlightenment? The prejudice contained in this question still haunts our ability to understand the powers of ritual practice in Zen or in any other religious tradition. Reducing ritual to mechanistic habit, we fail to understand how a practice of ritual can bring about a disciplined transformation of the practitioner, in this case how Zen ritual can give rise to Zen mind. The key, of course, is the gradual, even imperceptible, scripting of character through mental and physical exercise. In the Zen tradition, ritual is a thoroughgoing disciplinary program, imposed at first upon the practitioner until such time as the discipline is internalized as a self-disciplinary, self-conscious formation of mind and character.

Early anthropological and sociological efforts to understand ritual practices sensed some of this capacity in ritual. Emile Durkheim's notion that ritual is the communal means through which a culture's beliefs and ideals are communicated to individual members of the society captures part of what we would want to say today about ritual in Zen. Zen ritual does communicate the vision of Zen to its practitioners. One shortcoming of this understanding, as we can see it today, is that its construal of the goal of ritual is far too conceptual. Zen ritual does much more than communicate "beliefs and ideals." Beyond communicating meanings, Zen ritual actually does something to practitioners. It shapes them into certain kinds of subjects, who not only think certain thoughts but also perceive the world and understand themselves through the patterns impressed upon them by the repeated action of ritual upon their body and mind.

Ritual establishes a context of experience in which certain moods dominate and desires, emotions, states of mind, and actions come to the fore. Zen ritual need not be understood as aimed at one specific goal; several may be operating at the same time. Even if we take "enlightenment" to be the ultimate goal of Zen ritual practice, it is still important to see that these rituals serve multiple characteristics of "enlightenment" simultaneously. A particular Zen ritual may foster a sense of humility and selflessness while simultaneously giving rise to mindfulness, self-control, courage, or wisdom. If enlightenment is profound in its consequences, the ways of understanding its multiple features and characteristics must be sophisticated. It is also true that the effects of a single Zen ritual may be one thing for a novice practitioner while quite another for someone more advanced in the practice. Character differences also mean that what one practitioner might glean from a ritual to shape his or her character will be lost on another.

In contemporary ritual studies, the view that ritual goes beyond the task of expressing or communicating cultural values to actually effecting fundamental change in a person's perception of self and world is called the "performative" approach. Rituals have an effect on practitioners; they perform a transformative function that is not captured in either reductive interpretations or interpretations that remain at the level of belief or conception. In a persuasive effort to form a theory of Buddhist ritual, Robert Sharf draws upon the performative theories of Gregory Bateson and Erving Goffman that liken ritual to play.[17] Ritual, he concludes, makes effective use of imagination to foster change in practitioners. Ritual practitioners proceed in the ritual "as if" things were different than they seemed before entering the ritual. They imagine a state of affairs other than common sense would dictate and proceed as if something other than that were true. Zen practitioners engage in *zazen* as if they were enlightened buddhas, and in that act of imagination, something really changes.

As Taigen Dan Leighton (chapter 5) puts it, *zazen* practitioners understand this ritual as one that "enacts" the enlightenment of the Buddha already resident within the practitioner.[18] When you "enact" something, you act it out, acting *as if* it were already the case. If you act out that pattern attentively and long enough, then, to some extent at least, it becomes true of your mind through the patterning powers of repeated activity and mental focus. Thinking affects acting in some way, and acting helps shape who you become. This is a pattern we can see clearly in Stanley Tambiah's sophisticated work on Buddhist ritual.[19] There, thought and action are brought together in the realization that thinking is itself an act, one that, like all other acts, has consequences. Tambiah's performative theory of Buddhist ritual seeks to avoid the modern tendency to privilege thought over action in order to understand how in ritual these two forms of action are inherently coordinated.

This new development in contemporary thinking—sometimes called "post-Cartesian"—moves away from a predominantly mental orientation in analyzing human culture by recognizing the extent to which the mental and physical are intertwined or "nondual." Taking this perspective in thinking about Zen draws our attention to the ways in which Zen practice is a very physical, embodied practice, and to the ways in which Zen mind is a manifestation or extension of something even more basic—Zen ritual. One way to understand this transformation in our appreciation of Zen is to see it in terms of a difference between Western Cartesian and post-Cartesian interpretations of Zen. From an earlier perspective, an immersion in modern, Cartesian ways of thinking leads us to understand Zen as a highly refined discipline of the mind. In some sense at least, it obviously is a mental discipline of this sort. But from the point of view of post-Cartesian thought, Zen is not reducible to this mental discipline because every mental exercise practiced in Zen is set in a larger context of ritual that is fully embodied and profoundly physical (on this dimension of Zen ritual, see chapter 6). Zen rituals involve postures, gestures, and patterns of movement. To make sense of this basic dimension of Zen, we need to engage its fundamental corporeality by understanding Zen as a specifically *embodied* practice.[20]

As I sit practicing *zazen* in Eiheiji, no one has to remind me of this fact. What the senior monks at the temple are teaching me, and what I am mastering, is how to move and hold my body in positions appropriate to the ritual. Although a few suggestions are made about what to do with my mind, the instructions are overwhelmingly about the comportment of my physical existence. My teachers assume that, in time, the mind follows the body and that getting novices into the appropriate postures and movements makes possible the acquisition of appropriately "Zen" states of mind. Moreover, what I feel as I sit in meditation is primarily my body—and not just feelings more generally. At one moment I am completely focused on the patterns of my breathing, and at another moment, just my knees. Then my buttocks, then my back, and at some point, I return to conscious respiration. Whatever learning of Zen I accomplish takes place in and through my physical existence. Zen is embodied understanding, and the mental states that practitioners achieve through it are not separate from this physical framework.

Wittgenstein and Heidegger, two designers of post-Cartesian thought in the West, claim that our most basic grasp of the world—our most fundamental way of understanding it—is the practical mastery that we have of our physical, embodied world. Fundamental knowledge, they assert, is "know-how," the deep knowledge we have through routines and rituals that have long since taught us how to get around in the concrete dimensions of our world. To have a Zen understanding, in this sense, is to be able to do it in the most concrete and not necessarily conscious way. Molding physical habits and practices within the highly structured environment of the monastery trains the body to move and sense and feel in certain specifically Zen ways. The practices of Zen ritual are forms of practical understanding and knowledge. They constitute a particular way of acting and being in the world that defines Zen. It is the ritual dimension of Zen that most directly opens the vision of Zen to its well-honed practitioners. Sensing my own awkwardness at Eiheiji as I attempt to imitate authentic Zen movements, I am in awe of those who have so clearly mastered these rituals and who therefore have been initiated into the kinds of mindfulness that correspond to them.

When modern Protestants formulated their devastating critique of ritual as a way of engaging in religious practice, their intention, primarily, was to challenge the link between ritual and magic—the view that if you do the ritual then, magically or in recompense, the gods or angels will do something favorable for you. In formulating this now obvious critique, however, they failed to see all the ways in which ritual action is linked to understanding—how bodily movement and mental state are tied together. This perspective now provides ample ground for appreciating ritual, once it has been decoupled from magic, and for understanding the importance and power of ritual in Zen.

Zen masters have often stressed the idea that the state of mind through which ritual or any other practice ought to be performed is a state of "no mind" or "no thought." At first glance, you may sense irony here, since the most common criticism of religious ritual is that ritual tends to be "mindless" or "thoughtless," a pointless activity of "going through the motions" as though the appropriate results will emerge magically. But Zen Buddhists mean something very specific by "no mind" since it is commonly identified with the goal of awakening. For Lin-chi, for example, "no mind" is the condition of someone "who has nothing to do," that is, someone who has transcended all purposes and all striving in a joyful and powerful life of the spirit.

Some Zen rituals, performed in the spirit of meditation or mindfulness, are intended to help practitioners step up out of ordinary thought processes—everything from rational analysis to daydreaming and mental wandering—in order to engage in a discipline of attention that is nonconceptual and focused on the present moment. We might say that these forms of Zen meditation ritual are essentially the exercise or practice of attention in which abstracted states of mind, including important states like purposes, are set aside. In order to stress this goal in meditation, some Zen masters claim that meditative rituals are "nonpurposive," that is, they are not done for any reason beyond the act of doing them. Therefore, when asked what they are doing or what they hope to accomplish when they are sitting in *zazen*, Sōtō masters will often say that they are "just sitting" (*shikantaza*), and nothing more.

Nevertheless, in spite of the mental intention and attitude of "just sitting" in a purposeless manner, it is not difficult to see that the purpose remains in spite of their disclaimers. Indeed, if you lack the purposes of Zen, you will also lack everything else about Zen, including *zazen*. This is so because the purpose of casting off all purposes in an exalted state of no mind still stands there behind the scenes as the purpose that structures the entire practice, enabling it to make sense and be worth doing from beginning to end. From the point of view of our analysis, the Zen practice of ritual must be mindful, meaningful, and purposive at the same time that practitioners seek to transcend these mental states in an embodied state of no mind. It is also important to remember that *zazen*—the Zen ritual of meditation—is a communal activity. Every practitioner engages in it with a somewhat different purpose in mind, with a slightly different conception of what it means to do Zen, as well as with a wide range of maturity levels between participants. Although all practitioners receive instruction that brings them together as a community or as members of a larger tradition, ways of understanding and going about practice still vary to the extent that individuals vary.

As in other religious traditions, practitioners of Zen Buddhism take great pride and comfort in the ancient origins and genealogy of their rituals. The claim is typically made that their primary ritual practices descended from the early founders of Zen and have not changed substantially over the many centuries since then (see chapters 4 and 8). Monks understand themselves to be practicing the "Pure Rules" of the master Pai-chang, who is credited with establishing the order and procedures for Zen monastic life. The constancy of ritual in daily life—the fact that it always *seems* the same, day after day and year after year—is a source of great comfort and conviction, not just in Zen but in all religions. But that constancy of ritual in daily practice serves to help disguise the reality of change over time (see chapter 9). Although extremely difficult to see from the perspectives of practitioners, historians today have the tools to see how, in fact, Zen ritual has undergone continual transformation over its many centuries of time and in its movement from one culture to another. Studying the history of Zen practice and conception through its substantial archives, historians have begun to document how ritual evolved to suit new historical situations, even when the changes occurring were not noticeable to contemporary practitioners because the ritual order always appeared to maintain the solidity of timeless tradition.[21] Zen practitioners today, however, are beginning to realize that this historical truth about Zen ritual—that it is not timeless and changeless—verifies and upholds the basic Buddhist principle, which is that everything is subject to change, even those things that give the appearance of permanence.[22]

Chapter Summaries

In order to begin the process of understanding Zen ritual in the long and complex history of its unfolding, essays in this volume hone in on ways that ritual was understood and practiced in particular periods, particular schools, and particular texts. The following is a summary of the essays:

Chapter 1: T. Griffith Foulk's essay, "Ritual in Japanese Zen Buddhism," summarizes the modern scholarly opinion that throughout its history, the Zen tradition rejected religious ritual as a legitimate means of carrying out its unique Buddhist mission and subjects this view to a contemporary historical critique. The author's thesis is that modern Japanese Zen scholars constructed the antiritual theme in Zen in order to make Zen more relevant to the modern age in the eyes of both the ruling elite in Meiji/Taisho Japan and Western intellectuals who tended to be dismissive of religious ritual. Pushed in this direction by their own historical circumstances, modern Zen scholars portrayed the entire Zen tradition as antiritual in basic intent and practice in spite of the historical record that belies this view. Foulk proceeds to describe the history of Zen ritual and presents a catalog description of ritual activities that are practiced in contemporary Sōtō Zen.

Chapter 2: Mario Poceski's essay, "Chan Rituals of the Abbots' Ascending the Dharma Hall to Preach," describes a ritual tradition that clearly goes back to the very beginnings of Zen. These ritual occasions, sometimes daily and at other times less frequent, brought the entire assembly of monks together in a formal ceremony in which the abbot of the monastery would present a sermon on Zen doctrine or practice. One of Poceski's themes is that although these were the occasions most often valorized as expressions of the Zen master's spontaneity, in fact these sermons followed highly stylized and scripted patterns of Zen thought. Only certain doctrines and formats of delivery were appropriate for these sermons, and even the greatest of the early Zen masters rarely diverged from the "pre-existing templates" that were bequeathed to them by their predecessors. Although the talks would sometimes involve transgressions or critiques of the ritual order, in fact they validated and maintained that order by carefully setting their remarks within the all-encompassing sphere of Zen ritual. Poceski's essay carefully describes this ritual context, providing insight into the significance of Zen sermons.

Chapter 3: Albert Welter's essay, "Buddhist Rituals for Protecting the Country in Medieval Japan: Myōan Eisai's 'Regulations of the Zen School,'" provides a concrete analysis of Zen ritual in the earliest stages of Japanese Zen, including an important discussion of the reasons given for the practice of Zen ritual. Welter's thesis, although it is difficult for us to see this from the perspective of modern Zen, is that the function of ritual in Eisai's account of Zen is to serve the communal needs of the society as a whole and is not primarily a tool in the quest for individual enlightenment. Looking closely at Eisai's seminal text, "Promoting Zen for Protecting the Country," Welter shows the extent to which Zen monasteries were collective enterprises in the service of the moral and social order to the nation. Existing at the will of the Kamakura *bakufu* leaders, Zen institutions sought to fulfill their social/political roles, and one of the most important of these was to conduct rituals for protecting the country. As Welter describes them, Eisai's "sixteen types of ceremonies" show clearly all of the ways in which Eisai sought to fulfill his obligation as a Zen master to the government and to Japanese society as a whole.

Chapter 4: Steven Heine's essay, "Is Dōgen's Eiheiji Temple 'Mt. T'ien-t'ung East'? Geo-Ritual Perspectives on the Transition from Chinese Ch'an to Japanese Zen," approaches the formative period of the establishment of Zen ritual in Japan based on sources from China by way of the sacred space within which it is conducted. Heine's thesis is that, although it has long been thought that Dōgen sought to design his new Eiheiji temple after the Sung dynasty Chinese model of Mt. T'ien-t'ung, a study of the ritual layout of both plans reveals more differences than similarities. The "geo-ritual" perspective taken in this study compares how the geographical settings and social environments of the two temple sites affect the way in which they implement Zen ritual. The author's conclusion is that Dōgen did not attempt to duplicate the Chinese model in rural Japan but instead "adjusted it to the Japanese context" by taking local social, political, and economic conditions into account. These differences in the structural layout of the monasteries underscore the conclusion drawn elsewhere that Japanese Zen ritual diverged in a variety of significant ways from the models available in medieval China, even though Zen leaders in Japan typically proclaimed otherwise for the purpose of legitimation.

Chapter 5: Taigen Dan Leighton's essay, "Zazen as an Enactment Ritual," addresses what many today would consider the central ritual of Zen—*zazen*, or seated meditation. Although *zazen* is commonly understood by way of instrumental logic as a means or method for attaining enlightenment, from the Sōtō Zen perspective initiated by Dōgen and featured in this essay, the order of cause and effect is reversed—*zazen* is "the practice-realization of totally culminated awakening." In developing this approach to meditation, Leighton traces its roots to Vajrayana teachings that were influential not simply in Japanese Shingon, but also in Nichiren, Tendai, Jōdo, and Zen.

Upon that Buddhist foundation, the essay develops the "unity of practice and realization" by showing how this theme appears in Dōgen's instructions for meditation ritual (*Eihei shingi*), in his extended essays (*Shōbōgenzō*), and in direct teachings to his monks (*Eihei kōroku*). The essay claims that when meditation is taken as "the expression or function of buddhas," rather than as a technique of spiritual acquisition, an emphasis on meditative awareness in everyday life is made possible.

Chapter 6: Paula K. R. Arai's essay, "Women and Dōgen: Rituals Actualizing Empowerment and Healing," engages in ethnographic study of rituals practiced by nuns in the contemporary Sōtō sect of Zen. Through surveys and interviews conducted among Sōtō nuns in the Nagoya area of Japan, Arai has articulated the ways in which two quite different rituals "shape, stretch, and define" the identity of participants. Both rituals—*Anan Kōshiki* and *Jizō Nagashi*—seek to evoke in participants an awareness of their own Buddha nature and, along with that, a strong sense of their own free agency and power. Arai finds that the central themes of these two rituals are gratitude and interrelatedness and shows how elements in these sacred ceremonies bring these qualities out in the experience of the women who participate in them. In addition, these themes are linked to Dōgen's own Zen teachings as a natural expression of his claims about the Buddha nature in all beings.

Chapter 7: Michel Mohr's essay, "Invocation of the Sage: The Ritual to Glorify the Emperor," describes the history and contemporary standing of a political ritual practiced in most Japanese Zen monasteries and temples today. This hour-long ritual—*Shukushin* (Invoking the Sage)—is performed at least twenty-six times each year throughout Japan. Mohr's meticulous research takes us into the distant historical sources of this ritual in China and into the lives of current Japanese Zen ritualists whom the author has interviewed and filmed. Mohr traces the concept of the sage into classical Daoist sources and the practice of rituals on behalf of the well-being and long life of the Emperor through early Chinese Buddhist sources up through the Sung dynasty Ch'an school. Describing the ritual as it is performed today in Japan, the essay shows how continuity of ritual tradition is maintained in Zen even into the postwar era in which the Emperor's role in maintaining the prosperity and well-being of the nation is minimal.

Chapter 8: David E. Riggs's essay, "Meditation in Motion: Textual Exegesis in the Creation of Ritual," seeks to uncover the historical origins of *kinhin,* the ritual of walking meditation as it has been practiced in the Sōtō school of Japanese Zen. Practiced today between periods of *zazen,* the Sōtō style of *kinhin* entails an exceptionally slow pace of walking in order to coordinate each step with a full cycle of respiration. Although Sōtō monks typically attribute this practice to the founding figure, Dōgen and his teacher in China, Riggs finds the origins of the practice considerably later than this in the eighteenth-century Sōtō leader Menzan Zuihō's writings, the *Kinhinki*, a brief text describing the practice of *kinhin*, and the *Kinhinkimonge*, a commentary connecting this practice to traditional Buddhist texts. Riggs maintains that these two texts are the appropriate historical origins of the now widespread ritual of walking meditation. The essay provides a translation of both texts, as well as a discussion of their contents and implications.

Chapter 9: William M. Bodiford's essay, "Dharma Transmission in Theory and Practice," provides our best example of ritual transformation in the movement of Zen from one culture to another. After describing dharma transmission in East Asia by highlighting the theme of the family explicit in it and then focusing on transmission in the Sōtō school of Japanese Zen, Bodiford describes a newly created ritual for the confirmation of dharma transmission in the Sōtō sect of North America. This ritual—called the Dharma Heritage Ceremony—was constructed by and for Sōtō Zen priests active in North America at the first national conference of the Sōtō Zen Buddhist Association, which was held in 2004 in Oregon. The ritual was created in the recognition of participants that an "accessible Western ceremony" to recognize and confirm dharma transmission was essential to the ongoing success of their Zen practice in North America. In this essay, Bodiford asks, "What issues arise when Zen teachers attempt to transplant these various aspects of dharma transmission into twenty-first-century North America?"

I

Ritual in Japanese
Zen Buddhism

T. Griffith Foulk

Introduction

"Ritual" is a word, and like most words it has a number of different
meanings. Some of the meanings have developed over a long period of time in ordinary language, while others have been recently
posited by scholars in such fields as anthropology, sociology, and the
comparative study of religion who wish to use "ritual" as a technical term. In principle, there is nothing wrong with stipulating an
unambiguous, technical definition of ritual for use in a particular
discipline or area of study. All researchers and authors have the prerogative of coining terms as they see fit. Social scientists become
profoundly confused, however, when they conceive of ritual as a
single, identifiable mode of human behavior and seek to determine its essential characteristics by looking for a common denominator in all of the various activities that get called ritual in ordinary
language.

Speakers of European languages routinely refer to a wide range
of individual and group activities and modes of conduct as "rites"
or "rituals," and we are generally able to determine from context
exactly which meanings of those ambiguous words are in play at any
given time. Nobody really thinks that the obsessive hand-washing
ritual of a neurotic is identical, in its "essence" as ritual, to the mat-
ing rituals of animals, the social rituals of shaking hands, getting
married, and crowning kings, or the religious rituals of offerings,

prayers, and penance. Rather, we understand perfectly well that a variety of things are conventionally called rituals for different, albeit related, reasons. Etymological and historical study may identify root or intermediary meanings of the words "rite" and "ritual," which derive from the Latin *ritus*, but it is clear that their semantic range has been extended in so many different directions by analogy and association that there is no longer any single denotation or connotation that all uses of the words hold in common. Past, established meanings of the word "ritual" may be catalogued and analyzed through a process of historical and philological investigation. New meanings may be freely floated by poets or stipulated by scientists at any time, although there are no guarantees that any of those will catch on and become a part of the conventional lexicon. In all of this intellectual activity, I believe, the way to dispel confusion and attain clarity is to bear in mind the lesson of the Buddhist doctrine of emptiness: there is no such thing as ritual in and of itself—no single objective phenomenon, the essential nature of which we might reasonably hope to ferret out.

Although I present a survey of ritual in Japanese Zen in these pages, I make no claims (and harbor no unexamined assumptions) concerning the essential characteristics or identifying marks of ritual. For the purposes of this chapter, I am quite content to work within the established range of meanings of the ordinary English word "ritual," with all of its ambiguity. I see no need to stipulate a more precise, technical definition. Indeed, the multivalence of the ordinary word suits my purposes well, for Japanese Zen Buddhists engage in a wide variety of communal and individual ceremonies, practices, and modes of behavior that we can easily and reasonably call ritual in one sense or another, without worrying about identifying the common denominator that would be needed to group them all together in a single class.

There are, of course, problems of cross-cultural interpretation and translation that arise when thinking and writing in English about Japanese Zen ritual. The mainstream Chinese monastic tradition to which Zen is heir developed a rich vocabulary of technical terms pertaining to "Buddhist activities" (C. *foshi*, J. *butsuji*), but none of them correspond very closely in semantic range to "ritual." There is a tendency in European languages to apply the label "ritual" to behaviors that appear more formal or schematic than is necessary to achieve some particular end, or stylized behaviors that display no evident connection between means and ends. We are inclined to withhold the designation "ritual" from behaviors (even highly repetitive ones such as work on an assembly line) that have an obviously pragmatic function and to think of ritual as activity that either (1) has a symbolic or religious meaning to those who engage in it, (2) is motivated by a quasi-scientific but false understanding of the way things really work, or (3) is a manifestation of some obsessive-compulsive neurosis. The distinction between "practical" and "ritual" behavior is deeply embedded in European languages and is shared by people with very different points of view on religion. Skeptics who do not believe that God, ghosts, or other supernatural agents exist or operate in this world are likely to regard any formal, observable dealings with them as rituals that are grounded in superstition and have no real effect. Believers may view those same dealings as sacred rites which through some mysterious means do achieve real results in this world, or they may engage in them as an expression or reinforcement of faith in a God who does not respond in any immediately obvious way. Social scientists may call behavior that lacks a rational connection between means and stated ends "ritual" but nevertheless discover in it some unexpressed but beneficial sociological, psychological, or biological function that explains why people keep on doing it. None of these ways of thinking are native to the East Asian Buddhist tradition, but they have affected the manner in which modern scholars, Asian as well as Western, have interpreted that tradition.

The modern Japanese scholarly embarrassment with and denial of ritual in Zen Buddhism, certainly, is a direct result of Western influence on Japanese intellectuals in the Meiji period and later. Apologists such as D. T. Suzuki (Suzuki Daisetsu, 1870–1966) and Nukariya Kaiten (1867–1934) were eager to cast Zen as an East Asian and particularly Japanese form of philosophy, psychology, aesthetics, or direct mystical experience—anything but a religion encumbered by unscientific beliefs and nonsensical rituals. To the extent that Suzuki acknowledged the presence of ritual in Zen, he either dismissed it as a tolerant concession to superstitious popular religion, explained it as a form of psychological training, or assigned it a symbolic meaning that was consistent with rational, humanistic values. Westerners interested in Zen, by the same token, are often attracted to the "practices" of seated meditation (*zazen*), manual labor, and doctrinal study but uncomfortable with the "rituals" of offerings, prayers, and prostrations made before images on altars. There is nothing to prevent people from making distinctions of this sort, but it is important to recognize that they are fundamentally alien to the East Asian Buddhist tradition of which Zen is a part.

The East Asian Buddhist tradition itself has no words for discriminating what Westerners are apt to call "ritual" as opposed to "practice." The Japanese term that comes closest in semantic range to "ritual" is *gyōji*, which I translate as "observances," but that term encompasses a very broad range of activities that Zen clergy engage in, some of which we might prefer to call "ceremonies," "procedures," "etiquette," "training," "study," "meditation," "work," or the "ritual sacralization of everyday activities" (such as eating, sleeping, and bathing).

In the first two parts of this essay, I summarize and critique the modern scholarly view that the Zen tradition rejects Buddhist ritual, or that it merely tolerates various religious rituals as a kind of concession to "popular" demand. It is my contention that, with the exception of modern scholars, leaders of the Japanese Zen schools have never, either in actuality or in principle, rejected the monastic conventions and ritual practices that are characteristic of the mainstream of East Asian Buddhism. As I have demonstrated elsewhere, the Chan School in medieval China was not the iconoclastic sect that modern scholars make it out to be; it was an elitist movement that arose within the Buddhist sangha and competed successfully for leadership of it.[1] The so-called transmission of Zen to Japan in the Kamakura period (1185–1333), moreover, was a replication in that country of the most conservative, state-sanctioned monastic institutions of Song (960–1279), Yuan (1280–1368), and Ming (1368–1644) dynasty China.[2] The Japanese Zen School is thus heir to a wide range of practices and rituals, most of which are generically Buddhist, not uniquely "Zen," although they have often been regarded as such in Japan. More than any other branch of modern Japanese Buddhism, it preserves monkish procedures and rituals that can be traced all the way back to medieval Chinese adaptations of Vinaya materials that were originally translated from Indic languages.

In the third part of this essay, I present an overview of the full range of ritual activities that are practiced in various Japanese Zen institutions today, including the observances that most concern ordinary Zen temple priests and those that most often involve the laity.

Part One: The Apologetics of Ritual in Japanese Zen

Much of what we think about the so-called Chan/Zen tradition of Buddhism in East Asia is the product of modern Japanese scholarship, which set the basic parameters of the field of the "history of the Zen lineage" (*Zenshūshi*) in India, China, and Japan.[3] That field, also known simply as "Zen studies" (*Zengaku*), originated in Japan during the Meiji (1868–1912) and Taishō (1912–1926) eras, when scholars (a number of them Zen monks) began to apply Western methods of textual and historical criticism to traditional accounts of the Zen lineage (C. *Chanzong*, J. *Zenshū*) dating from Song dynasty China, which had been handed down within the Japanese Zen school.[4] They were especially fascinated by the Song hagiographies of the Tang dynasty (618–

906) Chan patriarchs (C. *zushi*, J. *soshi*), which are replete with dialogues (C. *wenda*, J. *mondō*) in which they employ apparently iconoclastic, antinomian, or sacrilegious sayings and gestures as opportune devices (C. *jiyuan*, J. *kien*) to bring their disciples to an understanding. Inspired by that literature, and responding to the social and political exigencies of the Meiji era, Japanese historians conceived the idea that the spiritual geniuses of the "golden age" of Zen in the Tang had been sectarian reformers who literally (not merely figuratively or rhetorically) rejected the conventional modes of merit-making, worship, morality, meditation, and sutra study that characterized the mainstream Buddhism of their day. The conceit that Zen is a mode of enlightened spirituality unencumbered by superstitious religious beliefs and practices not only played well in early twentieth-century Japan, it also struck a sympathetic chord among a number of intellectuals in the West and even a few in China, each of whom had their own culturally and historically specific reasons to find it attractive.

For centuries prior to the Meiji era, the major schools of Buddhism in Japan, with Zen at the lead, had established themselves as a religion of funerals and memorial services for ancestral spirits. Those rites consisted chiefly of the generation of merit (*kudoku*) through sutra chanting (*dokkyō*) and offerings (*kuyō*) to buddhas, capped by a dedication of merit (*ekō*) to the spirits of the dead and prayers for their well-being in the afterlife. During the Edo period (1600–1868), the Tokugawa shogunate established the so-called parishioner system (*danka seido*), under which every household in Japan was required to affiliate with and support a Buddhist temple where such ancestral rites were performed. With the collapse of the shogunate and the opening up of Japan to Western influences early in the Meiji era, Buddhism came under severe attack, not only for its close association with the old, discredited regime but for its "superstitious" beliefs and "unscientific" views of the world, which were blamed for retarding Japan's progress in the great march forward of civilization. At the height of the anti-Buddhist sentiment in the 1870s, it looked as though the religion might be entirely eradicated.[5] Buddhist institutions managed to survive, of course, but only after losing up to eighty percent of their temples. In every branch of the tradition, moreover, reformers emerged who strived to make their religion more relevant to the concerns of a rapidly modernizing society.

During the later Meiji and Taishō eras, when all of Japanese Buddhism was struggling to recover from the severe attack it had suffered upon the fall of the Tokugawa regime, leaders of the Zen tradition felt constrained to rationalize their faith and practice, dissociating those from merely "popular" Buddhist beliefs in spirits and karma that were castigated by the ruling elite as backward, superstitious, and antithetical to scientific and cultural progress. In their struggle to present Zen as relevant to the modern age, they promoted the Zen training monastery (*sōdō*), with its hierarchical social structure and rigorous communal discipline, as a model worthy of emulation in schools, industry, and the military. They touted the practice of collective labor (*fushin samu*) by monks in training (*unsui*), suggesting that it freed Zen monasteries from reliance on lay patronage and provided a model for Zen practice by lay people in the midst of their professional lives. They held up the practice of sitting meditation (*zazen*) as something that business, military, and government leaders could use to develop character and gain strength for the great task of nation building. Recalling that samurai rulers had patronized Zen during the Kamakura period, they pumped up the idea that the traditional "way of the warrior" (*bushidō*) was intimately connected with the spirit of Zen, going so far as to promote Zen practice as a means of preparing soldiers to sacrifice themselves for the greater good of the emperor and the state. They championed Japanese Zen masters, Dōgen Kigen (1200–1253) in particular, as native counterparts to the abstruse genius philosophers of the West, such as Kant and Hegel, and reveled in the notion that Western-style rationality could never penetrate the profound "nondual" wisdom (*satori*) manifested in the Zen discourse records and kōan collections. And, as nostalgia for things Japanese asserted itself in the wake of widespread Westernization, they began to claim that many of the "traditional Japanese" arts such as calligraphy, landscape gardening, and tea ceremony (all of which actually derived from the literati culture of Song and Yuan China) were manifestations of the spirit of Zen. The idea that Zen has nothing to do with Buddhist ritual first made its appearance in the company of apologetic notions such as these, although it was far from consistent with all of them.

Modern Japanese scholars have imagined a "pure Zen" (*junsuizen*) relatively free of Buddhist rituals for dealing with spirits and meeting the religious needs of lay patrons, which existed in the "golden age" of the Tang dynasty, especially in the Hongzhou school (*Hongzhouzong*) of Mazu Daoyi (J. Baso Dōitsu) and his disciple Baizhang Huaihai (J. Hyakujō Ekai, 749–814). The latter is traditionally credited with authoring a set of rules for Chan monasteries entitled *Baizhang's Rules of Purity* (*Baizhang qinggui*). No text by that name survives today, but an account of Baizhang's rules does appear in an early Song text entitled *Regulations of the Chan School* (*Chanmen guishi*).[6] Based on that text, modern scholars have posited that the characteristic features of Tang Chan monastic life were: group meditation (C. *zuochan*, J. *zazen*) in a sangha hall (C. *sengtang*, J. *sōdō*), public debate between a Chan abbot and his interlocutors in a dharma hall (C. *fatang*, J. *hattō*), individual instruction in the room (C. *rushi*, J. *nisshitsu*) of the abbot, and collective manual labor (C. *puqing zuowu*, J. *fushin samu*). These are said to be the essentials of "pure Zen."[7]

This view of the Chan tradition in the "golden age" of the Tang, however, is difficult to square with the well-documented circumstances of the Chan school in the Song and Yuan dynasties. A large and complex body of "rules of purity" (C. *qinggui*, J. *shingi*) for Chan monasteries survives from those periods, and the texts are inconsistent with the image of the "pure Zen" monastery that modern historians think existed in the Tang. The Song monastic codes contain procedural guidelines for many rituals, including worship of the Buddha, funerals, memorial rites for ancestral spirits, the feeding of hungry ghosts, feasts sponsored by donors, and tea services that served to highlight the bureaucratic and social hierarchy. The contents of the codes reflect the fact that Chan monasteries in the Song were large, public institutions that were regulated by the state and supported on a grand scale by lay patronage, land holdings, and various commercial ventures.

To mediate between the sparse description of Baizhang's system of monastic training found in the *Regulations of the Chan School* and the full-blown prescription of monastery organization and operation that appears in the Song and Yuan monastic codes, Japanese scholars have argued that the Chan institution "degenerated" between the Tang and the Song. They hold that by the time the oldest extant Chan code—the *Rules of Purity for Chan Monasteries* (*Chanyuan qinggui*)—was compiled in 1103, the "pure" institution founded by Baizhang had already begun to succumb to state sponsorship and lay patronage and that it had incorporated many "extraneous" elements from the mainstream Buddhist and native Chinese religious traditions. Kagamishima Genryū and Ogisu Jundō, for example, argue that Song period Chan became increasingly "syncretic" over time, being adulterated by the admixture of Tiantai, Huayan, Faxiang, and Pure Land (*jingtu*) teachings and practices, as well as Confucian and Taoist elements.[8] In Kagamishima's view, as Chan monasteries flourished with large land holdings and close ties with the aristocracy, the monks became secularized, shirking the rigorous practice of meditation in favor of cultural pursuits and material gain. The once lively, spontaneous practice of open debate between a Chan master and his students that is reflected in the records of the Tang patriarchs, Kagamishima says, devolved into an overly formalized, empty exercise, and sutra chanting services designed to produce merit for the satisfaction of the intentions of aristocratic lay patrons came to play an important role in monastery life.[9] From the standpoint of scholars such as Hu

Shih (1892–1962) and Yanagida Seizan (1922–2006), who have held that Shenhui's Heze school (*Hezezong*) and Mazu's Hongzhou school literally dispensed with the practice of seated meditation (*zuochan*) during the "golden age" of Tang Chan,[10] the fact that the Song Chan rules of purity included procedures for meditation might also be taken as a sign of degeneration.

The main sources that Kagamishima and other Japanese historians use to trace the evolution of Chan monastic institutions from the Song through the Yuan are the major rules of purity that survive from those periods.[11] The historical method they employ is one of diachronic comparison, which suggests that the later texts incorporate a greater number and variety of rituals than the earlier ones. The *Auxiliary Rules of Purity* (*Beiyong qinggui*) that was compiled in 1286,[12] for example, contains procedures for several rites that are not mentioned in the *Rules of Purity for Chan Monasteries* (*Chanyuan qinggui*),[13] compiled in 1103, including: sutra chanting services (*fengjing*) and prayer services (*zhusheng*) for the emperor; celebrations of the Buddha's birthday (*xiangdan*), enlightenment (*chengdao*), and nirvana (*niepan*); and memorial services (*ji*) for Bodhidharma, Baizhang, the founding abbot (*kaishan*), and various patriarchs (*zhuzu*). The *Imperial Edition of Baizhang's Rules of Purity* (*Chixiu baizhang qinggui*),[14] which was produced by decree of the Yuan emperor and compiled between the years 1335 and 1338, contains even more rites and more detailed procedural guidelines for carrying them out. Thus, scholars posit a continuous line of development from what appear to be the small, simple, independent Chan monasteries of the ninth century that are described in the *Regulations of the Chan School* to the large, complex, state-supported Chan monasteries that were regulated by rules of purity in the thirteenth and fourteenth centuries. And, in keeping with the notion that Chan in its original and pure form had no truck with Buddhist or state rituals, they describe that process as one of progressive "degeneration."[15]

Modern Japanese notions of the degeneration of Chan in the Song and Yuan dynasties are part and parcel of a view that Buddhism as a whole began to decline in China during the Song, that it became thoroughly syncretic and corrupt in the Ming dynasty (1368–1644), and that "authentic" Buddhism died out altogether in the Qing (1644–1912) dynasty. That opinion was voiced by many Japanese scholars in the Meiji and Taishō eras, and with such uniformity that a single example will suffice to represent the collective view. The following passage comes from *Outline of the History of Chinese Buddhism* (*Shina Bukkyōshi kō*) by Sakaino Satoshi (1861–1933), which was published in 1907. The book assays the history of all the major trends and schools in Chinese Buddhism from the first importation of the religion from India down through the Song and Yuan. In closing, Sakaino says:

The point that we should be especially aware of with regard to the last stage of Chinese Buddhism is the tendency toward fusion of the various teachings. The propensity for syncretism flourished not only within Buddhism, as was the case with Tientai and Chan, Huayan and Chan, or *nianfo* teachings and Chan. There was also a broad movement toward the combination of Buddhism and Confucianism, and a theory concerning the fusion of the three teachings—Buddhism, Confucianism, and Daoism—the development of which was, by the late Ming, quite phenomenal. From the Ming onward Buddhism progressively declined. At present, there is nothing to prevent us from saying that China has long since become a country without Buddhism. Even if there is some merely formalistic Lamaism, and some temples that retain their ancient names, because there is no longer anything worthy of being regarded as Buddhism, I see no need to say much about Qing dynasty Buddhism.[16]

Sakaino and most other Japanese scholars of his day imagined a golden age in the Tang and earlier when the various schools or family lines (*shū*) of Chinese Buddhism were "pure" and clearly separated from one another. They viewed the putative "mixing" of those lineages with each other, and with Daoism and Confucianism, as a kind of mongrelization that was degenerate and morally reprehensible.

Where did such attitudes come from? One key to understanding the disdain with which the Japanese viewed the Chinese Buddhism of recent centuries is the fundamental difference in the social organization of the Buddhist sangha in China and Japan. The various schools of Japanese Buddhism had a long history (going back to the Heian period) of maintaining independent monastic institutions, each with its own proprietary network of monasteries and hierarchy of clerics. In China, there was but a single Buddhist order, controlled by the state, so even when monks and nuns joined different schools (*zong*) that had specialized doctrines and practices, they shared a common career pattern of ordination and basic training, and they resided together in the same monasteries. Modern Japanese scholars who belonged to the various Tendai, Shingon, Pure Land, and Zen denominations all traced their spiritual lineages back to founding figures in Tang China. In writing the histories of their own schools in the Tang, they simply assumed (through a process of projection) that those had flourished in independent, sectarian monastic institutions. Although there was little concrete historical evidence from the Tang to support such views, neither was there much evidence that obviously refuted them. With regard to the Song and Yuan, however, Japanese scholars were confronted with clear-cut evidence (in the form of surviving rules of purity) of a Buddhist monastic institution that contained within it Pure Land, Tiantai, Tantric, Vinaya, and Chan teachings and practices, all apparently "mixed" together. In reality, the Buddhism of the Song was scarcely different from the Buddhism of the Sui and Tang in that respect, but the Japanese clung to their myths of original sectarian purity and labeled the Song as a period of incipient "syncretism" and decay.

Those attitudes on the part of modern Japanese scholars had some precedent in the history of Japanese Buddhism. In the Kamakura period, some Zen monks upheld the doctrine of the "equivalence of the three creeds [Buddhism, Confucianism, and Daoism]" (sankyō itchi), but others (e.g., Dōgen) rejected it; that debate, actually, was inherited directly from Song China. During the Edo period, when the Japanese were exposed to an infusion of Buddhism from Ming China instigated by the Chinese merchant community in Kyūshū, some Zen monks (e.g., Hakuin, 1685–1768) were dismayed by the apparent "mixing" of Zen and Pure Land elements that was rife on the mainland, while others (e.g., Kogetsu, 1667–1751) embraced it. Hakuin used the charge of "syncretism" to denigrate and blunt the influence of the newly imported Buddhism, which came to be known in Japan as Ōbaku Zen.

Early modern Japanese scholars of Buddhism were also sensitive to the nineteenth-century European judgment that the teachings of the historical Buddha, referred to as "original Buddhism" (genshi Bukkyō), was a rational and humanistic creed that had been corrupted by Mahāyāna polytheism and idolatry and reduced to utter ruin and moral decay by the syncretism and antinomianism of Tantra, especially Tibetan-style "Lamaism." Put on the defensive by the European philologists with whom they studied Sanskrit and Pali, the first generation of modern Buddhist scholars in Japan strained to defend the legitimacy of the Mahāyāna traditions to which they belonged.[17] In their eagerness to assert the "authenticity" of Japanese Buddhism, they sought to distance their own schools from the Qing Buddhism that had fallen under the influence of "Lamaism."

The Japanese disgust with the "syncretism" of Ming and Qing Buddhism may also have been influenced by nineteenth-century Euro-American ideals of racial purity and antipathy to miscegenation. The genealogical metaphor embedded in the very notion of "lineage" (C. zong, J. shū) in East Asian Buddhism was certainly conducive to conceptual associations of that sort. In any case, the notion that the Japanese people as a whole comprised a distinctive and superior "race" was a salient feature of Meiji ideology, and one that made it easier for Japanese Buddhist intellectuals to look down their noses at contemporary Chinese Buddhism. Ironically, their low opinion of the latter was shared by some Neo-Confucian intellectuals in China, such as Hu Shih, who blamed Buddhism—an "alien," superstitious religion—for China's failure to keep up with Western science and technology during the Qing.

In order to put the early modern Japanese dismissal of contemporary Chinese Buddhism into its proper historical context, it is important to understand that the Buddhist sangha (counting only ordained monks and nuns) in the late Qing dynasty and Republican period (1912–1949) was several times larger than its counterpart in Japan at the same time; the number of Buddhist temples in China was also at least twice as great.[18] China was hardly a "country without Buddhism" by any objective standard, and certainly not such a country in the opinion of Chinese Buddhists themselves. The demise of Chinese Buddhism that the Japanese had in mind, it seems, was something that had occurred on the spiritual, as opposed to the institutional or material, plane. The living flame of the dharma that had been passed from India to China and then Japan, in their view, had died out on the vast Asian continent and was kept burning only in Japan. That trope coincided nicely with the political and military ideology that Japan's destiny was to drive out the Western colonial powers and carry the torch of Asian civilization back to China and India.

The ambivalence that early modern Japanese Buddhist intellectuals felt toward China, the ancestral home of all their lineages, was especially acute for Zen scholars. Historians of the Tendai and Shingon schools could trace their traditions directly back to the golden age of Tang Buddhism. Those associated with the Jōdo and Jōdo Shin schools, too, could posit an ancestral line that led back through the Tendai school to the Tang. Historians of Zen, however, were forced to deal with the fact that their lineages had not been transmitted directly to Japan from Tang China but rather were offshoots of the Chan school of the Song. If the Chan monastic institution in the Song was already vitiated by syncretism, as many of them held, how could any of the pioneers who transmitted Zen from China in the Kamakura period have come into contact with the "pure" form of the religion that they allegedly promoted in Japan?

Sōtō Zen scholars have tried to resolve that dilemma by claiming that Dōgen, the founder of their school in Japan, rejected the worldly tendencies, aristocratic patronage, and syncretic doctrines that he found in continental Chan. What Dōgen actually transmitted to Japan, they argue, was not the Chan that he encountered in Song China but rather the pure Chan of Mazu and Baizhang that had flourished in China during the Tang dynasty.[19] Dōgen is said to have rejected ritual and stressed the exclusive practice of zazen. A passage from his *Bendōwa* (*A Talk on Cultivating the Way*) is frequently cited as proof:

From the start of your training under a wise master (*chishiki*), have no recourse to incense offerings (*shōkō*), prostrations (*raihai*), recitation of buddha names (*nenbutsu*), repentances (*shūsan*), or sutra reading (*kankin*). Just sit in meditation (*taza*) and attain the dropping off of mind and body (*shinjin datsuraku*).[20]

In the generations following Keizan Jōkin (1268–1325), however, Dōgen's pure Sōtō Zen supposedly became diluted by extraneous elements of esoteric ritual, folk religion, and various other concessions to popular demand, such as the performance of funerals and memorial services for lay patrons.[21] Dōgen's pure Zen was overshadowed for a long time, the story goes, but in the Edo period, partly in response to the threat of Ōbaku Zen, reformers such as Manzan Dōhaku (1636–1715) and Menzan Zuihō (1683–1769) began to study Dōgen's writings and restore the style of monastic training that he originally brought from Song China.

Another theory that makes use of the normative categories of "pure" versus "syncretic" Zen is one advanced by scholars such as Imaeda Aishin,[22] Takeuchi Michio,[23] and Martin Collcutt, who posit three stages in the transmission of Chan from China to Japan in the Kamakura period. As Collcutt explains:

> The first and largely syncretic stage, lasting for approximately fifty years, centered mainly on Hakata and Kyoto. Japanese Tendai monks who had journeyed to China were the principal agents. This stage was one of uneasy coexistence of Sung Zen teachings within the perimeter of the scholastic and esoteric framework of Japanese Tendai Buddhism. The only major exceptions to this initial syncretic pattern were the Kyoto monk Dainichibō Nōnin, a contemporary of Eisai, and Dōgen Kigen, who introduced Sōtō Zen teachings to Japan. Both these monks rejected accommodation with the established sects.[24]

Two monks held up as representatives of the initial, "syncretic" stage of transmission are Myōan Eisai (1141–1215) and Enni Ben'en (1202–1280). They are said to have made concessions to the established Tendai and Shingon schools, included facilities for esoteric Buddhist (*mikkyōteki*) rituals at their monasteries, performed prayer services (*kitō*) for lay patrons, and generally promoted a ritualistic, impure style of Zen. The second stage of acculturation is explained by Collcutt as follows:

> The syncretic phase was followed, during the second half of the thirteenth and early fourteenth centuries, by a period of consolidation

involving the vigorous introduction of what is frequently referred to as "pure" Chinese Zen to Kamakura monasteries by Chinese émigré monks. These monks were patronized by elite groups in Japanese society, especially the Hōjō regents. This stage saw the building of large-scale Zen monasteries on the Sung model, the imposition of characteristic Zen monastic regulations, and some diffusion of Zen-related Chinese culture.[25]

Collcutt considers Kenchōji in Kamakura, completed in 1253, to be one of the first examples of a full-scale Japanese Zen monastery built in the "pure" Song Chan style. The émigré monk Lanqi Daolong (1213–1278), installed by Hōjō Tokiyori as the founding abbot, is representative of this second stage. The third phase of acculturation, as Collcutt explains it, was one in which Chinese-style Zen took firm root in the religious, social, and political life of Japan:

> The beginning of the third stage of metropolitan Zen development can be dated from the opening decades of the fourteenth century, when Japanese disciples of émigré Chinese monks and Japanese monks who had studied in Chinese monasteries began to assume the headships of proliferating Japanese Zen monasteries. One of the most striking developments during this phase was the nationwide articulation of a system of official monasteries (*kanji*) known as the "Five Mountains" or *gozan* system.[26]

The monasteries in the Five Mountains system were dominated by Japanese Zen masters in the Rinzai lineage, which modern scholars further divide into "pure" and "impure" branches.

The line of Musō Soseki (1275–1351), for example, is stigmatized as having been overly intellectual and literary and too concerned with rituals for lay patrons. The founders of the so-called Ōtōkan line of Rinzai Zen,[27] on the other hand, are characterized as transmitters of pure Zen (*junsuizen*) who brooked no compromises and did not allow the Chinese-style monastic practice they established to be watered down by elements of native Japanese religiosity. They are described as heirs to the "original Zen of the patriarchs" (*honrai no soshi Zen*), meaning the Chan of the Tang patriarchs Mazu, Baizhang, and Linji. Daitō and Kanzan, in particular, are said to have lived frugally, stressed the practice of zazen, and shunned the elaborate ceremonies and literary diversions that had begun to sap the spiritual vitality of the major Rinzai monasteries in the Five Mountains system. Ōtōkan Zen purportedly stressed the "rigorous investigation of the self" (*koji kyūmei*) in the midst of seated meditation and all other activities. It is characterized as austere, disinclined to external display in the form of fine buildings or elaborate ceremony, free from the admixture of esoteric doctrine and ritual, and unconcerned with the popular propagation of religion. Ōtōkan Zen is further described as adhering to the principle of "a separate transmission outside of the teachings" (kyōge betsuden), and as using spontaneous, nonrational teaching "devices" (kikan), including kōans, shouts, and blows, rather than the intellectual explanation (richi) of Buddhist doctrines.[28]

Nevertheless, the story goes, by the end of the Muromachi period (1333–1573), even those streams of pure Rinzai Zen had been swamped by syncretic religious tendencies, the excessive involvement of leading monks in secular affairs, and the rise of mortuary sub-temples (tatchū), which resulted in the breakdown of communal monastic practice. With the advent of the parishioner system in the Edo period, moreover, Zen devolved almost entirely into "funerary Buddhism" (sōshiki Buppō). That dire situation was not helped by the invasion of another degenerate, syncretic form of Buddhism from Ming China, so-called Ōbaku Zen, which made use of the Pure Land practice of nenbutsu, or calling the Buddha Amida's name. Fortunately, a hero emerged to fight off Ōbaku syncretism, revive the pure kōan Zen (kanna zen) of the Ōtōkan line, and open training monasteries (sōdō) where the communal practices of zazen and manual labor were restored. That hero was Hakuin Ekaku (1685–1768), hailed since the Meiji as the single-handed restorer (chūkō) of Rinzai Zen and the spiritual ancestor of all living Rinzai masters (shike).

Holding up Dōgen and the Ōtōkan masters as the true, purist founders of their traditions, modern Japanese scholars have also been remarkably successful in convincing their fellow citizens, the rest of the world, and even themselves that contemporary (twentieth-century) Japanese Zen, in its essence, has nothing to do with beliefs in spirits and the rituals that are aimed at nourishing and propitiating them. One of the most influential early voices on this topic, in both Japan and the West, was that of D. T. Suzuki, who proclaimed in numerous publications that Zen was "emphatically against all religious conventionalism."[29] The following quotation is representative of Suzuki's mode of argument:

> Is Zen a religion? It is not a religion in the sense that the term is popularly understood; for Zen has no God to worship, no ceremonial rites to observe, no future abode to which the dead are destined, and, last of all, Zen has no soul whose welfare is to be looked after by somebody else and whose immortality is a matter of intense concern with some people. Zen is free from all these dogmatic and "religious" encumbrances.... As to all those images of various Buddhas and

Bodhisattvas and Devas and other beings that one comes across in Zen temples, they are like so many pieces of wood or stone or metal; they are like the camellias, azaleas, or stone lanterns in my garden. Make obeisance to the camellia now in full bloom, and worship it if you like, Zen would say. There is as much religion in doing so as in bowing to the various Buddhist gods, or as sprinkling holy water, or as participating in the Lord's Supper. All those pious deeds considered to be meritorious or sanctifying by most so-called religiously minded people are artificialities in the eyes of Zen.[30]

Suzuki knew full well, of course, that the very "artificialities" he denied in this passage are precisely the activities to which members of the Japanese Zen clergy (now, as in his day) dedicate most of their time, but he explained that as a concession to "popular religions":

How the hungry ghosts came to find their place in the scheme of the Zen conception of the world is a subject of special interest in the institutional history of Zen in China. Zen in its pure form has a tendency to become acosmistic, but in its "affirmative aspect" it accepts everything that is going on in the world of multiplicities. Even all the polytheistic gods including denizens of the air, of the earth, and of the heavens, and any other beings, who are living only in the realm of superstitional and traditional beliefs, are indiscriminately taken into the system of Zen. Each of them is permitted to have his or her place according to values given by the popular religions; and this is the reason why Zen has come to harbour so much of what I should call the Chinese Shingon element. The Dhāraṇī-sutras are recited; ancestors are worshipped; the prosperity of the ruling powers of the time is prayed for—although "to whom!" is the question still to be settled; the protection of the local gods is earnestly sought after; all the rituals in connection with the "departed spirits" are strictly observed; and all forms of exorcism are to a certain extent also practiced. The Feeding of Hungry Ghosts (*segaki*), which is observed at least twice a year during the Higan Season (lit., "other shore") is thus one of the excrescences added from the outside.[31]

Suzuki also explained the presence of such rituals in Zen monastic practice by assigning them a symbolic meaning that was consistent with rational, humanistic values. Thus, for example, he went on to argue that the ritual feeding of hungry ghosts (*segaki*) "is in reality sharing food, participating in the same staff of life, which symbolizes the idea of one grand community comprising all the spirits seen and unseen."[32] The ghosts, furthermore, "betoken the human desire to have, which never knows satiation. . . . We are all then hungry ghosts, though not necessarily departed spirits."[33] Sutra chanting, while admittedly conceived within the Buddhist tradition as a means of producing merit, is better interpreted as a form of meditation that "detaches one's mind from worldly concerns and self-centered interests."[34] The practices of "prayer-recitation, incense-offering, bowing, and so on," moreover, are simply an expression of gratitude and "appreciation of what the Buddhas, Bodhisattvas, patriarchs, teachers, and other personages have done for the Buddhist cause."[35] No reasonable Zen monk, Suzuki implies, would expect those beings to actually respond to the offerings and prayers directed to them.

Although Suzuki made the preceding arguments with respect to Zen monastic institutions that existed in Japan in the 1930s, the "pure Zen" that he conceived was, in its essence, an ahistorical, formless, spiritual entity. Thus, to back up his claims, he felt free to cite the exemplary behavior of various Chan and Zen masters who lived at very different times and places, as though the historical (not to mention textual) contexts in which they flourished were irrelevant. For example:

> When the importance of the spirit is emphasized, all the outward expressions of it naturally become things of secondary significance. Form is not necessarily despised [in Zen], but attention to it is reduced to a minimum, or we may say that conventionalism is set aside. . . . So Tanka (Danxia) burned a wooden image of Buddha to make a fire, and idolatry was done away with. Kensu (Xianzu) turned into a fisherman against the conventionality of monastery life. Daitō Kokushi (1282–1337) became a beggar and Kanzan Kokushi (1277–1360) was a cowherd.[36]

To bring this argument full circle, we need only add that another great free spirit of Zen, D. T. Suzuki himself, while living on the grounds of the Rinzai monastery Engakuji in Kamakura, held himself aloof from the daily, monthly, and annual rituals that its monks engaged in and boldly dismissed those as "excrescences" that had nothing to do with real Zen.

Views such as Suzuki's were widely accepted by intellectuals in Japan and the West. The British diplomat and historian George Sansom, for example, echoed contemporary Japanese academic sources when he wrote in 1931 that "a Zen teacher reads no sutras, he performs no ceremonies, worships no images, and he conveys instruction to his pupil not by long sermons but by hints and indications."[37] Sansom was stationed in Japan and could easily have observed the abbots of Zen monasteries engaged in all sorts of ritual, worship, and sermonizing if he had just taken a look, but he seems to have accepted the idealized description of "pure Zen" found in the modern scholarship at face value and simply repeated it for his English audience.

American Zen teacher Philip Kapleau harbored a similar set of misconceptions when he visited Japan some two decades later. In published excerpts from his diary, he wrote of his own first encounter with Zen monastic practice in Japan in 1953. The scene is the morning service at the Ryūtakuji training monastery (sōdō), which Kapleau visited with his American friend "P—":

> What a weird scene of refined sorcery and idolatry: shaven-headed black-robed monks sitting motionlessly chanting mystic gibberish to the accompaniment of a huge wooden tom-tom emitting other-worldly sounds, while the rōshi, like some elegantly gowned witch-doctor, is making magic passes and prostrating himself again and again before an altar bristling with idols and images.... Is this the Zen of Tanka, who tossed a Buddha statue into the fire? Is this the Zen of Rinzai, who shouted "You must kill the Buddha"?...The Kyoto teachers and S— were right after all....
>
> After breakfast the rōshi led us on an inspection tour of the monastery, set within a horseshoe of rolling hills in the quivering silence of a cultivated forest of pine, cedar, and bamboo and graced by an exquisite lotus pond—a veritable Shangri-la.... And what a view of Mt. Fuji, the majestic sentinel in the sky!...If only he doesn't mar it all by insisting we bow down before those images in the halls....
>
> O my prophetic soul!...he's brought us into the founder's room and is lighting incense and fervently prostrating himself before a weird statue of Hakuin.... "You too may light incense and pay your respects to Hakuin."...P— looks at me and I at him, then he explodes: "The old Chinese Zen masters burned or spit on Buddha statues, why do you bow down before them?"...The rōshi looks very grave but is not angry. "If you want to spit you spit, I prefer to bow."...We don't spit, but neither do we bow.[38]

Kapleau, we learn from his diary, had quit his job and gone to Japan in search of *satori* after attending dozens of lectures given by D. T. Suzuki (whom he refers to as "S—") and reading four of that scholar's books. There is little doubt that he and his American friend knew about Linji (J. Rinzai) and Danxia (J. Tanka) from the English writings of modern scholars such as Suzuki, Nukariya, and Hu Shih, all of whom gave the impression that the dialogues and anecdotes attributed to the Tang patriarchs in the classical (Song) histories of Chan were to be read literally, as historical documents.

That George Sansom was oblivious to what actually went on in the Japanese Zen monasteries of his day may be excused, perhaps, by the fact that his scholarly interest in Japanese culture was largely historical, not contemporary. Philip Kapleau's naive belief in the iconoclasm of Zen prior to his visit to Ryūtakuji is also understandable, given his reliance on the aforementioned scholars for information about the tradition. Inspired by the same sources, a number of Kapleau's contemporaries who belonged to the "beat generation" (e.g., Jack Kerouac) even saw in Zen the spiritual rationale for a life of hedonism and rebellion against social convention. No doubt their ardor for Zen would have cooled if they had known anything about the extreme emphasis on social etiquette, adherence to ritual forms, self-restraint, and conformity that actually characterizes Japanese Zen monastic training. But information about that training was not readily accessible to English-speaking audiences in the decades preceding or immediately following the Second World War. The only book on the subject was D. T. Suzuki's *The Training of the Zen Buddhist Monk*, which contains a rather abstract and idealized depiction of the Rinzai training monastery (sōdō) located at Engakuji in Kamakura in the 1930s. Suzuki's account is filled with quotations culled from the discourse records of the Tang Chan patriarchs, as if they themselves were the monks in training!

To this day, no ethnographic study has ever been published, in any language, that gives a detailed description of the organization and operation of the full range of contemporary Japanese Zen institutions. The only part of the Zen establishment that has been treated in either scholarly or popular literature has been the institution of the special training monastery (sōdō). There are several publications that combine drawings or photographs with explanatory text,[39] and some that describe the organization and operation of Zen monasteries in considerable detail.[40] In general, those works place a heavy emphasis on practices that are supposed to be characteristic of "pure" Zen: collective labor, meditation, kōan study, and individual interaction with a Zen master. They tend to gloss over the daily and monthly offerings and prayer services and the monthly and annual memorial services for deceased monks and laity, which in actuality occupy more of the monks' time and effort. And, they fail to explain the primary function of the training monasteries, which is to prepare members of the Zen clergy for their careers as specialists in mortuary rituals. Such works give the false impression that life in a training monastery is the norm for Zen monks. In reality, there are only about sixty Zen training monasteries in Japan and more than twenty-one thousand ordinary Zen temples. Although all Zen monks spend some time (a year or two, on average) in a training monastery early in their careers, less than five percent of the ordained Zen clergy is actively engaged in communal monastic discipline at any given time. The other ninety-five percent are ordinary temple priests who marry, raise families, and make a living by providing their parishioners (*danka*) with funerals and memorial services.[41]

In *The Training of the Zen Buddhist Monk*, D. T. Suzuki implied that contemporary Japanese Zen monasteries, with their daily periods of manual labor (*samu*), adhered to the same pattern of practice as their forerunners in the golden age of the Tang. Suzuki wrote that the Tang Chan practice of meditation in the midst of action "saved Buddhism from sinking into a state of lethargy and a life of mere contemplation," and he asserted that collective labor was still "one of the most essential features of the Zen life" in modern Japan.[42] In part, that argument deflected a criticism, often voiced in the West, that Buddhism was a "quietistic" or "nihilistic" religion. But Suzuki also maintained that collective labor in Tang Chan and Japanese Zen monasteries evinced a "democratic spirit":

> The term *puqing*, "all invited," means to have every member of the Brotherhood on the field. No distinctions are made, no exceptions are allowed; for the high as well as the low in the hierarchy are engaged in the same kind of work. There is a division of labour, naturally, but no social class-idea inimical to the general welfare of the community.[43]

Suzuki's invocation of democracy and social equality as Zen values was obviously an appeal to the sensibilities of his English-speaking audience, but he made similar assertions in his Japanese-language publications as well, and he was not alone in that respect. In 1929, for example, Inaba Meidō compared the role of labor in Chan and Christian (Benedictine) monasticism,[44] and he likened the egalitarian ideal expressed in the Chan principle of collective labor to that expressed in Tolstoy's utopian writings.[45]

The ostensible similarity between Zen and Western-style democracy or socialism, of course, was not an argument that played well with the right-wing nationalists and militarists who drove Japan into the Second World War. The more typical case made by Zen apologists in the prewar years was closer to one made by their predecessors in the Edo period. In 1940, for example, Fukuba Hoshū cited Hakuin's idea of "introspection in the midst of activity" to make the point that all productive members of society, be they military men, scholars, government officials, or merchants, could practice Zen while exerting themselves fully in the collective work of strengthening the nation.[46]

Over the course of the past century, ideology of this sort has proven quite effective in shielding the Zen establishment against attack, gaining support for it from leaders of business and government within Japan, and creating an interest in both Zen and "traditional Japanese culture" abroad. What the ideology has not done, for all of that, is reduce the emphasis on rituals for dealing with ancestral and tutelary spirits that has always been the cornerstone of Zen monastic training. Nor has it caused Zen priests to cease promoting mortuary rites among the laity or in any other way undermined the centuries-old relationship between ordinary Zen temples and their parishioners. The scholarly and monkish leadership that has produced the elitist view of "pure Zen" has done nothing to reform the training monasteries to bring them into conformity with the putative norm and has never tried to disabuse parishioners of their ostensibly misguided "popular" beliefs in spirits and karma. In effect, the post-Meiji portrayal of Zen as a mode of enlightened consciousness that transcends conventional Buddhist beliefs and practices has served as a kind of intellectual smokescreen behind which the Japanese schools of Zen have carried out their religious business as usual, perpetuating the funerals, me-morial services, and feeding of hungry ghosts that have been the ritual staples of the parishioner system from the Edo period down to the present.

Part Two: The History of Ritual in Japanese Zen

The so-called transmission of Zen from China to Japan in the Kamakura period is best understood as the replication on Japanese soil of the elite Buddhist monastic institution of Song and Yuan China. The mythology and ideology of the Chan lineage flourished within that institution, but it also contained many elements of generic and specialized Buddhist practice that, in China, were not identified as belonging to the Chan tradition. Moreover, it incorporated many aspects of Chinese culture that were not even Buddhist. The major Buddhist monasteries of the Song and Yuan, for example, imitated the architecture and ground plan of the imperial court; their internal bureaucratic structure was patterned after that of the state; and their social etiquette was basically that of the literati (scholar-bureaucrat) class, from which many leading prelates came. The philosophical, artistic, and literary dimensions of literati culture did admit to some Buddhist (and specifically Chan) influences, but on the whole they were more firmly embedded in the Confucian tradition. Nobody in Song or Yuan China, certainly, thought that the ubiquitous social ritual of drinking tea, the literati arts of calligraphy and ink painting, or the enjoyment of stone gardens (*shiting*) had any essential connection with Buddhism or Chan. When it was replicated in Japan, however, the entire package of Buddhist monastic forms, Chan literature and ritual, and literati culture eventually came to be identified as "Zen."

The monks who later became known as the founders of Zen in Japan, Eisai and Dōgen in particular, were quite explicit in their declarations that what they sought to transmit from China was not merely the lineage of Bodhidharma but true Buddhism in its entirety. That Buddhism can be summed up as comprising three fundamental modes of practice (C. *sanxue,* J. *sangaku*): morality (C. *jie,* J. *kai*), concentration (C. *ding,* J. *jō*), and wisdom (C. *hui,* J. *e*). Morality in Song Buddhism meant adherence to the 10 novice precepts (C. *shami shijie,* J. *shami jikkai*) and 250 precepts for *bhikṣu* (fully ordained monks) listed in the *Prātimokṣa* (C. *jieben,* J. *kaihon*) of the *Four Part Vinaya* (C. *Sifenlü,* J. *Shibunritsu*). Concentration comprised many techniques for focusing the mind, but for novice monks in basic training it took the form of communal seated meditation (C. *zuochan,* J. *zazen*) on the long platforms in a sangha hall (C. *sengtang,* J. *sōdō*). The cultivation of wisdom, at its most basic level, entailed the study of the Buddha's teachings as those were handed down in Mahāyāna sutras. The ability to read and recite sutras was a requirement for novice ordination. Sutra chanting (C. *fengjing,* J. *fugin*) was also the primary device for generating merit (C. *gongde,* J. *kudoku*) for dedication (C. *huixiang,* J. *ekō*) in conjunction with food offerings and prayers to buddhas, bodhisattvas, arhats, protecting deities, and ancestral spirits, which were the most common forms of ritual in Song Chinese Buddhism.

Once novice monks had gone through a period of basic training in the three modes of practice, they could begin to specialize. Some became experts in the Vinaya and the indigenous Chinese rules of purity that regulated monastic procedures and rituals. Those who wished to specialize in meditation gravitated to the Tiantai tradition, which preserved Zhiyi's compendia of methods for "calming and insight" (C. *zhiguan,* J. *shikan*) and maintained special facilities for the practice of various *samādhis* (C. *sanmei,* J. *zanmai*).[47] Becoming an heir in Bodhidharma's lineage of dharma transmission, which was the fast track to high monastic office within the Buddhist sangha, entailed mastering the literature of the Chan tradition and being able to reenact it in the ritual context of the "question and answer" exchange between master and disciple. As Chan adherents saw it, of course, it meant realizing and utilizing the wisdom of the Buddha inherent within oneself, not as a sutra exegete, but as one in full possession of the very "mind of buddha" (*foxin*).

Both Eisai and Dōgen, as I have noted in a previous publication, stressed adherence to moral precepts and the rules of monastic procedure and etiquette found in the Hīnayāna Vinaya.[48] They did so because they regarded the practice of morality, which had been treated rather lackadaisically by the Japanese Tendai and Shingon schools in the latter part of the Heian period (794–1185), as fundamental to the Buddhist path. They also emphasized the practice of communal seated meditation (*zazen*). Again, that was not because there was any particular association of meditation with the Chan lineage in China but rather because seated meditation was deemed fundamental to the basic training of all Buddhist monks there, whereas it was largely neglected by Japanese monks in the late Heian period. Dōgen actually criticized the use of the name "Chan/Zen lineage" (C. *chanzong*, J. *zenshū*) as a synonym for the lineage of Bodhidharma, arguing that what Bodhidharma transmitted to China was the Buddha Way (C. *fodao*, J. *butsudō*) in its entirety, not only the practice of meditation (C. *xichan*, J. *shūzen*).[49] In the emphasis that they placed on monkish morality, etiquette, and seated meditation, Eisai and Dōgen were scarcely distinguishable from Shunjō (1166–1227), another Japanese monk who had spent years training on the continent and then worked successfully to construct a Song-style monastery, named Sennyūji, in Kyoto.[50] Sennyūji was virtually identical in organization and operation to the monasteries founded by Eisai and Dōgen, but Shunjō had specialized in Vinaya exegesis in China and had not become an heir in the Chan lineage. Eisai and Dōgen, of course, were heirs to that lineage, so in addition to the three basic modes of Buddhist discipline mentioned above they worked to familiarize their Japanese disciples with the records of the transmission of the flame, the discourse records, and the kōan literature that served to distinguish the Chan tradition in China.

The claims of twentieth-century Sōtō school scholars that Dōgen rejected the "syncretic" aspects of Song Chan monastic practice and that he taught a form of "pure" Zen that consisted of an exclusive devotion to seated meditation are entirely groundless: they are nothing more than a projection of the modern Zen academic embarrassment with traditional modes of Buddhist ritual onto the founder of the school. As I have detailed elsewhere, every one of the ritual practices that Dōgen apparently dismissed in the famous passage from his *Bendōwa* that is quoted above—incense offerings (*shōkō*), prostrations (*raihai*), recitation of buddha names (*nenbutsu*), repentances (*shūsan*), and sutra reading (*kankin*)—was prescribed by him in great detail in his other writings.[51] Dōgen never criticized the *Rules of Purity for Chan Monasteries* (*Chanyuan qinggui*) for being "syncretic" or for any other reason. On the contrary, he held it up as a model for his disciples to follow, lecturing and commenting extensively on many of its provisions.

Nor does the notion that Keizan later embraced rituals that were originally spurned by Dōgen have any basis in historical evidence. All attempts to substantiate that view involve a faulty comparison of the *Eihei Rules of Purity* (*Eihei shingi*), a collection of six separate commentaries by Dōgen on various sections of the *Rules of Purity for Chan Monasteries* that was initially compiled in 1667, with *Preceptor Keizan's Rules of Purity* (*Keizan oshō shingi*), a set of procedures for calendrical and occasional rituals that was originally prepared by Keizan for his Yōkō Zen Monastery (*Yōkō zenji*) in Noto Province and only published under its present title in 1678.[52] Both texts came to be called rules of purity (*shingi*) in the Edo period (1600–1868), but beyond that they have very little in common. The idea that Dōgen wrote a comprehensive rules of purity in which he purposefully ignored or rejected many ritual practices that were later embraced by Keizan in the latter's rules of purity is a gross distortion of the historical record but one that is widely accepted by modern Sōtō scholars. Keizan is not criticized too harshly for diluting and sullying Dōgen's "pure" Zen, however, for he is regarded as a spiritual ancestor by a great many Sōtō clergy who trace their dharma lineages back to Dōgen through him. The general consensus among Sōtō scholars is that Keizan acted out of a combination of practical necessity and compassion for the common people. Since the Meiji era, Dōgen and Keizan have been honored in tandem as the two patriarchs (*ryōso*) of Sōtō Zen. Although that arrangement originated in what was basically a political settlement reached in the Meiji, it has since provided an umbrella under which Sōtō leaders can simultaneously hail the pure Zen of Dōgen as the essence of their tradition and continue, without fanfare, to uphold the practice of funerals and memorial services, which constitute the actual religious and economic foundation of contemporary Japanese Zen.

The notion that the founders of some Rinzai Zen lineages—Eisai, Enni, and Musō, for example—were "syncretists," whereas Lanqi, Daiō, Daitō, and Kanzan were "purists," similarly, is little more than a self-congratulatory fantasy promoted in the twentieth century by monk scholars who themselves belong to the Ōtōkan line, the sole surviving branch of the Rinzai lineage in Japan. As I have explained elsewhere, the facilities for practicing the four *samādhis* and rites of feeding hungry ghosts (*segaki*) that existed at Eisai's Kenninji and Enni's Tōfukuji—facilities that modern scholars have taken as evidence of a "syncretic" accommodation of Japanese Tendai and Shingon rituals—were all standard features of the Southern Song public monasteries that had Chan abbacies.[53] The prayer ceremonies (*kitō*) and sutra chanting services (*fugin*) that Eisai and Enni incorporated into their monastic routines, moreover, were not a concession to the "old Buddhism" of Japan: they derived from mainstream Song Buddhist monastic practice. There is no evidence whatsoever that either Daiō, Lanqi, or any other monk who trained in China and subsequently worked to propagate the Linji Chan lineage in Japan ever rejected the forms of Buddhist monastic discipline and ritual that were prevalent in the Song. In any case, the entire discussion of who built the first "pure" Zen monasteries in Japan, and the concomitant theory of three stages in the adoption of Chan, is based on the false premise that the Chan school in China was a sectarian movement that split off from the mainstream Buddhist institution and subsequently developed its own unique forms of monastic practice.

The Japanese Zen involvement in what is today disparagingly referred to as "funerary Buddhism" was not a corruption or watering down of a "pure" Chan practice imported from China, nor was it a concession to the religious needs or social demands of lay patrons. The Chan tradition in China had, at its very core, a vital concern with the commemoration and ritual nourishment of ancestral (patriarchal) spirits. Moreover, as William Bodiford has pointed out, the style of funeral rites promoted among the laity by medieval Zen monks was based on Song and Yuan Chinese monastic rules, not on preexisting Japanese customs,[54] and those funerary procedures "defined the standards that were emulated by other Japanese Buddhist schools."[55] Not only funerals, but a whole range of mortuary and ancestral rites that are now taken for granted by the parishioners of all Buddhist schools in Japan today were first introduced from China in the Kamakura period in conjunction with the so-called transmission of Zen.

Those rites were initially available only to emperors and the new warlord rulers of the country (the Hōjō clan) based in Kamakura: the few people with sufficient economic and political power to sponsor the construction and maintenance of large, Song-style (i.e., "Zen") monasteries. As noted above, modern scholars have identified Kenchōji in Kamakura, which had the fifth Hōjō regent Tokiyori (1237–1263) as its founding patron (kaiki), as one of the first "pure Zen" monasteries built in Japan. Although that category is itself confused and misleading, it is true that Kenchōji was modeled after the Ten-Thousand Years of Flourishing Imperial Rule Chan Monastery (Xingsheng wanshou chansi) on Jing Mountain (Jingshan) near the Southern Song capital of Hangzhou and that it was the first in Japan to have the words "Zen monastery" as part of its formal name: Kenchō Era Nation Promoting Zen Monastery (Kenchō kōkoku zenji). What is often overlooked or downplayed in modern scholarly accounts of Kenchōji is the fact that it was built as the ancestral mortuary temple (dannadera or bodaiji) of the Hōjō clan. As Collcutt notes, the merit of building the monastery was formally dedicated to "the longevity of the emperor, the welfare of the shogunal line and its ministers, peace under heaven, the repose of the souls of three generations of the Minamoto, of Hōjō Masako, and other deceased members of the Hōjō family."[56] It is clear from the survival of a mortuary portrait (chinzō) of Tokiyori that he was given a Buddhist funeral,[57] which entailed posthumously administering the precepts and shaving his head, thereby ordaining him as a monk. Tokiyori's son, Hōjō Tokimune (1251–1284), was ordained as a monk on the day of his death by the second abbot of Kenchōji, Wuxue Zuyuan (J. Mugaku Sogen, 1226–1286).[58] He, too, was given the funeral of a Chinese Buddhist abbot (C. *zunsu*, J. *sonshuku*), complete with cremation, the enshrinement of his ashes in a stupa, and the creation of a mortuary portrait (*shin*, a.k.a. *chinzō*) for use in the funeral itself and subsequent memorial services (*ki*).[59]

As Collcutt points out, "one means by which Zen monks extended their influence in society was by conduct of funeral services for important patrons."[60] It is not known exactly when the practice of monks conducting mortuary rites for lay men and women started in China, but there is an explicit reference to it in the *Rules of Purity for Huanzhu Hermitage* (*Huanzhu an qinggui*), written in 1317 by the eminent Chan master Zhongfen Mingben (1263–1323). Mingben stipulates that incense burning services on behalf of the deceased (*jianwang shaoxiang*) "should be the same for monks and lay people, men and women."[61] It is not clear from Chinese sources whether ordination of the deceased, which became the normal first step in funerals performed for lay people by Zen monks in Japan, was a part of lay funerals in the Song or Yuan. But it is difficult to imagine that émigré Chinese monks such as Lanqi and Wuxue would have initiated that practice in Japan if there had been absolutely no precedent for it in China.

What definitely did have a well-established precedent in China was the practice of dedicating the merit gained from founding and operating a Buddhist monastery to the ancestors and deceased family members of a single clan. Another good example of a Zen monastery built for that purpose is Rinsenji, which was founded in Kyoto in 1333 by the emperor Go-Daigo (1288–1339) as a memorial to one of his sons.[62] The Rinzai monk Musō Soseki was installed as founding abbot (*kaisan*). On the grounds of the main monastery, a mortuary sub-temple or "stupa site" (*tatchū*) was constructed that had a central worship hall (*shōdō*, literally "mortuary tablet hall") where offerings to the deceased were performed, a stupa (*tō*) for the emperor's son in an enshrinement hall (*shidō*) that was connected to the worship hall on one side, and a stupa for Musō (although he was still alive) in a founding abbot's hall (*kaisandō*) that was connected to the worship hall on the opposite side. Because there was an image of Maitreya (*Miroku*) installed in the worship hall, there were "three rituals" (*san'e*, literally "three assemblies") performed there, and the entire sub-temple was given the name San'e Cloister (*San'e-in*). In addition to the three connected structures just mentioned, the walled sub-temple compound of San'e Cloister included a stupa chief's quarters (*tassuryō*), which was the abbot's quarters (*hōjō*) of the cloister, and a kitchen-residence (*kuri*) that served to house and feed the small complement of monks whose job it was to tend the stupas and make regular offerings in the worship hall of food, drink, and merit produced by sutra chanting.

Kenchōji and Rinsenji are but two examples of the major Zen monasteries that were built as ancestral mortuary temples (*bodaiji*) in Kamakura period Japan. The large scale and high cost of such projects, as noted above, effectively limited them to clans that were at the very pinnacle of the social and political hierarchy. During the Muromachi period (1333–1573), however, not only the Ashikaga shoguns but members of the imperial family, warring states barons (*sengoku daimyō*), and wealthy merchants in urban areas such as Kyoto and Sakai (modern Osaka) found the wherewithal to patronize Zen abbots and establish their own ancestral mortuary temples, albeit on a somewhat more modest scale. Typically, the Zen institutions they supported were smaller regional monasteries and sub-temples that were built on the grounds of the major metropolitan monasteries. As the succeeding generations of abbots of those monasteries retired, they teamed up with wealthy lay patrons to have mortuary sub-temples (*tatchū*), which served initially as their retirement cloisters,[63] built for themselves and the ancestors of the founding patrons (*kaiki*).

Over time, the grounds of major Zen monasteries came to be crowded with scores of such mortuary sub-temples, each of which had its own abbot's quarters (*hōjō*) and kitchen-residence hall (*kuri*) in a walled compound. The vast sangha halls (*sōdō*) and kitchen-cum-administration buildings (*kuin*) that had once supported a large assembly of monks in Song-style communal training had all disappeared by the end of the sixteenth century.[64] Those facilities were no longer needed, for virtually all of the monks resided in mortuary sub-temples. The only observances that brought them all together at one time in the central buddha halls (*butsuden*) and dharma halls (*hattō*) of the main monasteries (*hon garan*) were major ceremonies such as the annual New Year's assembly (*shushō-e*) or Buddha's birthday assembly (*buttan-e*), and occasional rites such as the installation of an abbot (*shinsan-shiki*).

These developments took place largely within the rubric of the so-called Five Mountains (*gozan*) system of Zen monasteries that was centered in Kyoto and Kamakura and dominated by monks in Rinzai lineages. Sōtō Zen, meanwhile, spread in more remote rural areas, where it attracted the patronage of local power groups. In those areas, too, as Bodiford shows, "the regional dissemination of Japanese Zen Buddhism, and of the Sōtō school in particular, advanced hand-in-hand with the popularization of Zen funerals."[65]

Finally, during the Edo period, what had originated as the "Zen" (i.e., Chinese) style of funerals, memorial services, and lay family ties to ancestral temples became widely disseminated to the population at large with the advent of the state-mandated parishioner system (*danka seido*), a system that was conceived and implemented with the advice of prominent Zen clergy. All of the local Buddhist temples built during that period, not only those associated with the Zen schools, reiterated the architectural layout and ritual agenda of the Zen mortuary sub-temples, thus resulting in the style of "funerary Buddhism" that is widespread in Japan even today.

It was only in the Meiji period that scholar monks belonging to the Japanese Zen schools began to dissociate their tradition (in its "original" Tang form and timeless essence) from the funerals and memorial services that were, and remain today, its spiritual and economic lifeblood. Modern scholars belonging to other schools of Japanese Buddhism, too, have typically stressed the "pure" teachings and practices attributed to their founding patriarchs, such as Hōnen (Pure Land school), Shinran (True Pure Land school), and Nichiren (Nichiren school). They have conveniently ignored the fact that the rituals most frequently engaged in by lay parishioners at Pure Land, True Pure Land, and Nichiren temples in Japan today are not the trademark recitations of the *nenbutsu* ("Namu Amida Butsu") or *daimoku* ("Namu Myōhō Renge Kyō") but rather the funerals and services for ancestral spirits that were borrowed wholesale from the Zen tradition in the Edo period.

The modern Japanese Zen involvement with Buddhist ritual is most heavily indebted to the Song and Yuan rules of purity that found their way to Japan in the Kamakura period, but the history of that involvement is rather more complicated than one might expect. With the proliferation of mortuary sub-temples at the great metropolitan monasteries and the spread of ancestral memorial temples to the population at large, the Chinese style of communal monastic training that had originally been established in the Kamakura period had completely died out in both the Rinzai and the Sōtō schools by the middle of the seventeenth century. Just at that time, however, there was a new importation of Buddhism from the continent that began within the Chinese merchant community in Nagasaki and gained a following among the Japanese as so-called Ōbaku Zen. It received a huge boost when the eminent Chinese monk Yinyuan Longqi (1592–1673) came to Japan and was helped by the Tokugawa shogunate to build a large Ming-style monastery named Manpukuji in Uji, just south of Kyoto. In 1672, Yinyuan promulgated a set of ritual procedures for Manpukuji, entitled *Ōbaku Rules of Purity* (*Ōbaku shingi*),[66] that was based on earlier Song and Yuan rules of purity. When the Japanese saw the style of communal monastic training that was established at Manpukuji and other monasteries of the Ōbaku school, they were much impressed. Many monks who were interested in rigorous Buddhist practice gravitated to those centers. Leaders of the Sōtō and Rinzai schools of Zen were stimulated to initiate reforms that resulted in the reinstatement of many of the forms of communal monastic training that had been lost in the intervening centuries.

Like the Song Chinese Buddhist monastic institution that was replicated in Japan during the Kamakura period, the Ming Chinese style of monastic practice that took root in Japan in the Edo period as Ōbaku Zen was really just the latest iteration of mainstream Buddhist monasticism on the continent. As in the past, the Chinese monks who came to Japan from the Ming understood the Buddhist path as consisting of three fundamental modes of training: morality, concentration, and wisdom. Morality for them meant adherence to the 10 novice precepts and the 250 precepts for fully ordained monks listed in the *Prātimokṣa* of the *Four Part Vinaya*. They were shocked to find that, in Japan, most members of the Buddhist clergy had not received those precepts and were not subject to strict enforcement of the rules prohibiting alcohol and sex.[67] Concentration for the Chinese monks meant seated meditation. By the Ming, that was customarily practiced in a communal meditation hall (C. *chantang*, J. *zendō*) outfitted with sitting platforms around the walls and a large shrine in the center dedicated to the "sacred monk" (C. *shengseng*, J. *shōsō*) Mañjuśrī Bodhisattva (C. *Wenshu pusa*, J. *Monju bosatsu*), represented in sculpture as a monk seated in meditation. A device commonly used for concentrating the mind in this setting was the ancient meditation technique of "buddha-recollection" (C. *nienfo*, J. *nenbutsu*), which was made into a kind of kōan practice in which meditators would enquire of themselves, "*Who* is reciting the buddha name?" The third of the "three modes of training" was the cultivation of wisdom, which for Ming Chinese monks meant two things: study of the Buddhist sutras and study of the sayings of the patriarchs as recorded in the voluminous literature of the Chan school. As had been the case since the Tang and the Song in China, the ability to read and chant sutras was considered (along with precepts and meditation) basic to the training of all Buddhist monks. The study of Chan literature was considered a more advanced, specialized form of training, and the ability to penetrate and comment on the sayings of the patriarchs was understood to be the distinguishing mark of the Chan masters who were heir to the lineage.

When Yinyuan received the direct support of the Tokugawa shogunate in 1658, he set about establishing in Japan what he believed to be genuine Buddhist monastic practice, with a vital dimension of lay involvement as well. Manpukuji was constructed as a full-scale Ming-style monastery, complete with a main gate (*sanmon*), deva hall (*tennōden*), buddha hall (*butsuden*), dharma hall (*hattō*), meditation hall (*zendō*), refectory (*saidō*), mortuary hall (*shidō*), and abbot's quarters (*hōjō*). The ground plan, bureaucratic structure, principles of monkish etiquette, and routine of daily, monthly, and annual observances established at Manpukuji had evolved directly from the same Song and Yuan style of monastic organization and operation that had provided the model for Japanese Zen in the Kamakura period.

One feature of traditional Chinese monasticism that Yinyuan stressed at Manpukuji was the practice of communal labor (C. *puqing*, J. *fushin*). He dedicated a chapter of his *Ōbaku Rules of Purity* to that practice, declaring that it should be a "routine feature of monastery life."[68] Yinyuan lamented that

> in these latter times [monks] are frivolous and disdainful [of manual labor], liking only ease and idleness. They do not deign to wet their ten fingers with water. They take no responsibility for things. They neither pluck horizontal grasses [i.e., weeds] nor gather vertical grasses [i.e., wheat]. They think to themselves, "My study of Chan and practice of the way (C. *canchan biandao*, J. *sanzen bendō*) does not trifle with such things." How could they not remember the "old blackened pot" [the sixth patriarch Huineng], who hulled rice with the foot-driven mortar and pestle and became in the end a great vessel of the dharma, or Baizhang, who wielded a hoe and has ever since been a teacher of men?[69]

Yinyuan went on to say that because his community had received the "blessings of the nation" (C. *guoen*, J. *kokuon*) in Japan (i.e., generous support from the rulers), there was no need to engage in the labor of cultivating fields and gardens, but he nevertheless wanted the monks to engage in "minor work" (C. *xiaowu*, J. *shōmu*) such as picking tea leaves, sweeping the grounds, carrying firewood, moving earth, and so on. He then detailed the procedure whereby the labor steward (C. *zhisui*, J. *shissui*) should decide the tasks to be done, prepare the tools, and make a formal announcement of communal labor to the great assembly of monks. Only the aged and the ill were exempted. It is clear from this account in the *Ōbaku Rules of Purity* that manual labor was viewed as a beneficial mode of spiritual training for individual monks as well as a practical contribution to the daily operation of a monastery but that it had nothing to do with economic independence or the scorning of lay patronage.

The largest and most prominent of the ritual observances established by Yinyuan at Manpukuji was the "three platform precepts assembly" (*sandan kaie*), an eight-day-long extravaganza that was first performed in 1663. The "three platforms" were ordination platforms (*kaidan*) ritually established on three different days for administering: (1) the 10 novice precepts (*shami jikkai*) for initially leaving household life (*shukke*); (2) the complete (250) precepts (*gusokukai*) undertaken by novices becoming full-fledged monks (*dai biku*); and (3) the set of 10 heavy and 48 light bodhisattva precepts (*bosatsu daikai*) laid out in the *Sutra of Brahma's Net* (*Bonmōkyō*).[70] Lay people (*zaike*) were involved in preparatory rites that preceded the formal opening of the first platform: they took threefold refuge (*sanki*) in buddha, dharma, and sangha together with the monks and were also given, separately, the five precepts (*gokai*) and/or eight precepts (*hakkai*) for householders. Lay people were excluded, of course, from receiving the novice and complete precepts for monks, but they could be full participants in the third stage of the assembly, which entailed receiving the bodhisattva precepts. In Chinese Buddhism, and in the Ōbaku school of Zen in Japan, those precepts were used only to form karmic bonds between eminent monks and their followers (lay and monastic) and to instill an appreciation of Mahāyāna values. They differed from novice and full precepts in that they could be taken repeatedly and did not bring about any change in social, religious, or legal status. When the "three platform precepts assembly" was performed at Manpukuji for the second time in 1665, more than five hundred people received the precepts. The ritual was subsequently held at regular intervals thirty-two more times, the last being in 1922.[71]

Other noteworthy practices that were promoted in Edo period Japan by monks associated with the Ōbaku school include: publication of the entire Buddhist canon (*issaikyō*);[72] assemblies for the ritual release of living beings (*hōjō-e*); the ritual feeding of hungry ghosts (*sejiki*);[73] and various forms of self-mortification, such as burning off a finger as an offering to Buddha and copying sutras (*shakyō*) using one's own blood.[74]

The reform of Rinzai Zen in the Edo period manifested itself mainly in the conversion of small to medium-sized mortuary temples, especially ones with a single powerful patron family, into somewhat larger facilities that could support a number of monks engaged in regular meditation and other observances that went beyond the usual offerings to ancestral spirits.[75] Such conversions were referred to as "opening a [meditation] platform" (*kaitan*), as opposed to "founding a monastery" (*kaisan*), for they involved the construction of a Ming-style meditation hall (*zendō*) modeled after the ones found in Ōbaku monasteries. Meditation halls were used mainly for *zazen*; they were not designed, as the sangha halls (*sōdō*) of an earlier age had been, to also serve as dining halls and dormitories for the main assembly of monks (*daishu*). Thus, the existing kitchen-residence (*kuri*), one of the two main buildings at the typical Zen mortuary temple in the Edo period, also had to be expanded to allow for the feeding and housing of a larger community. The other main building in an Edo temple was called the abbot's quarters (*hōjō*), but in fact it had evolved into a "main hall" (*hondō*) where memorial images (*chinzō*) and mortuary tablets (*ihai*) for former abbots and the patron's ancestors were enshrined.

With the "opening of a platform," the main hall took on two additional functions: that of the buddha hall (*butsuden*) in a Chinese-style monastery, where daily services were held; and that of the dharma hall (*hattō*), where an abbot would take a high seat and preach to an assembly. Because an eminent Zen master was invited to lead such newly constituted monasteries, he needed private rooms that the existing kitchen-residences and nominal "abbots quarters" (main hall) could not provide, so an additional small residence called the "hidden quarters" (*inryō*) was also built for him and his personal attendant (*inryō jisha* or *inji* for short). Although they had no sangha hall proper, such monasteries in their entirety became known as "sangha halls" (*sōdō*), that is, as places where there was a sizable community of monks in training, not simply an abbot and a few disciples whose job it was to perform funerals and memorial services for lay households (*danka*). The formal name for such monasteries as they exist today in Rinzai Zen is "special training place" (*senmon dōjō*).

The conversion of mortuary temples into Rinzai sangha halls was often sponsored by feudal lords (*daimyō*) and other wealthy clans. An early example is Zuiganji, the mortuary temple of the Date clan, rulers (*hanju*) of the Sendai domain (*Sendai-han*). In 1636 the Rinzai Zen master Ungo Kiyō (1582–1659) assumed the abbacy and converted the temple into a sangha hall where the precepts were strictly observed and a regular schedule of twice daily meditation (*niji no zazen*), three daily sutra chanting services (*sanji no fugin*), and manual labor (*fushin samu*) was implemented.[76]

Another early example is Daianzenji, which was built in 1658 by Matsudaira Mitsumichi, fourth lord of the domain (*han*) of Echizen, to enshrine his ancestors. Mitsumichi invited Daigu Sōchiku (1584–1669), an eminent former abbot of Myōshinji, to serve as founding abbot (*kaisan*) in 1658. In 1659, shortly after his installation, Daigu composed a set of proscriptive rules (*kinsei*) for Daianzenji, which read in part:

> No wine inside the gate.
> No women allowed to stay, come, or go between evening bell and morning bell.
> No leaving the grounds without announcing it.
> No going out from the gate alone after evening bell.
> During winter and summer retreats, no leaving grounds unless on public business or taking care of sick monks; even then one must inform the abbot.
> No singing songs; no playing *go* or other games.[77]

These rules bespeak a concern with maintaining traditional monkish precepts as found in the Vinaya, but they say little about communal monastic training.

It was not until 1672, during the tenure of the fourth abbot Zen'in (n.d.), that a meditation hall (*zendō*) was built and Daianzenji was converted into a sangha hall.[78] That occasioned the composition of the *Everyday Rules for Myriad Pine Mountain (Banshōzan nichiyōki)*,[79] which was written sometime in the Enpō era (1673–1681). A schedule of daily, monthly, and annual ancestral offerings entitled *Mausoleum Officer's Record (Gozōdō densuki)*, dated 1748, drew on the *Rules of Purity with Various Dedications of Merit (Shoekō shingi)*[80] composed by the Rinzai monk Tenrin Fuin (n.d.) in 1566. Both the extant library at Daianzenji and catalogues of its holdings in the Tokugawa period reveal that the monks there studied the *Rules of Purity for Chan Monasteries, Rules of Purity for Daily Life in the Assembly (Ruzhong riyong qinggui)*,[81] *Imperial Edition of Baizhang's Rules of Purity*, and *Eihei Rules of Purity*, as well as Mujaku Dōchū's commentaries on those and his *Abbreviated Rules of Purity for Small Monasteries*. All of the rules, procedural manuals, and schedules of events that they used on a daily basis, however, were manuscripts written and handed down only at Daianzenji itself.

There are numerous other cases of clan mortuary temples (*bodaiji*) of Edo period *daimyō*, most of them branch temples (*matsuji*) of Myōshinji, being turned into sangha halls. Shōgenji, for example, was built in 1669 as the mortuary temple of the Satō clan, feudal lords (*ryōshu*) in the domain of Mino; it was turned into a sangha hall in 1847 by Zen master Settan Shōhaku (1800–1873). Sōgenji was built in 1698 by Ikeda Tsunamasa (1638–1714), lord of the domain of Okayama;[82] Zen master Gisan Zenrai (1802–1878) opened a sangha hall there toward the end of the Edo period. Some other mortuary temples of prominent clans that became sangha halls are: Myōkōji (Tokugawa clan, Owari-han); Heirinji (Matsudaira clan, Kawagoe-han); Daijōji (Date clan, Yoshida-han); Bairinji (Arima clan, Fukuchiyama-han); and Rinzaiji (Imagawa clan, Sunpu district).

It is clear from this data that the reform of Rinzai Zen that took place in the Edo period, while it did put a renewed stress on upholding moral precepts, communal seated meditation, and manual labor (all of which were prominent features of Ōbaku Zen), did not involve any rejection of "funerary Buddhism." On the contrary, it was centered in the mortuary temples (*bodaiji*) of powerful clans and actually gave a large boost to the funerals and memorial services that were their raison d'être. By building meditation halls and inviting eminent Zen masters to lead a sizable group of monks in communal training at their clan temples, the patrons of sangha halls certainly did not expect the routine of daily, monthly, and annual offerings to the spirits of their ancestors to be scaled back in any way. On the contrary, they regarded the extra expense and the sacred works of the "pure sangha" (*seishu*) it supported as means of generating far more merit (*kudoku*) than the usual recitation of sutras (*fugin*) alone—merit that could then be dedicated not only in thanks to the founding patriarchs of their dynasties but also to the future stability and prosperity of their respective regimes.

If one were to judge from modern scholarship on the history of Rinzai Zen in Japan, one might conclude that the reforms of the Edo period were almost entirely due to the heroic efforts of one man—Hakuin—who "revived a moribund school by returning to the Zen of the Song period that had been established in Japan by Nampo Jōmyō (Daiō Kokushi) and Shūhō Myōchō (Daitō Kokushi)."[83] Hakuin, we are told, stressed the practice of *zazen*, manual labor, and above all, hard mental "work" (*kufū*) on kōans, which he is credited with turning into a "system" of training.[84] In point of fact, Hakuin and a number of his followers in later generations were actively involved in the movement to open sangha halls at Rinzai temples, but they can scarcely be credited with starting that movement or inventing the forms of monastic practice that it incorporated. Indeed, it was only in the Meiji period, with the collapse of the Tokugawa regime and the disruption of Buddhist institutions that ensued, that representatives of "Hakuin Zen" succeeded in taking control of the abbacies of all the Rinzai training monasteries (*senmon dōjō*) and head monasteries (*honzan*) in Japan. Prior to that time, many of those institutions had abbots who belonged to other lineages, but the same modern scholarship that has pumped up Hakuin and the "pure" Zen of the Ōtōkan line has virtually ignored the other major contributors to the Rinzai revival of the Edo period, relegating them to obscurity as minor players in the historical drama it presents.

Chief among the Edo period Rinzai reformers who have been written out of modern history is Kogetsu Zenzai (1667–1751). Kogetsu left home as a novice monk at ten years of age; he later became a dharma heir of Kengan Zen'etsu (1618–1696), abbot of Tafukuji in Bungo. Kogetsu's teacher Kengan had trained under Chinese monks of the Ōbaku school, and like them he advocated strict adherence to monkish precepts (*kairitsu*). Kogetsu shared that concern: in 1699, at age thirty-three, he participated in a "three platform precepts assembly" (*sandan kaie*) that was held at the Ōbaku head monastery Manpukuji for the ninth time since its founding, receiving the complete precepts (*gusokukai*) of a full-fledged *bhikṣu*. Kogetsu also shared the Ōbaku interest in promoting Buddhist sutras: he engaged in copying the massive *Great Perfection of Wisdom Sutra* (*Dai hannya kyō*) and strived to obtain a copy of the entire Buddhist canon (*issaikyō*) from China. A number of successors in Kogetsu's lineage were instrumental in converting ordinary mortuary temples into sangha halls. For example, Seisetsu Shūcho (1745–1820), a "grandson" dharma heir of Kogetsu, became the abbot of Engakuji in Kamakura and converted the founding abbot's stupa sub-temple into a sangha hall. Later, Seisetsu moved to Kyoto and was instrumental in establishing sub-temple sangha halls at Shō-kokuji and Tenryūji, two other high ranking monasteries in the shogunate's head/branch system. His dharma heir Sengai Gibon (1750–1837), famous for his irreverent ink paintings, opened a sangha hall at Shōfukuji in Fukuoka. In reality, the followers of Hakuin who opened sangha halls in the Edo period were no less involved in "funerary Buddhism" and no less influenced by elements of Ōbaku-style communal monastic practice than Kogetsu and his followers. The latter, however, have been dismissed by modern scholars as "syncretists" who were "overly intellectual" (*rikutsuppoi*).

Another leader of the Edo movement to reform Rinzai Zen whose impact has not been fully recognized in modern histories is Mujaku Dōchū (1653–1744), a scholarly monk who twice served as abbot of Myōshinji. Inspired by the *Ōbaku Rules of Purity*, Mujaku launched an exhaustive comparative study of all of the Song and Yuan rules of purity that were available to him. Two outstanding products of that research were his *Commentary on the Imperial Edition of Baizhang's Rules of Purity* (*Chokushū hyakujō shingi sakei*), which he worked on from 1699 until 1718,[85] and his *Encyclopedia of Zen Monasticism* (*Zenrin shōkisen*),[86] preface dated 1741. Neither Myōshinji nor any of the other major metropolitan monasteries were interested in a radical overhaul, however, and there were no serious attempts to reconstruct the communal life of Song-style monasteries in the same form, or on the same grand scale, that had once existed at those places in the Kamakura period. The reforms that Mujaku pushed for came to fruition only on a smaller scale, at the mortuary temples that were transformed into sangha halls. His most influential work thus turned out to be the *Abbreviated Rules of Purity for Small Monasteries* (*Shōsōrin ryaku shingi*),[87] published in 1684.

The Sōtō school response to Ōbaku Zen was similar in many respects to that of the Rinzai school, but it played itself out differently at the institutional level. In the Edo period, the major Rinzai monasteries of Kyoto and Kamakura—for example, Kenninji, Tōfukuji, Nanzenji, Tenryūji, Shōkokuji, Daitokuji, Myōshinji, Engakuji, and Kenchōji—were all head monasteries (*honzan*) that had sizable networks of branch temples (*matsuji*) scattered around the country. The Sōtō school, likewise, had a number of head monasteries, such as Eiheiji, Sōjiji, and Daijōji, that boasted large numbers of affiliated branch temples. In both the Rinzai and the Sōtō networks, the vast majority of branch temples were local mortuary temples that, as mandated by the Tokugawa regime, each had numerous patron households (*danka*) associated with them. Historically, however, the Sōtō school had lagged behind the

Rinzai in garnering support from the highest levels of the social hierarchy at the geographical centers of political power, concentrating instead on building its patronage base in provincial centers and more remote rural areas. The expression "Rinzai warrior (*bushi*), Sōtō farmer (*hyakushō*)" has some historical truth to it, but not because of any significant differences in their approach to Buddhist practice. Rather, it was because aristocrats and warlords in the Kamakura and Muromachi periods, and the lords (*daimyō*) of feudal domains (*han*) in the Edo period, did tend to select prominent Rinzai monks as the founding abbots of their clan mortuary temples, whereas Sōtō monks had to rely on larger numbers of less wealthy patrons. That meant that would-be reformers of Sōtō Zen did not have as much access to the kind of high-level patronage that was needed to turn a mortuary temple into a sangha hall capable of supporting a sizable community of monks. On the other hand, the leaders of Sōtō head monasteries proved less resistant to change than their counterparts at the major Rinzai head monasteries in Kyoto and Kamakura and thus were able to overhaul their institutions along the lines of Manpukuji and other Ōbaku monasteries.

The initial impulse of Sōtō reformers was to emulate the Ōbaku style of rigorous communal monastic discipline, but as time went by they increasingly strived to trump Ōbaku Zen by holding up an earlier model as more authentic: that of the Song and Yuan institutions that Dōgen and Keizan had based their rules of purity on. The impulse to study those rules and reimplement them at major Sōtō monasteries became known as the movement to "restore the old" (*fukko*).

Two pioneers of that movement were Gesshū Sōko (1618–1696) and his disciple Manzan Dōhaku (1636–1715). Having studied with Yinyuan, the Chinese founding abbot of Manpukuji, Gesshū wanted to produce a counterpart to the *Ōbaku Rules of Purity* that could be used to facilitate communal training and hold formal retreats (*kessei*) at the Sōtō monastery Daijōji (a.k.a. *Shōju Grove*), where he was abbot. Thus, in 1674, he consulted Dōgen's commentaries on various aspects of the *Rules of Purity for Chan Monasteries*, drew on the *Procedures for Observances at Tōkoku Mountain Yōkō Zen Monastery in Nō Province* (*Nōshūtō-kokuzan Yōkōzenji gyōji shidai*) that had been written by Keizan in 1324 to regulate that one monastery, and together with Manzan compiled the *Guidelines for Shōju Grove* (*Shōjurin shinanki*).[88] In 1678, Gesshū and Manzan edited the *Procedures for Observances at Tōkoku Mountain Yōkō Zen Monastery in Nō Province* and published it as *Preceptor Keizan's Rules of Purity* (*Keizan oshō shingi*).[89] All of those works had a great influence on subsequent Sōtō ritual manuals.

Some of Dōgen's writings on monastic procedure and ritual had been incorporated in his *True Dharma Eye Collection* (*Shōbōgenzō*),[90] but others had been handed down independently. In 1667, six separate commentaries that Dōgen had written on the *Rules of Purity for Chan Monasteries* were pieced together and published by Kōshō Chidō (?–1670), the thirtieth abbot of the Sōtō head monastery Eiheiji, under the title *Rules of Purity by Zen Master Dōgen, First Patriarch of Sōtō in Japan* (*Nichiiki Sōtō shoso Dōgen zenji shingi*).[91]

Another Sōtō reformer of major importance was Menzan Zuihō (1683–1769), who published his *Rules of Purity for Sangha Halls* (*Sōdō shingi*) in 1753.[92] In preparing that text, Menzan consulted Dōgen's newly compiled *Rules of Purity* (*Shingi*), Preceptor Keizan's Rules of Purity, the *Ōbaku Rules of Purity*, and all the extant Song and Yuan Chinese rules of purity. He presented his research findings in a companion volume entitled *Separate Volume of Notes on the Sōtō Rules of Purity for Sangha Halls* (*Tōjō sōdō shingi kōtei betsuroku*),[93] published in 1755. He also researched the arrangement of Zen monastery buildings and sacred images used in Dōgen's and Keizan's day, publishing his findings in 1759 in the *Record of Images Placed in the Various Halls of Sōtō Monasteries* (*Tōjō garan shodō anzōki*).[94]

Yet another reformer whose work has had a direct influence on contemporary Sōtō Zen practice is Gentō Sokuchū (1729–1807), the fiftieth abbot of Eihei. In 1794, a year before assuming that position, he edited the *Rules of Purity by Zen Master Dōgen, First Patriarch of Sōtō in Japan* and published it with the title *Revised and Captioned Eihei Rules of Purity* (*Kōtei kanchū eihei shingi*). That edition, which circulated widely and became the standard, is commonly referred to as the *Eihei Rules of Purity* (*Eihei shingi*) or *Large Eihei Rules of Purity* (*Eihei dai shingi*).[95] In 1805, Gentō wrote the *Small Eihei Rules of Purity* (*Eihei shō shingi*).[96] In preparing that manual, he too consulted all the extant Song and Yuan Chinese rules of purity, but he gave precedence to the *Rules of Purity for Chan Monasteries* on the grounds that it was the text relied on by Dōgen.

The Sōtō school today has two head monasteries (*honzan*), Eiheiji (founded by Dōgen) and Sōjiji (founded by Keizan), both of which have been recently reconstructed to conform closely to the layouts of the great public monasteries that Dōgen encountered in Song China and strived to replicate in Japan.[97] Sōjiji, after burning down at its original location on the Noto Peninsula in 1898, was rebuilt along the lines of a Song monastery in Yokohama in 1907. Eiheiji remains at the site of its original construction in Echizen (modern Fukui Prefecture). The oldest building at Eiheiji, however, is the main gate (*sanmon*), which was built in 1749 in the Ming Chinese style, with images of the four deva kings (*shitennō*) enshrined at ground level (two on each side of the central portal) and an arhats hall (*rakandō*) on the second floor. The gate has not been replaced with a "proper" Song-style building, but the Ming-style meditation hall (*zendō*) and refectory (*saidō*) that Eiheiji had in the mid-eighteenth century were later replaced by a Song-style sangha hall (*sōdō*), where monks in training eat, sleep, meditate, and perform religious services, and a Song-inspired kitchen-cum-administration building (*kuin*).

The oldest extant ground plan of Eiheiji, dated 1802, shows a sangha hall with attached common quarters (*shuryō*) and a large kitchen-residence (*daikuri*) opposite it where the administration hall now stands. Gentō, the fiftieth abbot who edited and reprinted the *Large Eihei Rules of Purity* and compiled the *Small Eihei Rules of Purity*, wrote a short text in 1796 commemorating the rebuilding of the sangha hall and setting down rules for its use. Entitled "Admonition on the Rebuilding of the Sangha Hall at Eiheiji" (*Eihei saiken sōdō kokuyūbun*), the text begins by praising Dōgen for building the first sangha hall in Japan, then explains:

> The monastic practices (*sōrin gyōhō*) associated with [the sangha hall] are many. It is there that bowls are spread out (*tenpatsu*) for the two daily meals—the morning gruel (*shuku*) and midday repast (*sai*); it is there that the four periods of sitting meditation (*shiji zazen*) are energetically practiced; it is there that [monks] sleep (*tamin*) in the middle of the night; it is there that sutra reading (*kankin*) is held when required (*rinji*); it is there that recitations of prayers (*nenju*) are performed on the "three" and "eight" days of the month [3rd, 8th, 13th, 18th, 23rd, 28th]; and it is there that tea is served (*senten*) upon the binding and release of retreats (*ge no kekkai*). It is the place where the majority of monks in the assembly are to reside.[98]

The construction of the sangha hall at Eiheiji was emblematic of the movement to break away from the Ōbaku school model and "restore the old rules of the patriarchs" (*soki fukko*), but it is clear from this document that the so-called "old" ways of Song-style practice were actually new to the monks of Eiheiji in 1796. All of the sangha hall observances listed by Gentō, however, have been practiced routinely at Eiheiji and Sōjiji from at least the Meiji era down to the present.

Part Three: Ritual in Contemporary Japanese Zen

To understand the various modes of ritual performance found in contemporary Japanese Zen, it is necessary to know something of the institutional settings in which they take place. In the following pages I present an overview of those settings. I then summarize the full range of observances found in Zen training monasteries and detail the most common and widespread ritual practices in Japanese Zen today: those performed on a regular basis at ordinary Zen temples and those that directly involve the laity.

The Zen Institution in Contemporary Japan

At present, there are twenty-two comprehensive religious corporations (*hōkatsu shūkyō hōjin*) registered with the Japanese government that are recognized as belonging to the Zen tradition (*Zenkei*).[99] Those include: the Sōtō school (*Sōtōshū*); fifteen separate corporations that identify themselves as branches *(ha)* of the Rinzai school (*Rinzaishū*); the Ōbaku school (*Ōbakushū*); and five small corporations that have splintered off from the Sōtō and Rinzai organizations. Each of the twenty-two Zen denominations has a number of temples affiliated with it, ranging from 14,664 in the Sōtō school to 3,389 in the Myōshinji branch of the Rinzai school (*Rinzaishū Myōshinjiha*), 455 in the Ōbaku school, a few hundred in the smaller Rinzai denominations, and just a handful in the smallest of the corporations.

The individual temples (*jiin*) that make up the Zen comprehensive religious corporations can be divided into four different types: head temples (*honzan*), mortuary sub-temples (*tatchū*), training monasteries (*sōdō*), and ordinary temples (*ippan jiin*). These distinctions are not made in the statistics published by the Japanese government; they are a product of my own analysis.[100] The nomenclature I employ, however, has long been in use within the Zen tradition.

All but the very smallest of the Zen corporations has a head temple (*honzan*) that serves as its administrative center and typically gives the corporation its name. Historically, the most famous of the Rinzai head temples are Kenninji, Tōfukiji, Nanzenji, Tenryūji, Shōkokuji, Daitokuji, and Myōshinji in Kyoto, and Kenchōji and Engakuji in Kamakura. The Sōtō school, for historical reasons that are peculiar to it, has two head temples (*ryōhonzan*), Eiheiji in Fukui and Sōjiji in Yokohama, and a separate Administrative Headquarters (*shūmuchō*) located in a Tokyo high-rise. The Ōbaku school's head temple is Manpukuji, situated in the town of Uji, just south of Kyoto.

Mortuary sub-temples (*tatchū*) are found mainly within the precincts of Rinzai head temples, especially in Kyoto. Occupying their own small, walled compounds, they originated in the medieval period as shrines dedicated to maintaining a stupa (*tō*) and performing memorial services for a particular Zen master who was one in the series of former abbots (*zenjū*) of the central monastery. As discussed in Part Two, they were paid for by wealthy lay patrons, who enshrined their own ancestral spirits there as well and had the small contingent of resident monks perform routine merit-dedicating services for them. The two main buildings of mortuary sub-temples, the abbot's quarters (*hōjō*) and kitchen (*kuri*), often featured the finest in Japanese-style architecture and were lavishly appointed with beautiful works of art and surrounded by tranquil gardens. A great many sub-temples were destroyed early in the Meiji period. Those that survive at Rinzai head temples in Kyoto have largely lost the single-family patronage they once had. Many have taken on additional households as parishioners. Some have opened their gates to tourism as a source of income. In the process, their fine old buildings, works of art, and gardens have become emblematic around the world not only of Zen but of traditional Japanese culture. Visitors, especially those that receive pamphlets in English, are typically fed some Suzuki-esque propaganda about how the Song literati paintings embody Zen spirituality and how the gardens are used for meditation or "represent" meditative states; they are never told that what they are seeing is actually the private mortuary chapel of some wealthy clan of the feudal past.

Monasteries (*sōdō*) are places where groups of trainee monks (*unsui*), ranging in number from a dozen to more than a hundred, engage in communal monastic discipline under the guidance of one or more senior teachers (*rōshi*). The primary function of these institutions is to expose young monks to traditional forms of Zen Buddhist practice, including zazen, kōan introspection, and doctrinal study, and to prepare them as ritual specialists for the careers they will have as ordinary temple priests. As explained in Part Two, the training monasteries that exist today perpetuate an Edo period revival, albeit on a more modest scale, of forms of communal monastic practice that had originally been introduced to Japan from China in the Kamakura period but had died out in the interim. At present, there are thirty-eight Rinzai training monasteries in operation. All but one of the fifteen Rinzai head temples has a training monastery located on its grounds in a mortuary sub-temple converted to that purpose. The remaining twenty-four Rinzai training monasteries, eighteen of which belong to the Myōshinji branch, are scattered around the country. The two flagship institutions of the Sōtō school are the head temple training monasteries (*honzan sōdō*) of Eiheiji and Sōjiji, which have gone to great lengths over the past century to replicate the large-scale Song-style institutions that the patriarchs Dōgen and Keizan originally established in the Kamakura period. In addition, the Sōtō school operates twenty-two smaller training monasteries and three nuns training monasteries (*nisōdō*). The head temple of the Ōbaku school, Manpukuji, is a training monastery in its own right.

Head temples, memorial sub-temples, and training monasteries get virtually all of the attention in popular and scholarly literature dealing with the Zen establishment in Japan, but in actuality they are merely the tip of an institutional iceberg that is composed largely of ordinary temples (*ippan jiin*). The vast majority of Zen clergy reside in ordinary temples, where they hold the traditional title of abbot (*jūshoku*) but are in fact married men who raise families and have no young monks (*kozō*) serving under them save their own sons. Ordinary temples generally have a number of lay households associated with them as parishioners (*danka*); the numbers range from two or three dozen households in small towns and rural areas to three or four hundred in cities. The primary function of an ordinary Zen priest is the daily nourishment of the many spirits (ranging from buddhas, patriarchs, and devas to former abbots and the ancestors of patrons) that are enshrined in his temple and the performance of funerals (*sōgi*), annual memorial services (*nenki*), and prayer services (*kitō*) for his parishioners. Ordinary temples are supported largely by donations (actually fees for priestly services) from parishioners. A percentage of their income is passed on to their respective head temples as dues for membership in the comprehensive corporation. A relatively small number of ordinary Zen temples (about six hundred) have meditation groups (*zazenkai*) that meet on a biweekly or monthly basis and give lay people a chance to get a taste of a monastic-style Zen practice.

In addition to the four types of temples discussed above, there are a number of educational institutions (*kyōiku kikan*) that are run by religious corporations belonging to the Zen tradition. The Sōtō school has by far the most, with five universities, three research centers, two junior colleges, seven high schools, and three middle schools. The Myōshinji branch of the Rinzai school operates one university, two research centers, one junior college, and one high school. Many of the faculty members and researchers at the Zen universities are themselves ordained members of the Zen clergy. The universities are coeducational and open to students from all backgrounds, and their curricula are fairly diverse and secular, but they do put an emphasis on sectarian studies (*shūgaku*) and the education of the sons of Zen priests who will eventually succeed their fathers as the abbots of ordinary temples. Zen universities came into existence during the Meiji period and, like all other religious and state-run institutions of higher learning in modern Japan, were founded on a Western model. Since that time, they have been centers of the modern academic study of the "history of the Zen lineage" (*zenshūshi*)—a field that has done a wonderful job of providing all sorts of research tools and has produced a large amount of fine critical scholarship, but that has also been responsible for inventing and promoting the apologetic and misleading ideal of an iconoclastic "pure" Zen that, in its essence, has nothing to do with ritual.

In addition to the institutions described above, the Administrative Headquarters of Sōtō Zen Buddhism (*Sōtōshū shūmuchō*) organizes and supports such groups as a National Sōtō School Youth Association (*Zenkoku Sōtōshū shōnenkai*) and Sōtō School Women's Association (*Sōtōshū fujinkai*). It includes within its offices a Publications Division (*shuppanbu*) and Education Division (*kyōkabu*) that reach out in various ways to lay followers in Japan and abroad. The Myōshinji branch of the Rinzai school mounts similar efforts, although on a lesser scale.

Training Monasteries

The sixty or so Zen training monasteries operating in Japan today preserve many of the traditional forms of Buddhist monastic ritual that were originally imported from Song and Yuan China in the Kamakura period and reimported from Ming China in the Edo period. Daily observances (*gyōji*) at those monasteries include: (1) three periods of sitting meditation—dawn zazen (*kyōten zazen*), midmorning zazen (*sōshin zazen*), and evening zazen (*kōkon zazen*); (2) various sutra-chanting services (*fugin*)—the morning service (*chōka fugin*), midday service (*nitchū fugin*), kitchen service (*sōkō fugin*), meditation hall service (*dōnai fugin*), and evening service (*banka fugin*); (3) three meals—morning gruel (*shuku*), midday main meal (*sai*), and evening "medicine" (*yakuseki*); (4) early morning cleaning (*sōji*); and (5) depending on the day, either collective labor (*fushin samu*), such as gardening, weeding, and cutting wood, or lectures on Zen texts (*hōyaku* or *teishō*).

The practice of zazen in training monasteries is a highly formal, ritualized affair. Individual places on the meditation platforms (*tan*) in a Sōtō sangha hall (*sōdō*) or Rinzai meditation hall (*zendō*) are arranged by seniority, and there is a set procedure for filing in and out as a group, positioning one's hands, turning one's body, bowing to neighboring and opposite places, taking one's seat, donning one's formal monks robe (*kesa*), and so forth. Enshrined in the center of every sangha hall and meditation hall is an image of Monju Bosatsu (the bodhisattva Mañjuśrī) dressed as a monk, sitting in meditation on an altar. Known as the "sacred monk" (*shōsō*), he is regarded as the most senior member of the assembly (followed by the abbot) and as the protecting deity of the hall. He has his own attendant (*jisha*), who offers tea and incense to him daily. The monks bow to him whenever they enter or leave and engage in daily services in which they make prostrations and chant dharanis to produce merit (*kudoku*) for dedication (*ekō*) to him. However dismissive D. T. Suzuki may have been about "all those images of various Buddhas and Bodhisattvas and Devas and other beings that one comes across in Zen temples," even he could not claim that Monju Bosatsu found his way into the training monasteries as an "excrescence added from the outside" or as any kind of concession to "popular" religiosity. The sacred monk was a standard feature of the communal meditation facilities found in all Chinese Buddhist monasteries from the Song through the Ming, facilities that were generally off-limits to anyone but properly ordained monks.

Westerners tend to think of meditation as a self-absorbed, psychologically oriented exercise, but as it is practiced in Japanese Zen monasteries it is the social ritual par excellence, epitomizing the regimentation, extreme concern for etiquette (*igi*), and sacrifice of individuality that is characteristic of the monastic regime in general. In zazen, maintaining the correct posture, regardless of pain or drowsiness, is stressed above all else. No matter what inner turmoil one feels, one must remain without moving in the cross-legged, eyes-lowered posture of a sitting buddha, *looking* alert, calm, and collected. Hall monitors patrol with sticks (*kyōsaku* or *keisaku*), correcting the postures of sitters and hitting their shoulders in a ritualized manner (punctuated by bows before and after) to wake them up and stimulate their efforts.

At Rinzai monasteries, where the monks in training (*unsui*) engage in the contemplation of kōans (*kanna*) under the guidance of the Zen master (*rōshi*), the periods of zazen are the times when (as signaled by a bell) they may go to the master's quarters (*inryō*) for the highly formalized rite of individual consultation (*dokusan*). The rite of "entering the room" (*nisshitsu*) is also preserved in Sōtō monasteries, where it takes place at the discretion of the abbot, not during periods of zazen. Based on the Ōbaku model, it is a semipublic ceremony in which the monks take turns approaching the abbot's seat and engaging in a "question and answer" (*mondō*) exchange; they may, but do not have to, "raise" (*nentei*) a kōan as a topic of discussion.

Sutra-chanting services (*fugin*) take up more of the time of monks in Zen monasteries than any other kind of observance. They are regarded as a vital part of the daily (as well as monthly) routine, for it is through them that all the spirits enshrined on altars in various monastery buildings are nourished and propitiated. The spirits so feted typically include: the Buddha Śākyamuni; his disciples, the arhats; the successive generations of patriarchs in the Zen lineage; the founding and former abbots of each particular monastery; various devas and spirits identified as protectors of the Buddha-dharma and the monastery; the founding patron of the monastery; and the ancestors of current lay patrons. The basic ritual procedure in a sutra-chanting service is to generate merit (*kudoku*) by chanting sutras or dharanis and then to offer it to a spirit or spirits by means of a formal verse for the dedication of merit (*ekōmon*). Merit (Skt. *puṇya*), as interpreted in the East Asian Buddhist tradition, is literally the "virtue" or "power" (C. *de*, J. *toku*) that results from good "works" or "deeds" (C. *gong*, J. *ku*). It is the fruit of good karma (actions), conceived as a kind of spiritual energy that can be saved, invested, spent, or given away like cash. In the East Asian context, the Buddhist transfer (C. *huixiang*, J. *ekō*) of merit is also understood as an "offering of nourishment" (C. *gongyang*, J. *kuyō*) to spirits, one that is akin to generic (not uniquely Buddhist) offerings of food and drink on an altar where the mortuary tablets of ancestral spirits are enshrined. In Zen monasteries and temples, the recipients of merit in sutra-chanting services are generally represented on an altar with some kind of icon—a sculpture, painting, or tablet—and the dedication of merit is generally coupled with offerings of incense and (in more elaborate rites) food and drink.

The morning service (*chōka fugin*) is the most important daily observance in a training monastery, as indicated by the fact that it is the only one that every single member of the community must attend. In Sōtō monasteries, the morning service consists of five separate rites: (1) buddha hall sutra chanting (*butsuden fugin*), (2) sutra chanting for arhats (*ōgu fugin*), (3) patriarchs hall sutra chanting (*sodō fugin*), (4) sutra chanting for founding and former abbots (*kaisan rekijū fugin*), and (5) mortuary hall sutra chanting (*shidō fugin*). All five are actually performed in one place, the main hall (*hondō*), but the abbot approaches the altar and burns incense five times while the assembly of monks chant sutras, and there are five different dedications of merit that are recited by the cantor (*ino*). The first of those, which is for the buddha hall sutra chanting, reads as follows:

> Having chanted the *"Universal Gateway of Avalokiteshvara Bodhisattva" Chapter of the Lotus Sutra*, the *Great Compassionate Mind Dharani*, and the *Marvelously Beneficial Disaster-Preventing Dharani*, we reverently offer the merit generated thereby to: our Great Benefactor and Founder of the Doctrine, the Original Teacher Śākyamuni Buddha; to the Eminent Ancestor Jōyō Daishi [Dōgen]; and to the Great Ancestor Jōsai Daishi [Keizan]; may it adorn their awakening, the unsurpassed fruit of buddhahood. We further offer it to all the dharma-protecting devas; to the dharma-protecting saints; to the earth spirit of this place and to the monastery-protecting spirits; to the Bodhisattva Jōhō Shichirō Daigen Shuri; and to the tutelary deities enshrined in all halls.
>
> What we desire is peace in the land, harmony among all nations, prosperity and longevity for donors throughout the ten directions, tranquility within the monastery, and ample sustenance for the community; may sentient beings throughout the dharma realm equally perfect omniscience.

The final verse for the dedication of merit in the morning service, that for the mortuary hall sutra chanting, reads as follows:

> We humbly beg the three treasures (*sanbō*) for their attentive concern.
>   Having chanted the *Verse from the "Lifespan of the Tathāgata" Chapter of the Lotus Sutra*, we transfer the merit generated thereby to the teachers <Names>, head seats <Names>, trainee monks <Names>, and other deceased monks of this monastery; to the departed spirits of every member of the sangha throughout the dharma realms; to the founding patron <Name> of this monastery; to the spirits of martyrs of every nation; to the patrons associated with the mortuary hall of this monastery; to the six close kin and seven generations of parents of the pure assembly gathered at this monastery; and to sentient beings throughout the dharma realm.
>   May they all attain complete awakening (*bodai*).

As seen in these examples, the basic elements found in most verses for dedicating merit are: (1) an invocation; (2) a statement of how the merit was generated; (3) a declaration of who is to receive the merit; and (4) an indication of the purpose of the dedication, and/or a formal prayer in which some specific benefit is requested in return.

Western practitioners of Zen sometimes understand the chanting of sutras and dharanis itself to be the main ritual performance and the verse for the dedication of merit as some sort of closing gesture or coda. That view allows those who are uncomfortable with "ritual" (but happy to "practice") to rationalize that the purpose of the chanting is to learn or spread Buddhist doctrines or (in the case of nonsensical dharanis) that it is a device for focusing the mind in meditative concentration. The underlying assumption is that "merit" is a magical, superstitious, or at best symbolic kind of thing that no rational, scientifically minded person could take seriously as actually existing. In the East Asian Buddhist tradition of which Japanese Zen is a part, however, people do believe in merit. It is as real to them as, say, money—that other symbolic, magical thing that has no substantial existence but nevertheless serves to organize human societies and get things done. There is no doubt that the main purpose of sutra-chanting services in Zen is the production of merit and that the formal dedication of that merit is the performative heart and defining moment of the ritual.

Scholars of religion, art historians, and anyone else who wonders what "all those images" are doing in Zen monasteries can do no better than actually read the verses for the dedication of merit that are used when making offerings to the beings enshrined. The verses shed light on the status of those beings in the

Buddhist spiritual hierarchy and the human relationship to them, for merit is either given "up" as an offering to buddhas and patriarchs, "across" as support for fellow monks who have died, or "down" as salvation for poor unfortunates such as hungry ghosts and disconnected spirits who have no living relatives. The verses also reveal what the monastic community hopes to gain by enshrining and nourishing each spirit. The arhats, for example, are enjoined to "please use your three awarenesses and six supernatural powers to turn the age of the end of the dharma (*mappō*) into the age of the true dharma (*shōbō*); use your five powers and eight liberations to lead living beings to the unborn; continuously turn the two wheels (*nirin*) of the monastery; and forever prevent the three disasters from afflicting the land."[101] The "two wheels" referred to here are the wheel of food (*jikirin*) and wheel of dharma (*hōrin*), so we may infer that one function of the arhats is to help keep the monastery kitchen well supplied.

Meals in Zen training monasteries, known generically as "handling bowls" (*gyōhatsu*), are highly ritualized affairs. That is especially true of meals served on the platforms in a sangha hall (or meditation hall) in the manner prescribed in Song and Yuan rules of purity, but even the "simplified meals" (*ryaku handai*) that are served at long low tables in a kitchen (*kuri*) have quite an involved etiquette. The monks must set out their bowls, receive the food, make a small offering of rice to hungry ghosts, eat, and finally clean and put away their bowls, all in a minutely prescribed manner, either in unison or (in the case of the actual serving of food) in order of seniority. The meal is punctuated by the group chanting of a number of verses that serve to sanctify it but otherwise is taken in complete silence. The following verses are used in Sōtō monasteries:

> *Verse upon Hearing the Meal Signal* (*Montsui no ge*)
>   Buddha was born in Kapilavastu,
>   enlightened in Magadha,
>   taught in Varanasi,
>   entered nirvana in Kushinagara.

> *Verse for Setting Out Bowls* (*Tenpatsu no ge*)
>   Now we set out Buddha's bowls;
>   may we, with all living beings
>   realize the emptiness of the three wheels:
>   giver, receiver, and gift.

> *Ten Buddha Names* (*Jūbutsumyō*)
>   In the midst of the three treasures which verify our understanding, entrusting ourselves to the sangha, we recall (*nen*):

Vairochana Buddha, pure Dharmakāya.

Lochana Buddha, complete Sambhogakāya.

Śākyamuni Buddha, of myriad Nirmānakāyas.

Maitreya Buddha, of future birth.

All buddhas throughout space and time.

The Mahāyāna *Sutra of the Lotus of the Wondrous Dharma.*

Mañjuśrī Bodhisattva, of great holiness.

Samantabhadra Bodhisattva, of the great vehicle.

Avalokiteśvara Bodhisattva, of great compassion.

All honored ones, bodhisattvas, mahāsattvas.

Great perfection of wisdom.

Food Offering Verse (*Sejiki ge*) [at breakfast]

This morning meal of ten benefits

nourishes us in our practice.

Its rewards are boundless,

filling us with ease and joy.

Food Offering Verse (*Sejiki ge*) [at midday meal]

The three virtues and six tastes of this meal

are offered to buddha and sangha.

May all sentient beings in the universe

be equally nourished.

[When the preceding verses have been chanted, the food is served. Prior to eating, the following verses are chanted.]

Verse of Five Contemplations (*Gokan no ge*)

We reflect on the effort that brought us this food and consider how it comes to us.

We reflect on our virtue and practice, and whether we are worthy of this offering.

We regard greed as the obstacle to freedom of mind.

We regard this meal as medicine to sustain our life.

For the sake of enlightenment we now receive this food.

Verse of Food for Spirits (*Saba ge*) [at midday meal only]

Oh spirits, we now give you an offering;

this food is for all of you in the ten directions.

Bowl Raising Verse (*Keihatsu no ge*)

First, this is for the three treasures;

next, for the four benefactors;

finally, for the beings in the six realms.
May all be equally nourished.
The first portion is to end all evil;
the second is to cultivate every good;
the third is to free all beings.
May everyone realize the buddha way.

[When the preceding verses have been chanted, monks begin
eating. When finished, while washing bowls, they chant the
following.]

Verse of the Rinse Water (*Sessui no ge*)
    The water with which we wash our bowls
    tastes like ambrosia.
    We offer it to the many spirits;
    may they be satisfied.
    On ma ku ra sai so wa ka.

Not only meals but various other activities in the daily life of Zen monks
in training are regulated and sanctified by a prescribed etiquette (*igi*), special
procedures (*sahō*), and the chanting of verses, such as the *Verse for Donning
Robes* (*Takkesa ge*), *Face Washing Verse* (*Senmen no ge*), *Verse for Entering the
Bath* (*Nyūyoku no ge*), and *Verse for the Toilet* (*Senjō no ge*). The mealtime ritual,
verses, and other procedures for the ritualization of otherwise ordinary daily
activities do not have their origins in any uniquely "Zen" application of the
practice of mindfulness to everyday life, as modern scholars sometimes argue.
All of those procedures can be traced back to mainstream, generic Buddhist
monastic practices in Song and Yuan China.

Monthly observances at Zen training monasteries are mostly sutra
chanting and offering services for spirits who already receive dedications of
merit on a daily basis, monthly memorial services (*gakki*) for important patriarchs in the Zen lineage, and certain other rites pertaining directly to the
monastic vocation. In Sōtō monasteries, on the 1st and 15th days of every
month, there are: a service of prayer sutra chanting (*shukutō fugin*), which
originally entailed (and still does entail in Rinzai monasteries) dedications of
merit to the emperor; a special sutra chanting for tutelary deities (*chinju fugin*);
a small convocation (*shōsan*) for instruction in the abbot's quarters; special
offerings to the arhats (*rakan kuyō*) and the main object of veneration (*honzon
jōgu*), usually Śākyamuni; a touring of the sangha hall by the abbot and a tea
service there (*jundō gyōcha*); and an abbreviated *poṣadha* (*ryaku fusatsu*), a traditional Buddhist monastic rite of confession and purification. On days of the

month ending in "1" (the 1st, 11th, and 21st), there is a formal reading of common quarters rules (*sendoku shingi*). On days ending in "3" and "8" (the 3rd, 8th, 13th, 18th, 23rd, and 28th), there are sangha hall recitations (*sōdō nenju*), in which the *Ten Buddha Names* are chanted (a form of *nenbutsu* practice) and the following recitation text (*nenjumon*) is intoned:

> From the time that our Great Teacher the Tathāgata entered final nirvana until the present [2006], already [2,492] years have gone by. When this day has passed, our remaining lives will also be one day shorter. We are like fish in scant water: what pleasure can be taken in this? All you in the assembly should exert yourselves with vigor, as if trying to save yourselves when your head is on fire. Just reflect on impermanence and be careful not to engage in self-indulgence.
>
> We recite (*nen*) buddha names to create karmic conditions so that the earth spirit of the monastery may protect the dharma and bring peace to people, and that donors in all ten directions may have greater good fortune and increased wisdom.

On days ending in "4" and "9," the monks shave their heads (*jōhatsu*), take baths (*kaiyoku*), do their own laundry and mending and other individual chores. On the 5th day of every month, there is a special sutra chanting for Idaten (*Idaten fugin*), the tutelary deity of the kitchen, and a monthly memorial service (*gakki*) for Bodhidharma, first patriarch of the Zen lineage in China. On the 29th of every month, there is a monthly memorial service for the Two Patriarchs of the Sōtō lineage in Japan, Dōgen and Keizan. The monthly memorials involve special offerings of "decoction, sweets, and tea (*tōkasa*) and rare delicacies (*chinshū*)" in addition to the merit produced by sutra chanting.

The most important annual observances at all Zen monasteries and temples are: (1) the New Year's assembly (*shushō-e*) held on the first three days of January; (2) the Bon festival assembly (*urabon-e*), which was traditionally centered on the 15th day of the 7th month of the lunar calendar but has been celebrated at somewhat different times (e.g., July 15th or August 15th), depending on local custom, since the adoption of the Gregorian calendar in the Meiji era; (3) the Other Shore (i.e., *nirvāṇa*) assemblies (*higan-e*) held on the vernal and autumnal equinoxes; (4) the so-called "three Buddha assemblies" (*san butsu-e*): the Buddha's birthday assembly (*buttan-e*) on April 8, awakening assembly (*jōdō-e*) on December 8, and nirvana assembly (*nehan-e*) on February 15; and (5) annual memorial services (*nenki*) for the founding abbot (*kaisan*) and important patriarchs such as Bodhidharma, Huike, Linji, Dōgen and Keizan.

At training monasteries, the New Year's assembly is occasion for the revolving reading of the *Great Perfection of Wisdom Sutra* (*tendoku daihannya*), a colorful rite that involves riffling through all six hundred fascicles of the text while reciting dharanis. The dedication of merit reads as follows:

> This dharani (*sōji*) [i.e., the sutra] is akin to a wonderful medicine that treats the whole collection of illnesses of delusion. It is also like heavenly ambrosia: those who imbibe it always experience ease and joy.
>
> We humbly beg the three treasures for their attentive concern.
>
> Having done revolving reading (*tendoku*) of the golden text of the six hundred scrolls of the *Great Perfection of Wisdom Sutra* and chanted the *Heart of Great Perfect Wisdom Sutra* and the *Marvelously Beneficial Disaster-Preventing Dharani*, we dedicate the merit accumulated thereby to all the buddhas and bodhisattvas of the perfection of wisdom assembly, to the sixteen good spirits, to all dharma-protecting devas, and to this monastery's earth spirit and tutelary deities enshrined in all halls, that it may increase their majestic light and incalculable ocean of merit.
>
> What we pray for is that the true dharma may flourish, that there will be peace in the land and harmony among all nations, that living beings may be tranquil, that the monastery may thrive, that donors and believers may rely on worship, that the assembled monks may be at peace, and that all conditions may be favorable.

Revolving reading is understood as an efficient way of generating a great deal of merit, for the entire *Great Perfection of Wisdom Sutra* "counts" as having been read, but the monks do not have to actually chant it. Even people who wish to deny the centrality of merit production and dedication in Zen practice would have a hard time rationalizing this rite, for it cannot be explained away as an educational or meditative exercise. It is, however, quite theatrical.

The New Year's assembly in training monasteries is also a time for formal salutations (*ninji gyōrei*) in which the abbot, monastic officers, and ordinary monks in training visit each other's quarters and exchange formal congratulations and thanks. Lay patrons are greeted (*gakyaku settai*), and there is a special tea service in the sangha hall (*sōdō dokui cha*), following the procedures first introduced to Japan by the Song and Yuan rules of purity.

In training monasteries and ordinary Zen temples alike, the Bon festival and Other Shore assemblies are occasions for holding major public "feedings of the hungry ghosts" (*segaki-e*), also called "food-offering assemblies" (*sejiki-e*). Because those are primarily aimed at the laity, they are explained in the following section.

The three Buddha assemblies are major events in the ritual calendars of head temples and training monasteries. All three are marked by the same elaborate offerings of food and drink on special altars that are set up in front of images of the Buddha Śākyamuni, coupled with special sutra-chanting services for the generation and dedication of additional merit. For the nirvana assembly (*nehan-e*) on the 15th day of the 2nd month, the traditional East Asian date for the Buddha's death, a nirvana image (*nehanzō*) is hung that shows him prone and surrounded by grieving arhats, bodhisattvas, devas, and animals. For the Buddha's birthday, traditionally celebrated on the 8th day of the 4th month, an image of the newborn Buddha is set in a bowl under a flower trellis and bathed with sweet tea by senior monastic officers, who first leave their ranks and burn incense (*shuppan shōkō*). The Buddha's attainment of awakening (*jōdō*), said to have taken place on the 8th day of the 12th month (*rōhatsu*), is preceded by a week-long intensive training period (*sesshin*) in which the hours spent in zazen are increased dramatically, many usually scheduled daily activities are suspended (but not the daily sutra-chanting services), and (at some Rinzai monasteries) the monks are not allowed to lie down to sleep for the entire time.

Other annual observances that are unique to training monasteries are the opening (*kessei*) and closing (*kaisei*) of the two annual ninety-day retreats (*ango*), the registration (*kata*) and send-off of (*sōan*) monks in training, various rites that involve the appointment and retirement of officers in the monastic bureaucracy, and a number of special tea services. All of those rites perpetuate the modes of Chinese Buddhist monastic practice that were originally introduced to Japan by monks such as Eisai, Enni, Dōgen, and Lanqi.

Ordinary Temples and Rituals Involving the Laity

The abbots of ordinary Zen temples are mainly concerned with performing services for their lay parishioners (*danka*), but the one daily rite that they feel most constrained to carry out if at all possible is the morning service (*chōka fugin*), in which all the spirits enshrined on the premises are propitiated with offerings of merit. In most cases, it is the abbot alone who wakes up early (at 5:00 or 6:00 AM) to take care of that sacred duty. In Sōtō school temples, the solitary abbot will burn some incense before the altar and perform an abbreviated morning service (*ryaku chōka fugin*), which employs the following verse for the dedication of merit:

> Having chanted the *Heart of Great Perfect Wisdom Sutra*, we reverently offer the merit generated thereby to our Great Benefactor and

Founder of the Doctrine, the Original Teacher Śākyamuni Buddha, to
the Eminent Ancestor Jōyō Daishi [Dōgen], to the Great Ancestor
Jōsai Daishi [Keizan], to the successive generations of buddhas and
ancestors who transmitted the flame, to the founding abbot of this
monastery, Great Teacher <Name>, to the various former abbots,
and to the eternal three treasures in the ten directions, that we may
repay their compassionate blessings. We further offer it to the tutelary deities of this monastery, all the dharma-protecting devas and
good spirits.

What we pray for is the flourishing of the true dharma, harmony
among all nations, tranquility within the monastery, and that all
conditions may be favorable.

Some ordinary temple priests also make an effort to do a little zazen each
morning, or to incorporate some of the mealtime verses in their family's daily
routine, but they are in the minority.

As I have stressed throughout this essay, funerals and memorial services
are the mainstay of the Zen tradition in Japan and its most important contribution to Japanese Buddhism at large. Let us examine in detail, then, the
procedure for the funeral of a lay follower (*danshinto sōgi hō*) as it has been
handed down in the Sōtō Zen tradition (the Rinzai lay funeral scarcely differs).[102] What is most striking about the procedure is that it is based entirely on
the funeral of a Buddhist monk as it was practiced in Song and Yuan China.

As soon as a Zen priest hears that one of his parishioners (*danka*) has
died, he goes to the home of the deceased and performs a sutra chanting at
the time of death (*rinjū fugin*), commonly known as "pillow sutras" (*makur-
agyō*). He chants the *Last Teaching Sutra* (*Yuikyōgyō*) and *Verse of Homage to
Buddha's Relics* (*Shariraimon*), both of which are closely associated with the
death (*nirvāṇa*) of Śākyamuni Buddha, and dedicates the merit as follows:

Having offered incense, flowers, lamps, candles and pure water,
and having chanted the *Sutra of the Condensed Teachings Left by
Buddha Upon His Final Nirvana* and *Verse of Homage to Buddha's
Relics*, we dedicate the merit accumulated thereby to the newly deceased spirit. What we pray for is that, as the karmic conjunction
of the four elements fades, this merit may adorn his/her place of
karmic retribution.

On the night before the funeral (*sōgi*), there is an all-night vigil (*tsuya*) at
which relatives and friends console each other and reminisce about the deceased. The priest performs an all-night vigil sutra chanting (*tsuya fugin*).

On the day of the funeral, the deceased is given tonsure (*teihatsu*), just as if he/she were alive and undergoing ordination as a monk or nun. Before shaving the head of the "ordinand," the priest recites the following verse three times:

> Throughout the round of rebirth in the three realms, the bonds of love (*on'ai*) cannot be severed; to cast off human obligations (*on*) and enter into the unconditioned is the true repayment of blessings (*hōon*).

This sounds appropriate for a funeral, but the "severing of bonds" that the verse refers to is that of cutting off ties with family members and entering the Buddhist sangha. The priest takes the razor, infuses it with incense smoke, gasshos while holding it between the thumbs and index fingers of both hands, and recites three times the *Verse of Tonsure* (*Teihatsu no ge*):

> In shaving off beard and hair, we pray that all living beings should forever be free from mental afflictions and in the end attain nirvana.

Next, the deceased is given the precepts (*jukai*), just as in the ordination rites for a living person. The priest strikes the precept clappers three times and says:

> O layman (*shinji*)/laywoman (*shinnyo*) <Name>, who has recently returned to the source: if you wish to take refuge in the precepts, you must first make repentance. Although there are two procedures for the two types of repentance, we have a *Repentance Verse* (*Sangemon*) secured and maintained by the prior buddhas and handed down by the patriarchs which completely extinguishes karmic hindrances; you should repeat it after me: I now entirely repent all the evil actions I have perpetrated in the past, arising from beginningless greed, anger, and delusion and manifested through body, speech, and mind.

Following this repentance, the priest gives the precepts of three refuges (*sankikai*):

> Having made repentance for the three spheres of karma—body, speech, and mind—you have attained great purification. Next you must reverently take refuge in the three treasures: buddha, dharma, and sangha. The three treasures are of three kinds, each of which has its own merit, namely: the three treasures as a single essence; the three treasures as manifested [by the Buddha]; and the three treasures as maintained [by humans]. When you take refuge but once, all three kinds of merit shall be fully realized.

The priest then sprinkles water in three directions, in front of the mortuary tablet (*ihai*) and to its right and left. He strikes the precept clappers once and recites:

> Hail refuge in buddha,
> Hail refuge in dharma,
> Hail refuge in sangha.
>
> I take refuge in buddha, honored as highest,
> I take refuge in dharma, honored as stainless,
> I take refuge in sangha, honored as harmonious.
>
> I have taken refuge in buddha;
> I have taken refuge in dharma;
> I have taken refuge in sangha.

The conferral of precepts has thus been completed. From this time forth the true and perfect awakening of the Tathāgata shall be the great teacher of layman/laywoman <Name>, who has recently returned to the source, and he/she shall not take refuge in other paths, for we hail great pity, great compassion, and great mercy.

Having taken refuge in the three treasures of buddha, dharma, and sangha, next you must receive the three sets of pure precepts (*sanju jōkai*). First are the precepts of restraint. Second are the precepts of adopting good qualities. Third are the precepts of benefiting all living beings.

Next, you must receive the ten major precepts of restraint (*jūjū-kinkai*). First is the precept not to kill living beings. Second is the precept not to steal. Third is the precept not to engage in sex. Fourth is the precept not to engage in false speech. Fifth is the precept not to deal in alcoholic beverages. Sixth is the precept not to point out the transgressions of others. Seventh is the precept not to praise oneself and denigrate others. Eighth is the precept not to be stingy with the dharma or material things. Ninth is the precept not to give rise to anger. And tenth is the precept not to disparage the three treasures.

The aforementioned three refuges (*sanki*), three sets of pure precepts (*sanju jōkai*), and ten major precepts of restraint (*jūjūkinkai*) have been secured and maintained by the prior buddhas and handed down by the patriarchs. I now give them to you. Beginning with your present body and continuing until you obtain the body of a buddha, you should uphold these things well.

Having administered the preceding set of sixteen precepts, the priest next gives the deceased a lineage certificate (*kechimyaku*). He raises the certificate, infuses it with incense smoke, and says:

> This is the lineage certificate of the great bodhisattva precepts (*bosatsu daikai*) correctly transmitted by the buddhas and patriarchs. Buddha after buddha and patriarch after patriarch, successor after successor have inherited it, and it has come down to me. I now give it to layman/laywoman <Name>, who has recently returned to the source. Beginning with your present body and continuing until you obtain the body of a buddha, you should reverently protect it.

He places the lineage certificate in front of the deceased (*reizen*, literally "before the spirit") and recites:

> When living beings receive Buddhist precepts, they enter the rank of all the buddhas. When one's rank is the same as the greatly awakened, truly one is a child of all the buddhas. Hail great pity, great compassion, and great mercy, which embrace us.

With this, the ordination of the deceased is complete, and he or she can be given what is basically the traditional funeral of an ordinary Buddhist monk or nun (but not an abbot), as detailed in the Song and Yuan rules of purity and applied in the funerals of all Zen clergy today. At most ordinary Zen temples, the abbot can handle the ordination procedures with relatively little assistance, but the funeral proper requires the participation of at least five or six more priests. Thus, the abbots and assistant abbots of neighboring temples form cooperative groups for the purpose of performing funerals and other major rituals at each other's temples.

The funeral proper involves, at the outset, a chanting of sutras and dedication of merit upon encoffining the deceased (*nyūkan fugin*). Next there is a recitation before the coffin (*kanzen nenju*), in which the priest serving as cantor (*ino*) intones:

> We are painfully aware that birth and death give way to each other; that cold and heat vary reciprocally. They come like lightning flashing in a vast sky; they go like waves calming on a great sea. Today, that is the case with layman/laywoman <Name>, who has recently returned to the source. His/her karmic conditions supportive of life are exhausted, and his/her ordained lifespan has suddenly expired. Understanding the impermanence of all things, he/she takes nirvana as ease. I respectfully request the pure assembly

present here to humbly chant the glorious names of the various sacred beings that the great blessings accumulated thereby may adorn the path of awakening. I respectfully invite the pure assembly to recite.

The entire assembly of clergy then recites the *Ten Buddha Names*.[103] Next, the cantor initiates chanting of the *Verse of Homage to Buddha's Relics*. The clergy chant in unison three times, and the cantor recites the dedication of merit:

Having performed recitations (*nenju*) and chanted sutras, we dedicate the merit to layman/laywoman <Name>, who has recently returned to the source. We humbly pray that his/her spirit may cross over to the Pure Land; that his/her karmic afflictions will fade away, that the lotus will open its highest grade of blossom, and that Buddha will bestow prediction of a birth.

Modern scholars who tout the notion of a "pure" Zen find it difficult to accept what is obvious here: the presence of Pure Land motifs in the funerals of Zen monks and lay people. Actually, the chanting of the *Ten Buddha Names*, which is a form of *nenbutsu* practice, is not limited to funerals: it is ubiquitous in the daily services performed in all Zen monasteries, being a part of the mealtime liturgy, monthly recitations (*nenju*), and various other litanies.

The recitation before the coffin is followed by a recitation upon lifting the coffin (*kokan nenju*), a "guiding dharma phrase" (*indō hōgo*), and a recitation at the funeral site (*santō nenju*). All of the recitations (*nenju*) involve chanting the *Ten Buddha Names* and a dedication of merit similar to the one quoted above. The funeral reaches a climax with what are called the three buddha rites (*san butsuji*): an elaborately orchestrated offering of decoction (*tentō*) to the deceased, an equally involved offering of tea (*tencha*), and the wielding of the torch (*hinko*) used to ritually start the cremation. A separate monk officiant is required to take the lead in each of those rites. When all of the preceding ceremonies are finished, at the end there is a sutra chanting for placing the tablet (*an'i fugin*) of the deceased in the temple's mortuary hall (*shidō*).

Funerals in the Japanese Zen tradition are the most involved, dramatic, and expensive of rites involving the dead, but they are certainly not the last. The typical parishioner household associated with an ordinary Zen temple has a buddha altar (*butsudan*) in the home. The altar contains an image of a buddha, most often Śākyamuni, flanked by memorial tablets (*ihai*) bearing the names of deceased family members. The altar is decorated with candles and flowers, has a stand or shelf for offerings, and a brazier for burning incense. Family members (usually the woman of the house) may make offerings of food and drink to the spirits on a daily basis, on the monthly return of their death days (*maitsuki no meinichi*), or less often. On the anniversaries of their death days (*shōtsuki meinichi*), during the week of the midsummer Bon festival (*o-bon*), and in conjunction with the Other Shore (*o-higan*) memorial rites that are held on the spring and fall equinoxes, it is customary to invite the temple priest to the home to perform sutra-chanting services (*fugin*) before the altar. At such time, the entire family is ordinarily present for the service. The priest makes offerings to the Buddha, chants scriptures to produce merit (*kudoku*), and dedicates (*ekō*) the merit to the deceased. Priests of the Sōtō school generally use the following *Abbreviated Dedication of Merit for Householders (Zaike ryaku ekō)* in this context:

> We humbly beg the three treasures for their attentive concern.
> Having chanted sutras and dharanis, we dedicate the merit gener-
> ated thereby to the spirit of <dharma Name of deceased>, that it may
> adorn his/her place of karmic retribution.[104]

Usually the household provides the priest with refreshments or a meal. There is always a monetary donation in return for the services rendered.

Many parishioner households also maintain their own graves (*haka*) in the cemetery (*bochi*) of the Zen temple they are affiliated with, as well as mortuary tablets (*ihai*) bearing the names of deceased family members in a mortuary hall within the temple itself. Actually, the English words "cemetery" and "grave" are poor translations of *bochi* and *haka*, because nobody is buried in a *bochi* (virtually all Buddhist funerals in Japan today involve cremation), and the "gravestones" do not mark the resting place of individuals: they are stone stupas dedicated (in a prominent inscription on the front) to "all the ancestors" (*senzo daidai*) of a particular family, with the names and death dates of individual family members inscribed in smaller letters on the sides and back of the one monument. Ashes of the deceased may be placed in a cavity under or within the stupa, which consists of several moveable stones resting one upon the other, or may be enshrined in a small box in the mortuary hall, near the tablets.

When parishioners visit their family graves and mortuary hall tablets on the anniversaries of death days, they often request that the temple priest perform a sutra-chanting service. In Sōtō temples, the following *General Dedication of Merit (sōekō)* is used in the rite of sutra chanting for patrons' ancestors (*dannotsu senmō ruidai fugin*):

> The clear cool moon of bodhisattvahood floats in the sky of utter
> emptiness; when the water of the minds of living beings is pure, the

reflection of awakening appears in it. We humbly beg the three
treasures for their attentive concern.

Having chanted sutras and dharanis, we dedicate the merit generated thereby to the spirits of all the generations of deceased members of the family of <dharma Name>; to his/her six close kin
and seven generations of parents; to the myriad spirits of the triple
world, including those with and those without connections to the
living; and to the entire class of sentient beings in all dharma realms.

What we desire is that their benightedness of futile kalpas will
now be extinguished; that the marvelous knowledge of true emptiness will hereby appear to them; and that they will immediately
comprehend non-arising and quickly bear witness to the fruit of
buddhahood.[105]

In this verse for the dedication of merit, as is common in many Mahāyāna
liturgies, the specific wishes of the sponsor of the rite (in this case, the well-
being of one family's ancestors) are coupled with universal prayers for the
salvation of all living beings. That expression of generosity, paradoxically, does
not dilute or reduce the offering of merit to specifically named recipients but
rather intensifies it, for giving itself is deemed a highly meritorious act.

The most popular times to visit family graves at a temple are during the
Bon and Other Shore festivals. On those occasions, parishioners find themselves in the company of many other families come for the same purpose. Many
Zen temples hold a feeding of the hungry ghosts (*segaki-e*) at this time. A special
altar for making offerings to "all the spirits of the three realms" (*sangai banrei*)
is set up at the rear of the main hall (*hondō*), opposite the central Sumeru altar
(*shumidan*) on which Śākyamuni Buddha is permanently enshrined, and an
esoteric rite known as opening the ambrosia gate (*kai kanromon*) is performed.
This requires the participation of at least six or eight priests, so each abbot calls
on his usual cohort of cooperating colleagues; their ranks may also be aug-
mented by a few monks in training on leave from their monasteries.

The ambrosia gate ritual begins with an invocation of the three jewels
(*bushō sanbō*). That is followed by the recitation of a vow of invitation (*chōshō
hotsugan*), which goes as follows:

By all the members of this assembly:
    Giving rise to the thought of awakening, we present a vessel of
    pure food, offering it to all the hungry ghosts in every country of the
    innumerable lands in the dharma realm throughout all space in
    the ten directions. Please come and gather here, you departed long
    ago, and all spirits, from earth gods of mountains and rivers to

demons and wraiths of barren wastes. Taking pity on you all, with this food we feed you now.

We pray that every one of you, having received this food of ours, offers it in turn to all the buddhas, holy ones, and sentient beings throughout all realms of empty space, that all may be satisfied. We also pray that your bodies, conveyed by this dharani-food, may leave suffering behind and gain liberation; that you may attain the joy of birth in heavens; that you may, in accordance with your wishes, be delivered to one of the Pure Lands in the ten directions; that you may give rise to the thought of awakening, practice the path to awakening, and in the future become buddhas; that you may never backslide; and that whoever first attains the way may vow to lead the others to liberation as well. We also pray that day and night without cease you shall protect us and completely answer our prayers.

May the merit generated by giving this food be dedicated to sentient beings of the dharma realm, so that those various beings may exist in equality, and together dedicate these blessings to the dharma realm of suchness, to supreme awakening, and to omniscience, with the prayer that together with all sentient beings we may quickly attain buddhahood and not seek any other rewards.

May all sentient beings of the dharma realms, conveyed by this rite, swiftly attain buddhahood.

Next comes the recitation of a series of dharanis or magical spells, each chanted three times: Dharani for Inviting the Cloudlike Hosts of Spirits (*Unshū kijin chōshō darani*); Dharani for Breaking Down the Gates of Hell and Opening Throats (*Ha jigokumon kai inkō darani*); Dharani for Sanctifying the Food with the Unimpeded Radiance of Innumerable Virtues (*Muryō itoku jizai kōmyō kaji onjiki darani*); Dharani for Bestowing the Ambrosial Taste of the Dharma (*Mō kanro hōmi darani*); Dharani for Contemplating Vairocana through the Graph "Mind" on a Disk of Water (*Birushana ichiji shin suirin kan darani*); Dharani for Invoking the Precious Names of the Five Tathāgatas (*Go nyorai hōgō chōshō darani*); Dharani for Producing the Thought of Enlightenment (*Hotsu bodaishin darani*); Dharani of Giving the Bodhisattva Samaya Precepts (*Ju bosatsu sammayakai darani*); Secret Root Dharani for Dwelling in the Great Jewelled Pavilion (*Daihō rōkaku zenjū himitsu konpon darani*); and Dharani for Initiation into the Mantra of the Radiance of the Buddhas (*Shobutsu kōmyō shingon kanchō darani*). The last, to give some idea of what these spells are like, goes as follows:

Abogya
bei rosha no
maka bodara
mani han doma
jin bara hara bari
taya un.

The Chinese characters in which the dharanis are written are mere phonetic representations (transliterations) of Indic words, so they do not form sentences with any discernible syntax or semantic value. To Chinese and Japanese ears, dharanis are just a series of sounds, although people familiar with Buddhist texts may recognize an occasional word such as "rosha no" (Skt. *Locana*) or "maka" (Skt. *mahā*). Even in their original Indic languages (Sanskrit, Prakrit, etc.) dharanis were valued more for the magical power they were believed to embody phonetically than for the "meaning" of the words and phrases they employed. In any case, to the lay parishioners who attend a feeding of the hungry ghosts, even the prayers that precede and follow the dharanis are virtually incomprehensible, although their meaning is perfectly clear to the priests who perform the rite. The ambrosia gate service ends with the recitation of a *Verse for Dedicating Merit* (*Ekō ge*):

> With the good karma gathered in this practice, we repay the virtuous toils of our fathers and mothers, that the living may be blessed with joy and long life without distress, and the deceased freed from suffering and born in the Pure Land. May the four benefactors, sentient beings in the three classes of existence, and those born in the three evil destinies and eight difficulties all be able to repent their transgressions, purify their defects, entirely escape the round of rebirth, and be born in the Pure Land.

In other words, the entire feeding of the hungry ghosts, for all of its expression of universal compassion for disconnected spirits (*muen botoke*) who have no living descendants to nourish and care for them, is conceived as a powerful device for generating merit that is then dedicated to the ancestors of the lay parishioners whose donations sponsor the rite (and, as is the norm noted above, to all sentient beings).

Modern scholars such as D. T. Suzuki have described the feeding of hungry ghosts as a "Shingon element" that does not really belong in Zen and as an "excrescence added from the outside" in response to popular demand, but neither of those judgments stands up to historical criticism. The ambrosia gate rite as it is practiced in Zen temples today comes directly from Yuan and

Ming dynasty China, where it was part and parcel of the mainstream monastic Buddhism that was dubbed "Zen" after its importation into Japan. Moreover, it is clear that most lay people have only a very vague notion of what is going on in the rite. As far as they are concerned, their own departed loved ones are the focus of the proceedings. At the conclusion of the ambrosia gate service, they line up and burn incense one by one at the altar to "all the spirits of the three realms," but each has their own family members in mind. Next to that altar there is a large stack of freshly inscribed "stupas" (*sotoba*)—long wooden plaques, each of which is dedicated to "all the generations of ancestors" of one of the families in attendance. After burning incense, each family carries their wooden stupa to the cemetery and sets it up next to the family grave. The ambrosia gate, in short, is not a concession to the laity; it is an esoteric rite that is maintained by the Zen clergy for its own purposes and marketed to the laity as a particularly potent form of ancestor worship. That model, of course, can be traced all the way back to medieval China.[106]

The focus on the clan (or household) in the operation of ancestral mortuary temples (*dannadera* or *bodaiji*) as they developed in Zen and spread throughout Japanese Buddhism has not been very conducive to any kind of congregational spirit. As we saw in the case of the Feeding of the Hungry Ghosts, although a large number of parishioners may gather at an ordinary temple for a public rite, they do not necessarily feel any sense of common purpose or group identity. It is true that in some rural areas, the local temple (Zen or otherwise) sometimes plays the role of a community center: a place where various farmers' groups, women's and youth clubs, and hobby (e.g., tea ceremony, painting, calligraphy, singing) groups can meet. For the most part, however, people approach Buddhist temples for their own reasons and at times of their own choosing, either as individuals or with family members. Lay people are free to enter the main halls (*hondō*) of Zen temples and to pray before any of the sacred images enshrined there. Such activities do not require the presence of the priest or the making of a donation, although a box for coin offerings is available.

On New Year's Eve, it is customary for the parishioners of ordinary Buddhist temples, Zen included, to visit their local temple at midnight for the ringing of the large outdoor bell (*joya no kane*). The bell is rung 108 times, symbolizing purification of the 108 afflictions (*bonnō*) that are the cause of all suffering.[107] The Japanese, in general, associate both Buddhist and Shintō New Year's observations with a purification of the misdeeds and pollutions of the previous year.

The Buddha's birthday celebration, also known as the "assembly for bathing the buddha" (*kanbutsu-e*), is the most popular of the three Buddha assemblies. Commonly called the Flower Festival (*hana matsuri*), it entails setting up an image of the baby Buddha in a bowl underneath a trellis covered with flowers, representing the Lumbini grove in which Śākyamuni was said to have been born. Lay participants, including many children, pour sweetened tea over the image, thereby reenacting the legendary bathing of the newborn Buddha by the devas.

Occasional (special) rituals that many parishioners attend include the ceremony of installing a new abbot (*shinsanshiki*), the dedication of new sacred images or stupas (*zōtō kaigen*), and the ceremony of giving precepts (*jukai-e*). The last, which is often a week-long event at Sōtō temple, was originally modeled after the Ming-style precept ceremonies of the Ōbaku school. What it involves today, basically, is administering the bodhisattva precepts to lay followers.

In times of personal crisis, parishioners may ask ordinary Zen temple priests to perform special prayer services (*kitō-e*) for them in exchange for donations. Prayer services involve the production of merit by chanting sutras and dharanis and a subsequent dedication of merit to various deities, coupled with prayers (*kitō*). They are different from sutra-chanting services, however, in that they are not construed as acts of veneration or devotion but are explicitly motivated by the desire to bring about specific boons for designated recipients. The offerings involved tend to be reduced in significance to a kind of mechanical procedure meant to ensure the efficacy of the prayers. The desired ends are sought through the direct manipulation of spiritual forces rather than by supplicating deities believed to have the power to help. As noted above, some modern scholars explain the presence of prayer services in Japanese Zen as a kind of "syncretism" or borrowing of elements from the Shingon tradition and thus as something not proper to "pure" Zen. Such prayers, however, just like the recitation of buddha names (*nenbutsu*) and the feeding of hungry ghosts, are as integral a part of the Zen tradition as taking precepts, sitting in meditation, and chanting sutras. That is to say, they are all elements of the mainstream Chinese Buddhist monasticism that became known as "Zen" in Japan.

Having outlined in broad fashion the religious practices engaged in by parishioners of Zen temples, let me note in closing that there is little in all of this to distinguish them from the parishioners of other schools of traditional Japanese Buddhism. The domestic buddha altars (*butsudan*) set up by lay followers of other schools have different main objects of veneration (*honzon*) and admit to minor variations in arrangement, but the fundamental practice of enshrining memorial tablets for deceased family members is exactly the same. Likewise, the sutras and dharanis chanted by the priests of other schools vary somewhat from those used in Zen, but the basic idea of generating merit and dedicating it to ancestral spirits is identical. Architecturally, as noted in Part Two, most ordinary Buddhist temples in Japan have similar layouts of buildings and grounds, which derive from the mortuary sub-temples of the Zen tradition. The annual rituals that attract the greatest participation from parishioners in all schools of Buddhism—the Bon, Other Shore, and Flower Festival assemblies—are also the same. In each school, to be sure, there are a relatively small number of lay followers who get involved in specialized practices that are unique to the particular tradition in question. In the case of Zen, those are the practicing laymen (*koji*) and practicing laywomen (*daishi*) who belong to zazen groups (*zazenkai*) at ordinary temples or train together with monks at a monastery. The basic rituals that most parishioners are exposed to, however, vary little from one ordinary Buddhist temple to another, regardless of denominational affiliation. As explained above, that is due to the widespread influence in Japan of Zen-style mortuary practices.

2

Chan Rituals of the Abbots' Ascending the Dharma Hall to Preach

Mario Poceski

Rituals that frame the public lectures given by Chan/Zen teachers occupy a central place in the liturgical programs and everyday routines of monasteries affiliated with the various Chan/Zen traditions in East Asia, both past and present. These rituals are usually subsumed under the general category of "ascending the [Dharma] hall [to deliver a public sermon]" (C. *shangtang*, J. *jōdō*, K. *sangdang*).[1] Traditionally, they were enacted at formal occasions when the abbot of a Chan monastery ascended the high seat or dais in the Dharma hall (C. *fatang*, J. *hōdō*, K. *pŏpdang*) to deliver a sermon on Chan doctrine and provide instructions about spiritual cultivation. While these lectures were ostensibly geared toward the monastic assembly, typically they were public occasions that were also attended by laypeople. In them, a Chan abbot would give a formal address on select aspects of Chan teachings and practices, usually peppered with copious quotations from canonical texts and classical Chan records. Typically, the sermons were (and still are) delivered in a stylized manner, following a prescribed ritual pattern, and they were preceded and followed with customary ceremonial acts such as bows, invocations, and chants that are part and parcel of the liturgical repertoire of East Asian Buddhism. At times, the ceremonial events also included questions from the audience.

Many popular and scholarly publications dealing with Zen history and teachings evoke the various Chan/Zen traditions' (Chinese and Korean, Rinzai and Sōtō, etc.) penchant for dissociating themselves from reliance on the medium of language and highlight their misgivings about traditional Buddhist forms of worship and practice. Closely related to that are the occasional accounts about the Chan/Zen teachers' injunctions against conventional sermonizing and their summary dismissal of the formulaic rituals linked with it. These are key elements that shape the well-attested—and often unduly romanticized—images of Chan antiritualism.[2] They are part of a traditionalist narrative about the Chan school's iconoclastic ethos, symbolized by the purportedly spontaneous and free-spirited interactions between Chan teachers and students. Such images of the Chan teachers' untrammeled, emblematic manifestations of Chan insight are partially based on traditional lore, especially the well-known "encounter dialogue" stories. Popular anecdotes of this type exemplify the classical Chan teachers' putative rejection of established monastic mores and their adoption of unconventional communication strategies and pedagogical devices.

These stories about the Chan monks' unconventional spiritual exploits and peculiar pedagogical techniques were codified by the influential Chan chronicles composed from the early Song period (960–1279) onward, such as *Jingde chuandeng lu* (Jingde [era] Record of the Transmission of the Lamp, compiled in 1004), and have ever since been a central component of Chan literature and a focal element of Chan ideology. The iconoclastic images of Chan teachers as inimitable spiritual virtuosi who eschew traditional forms of preaching, as gleaned from these texts, are further refashioned through the prism of the ideological suppositions and sectarian biases of later Zen traditions (primarily in Japan, but also elsewhere). Finally, there are our modern reimaginings of ancient texts, teachings, and traditions in light of our own intellectual predilections, religious sensibilities, and cultural preconceptions.

This chapter is meant to serve as an historical survey of the Chan rituals subsumed under the category of *shangtang*. In order to provide a historical context for the emergence of these forms of Chan ritual, I start with a brief review of the preaching rituals current in medieval China, which served as templates for the development of liturgical models distinctive of the Chan school. That is followed by an examination of the sermons of Chan teachers who flourished during the Tang era (618–907), when the Chan school evolved into a distinct tradition within Chinese Buddhism and when the term *shangtang* was first used in a technical sense to denote the sermons of Chan teachers. The next section takes us to the Five Dynasties (907–960) and early Song periods, when we are first confronted with a seemingly conspicuous subversion of traditional ritual forms and an emergence of what at first sight appears to be an iconoclastic form of antiritualism.

The most detailed premodern descriptions of Chan rituals appear in the monastic codes belonging to the "pure rules" or "rules of purity" genre (C. *Chan qinggui*, J. *Zen shingi*), which is discussed in the longest section of this chapter. The following section concisely comments on key subsequent developments, including the preaching rituals enacted in contemporary East Asian Buddhism, especially within the context of the Korean Sŏn tradition. All of them point to the enduring influence of time-honored ritual forms that basically go back to the Song period. The chapter ends with brief reflections on the manner in which the study of the historical trajectories of particular ritual forms such as *shangtang* shed light on the process of identity formation within the Chan tradition, a central element of which was negotiating the lines of demarcation and the points of convergence between Chan and the rest of Buddhism. While the public performance of specific ceremonial forms and stylized verbal and physical acts highlighted central aspects of Chan ideology, at their core Chan rituals were based on conventional Buddhist prototypes. Throughout history, the differences between them—at the levels of form and content, essence and function—were perhaps not more prominent or significant than their intersections and commonalities.

Preaching Rituals in Medieval Chinese Buddhism

Preaching was among the primary means of communicating the teaching of Buddhism and propagating the religion in medieval China. As can be seen from numerous monastic biographies, it was usual for young monks to travel to various monasteries and listen to the lectures of different Buddhist teachers. The study of canonical texts and philosophical doctrines during monks' formative years was prevalent among the clerical elite, and this customary pattern is also evident in the biographies of noted Chan teachers, which often mention the texts and doctrines they learned during their youth.[3] In the process of becoming Dharma teachers (*fashi*), monks trained in the art of delivering public sermons, in addition to mastering the doctrines of canonical texts and related exegetical traditions. Creative textual interpretation and innovative expository style were areas where a charismatic or intellectually gifted monk could leave his personal mark, thereby procuring personal recognition and attracting disciples and patrons.[4]

Usually Buddhist lectures were public affairs, but there are also records of private instructions given only for the benefit of a select group of disciples. One such example is the story of the Korean monk Wŏnch'ŭk (613–696) bribing a doorkeeper at a monastery in the Tang capital Chang'an to secretly listen to a lecture of the famous translator and exegete Xuanzang (602–664).[5] Preaching also took place in the form of debates, at times among Buddhist monks espousing different doctrinal viewpoints but also among representatives of the main religious traditions (namely, Buddhism, Confucianism, and Daoism).[6] Especially prominent were the public debates between representatives of Buddhism and Daoism, which were occasionally held at the imperial court in the presence of the emperor and the high officials.

Commonly, the public lectures were expositions of popular canonical texts, such as the *Lotus* and *Huayan* scriptures. It was not uncommon for there to be a series of lectures on a given text, frequently sponsored by lay patrons. At times, the lecture series were also commissioned by the imperial court and the emperor.[7] These lectures were delivered by learned monks who specialized in scriptural exegesis, whose public talks typically drew sizeable audiences of monks and laypeople. These monks formed a distinguished segment of the Buddhist clergy, and they were esteemed for their learning and eloquence. Sometimes they were assisted in their lecturing by monks who served as assistant lecturers (*dujiang*, sometimes also rendered as "cantor").[8] Records of the lives and accomplishments of the best known among the Buddhist scholiasts and lecturers were preserved for posterity, as they were included in the influential collections of biographies of eminent monks, the oldest extant example of which is Huijiao's (497–554) *Gaoseng zhuan* (Biographies of Eminent Monks, compiled in 519). There these monks' biographies are collected under the category of exegetes (*yijie*).[9] Huijiao's text also includes two related categories of biographies of monks, which highlight a prevalent emphasis within Chinese Buddhism on memorizing and enunciating the sacred texts: chanters of scriptures (*songjing*) and reciters of scriptures (*jingshi*; literally "masters of scriptures").[10]

In the diary of his travels in Tang China, the Japanese monk and pilgrim Ennin (799–852) makes frequent references to public Buddhist lectures, which attests to their popularity. Ennin's description of a scripture lecture he witnessed in the eleventh lunar month of 839 at a monastery in Shandong, run and patronized by Korean immigrants, highlights the ritual solemnity and stylized format of these lectures:

> At 8 A.M. they struck the bell for the scripture lecturing, apprising the group, after which the congregation spent quite a little time entering the hall. At the moment the bell sounded for the congregation to settle down, the lecturer entered the hall and mounted to a high seat, while the congregation in unison called on the name of the

Buddha. Their intonation was wholly Korean and did not resemble the Chinese sounds. After the lecturer had mounted to his seat, the invocation of the name of the Buddha stopped. A monk seated below him chanted in Sanskrit, entirely in the Chinese manner, the one-line hymn, "How through this scripture," etc. When he reached the phrase, "We desire the Buddha to open to us the subtle mystery," the crowd chanted together, "The fragrance of the rules, the fragrance of meditation, the fragrance of deliverance," etc. After the singing of the Sanskrit hymn had ended, the lecturer chanted the headings of the scripture and, dividing them into the three parts, explained the headings.[11]

As he continues his account of the preaching ritual, Ennin reveals that the lectures were supported by lay patrons, who presumably also attended the ceremonies. That indicates that the lectures were—in addition to their religious and educational functions—a source of income for the monastic community. The text then goes on to tell us that a formalized debate, which also involved monks from the audience, was part of the preaching ritual, although unfortunately it does not provide additional details about the questions asked and the answers given by the debate participants. It is noteworthy that Ennin found the preaching rituals familiar, since they differed in only minor details from those in his native Japan. This points to the presence of a common ritual framework throughout the Buddhist world of East Asia.

After that the *weina* (K. *ina*) came in front of the high seat and read out the reasons for holding the meeting and the separate names of the patrons and the things they had donated, after which he passed this document to the lecturer, who, grasping his chowry, read the patrons' names one by one and made supplications for each individually. After that the debaters argued the principles, raising questions. While they were raising a question, the lecturer would hold up his chowry, and when a questioner had finished asking his question, he would lower it and then raise it again, thank [the questioner] for his question, and then answer it. They recorded both the questions and the answers. It was the same as in Japan, except that the rite of [pointing out doctrinal] difficulties was somewhat different. After lowering his hand at his side three times and before making any explanation, [a debater] would suddenly proclaim the difficulty, shouting with all his might like a man enraged, and the lecturer would accept the problem and would reply without raising problems in return.[12]

Ennin ends his account with a description of the closing ceremonies, which included additional readings from the scripture, chanting of hymns and invocations, and solemn departure from the lecture hall by the preacher and the congregation.

The collections of monastic biographies also describe a class of preachers called "proselytizers" (*changdao* or *changdao shi*). The proselytizers were usually itinerant monks who propagated Buddhist teachings to diverse audiences, often without relying on a specific text, a point of similarity with the Chan teachers. On many occasions they used edifying stories—including those belonging to the popular Buddhist genres of *jātaka* (*bensheng*), *avadāna* (*piyu*), and *nidāna* (*yuanqi*)—to illustrate the workings of the law of karma and to highlight key Buddhist virtues. Their lectures were often held during festivals or in conjunction with vegetarian feasts. *Gaoseng zhuan* defines this group of preachers as those who "excel at educating and enlightening the minds of the multitude by propagating and chanting the principles of Buddhism."[13] According to the text, a successful proselytizer was supposed to posses four basic qualities: good voice, debating skills, natural gift, and extensive learning.[14]

The proselytizers were a diverse group, and they preached to varied audiences. Some of them presented their sermons in a simple language that was accessible to the masses. Others were adept at presenting Buddhist teachings in ways that appealed to the educated elites, lay and monastic. The author of *Gaoseng zhuan* suggests that they employ strategic adaptations of their religious teachings in response to the varied needs, predilections, and levels of sophistication of their diverse audiences. When preaching to monastic audiences, they should talk about impermanence and suffering and explain the principle and practice of repentance. If teaching to kings and sophisticated layman, they should quote the secular classics and use beautiful language and refined expressions. Finally, when addressing an uneducated audience of common people, they should use local words and expressions and simply censure vice in ways that commoners can relate to.[15]

Additional information about preaching rituals in Tang China, especially some of their popular formats, can be found in the Dunhuang manuscripts. Some of the Dunhuang sources contain transcripts of popular lectures and sermons, which are referred to by a variety of names, including "scripture lecturing texts" (*jiangjing wen*), "popular lectures" (*sujiang*), and "seat-settling texts" (*yazuo wen*). The importance of these sources is that, in addition to providing information about the narrative contents of the lectures, they also shed light on their performative contexts. That is a feature they share with other related Dunhuang genres written in prosimetric form, such as the narratives on karmic circumstances (*yuanqi*) and the transformation texts (*bianwen*).[16] In the annotation and remarks written in the margins of the Dunhuang manuscripts, we see the interpolation of brief instructions and reminders that served to aid the public performance of the sermons and popular lectures. That includes presentation aids such as recitation cues, notations that indicate places where the preacher/performer can elaborate beyond what is written in the main text, and prompts about interpolating liturgical elements such as invocations of the Buddha's name.[17]

A Dunhuang manuscript preserved in the Pelliot collection summarizes the main elements that composed a popular lecture in terms of liturgical program with a tripartite structure.[18] First, there was an introductory part that consisted of recitation of Buddhist chants (which were presumably intoned in Sanskrit) and invocation of the name of bodhisattva Guanyin, followed by recitation of a seat-settling text. Next, there was the lecture proper, which was highly ritualized; besides explanations of the particular scripture (the *Vimalakīrti Scripture* in the case of the Dunhuang manuscript), there was also the chanting of an opening eulogy and invocations of the Buddha. The lecture concluded with a eulogy of the Buddha, making of vows, and transference of merit.[19]

Sermons in Tang Chan

Within the early Chan tradition, the preaching of sermons was the main medium of religious instruction. Chan teachers stood apart from scriptural exegetes by their eschewal of methodical lecturing on canonical texts. At the same time, their discourse was unabashedly elitist; with some exceptions, they shied away from the aforementioned efforts of conventional proselytizers to reach the masses by offering popular lectures on common themes such as karmic recompense and the salvific powers of the Buddhas and bodhisattvas. Instead, Chan teachers experimented with their own idiosyncratic ways of explicating various aspects of Buddhist doctrine and practice, although they still continued to rely on canonical sources and frequently imbedded copious scriptural quotations and allusions in their public lectures and private instructions.

Some of the teachings of early Chan were written down in the form of treatises, but the major format for disseminating doctrines and offering guidance about spiritual cultivation was the sermons of Chan teachers.[20] Some of the sermons were transcribed by disciples and were eventually included as parts of the records of noted Chan teachers, such as Shenhui (684–758), Mazu Daoyi (709–788), Huangbo Xiyun (d. 850?), and Linji Yixuan (d. 866).

Arguably the best-known Chan text of all time, *Liuzu dashi fabao tanjing* (usually abbreviated to *Liuzu tanjing*, *Platform Scripture on the Sixth Patriarch*), is for the most part a collection of sermons attributed to Huineng (638–713), the putative "sixth patriarch" of Chan.[21] Here is a sample excerpt from one of Huangbo's sermons, included in *Wanling lu* (*Wanling Record*), one of the two collections of his sermons and discussions compiled by the noted official and lay Buddhist Pei Xiu (787?–860):

> [Huangbo] ascended the [Dharma] hall and said [to the assembly]: "Mind is Buddha. From all the Buddhas at the top, all the way down to the squirming creatures, each and every one has Buddha nature. Therefore, Bodhidharma came from India and only transmitted the teaching of One Mind. He directly pointed out that all living beings are originally Buddhas, without having to rely on spiritual cultivation. Only like now, if you come to know your own mind, perceive your own original nature, then there is no need to seek anything else."[22]

In the records of Tang-era Chan teachers, their sermons are also often presented as a response to a question from the audience; at times, the sermon is punctuated with follow-up questions. That is a format that was familiar in medieval Chinese Buddhism, also appearing in numerous non-Chan texts. This conventional question and answer format—not to be confused with the well-known "encounter dialogue" model that is the hallmark of post-Tang Chan literature—resembled the dialogues between the Buddha and his disciples presented in the scriptures. It also had counterparts in classical Chinese works such as the *Analects of Confucius* (*Lunyu*) and *Mencius* (*Menzi*). Many of the questions addressed to Chan teachers—especially in the records of Baizhang Huaihai (749–814) and Huangbo—point to their audiences' familiarity with canonical texts. Some questions contain quotations from scriptures or extra-canonical works, while others simply ask for explanations of well-known scriptural passages. Here is an example from Baizhang's record, which also appears in the records of Huangbo, Linji, and other later Chan teachers, including Caoshan Benji (840–901) and Dahui Zonggao (1089–1163).

> A monk asked: "How is it that Excellence of Great Universal Wisdom Buddha sat at the site of awakening for ten eons without the Buddha-dharma appearing to him, and without him achieving Buddhahood [as described in the famous passage from the *Lotus Scripture*]?"[23]

Transcripts from the Tang period convey significant information about the contents of Chan sermons, but there is little information about their ritual format. Typically, the sermons are simply prefaced by a terse phrase such as "[Chan teacher so-and-so] instructed the assembly, saying" (*shihzhong yun*, or often simply *shihzhong*) that marks the beginning of the sermon, without additional information about the circumstances and the ceremonial procedures that presumably accompanied the sermon. The commonly used phrase *shihzhong* is usually synonymous with *shangtang* (which, as noted above, literally means to "ascend the [Dharma] hall").[24] In Chan texts the two terms are used interchangeably; they both refer to a formal occasion during which a Chan teacher would address his disciples in the lecture hall of the monastery for the purpose of elucidating the essentials of Buddhist doctrines and soteriology, inspiring them, resolving their doubts about his teachings, and encouraging them to persevere in their practice.

Among the earliest explicit mentions of the ceremonial format of Chan sermons is a pithy passage from *Chanmen guishi* (Regulations of the Chan School). This brief text is appended to Baizhang's biography in *Chuandeng lu*. Supposedly it recounts Baizhang's monastic innovations that led to the establishment of a distinctive system of Chan monasticism. This is among the earliest mentions of the Baizhang legend; the text's account of the establishment of a "Chan monastery" is historically significant because it served as a forerunner for the monastic manuals that belong to the Chan rules of purity genre (see below):

> All the monks in the monastery should attend the morning practice and the evening assembly. When the Elder (i.e., the abbot) enters the [Dharma] hall and ascends to the high seat to preside over the meeting, all the monks should stand on the sides in files and listen [attentively to what is said]. At that time, the monks can raise questions about the essentials of the teaching and engage in an open and alive dialogue with the Elder, so that it is shown how to abide in accord with the Dharma.[25]

This passage suggests that formal sermons and discussions with the abbot were central events in the life of a monastic community. While the text implies that the sermons were solemn affairs and important communal functions attended by the whole congregation, because of its terseness and ambiguity this passage is not particularly illuminating regarding the contents and format of the sermons, including the ceremonial proceedings that presumably were integrated into them. Moreover, nothing in the passage can at face value be taken to point to a practice or procedure that was unique to the Chan school. This kind of equivocal description of common Buddhist practices or institutions, depicted as elements of supposedly distinctive "Chan monastic life," is a characteristic of the texts as a whole. That itself points to the fuzzy boundaries that separated Chan from the rest of Chinese Buddhism and the ambiguities that were imbedded in that relationship. While the unknown author's stated purpose was to document the establishment and institutional underpinnings of distinct Chan monasteries, he pretty much ended up describing a generic Chinese Buddhist monastery. From this we can hypothesize that the preaching rituals enacted by Chan monks were for the most part similar to those of other Buddhist groups and teachers.

While we do not have detailed Tang-period descriptions of the rituals programs enacted at monasteries led by Chan teachers, occasionally early Chan texts contain passages that shed light on some of the ceremonial practices that accompanied the sermons of Chan teachers. For instance, the *Platform Scripture* alleges to be a record of sermons given by Huineng at Dafan monastery (in present-day Guangdong), recorded by a disciple called Fahai.[26] The text begins with a description of Huineng ascending the high seat in the lecture hall to deliver a sermon to a large audience composed of monastics and laypeople, which also included a number of government officials and Confucian scholars.

> The Great Master Huineng ascended the high seat at the lecture hall
> of Dafan monastery, and then expounded the teaching of the great
> perfection of wisdom and transmitted the formless precepts. At that
> time, there were over ten thousand monks and nuns, monastic
> and lay followers assembled below his seat. The prefect of Shaozhou,
> Wei Ju, over thirty officials from various departments, and over thirty
> Confucian scholars implored the Master to preach on the teaching
> of the great perfection of wisdom. The prefect then asked the monk
> Fahai to record his words, so that they might become known to
> later generations and be of benefit to students of the Way, in order
> that they might receive the pivot of the teaching and transmit it
> among themselves, taking these words as their authority.[27]

This introductory paragraph is followed by a long sermon that starts with the famous story of Huineng's early life and spiritual quest, followed by peculiar explanations of meditation (*ding*) and wisdom (*hui*). After that, the text records Huineng's transmission of the "formless precepts" (*wuxiang jie*). While the text exhibits a partiality for content over form, mainly recording the doctrinal explanations imbedded in the rite rather than describing the ritual acts, it still shows the extent to which within the early Chan movement public preaching was formalized and connected with popular ritual forms. Huineng is depicted as starting the precept transmission rite in a customary way by bestowing to his audience the refuge in the Buddha (the first of the Three Refuges of Buddhism), but with an innovative twist that reflects the text's embrace of symbolic exegesis (*guanxin shi*, sometimes also rendered as "contemplative analysis"), an exegetical strategy that involved redefining traditional Buddhist concepts, practices, and rubrics in a metaphorical manner peculiar to the nascent Chan school (also found in other early Chan texts, such as the manuscripts of the Northern school and the records of Shenhui):[28]

> Virtuous friends, you must all with your own bodies receive the formless precepts and recite in unison what I am about to say. It will make you see the threefold body of the Buddha in your own selves. "I take refuge in the pure *dharmakāya* Buddha in my own physical body. I take refuge in the ten thousand hundred billion *nirmānakāya* Buddhas in my own physical body. I take refuge in the future perfect *sambhogakāya* Buddha in my own physical body." (Recite the above formula three times).[29]

While the text goes on to provide a detailed explanation of the three bodies of the Buddha, it is noteworthy that in the above passage Huineng is vouchsafing the ritual efficacy of the refuge formula he bestows on his audience: he tells them that the result will be nothing less than *seeing* the three bodies of the Buddha within oneself. After the explanation of the three bodies, the rite continues as Huineng leads the audience into a protracted ritual program that includes: (1) reciting the bodhisattvas' four great vows, (2) conferring formless repentance that obliterates the karmic burden of unwholesome acts, and (3) finally bestowing the formless precepts of the three refuges.[30] In each case, he leads the audience in the chanting of ritual formulae and than goes on to present his peculiar explanations of the basic concepts and actions associated with that part of the rite. It is only after these rituals that Huineng begins his exposition of the great perfection of wisdom (*mahā-prajñāpāramitā*).

Similar emphasis and appreciation of ritual efficacy is also evident in the records of Shenhui. Much of Shenhui's preaching was done from ordination platforms or altars (*jietan*), which were popular at the time. The ordination platforms were initially instituted and promoted by the famous Vinaya teacher Daoxuan (596–667) as part of his efforts to reinvigorate the monastic order.[31] They represented a hallowed ritual space graced with the Buddha's presence. As such, they were infused with religious significance and served as powerful venues for preaching and other ritual performances, in addition to their central function as sanctuaries for monastic ordinations and the transmission of precepts. By addressing his audience from the ordination platform, presumably at the beginning of ordination ceremonies, Shenhui was able to infuse his sermons with the authority of the Buddha as he strove to promote his version of Chan orthodoxy.[32]

It seems safe to presume that the ritual framework provided by the ordination platform impacted both the format and contents of Shenhui's public sermons. For instance, at the beginning of *Tanyu* (Platform Sermon), Shenhui starts his sermon by leading his audience through a series of conventional ritual procedures that focus on repenting past transgression and paying homage to the Buddhas, with the intention of engendering *bodhicitta* (*puti xin*), the initial aspiration to realize Buddhahood that marks the beginning of the bodhisattva path.[33] In *Putidamo nanzong ding shifei lun* (Treatise on the Determination of Truth and Falsehood Concerning Bodhidharma's Southern School), Shenhui takes the reliance on ritual expediency a step further as he extols the virtue of reciting the *Diamond Scripture*, a canonical text championed by him in response to the Northern school's advocacy of the *Laṅkāvatāra Scripture*. After proclaiming the cultivation of the perfection of wisdom to be the fundamental source of all practices, Shenhui tells his audience that if they want to realize the *dharmadhātu* (*fajie*, realm of reality) and perfect the samādhi of single practice (*yixing sanmei*), they must first recite the *Diamond Scripture* and learn the perfection of wisdom.[34]

With the emergence of Mazu's Hongzhou school as main representative of the Chan movement in the decades following An Lushan's (d. 757) rebellion, mass convocations such as those featuring Shenhui's sermons at the ordination platform came to an end, along with the popular rituals that accompanied them. Even so, public preaching continued to be in vogue among Mazu's followers, although we have no information about the ritual procedure associated with it. Chan texts from the late Tang period that deal with monastic life—such as Guishan Lingyou's (771–853) *Guishan jingce* (Guishan's Admonitions) and Xuefeng Yicun's (822–908) *Shi guizhi* (Teacher's Regulations)—indicate that on the whole the monastic mores and practices observed at monasteries led by Chan teachers did not substantially deviate from those at conventional monastic establishments.[35] Therefore, it seems safe to presume that some sort of traditional Buddhist rites were integrated into the formal sermons of Chan teachers, even if there was a move away from mass proselytizing and facile reliance on ritual efficacy as evidenced in the case of Shenhui. Accordingly, the importance of ritual was somewhat downplayed as it was relegated to the category of expedient means (C. *fangbian*, Skt. *upāya*), even as it remained an integral part of monastic routines.

Iconoclastic Interlude

The preaching rituals discussed in the previous section do not tally with popular images of Tang-era Chan as an iconoclastic tradition and of Chan teachers as a new type of indomitable religious leaders who discarded received traditions and subverted mainstream Buddhist mores, including formal monastic practices and liturgical procedures. In terms of historical chronology, the radicalized images of Chan teachers as unconventional spiritual virtuosi— expressed in the classical encounter-dialogue stories that depict their ostensibly eccentric acts and inscrutable verbal rumblings—were first affixed to Mazu and his disciples, collectively known as the Hongzhou school, and from the early Song period onward they became hallmarks of Chan literature and ideology. As I have shown in a previous publication, the attribution of an iconoclastic ethos to the Hongzhou school is historically unwarranted, since it is based on fictionalized accounts of the lives and teachings of Mazu and his disciples that first appear in post-Tang sources.[36] The encounter-dialogue format did not even exist during the Tang period, let alone at the time being the main medium of religious instruction within the Chan school.

But what do we make out of similar stories featured in the records of Chan teachers from the Five Dynasties period (907–960), when the encounter-dialogue format first appeared, as evidenced by the compilation of *Zutang ji* (*Patriarchs' Hall Collection*) in 952? Here is an example of that kind of story that pertains to the present topic of preaching rituals, coming from the record of Fayan Wenyi (885–958), who was retroactively recognized as the "founder" of the Fayan school of Chan. The brief account allegedly describes his first formal address as a newly installed abbot of a monastery in Jiangxi:

> When Fayan arrived at Linchuan, the prefectual governor invited him to take up residence at Chongshou temple. On the first day of holding a formal assembly [as abbot], Fayan was sitting in the tea hall, and did not leave even as the fourfold assembly at first gathered around the Dharma seat. At that time, a monk told the master, "The fourfold assembly is already gathered around your reverence's Dharma seat [and they are waiting to hear you preach]."
>
>   Fayan said, "Those assembled are retreating from calling on true virtuous friends." After a while, [Fayan] ascended the [abbot's] seat. The assembly paid their respects and [formally] requested [Fayan to preach].

Fayan said to the assembly, "Since you are all already here, I have no choice but to say something. I will recommend to you an expedient presented by the ancients. Take care." He then came down from the [abbot's] seat.[37]

Here we find Fayan subverting formal monastic procedures. His dramatic performance seems to express an ambivalence, perhaps a feigned one, about his newly assumed duties as an abbot, among which especially important was the delivery of edifying sermons for the benefit of the resident monks and the visiting laypeople. This kind of story is typical of Chan records from that period. They often feature Chan teachers' seemingly bizarre acts and perplexing utterances that—from a traditionalist Chan/Zen point of view, at least—supposedly challenged received values and interrupted their disciples' habitual patterns of thought and action, at times even catalyzing their experience of awakening.

In these accounts, the Chan teachers' supposedly ingenious dispensations of idiosyncratic insights and their curious styles of hands-on teaching take place in all sorts of situations. However, a preponderance of them is set in the Dharma hall at the occasion of giving a formal sermon. Here is a similar example from the record of Fayan's older contemporary Yunmen Wenyan (864–949), who also came to be celebrated as a "founder" of Chan schools that bear his name. In this vignette, Yunmen also appears to manifest a disdain for ritual formalism and subverts conventional ways of doing things. Once again, a communal occasion that is supposed to be a formal sermon is subverted and turned into a sort of antisermon. As he ostensibly undercuts the established procedures of public preaching, Yunmen is even more demonstrative in the application of a peculiar brand of Chan pedagogy, and he lives up to his reputation as one of the most forceful Chan teachers:

Having ascended the [Dharma] hall [for a formal sermon, Yunmen] said: "Today I shall bring up a case for you [from the teachings of the Chan school]." The whole assembly listened attentively. After a while, a monk stepped forward and bowed. Just as he was about to ask a question, the master went after him with his staff, saying: "You are like those who destroy Buddhism, those monks who receive donated food on the long bench [in the monks' hall, and say] 'What's there to talk together about?' What a bunch of roughnecks!" With his staff, the master at once chased them out of the hall.[38]

As we try to make sense of these stories within the context of the Chan school's historical evolution during the Tang-Song transition, we may want to be wary about following the lead of the somewhat naïve traditionalist inter-pretations, namely, reading the stories as factual depictions of the mystifying ways in which tenth-century Chan teachers spontaneously manifested their rarefied wisdom. However, perhaps we may also want to pause before moving into an opposite extreme direction, that is to say, going along with a recent scholarly tendency to simply portray them as pious works of religious fiction, which "served polemical, ritual, and didactic functions in the world of Song Chan" but had little to do with the lives and teachings of their main protago-nists.[39] After all, the Song editors of the Chan chronicles and records of sayings did not simply invent these stories, since they primarily compiled materials that were already in circulation. Some of the stories that feature noted tenth-century monks were already in circulation while they were still alive or soon after their death, although it is true that many of them cannot be traced back earlier than the Song period.

Was there really a marked iconoclastic turn during the tenth century, as Chan teachers such as Fayan and Yunmen began dispensing their supposedly unique insights by engaging in spontaneous, unscripted interactions with their students, in the contexts of both formal sermons and other situations, as suggested by these stories? If that was the case, their iconoclastic approach stands in stark contrast to the rigid formalism evident during the subsequent Song period (see next section). Considering the lack of research on the crucial Five Dynasties period and the decades that immediately preceded and followed it, we are not yet in a position to draw firm conclusions about the complex historical trajectories and manifold changes that the Chan school underwent in the course of the Tang-Song tradition. Those transformations were reflected in the development of Chan literature, doctrines, contemplative and liturgical practices, and monastic institutions, with significant ramifications for the sub-sequent history of Chinese Buddhism. However, putting aside for the moment the uncertain provenance of the encounter-dialogue stories and the questions about their reliability as sources of information about preaching events that transpired at Fayan's and Yunmen's monasteries, I would like to suggest that both Chan teachers are somewhat improbable iconoclasts. Notwithstanding the radical rhetoric and dramatic storytelling associated with them as evi-denced in traditional Chan lore, their historical personas as prominent and well-connected ecclesiastics do not quite fit into the popular mold of a novel type of religious radicals or countercultural heroes bent on subverting the status quo. By their time, Chan was already the main tradition of elite Chinese Buddhism, and they both occupied positions of power and privilege at the very top of the Buddhist ecclesiastic structures, in the kingdom of Southern Han (917–971) in Yunmen's case and in Southern Tang (937–975) in the case of Fayan.

For instance, the success of Yunmen's clerical career and his prominence as a Chan teacher were closely intertwined with the patronage he received from Liu Yan (r. 918–942), the ruler of the Southern Han. Yunmen first came to prominence when the new emperor invited him to the capital in 918 and bestowed on him the honor of a purple robe. The following year, Yunmen assumed his first abbacy and began his teaching career when the emperor installed him as an abbot at Lingshu monastery. Subsequently the emperor honored Yunmen by inviting him to the imperial palace and giving him the office of Inspector of the Monks in the Capital. The emperor also made regular donations to Yunmen's monastery a few times per year.[40] Therefore, Yunmen's apparent antiritual move, evident in his subversion of established ceremonial functions that were symbolic markers of the religious authority and social stature of the abbacy, as depicted in the above story about his public "sermon," was predicated on his possession of a prominent, officially sanctioned ecclesiastical position, along with his standing as a notable Chan teacher. (We should also bear in mind that even under the best scenario, there was probably a considerable discrepancy between the actual events, their subsequent recounting within the context of an oral tradition, and eventually their writing down in accord with a formulaic literary model).

By symbolically crossing over established religious and institutional boundaries, codified by means of external markers and preset forms of ritualized behavior, Yunmen was essentially asserting his status as an abbot and a Chan teacher, with all the authority and power that entails. In all probability, his behavior was also shaped by his audience's horizons of expectation, which were to some extent formed by apocryphal stories that retroactively attributed similar patterns of behavior to Mazu and the other great Chan teachers from the Tang period. At any rate, by engaging in a public performance of that kind, Yunmen reaffirmed the divide between himself—in his dual role as an abbot and a living representative of a Chan lineage that allegedly went back to the Buddha himself—and an audience composed of ordinary monks and laypeople, which relied on his edification and sought his sanction of the spiritual understanding of individual members.

In view of that, we might want to look at these stories not simply as records of spontaneous manifestation of Chan's free spirit and inscrutable essence, even if we are not inclined to preclude the possibility that in some instances there were elements of that. It seems prudent to view these kinds of records of Chan "sermons" as one-sided depictions of what in all likelihood were contrived performances that fitted into preexisting templates of behavior deemed apt for Chan teachers, even if in them there was some scope for individual expression and creativity. In that sense, these types of public performances

involved surface transgressing of established ritual forms associated with formal preaching; but in the end they were variations on the theme of the ritual
antiritualism, which is emblematic of the Chan tradition as a whole.[41] Notwithstanding the apparent radicalization of Chan school's rhetorical posturing
during the tenth century, in all likelihood the iconoclastic interlude was more
apparent than real, largely an imagined construct that in due course came to
occupy a central place in the construction of normative Chan history by means
of a series of interpretative distortions.

Song-era Schematizations of Shangtang

During the Song era, there was an upsurge in formalism within the Chan
tradition. That included increased systematization of monastic life and ongoing ritualization of various aspects of daily routine and religious practice. These
developments were part of a multifaceted transformation and far-reaching
consolidation of the Chan school within a larger context of realignment of
Chinese Buddhism, which involved creation of distinctive rhetorical styles and
novel literary genres such as the transmission of the lamp chronicles and the
gong'an (J. kōan) collections. These developments were linked to the emergence
of distinctive methods of meditative praxis, epitomized by the "investigating
the critical phrase" (kanhua) approach championed by Dahui. Significant developments in the institutional arena included the emergence of select monastic establishments that for the first time bore the official designation of a
"Chan monastery" that was granted by the imperial government.

The officially designated Chan monasteries were the most elite monastic
establishments in the Song empire, which reflected the status of the Chan
school as the predominant and most influential (although not the only) tradition of elite Buddhism. That was accompanied by a codification of detailed
rules and procedures for these monasteries, as evidenced by the growth of the
Chan rules of purity genre, which built upon a long tradition of writing on
monastic life and discipline that flourished in medieval China. These texts
provide detailed regulations for various facets of monastic life and discipline,
along with descriptions of diverse functions and formal procedures, including
preaching rituals. They also stipulate the duties and proper procedures associated with an array of monastic offices that attests to the growth of a fairly
complex monastic bureaucracy, which was central to the smooth operation of
the large Chan monasteries.[42]

The Chan school's success in becoming the main tradition of elite Buddhism in the Chinese realm was largely predicated on the development of a

distinct ideology that bolstered its religious legitimacy and anchored its in-stitutional authority. A key part of that was the Chan school's oft-repeated claim to uniqueness as a "special transmission outside of the [canonical] teachings," with the implied assertion that Chan was the highest and most authentic expression of Buddhist spirituality. That was based on the widely accepted myth of the Chan school's exclusive origins as a direct transmission of the timeless essence of the Buddha's enlightenment, brought to China via a lineage of Chan patriarchs. This myth of origins was a central element of the tradition's pseudo-history, narrated through the hagiographies of the Chan patriarchs recorded in the transmission of the lamp chronicles. The roots of the Chan school's conception of a patriarchal lineage went back to the Tang period, but the notion of lineage underwent further development and became fully institutionalized during the Song period.

The Chan school's rise to preeminence enhanced the status and authority of the abbots of monasteries associated with it, both within the confines of the Buddhist monastic community and beyond in the general world of Song so-ciety. That was reflected in the formalization of their official status and reli-gious functions. During this period, formal membership in the Chan lineage, substantiated by an official inheritance certificate that was acknowledged by the government, became an indispensable requirement for assuming the ab-bacy of any large officially designated Chan monastery. As last-generation representatives of a patriarchal lineage that according to Chan mythology went back to the historical Buddha, in theory (even if perhaps not always in actual practice), the Chan abbots assumed the roles of living embodiments of the highest Buddhist virtues and bearers of the torch of enlightenment.

The formalization of the status and role of the Chan abbotship was re-flected in the codification of preaching rituals, which took the form of highly structured ceremonial performances held in the monastery's Dharma hall, a building that was architecturally similar to the Buddha hall. The primary function of the Dharma hall was to serve as a venue for the abbot's formal lectures, and it was also used for the inauguration of new abbots.[43] The abbot's sermons were stylized public events that occupied a central place in the mo-nastic calendar. They were replete with symbolism and infused with conven-tional ritual elements such as formal processions, bows, prostrations, and invocations. While they were apparently organized as teaching venues for the resident monastic congregation, they were also a major draw for lay patrons, who attended the festivities and made generous monetary contributions to the monastery and the monks. The monastic codes and manuals from the Song and subsequent dynasties provide diverse classifications of Chan sermons, based on the events that occasioned them and on their scheduling pattern.

Some of the sermons were part of the regular monastic schedule, while others were held on special occasions, such as the emperor's birthday. Here are some of the main designations:

1. fortnightly sermons (*danwang*), held on new moon and full moon days, traditional Buddhist observance days, which coincided with the first and fifteenth days of each lunar month;
2. sermons held on a fifth day (*wucan*), given four times a month, typically on the fifth, tenth, twentieth, and twenty-fifth days of the lunar month, although there are other variations on this pattern;
3. the nine sermons (*jiucan*), held every three days;
4. sermons held in honor of the emperor's birthday (*shengjie*), during which the monastic congregation offered their best wishes and prayed for the emperor's longevity and good health (*zhusheng*);
5. sermons that commemorated the passing away of an emperor (*daxing zhuiyan*), held in order to offer prayers and seek blessings on behalf of the late emperor;
6. sermons occasioned by abbot's going away from the monastery (*chudui*), held upon the abbot's return from outside preaching engagements;
7. sermons held in accord with events (*yinshi*), which were irregularly scheduled in response to specific circumstances, such as external events that threatened the peace and prosperity of the monastery and the surrounding community;
8. sermons held to express gratitude to the head monastic officials (*xie bingfu*).[44]

Among Song-era texts, a fairly detailed description of the formal procedure of "ascending the hall" is included in *Chanyuan qinggui* (*Rules of Purity for Chan Monasteries*), the oldest full-fledged Chan monastic code compiled in 1103 by Changlu Zongze (d. 1107?). According to the author's preface, he compiled the text in order to codify a comprehensive and authoritative system of regulations and procedural guidelines for monasteries associated with the Chan school.[45] Notwithstanding the explicit affirmation of a unique pattern of Chan monastic life, the monastic regulations presented in this and subsequent Chan monastic codes are largely based on the Vinaya and related commentarial literature; in addition, they also include many common Buddhist and Chinese customs.[46] Therefore, the rules for Chan monasteries do not represent a radical departure from the rest of Chinese Buddhist monasticism or function as definitive markers of institutional independence on the part of the Chan school. In fact, they exemplify the Chan school's institutional

conservatism and its embrace of the role of embodiment of Buddhist orthodoxy within the social and religious mainstreams of Song China. These kinds
of conservative attitudes are evident in Zongze's description of the ascending
the hall ceremony, which is found at the beginning of the second fascicle of
his code. Here is the initial section that describes the convocation of the
monastic assembly in the Dharma hall:

> On the fixed dates when the abbot ascends the seat in the Dharma
> hall to give the morning sermon, nobody is to leave the convoca-
> tion after the early morning meal. At dawn, after the signal for
> "opening of the quiet" is given, the chief seat leads the assembly to
> the Sangha hall. After hearing the first drum sequence, the chief seat
> and the assembly enter the Dharma hall in an orderly procession,
> following the order of seniority, and each with his side to the center
> position. The position closest to the Dharma seat is the most senior.
> The chief seat, scribe, sutra curator, guest master, and bath master
> form their own row in front of the assembly, standing in the pro-
> scribed order. The remaining chief officers simply take their posi-
> tions among the assembly. The retired elderly abbots take their seats
> in front of the chief seat, leaving two empty positions between them
> and him. These retired elderly abbots stand facing south, but with
> their sides turned slightly to the center. At the sound of the second
> drum sequence, the four administrators [the prior, rector, cook, and
> superintendent] enter the hall, walking in order of their respective
> ranks. They stand at their bowing mats by the Dharma hall's door on
> the south side and face the Dharma seat. The prior takes his posi-
> tion on the east side of the hall. When the postulants hear the first
> sequence of the drum, they form a row in front of the storage hall and
> stand waiting. At the second drum sequence they follow the ad-
> ministrators into the Dharma hall to attend the sermon. Inside the
> Dharma hall, they bow to all present and move to the east side of
> the hall, where they stand facing the west. The position farthest to the
> north should be the most senior position. (The postulants attend-
> ing the sermon must wear shoes and socks.)[47]

The ceremonial occasions of the abbot's formal sermons were key events
in the monastic calendar that brought together the whole community. While
the congregating of all resident monks symbolized the unity of their religious
community, the formal staging of the event also highlighted the hierarchical
stratification imbedded in it. The careful description of the monks' entry
sequence into the Dharma hall prior to the formal sermon and their positions

within the hall provide clear clues about the various participants' status within the monastic community, with the abbot occupying the highest position and wielding unquestioned authority. The whole event is carefully choreographed, with each member of the monastic community entering in a strictly pre-scribed sequence that reflects his rank and status. The postulants enter the hall last, which symbolizes their lowly standing within the monastery.[48]

Within the ritual context of the Dharma hall, the symbolic center of power and marker of supreme status is the abbot's ceremonial chair, called the Dharma seat (*fazuo*). Placed on a centrally positioned, elevated dais, the abbot's seat evokes the preaching thrones of the Buddhas and bodhisattvas described in the scriptures. Further analogy is that of the emperor's throne in the audi-ence hall at the imperial palace. The position of each participant in relation to the abbot's seat correlates with his rank and status within the monastic com-munity. The closer a monk is situated to the abbot's seat, the higher is his status, with the retired abbots occupying the highest position (after the current abbot), followed by the high-ranking monastic officials. This kind of arrange-ment reflects a system of hierarchical stratification formed under the influence of two disparate models of social organization. First, there is the influence of the Vinaya (the monastic code of discipline), according to which monks should be seated in order of seniority, based on the time of their ordination, and junior monks should pay respects to their seniors. Second, there is the Chinese bu-reaucratic model with its clearly designated ranks and offices, which are care-fully observed in various ceremonial events at the imperial court and other formal functions.

Just as Buddhist devotees bow and worship the Buddha, and in slightly different context court officials pay their respects to the emperor by per-forming similar ceremonial acts, in the Dharma hall everybody reverences the abbot. The monks and the lay attendees worship the abbot as a living Chan patriarch who transmits the flame of the Buddha's enlightenment, but they also pay him respects in his official capacity as the supreme leader of the monastic community, with an undisputed power and authority to influence all aspects of its operation. Here is the text's description of the prescribed manner in which members of the monastic congregation worship the abbot, thereby acknowledging his religious authority and official status:

> At the third sequence of the drum, the attendant informs the abbot that it is time to enter the [Dharma] hall. Everyone bows in unison to the abbot, and the abbot ascends the Dharma seat and stands in front of the Chan chair. First the attendants bow. (The attendant who carries the incense now ascends towards the Dharma seat on the east

side not far from the seat, and stands facing the west with his side to the center). Then the chief seat and the assembly turn to face the Dharma seat, bow, and return to their positions. The administrators then step forward and bow, standing opposite and facing the chief seat. The one standing closest to the Dharma seat is the most senior. Then the novices and the postulants turn to face the Dharma seat, bow, and return to stand in their positions. (In the tradition of Lushan Yuantong [1027–1090], the postulants enter the Dharma hall in a single file, bow, and stand in the east section divided into three rows. The administrators then bow and remain standing. At this point the three rows of postulants, beginning with the southern-most position, walk one after another toward the Dharma seat and stand in an east-west row in front of the abbot. After they bow again, the one with the easternmost position leads the postulants back to their original position in three rows on the east side of the hall, where they bow once more and remain standing.) The guest master then leads the donors to stand in front of the administrators. The administrators, as well as the assembly, remain standing in a straight line with their sides to the center, listening to the abbot's sermon. When the abbot descends from the Dharma platform to exit the Dharma hall after the sermon, all those present bow simultaneously and, beginning with the chief seat, enter and circumambulate the Sangha hall. Everyone then remains standing in the Sangha hall until the abbot enters. Then the administrators circumambulate the hall.[49]

Chanyuan qinggui provides no description of the general character and specific contents of the actual sermons. However, from other sources—such as the records of sayings of Song monks and the *gong'an* collections—we know that they were highly stylized presentations, far removed from the romanti-cized images of Chan teachers spontaneously manifesting their unconven-tional wisdom, which according to popular lore included extemporaneous repartee, inscrutable proclamations, emblematic gestures, and other forms of uncontrived interactions with the audience. Usually, the primary sources and models for the sermons were the teachings of the famous Chan teachers from the Tang and Five Dynasties periods, as presented in their records of sayings and the transmission of the lamp chronicles. The pithy sayings and dramatic actions of the ancient patriarchs were evoked and ritually reenacted by the abbot in the course of the sermon, thus drawing a connection with the glories of the bygone Tang era, when the Chan tradition supposedly reached the pinnacle of its brilliance and perfection.[50]

Often the sermon revolved around a specific Chan case, typically a well-known encounter dialogue that featured a famous Chan teacher from the past. In such cases, the sermon was an exegesis of a sort on the case, replete with stylized yet seemingly radical rhetorical flourishes deemed characteristic of the classical Chan style, along with witty rejoinders. The sermons were also peppered with abstruse allusions and metaphors that appealed to a culturally sophisticated and classically educated literati audience, which was a key recipient of Chan teachings and important sources of political and economic patronage. The lay audience is explicitly mentioned in the above passage, which indicates that the lay donors were not only present at the sermons but were included in the ceremonial functions that preceded it. The preaching ritual's ending follows a similar ceremonial pattern as its beginning. The following passage also points to the inclusion of optional elements in the ceremony, such as serving tea after the sermon:

> If the monastery serves tea after the sermon, the abbot sits in his position and the administrators stand outside the door. After the tea is finished, the abbot stands up and the bell to exit the hall is rung. If there is no tea, the administrators circumambulate the hall and exit, merely waiting for the abbot's bow before withdrawing. Sometimes, after the three strikes of the bell to exit, the abbot ascends the platform inside the hall. In the morning, according to custom, there is a break from the sermon; but if the abbot is scheduled to preach, then after the sermon there is no circumambulation of the Sangha hall.[51]

The concluding part of the section on *shangtang* in *Chanyuan qinggui* makes it clear that attendance of the abbot's sermon was compulsory for all residents of the monastery, with a couple of exceptions for monastic officers who were precluded from attending because of their official duties. There were penalties for nonattendance; monks were also prohibited to cause disturbance by being late and entering after the abbot had commenced the sermon.

> Whenever the abbot ascends the seat in the Dharma hall, all must attend, with the exception of the chief of the assembly quarters and the Sangha hall monitor. Whoever violates this rule will be subject to the monastery's penalty. It is best to avoid this offense. If a monk is detained because of some extraneous business or an emergency, and not due to his own indolence, then he may arrive a bit late. But if the abbot has already ascended his seat in the Dharma hall, the monk should not enter, and he should avoid letting the abbot see him. All

those who attend the sermon should not wear hats or sleeve-like cowls (including the abbot). If a person should ask an unintentionally amusing question, no one should burst out laughing, or even break a slight smile. They should maintain a demeanor of sincerity and solemnity while listening to the abbot's profound teaching.[52]

The concluding sentences reiterate the great importance of the preaching ritual in the religious life of the monastic community. They also once more highlight its ceremonial decorum and solemn character. Here we are far removed from the popular depictions of Chan monks as iconoclastic characters bent on subverting established mores and rejecting conventions. Even any semblance of humor is expunged from the preaching event, and an unintended insertion of it into the proceedings must be ignored without even registering a silent smile on the monks' faces. They are simply expected to dignifiedly stand in rapt attention, solemnly present, absorbing every word of the abbot's profound sermon (although, needless to say, in actual practice it did not always work that way).[53] To sum up, there was little room for unscripted improvisation or spontaneous action in the Chan sermons of the Song era. They were highly formal events that reaffirmed the status of the abbot as a living patriarch, legitimized existing institutions and the structure of the monastic hierarchy, underscored other central aspects of Chan ideology, attracted the laity and motivated its generous donations, and of course provided religious inspiration and instructions about the pursuit of the Chan path of practice and realization.

Later Developments

The Chan teachings, practices, institutions, and literary genres that became fully developed and formalized during the Song period remained normative during the succeeding epochs of Chinese history. From the vantage point of subsequent history, the ideological constructs and the traditions of the Song era can be regarded as standards of Chan orthodoxy and established models of orthopraxis, not only in China but also throughout East Asia. That remained the case even though at its core Song Chan embraced an imagined vision of Tang Chan as the classical paradigm. The Chan traditions of Korea and Japan also came to be based on Song models. That influence continues down to the present time throughout East Asia, notwithstanding peculiar regional developments and later innovations.

In the case of Japan, the initial transmission of Zen took place during the Song period. A central legitimizing claim of early Zen pioneers such as Eisai

(1141–1215) and Dōgen (1200–1253) was that they were directly transmitting the orthodox teachings and practices of Song Chan, learned during their study in China. That included the various monastic conventions and ceremonial practices, including preaching rituals. Dōgen is especially noteworthy for his strict emphasis on monastic decorum and proper ritual form. Under his influence, there was a notable move within his Sōtō school toward further ritualization of Zen practice, which not only included ceremonial functions, such as daily liturgies and formal sermons, but also came to include virtually all aspects of priestly life, even mundane activities such as taking a bath. Meditation was not spared from this shift in focus and associated reconstituting of Zen practice, as it became formalized as a ritual expression of Zen awakening.[54]

In the Korean case, Chan was initially transmitted during the unified Silla dynasty (668–935) by monks who traveled to China to study with noted Chan teachers, mostly students of Mazu. However, during the Koryŏ period (937–1392), Song style teachings and practices, especially as represented by the Linji school and its *huatou* method of meditation, became chief models for the Korean Sŏn tradition. The widespread and enduring influence of ritual models and teaching procedures formalized within the context of Song Chan—as written down in the Chan monastic codes and as passed down by generations of monks—accounts for the commonality of basic elements constitutive of preaching rituals across the various Chan/Zen schools and traditions throughout East Asia. Needless to say, there were (and still there are) deviations from normative models, which reflected adaptations to local conditions and responses to changing historical predicaments and diverse social milieus.

Changes in monastic practices and rituals were also brought about by way of occasional efforts to reform or revive Chan/Zen traditions that were perceived to be moribund, corrupt, or simply in need of suffusion with new spirit and energy. Typically, revival efforts were initiated in response to existing conditions, but they were cast in terms of a return to hallowed precedents set during a glorious golden age, usually that of the great Chan teachers from the Tang era. At times, a central theme of those developments was the revival of classical rhetorical styles and teachings stratagems, exemplified by the ascending the hall ceremony. A case in point is the revival of the paradigmatic Chan practice of encounter dialogue in seventeenth-century China, which involved a reinvention of tradition on the basis of the *gong'an* stories contained in classical Chan literature. The reenactment of the iconoclastic acts featured in those stories was presented as a hallmark of putative reemergence of an authentic Chan style of teaching and practice.[55] Especially pertinent to our discussion is the manner in which at the time some Chan teachers reimagined a celebrated past by formulaic manifestations of an allegedly ancient Chan spirit in the context of formal sermons in the Dharma hall.

The infusion of archaic, textually derived elements into the public sermons of Chan teachers during the late Ming (1368–1644) and early Qing (1644–1911) periods involved mimicking the iconoclastic teaching style of classical Chan teachers, especially the shouting at and beating of students in response to their questions, which became a central element of the ascending the hall ceremony. While these kinds of improvisations, centered on an antinomian model of presentation enshrined in authoritative texts, were meant to convey a genuine Chan spirit, they elicited strong criticism in some quarters. The Chan teachers in question were taken to task for their contrived and romanticized reinvention of archaic religious ideals through the artful manipulation of textual models. Many literati viewed this kind of Chan performance as highly artificial and degenerate, hardly different from the dramatic entertainment offered by theatrical programs. They accused the Chan teachers of merely putting up a show, equipped with all the props and elements of a dramatic performance, thereby beguiling a captive but unsophisticated audience and vulgarizing the true Chan spirit. According to them, the Chan teachers were guilty of acting irresponsibly in ways that resembled actors in popular dramas, and they summarily dismissed their claims to a genuine Chan insight.[56]

The ongoing interplay between the form and contents in the context of public Chan sermons and the occasional tensions it engenders are recurrent themes in Chan history. Since for reasons of space it is impossible to cover all pertinent developments and thematic variations apparent in late Chan history, I will end with a modern description of the ascending the hall ceremony that highlights the deeply seated formalism of Zen ritual and its continuing centrality in Zen monastic life. The example comes from Robert Buswell's study of Zen monasticism in contemporary Korea, based on his experiences at Songgwang monastery during the 1970s. Here is his description of the ritual sequence of events that precede the beginning of the Zen (Sŏn) teacher's formal sermon:

> Once the audience is settled and still, the Sŏn master enters from this center door and takes his regular seat amid the assembly. His attendant enters simultaneously from a side door at the front of the hall, as is appropriate to his status, and takes his seat next to the dais. The monk coordinating the ceremony, usually the verger or a senior monk, strikes the mokt'ak once. The audience then rises and recites in unison a short series of verses. The assembly resumes its seats and listens silently as the monk coordinating the ceremony and

an assistant perform a ten-minute ritual. After that ritual is finished, two monks from the audience, usually the master's attendant and one of the younger meditation monks, come forward and prostrate themselves three times before the Sŏn master as an invitation to him to deliver his lecture. The master bows with palms together once at his seat in response, rises, and walks to the dais accompanied by the two monks.... After the master is seated, the verger will lead the monks in special bowing and chanting, three times requesting formally that the master impart his wisdom to them. The rector then strikes the chukpi three times, initiating some three minutes of silent meditation in order to get the monks into the appropriate frame of mind for hearing the lecture. When the rector strikes the chukpi three times to end the period, the audience, which had been facing directly forward throughout this time, turns slightly toward the dais. The master then raises his Sŏn staff (*chujangja*) and strikes it hard against the dais three times to mark the beginning of the lecture.[57]

The contents of the sermon itself are as formulaic as the rites that precede (and follow) them. Relying on written notes prepared in advance, the Zen teacher delivers a carefully scripted and exceedingly stylized performance that includes recitation of poems composed in literary Chinese, shouting, making enigmatic statements, posing rhetorical questions to the audience, pausing in silence, and looking in the four directions. The sermon ends with another ritual sequence that includes the Zen teacher hitting the staff on the dais, followed by the congregation's chanting of the Buddha's name and recitation of the four bodhisattva vows.[58] The whole preaching ceremony treads on a familiar ground and in general accords with the earlier models discussed above. Once again, we are as far removed from the extemporaneous homilies popularly associated with the teachings of the Zen masters as we can possibly imagine. Buswell also makes note of the monks' occasionally not very enthused reactions to Zen teachers' highly conventional and lackluster presentations. They include complaints about the abbot droning on and repeating discredited legends, or simply succumbing to boredom and falling asleep, only to be woken up by the rector whose duty is to keep the audience awake during the often tedious sermon.[59]

Concluding Remarks

Historically grounded studies of the performative features and socioreligious functions of Chan rituals—including those associated with the abbots' formal

sermons and other types of public addresses—shed light on the Chan traditions' ongoing appropriation and adaptation of basic forms of Buddhist ritual.
The evolution and codification of ceremonial procedures was an integral part of
a larger process of identity creation, and it generally unfolded in ways that
bolstered the Chan school's religious legitimacy and reinforced its principal
position within the wider Buddhist milieu. This process especially gathered
speed and became formalized during the Song period, but there are precedents
that take us back to the Tang and Five Dynasties eras. The gradual development
of distinct styles of Chan sermons involved the introduction of innovative
features that brought into relief significant distinctions in terms of contents
and ritual form, even if Chan preaching rituals remained grounded in their
pan-Buddhist prototypes.

The establishment of the ascending the Dharma hall ceremony as a
principal religious event, while related to the traditionally central function of
public preaching in Chinese Buddhism, strengthened the Chan school's ideological claims to unsurpassed spiritual pedigree and institutional distinctive-
ness. In addition, there were its educational and social balancing roles within
the context of the monastic community. Like the rituals of other traditions,
this type of ritual mirrored the organization and values of the culture from
which it emerged.[60] The Chan abbots' assumption of religious authority and
the wielding of power linked with it, unmistakably marked by their public
performance of preaching rituals, largely revolved around their presumed
status as living patriarchs and bearers of the wordless and timeless flame of
awakening. From the Song period onward, by means of distinct styles of sermonizing that involved the use of recognizable Chan idiom and the performance of stylized gestures and utterances, the Chan abbots purportedly
manifested their personal insight, but they also underscored their exalted
status as putative members of the Chan lineage, in addition to their positions as
heads of the monastic community.

In light of the roles (albeit secondary ones) that evolving ritual forms
played in the development of the Chan school's religious identities, the historical analysis of Chan rituals has to concurrently move in two directions and
account for two sets of interrelated issues. On one hand, there is the broad
historical context of the Chan school's selective adoption of key elements of
popular Buddhist ceremonials and rites, including those associated with public
lectures, which had wide currency in China and the rest of East Asia. This helps
us appreciate the close links between the Chan school and the rest of East Asian
Buddhism, thereby undermining the mythos of the Chan school's uniqueness
and singularity. The shared common ground is reflected in the analogous
patterns of monastic life and practice, including ritual performances, which

made "Chan monasteries" barely distinguishable from other non-Chan establishments of similar size and function. That was the case despite the subitist rhetorical flourishes and iconoclastic posturing occasionally adopted by various Chan/Zen teachers and traditions. That includes the oblique critiques of ritualism as empty formalism and deviation from authentic practice found in Chan literature—that are further hyperbolized and decontextualized in popular (and sometimes scholarly) works on Zen—which are typically ascribed to Chan teachers who were steeped in the performance of rituals.[61]

On the other hand, Chan ritual developed certain features unique to the Chan school, which helps us to better appreciate the ways by which the tradition carved its identity as a distinct school of Buddhism and a key player in the Chinese (and more broadly East Asian) religious landscape. The same can be said of the relationship between ritual and other aspects of Chan praxis. From the Song period onward, those distinctive elements reinforced the Chan school's claims to orthodoxy and highlighted the Chan teachers' unique standing among the monastic elite. The preaching rituals thereby bolstered the religious authority of the Chan teachers and enhanced their privileged social status. But even as these public performances reaffirmed their position at the apex of the ecclesiastic hierarchy, they also facilitated the communication of specific religious teachings and the articulation of distinct perspectives on issues of ultimate import.

3

Buddhist Rituals for Protecting the Country in Medieval Japan: Myōan Eisai's "Regulations of the Zen School"

Albert Welter

The author would like to acknowledge the Social Science and Humanities Research Council of Canada's support for research on which the current study is based.

Introduction

The purpose of religious ritual is normally understood within the soteriological context of the religion in question. Until recently, this has been especially true in depictions of Zen Buddhism that place great emphasis on monastic rituals aimed at initiating the experience of awakening, or *satori*, in practitioners. As a result, in the Zen context, monastic ritual has often been considered in terms of the operation of the monastery and its aim of promoting enlightenment for individual members. Zen monastic rituals such as seated meditation (*zazen*) and *kōan* study have normally been emphasized in this regard, but even such mundane activities as cooking, cleaning, and weeding the garden are often presumed to be part of the heuristic program for engendering *satori*. While this explanation may make sense in terms of the modern project to rehabilitate

Zen and promote it to international audiences, how does it square with the aims and purposes of Zen ritual in medieval Japan?

This essay challenges the individualistic presuppositions that characterize many contemporary interpretations of Zen monastic training. While the goal of *satori* is inherent in Zen, as in other forms of Buddhist monastic training, this was not the *raison d'être* of the medieval Zen monastery. Rather than individually driven, Zen ritual, even *zazen*, was viewed as a collective activity serving the needs of the broader social community and government political aims. Regularly scheduled daily and annual rituals and ceremonies at Zen monasteries were designed to fulfill public spiritual and religious goals in accordance with social and political expediency. As members of a Zen monastic community, individuals performed designated rituals and ceremonies, but the rationale for their doing so was not individual but communal, even "national" (if the use of this term may be allowed for a period prior to the rise of nation-states). The very existence of the Zen monastery as an institution was to participate in communal aims, under government sanction.

The political and communal nature of Zen monasteries is nowhere so clear as in the Japanese Rinzai Zen pioneer, Myōan Eisai's (a.k.a. Yōsai) *Promoting Zen for Protecting the Country (Kōzen gokokuron)*. In this document, Eisai argues for the Heian and Kamakura elite to adopt Zen, newly introduced in Japan as an independent school, as best suited for preserving and maintaining the imperial mission. Eisai stipulates how rituals performed at Zen monasteries commemorating imperial birthdays, invoking the names of the buddhas, repaying the emperor's kindness, and so on, are all designed to enhance the imperial cause and the fortunes of the Japanese state. In addition, the essay explores how daily rituals at Japanese monasteries implicitly drew upon the rigorous moral agenda demanded of participants. A strictly observed ethical framework served as the basis for moral purification and the rationale for the broader place Zen occupied within society. As a moral beacon, the Zen monastery functioned as a transforming influence beneficial to society as a whole. To Eisai, this provided a major justification for Zen's appearance on Japanese soil. In short, the communal and state-imperial understanding of the function of ritual at Zen monasteries was a major aspect of the status Zen enjoyed and the rationale for its existence. Martin Collcutt, writing on Eisai's aims for the Rinzai monastic institution, comments:

> Eisai and his immediate disciples were not engaged by the shoguns and their retainers as teachers of Zen meditation or philosophy. Their principal function was to conduct invocations and prayers for the memory of the deceased or the intention of the living, and to

make appropriate incantation in time of warfare, drought, or natural disaster. Their religious function, therefore, hardly differed from that of the Tendai or Shingon priests who had previously performed these very same activities.[1]

Eisai's assumption of Tendai authority as "Chief Seat of the Buddhist Religion for Ensuring the Security of the Country" (chingo-kokka no dōjō), the designation given the religious ideology selected as the spiritual safeguard for Japan, was not based on the pretext that the spiritual role of Zen differed from Tendai but that Zen fulfilled that role where Tendai had failed. Rather than forge new ground, Eisai was intent on fulfilling prevailing assumptions governing the role of religion in medieval Japanese society. As I have written elsewhere,[2] the role of religion in medieval Japan was predicated on an ideology espoused in Mahayana scriptures, particularly the Ninnō gokoku hannya-kyō (Prajnaparamita Sutra Explaining How Benevolent Kings Protect Their Countries, or simply, the Ninnō-kyō [Sutra of Benevolent Kings]).[3] Along with the Myōhō renge-kyō (Sutra of the Lotus Blossom of the Fine Dharma, better known simply as the Hokke-kyō, the Lotus Sutra),[4] and the Konkōmyō-kyō (Sutra of the Golden Light),[5] the Ninnō-kyō provided the foundation of Buddhist ideology in Japan, collectively known in Japan as the "three sutras for the protection of the country" (chingo kokka no sambukyō).[6] The ideology promoted in these scriptures was amply evident throughout the Heian period (794–1185).

While it is commonly supposed that early Kamakura bakufu leaders were attracted to Zen for spiritual reasons and for its discipline and a rough and ready call to action that was part and parcel of samurai life, nothing could be further from the truth.[7] Early Zen patrons looked to Zen for largely the same reasons that previous Japanese leaders had looked to Tendai and Shingon, to honor the dead, ensure victory in warfare, and alleviate sufferings associated with drought and natural disaster. Far from a revolutionary doctrine, Eisai's Zen was a conservative reaction to the intemperances of contemporary monastic life, a return to the basics of Buddhist teaching as understood in medieval Japan. As such, it represented a return to moral foundations, in the belief that such return would produce tangible, salutary effects for the country as a whole, particularly as directed by its rulers.

A central feature of Eisai's conservatism was a return to the monastic discipline central to the Buddhist enterprise. The purpose of monastic renewal, according to Eisai, was not primarily for the edification of individual practitioners but for the enhancement of the country. Stated differently, the primary aim was not the enlightenment of the monastic clergy but the moral enhancement of the society in which the clergy functioned and for whom it served. In practice, this relegated the monastery to an arm of the secular bureaucracy, whose interest monastic institutions and rituals were designed to serve. Again, this is highly reminiscent of parameters established by Saichō, who conceived the religious (i.e., Buddhist) nature as the treasure of the nation, possessed by the highest Buddhist (i.e., Tendai) adepts; the purpose of monastic training on Mt. Hiei was explained in terms of the service that Tendai monks rendered in safeguarding the nation.[8]

One section of the *Kōzen gokokuron*, section eight, "The Established Regulations of the Zen School" (*Zenshū [kenritsu] shimoku*),[9] lay at the heart of Eisai's reform agenda. In this section, Eisai outlines the aims and function of Zen ritual in detail, implicitly suggesting the validity of Zen practice over all others. In this regard, section eight is the cornerstone of Eisai's vision for the renewal of Japan based on the moral superiority and spiritual efficacy of Zen institutional practice. The present study is a description and analysis of the rituals for protecting the country at Zen monasteries, focusing on Eisai's reform program in section eight. As a prelude, I compare Eisai's orientation toward ritual observances at Zen monasteries to the influential Song dynasty Chinese guide for Chan ritual, the *Chanyuan qinggui* (Rules of Purity for the Chan Monastery). Following a description of Eisai's ritual program, I embark on an analysis of the theoretical basis for such a program, exploring the adaptation of Buddhist ritual usage to Confucian suppositions regarding the role of ritual in society, focusing on the widespread use of incense offering in Buddhist ceremonies.

The *Kōzen gokokuron* and *Chanyuan qinggui*: Convergent Aims and Divergent Purposes

While it is true that recent studies on Chan and Zen ritual have emphasized actual practice at Chan and Zen monasteries and the impact of monastic institutions on society,[10] it is interesting to observe that the explicit articulation of the Zen monastic ritual program and its social implications have been evident all along in works like Eisai's *Kōzen gokokuron* and, more particularly, the *Chanyuan qinggui* (Rules of Purity for the Chan Monastery).[11] The *Chanyuan qinggui*, the oldest intact monastic code for the Chan institution, was an influential work whose stipulations provided the basic framework for operations at Song Chan monasteries. Zen pioneers in Japan eagerly adopted it as the model for the Zen monastic institution in Japan. Eisai explicitly stipulates the *Chanyuan qinggui* (J. *Zen'en shingi*) as his model at the outset of section eight. As such, it serves as the basis for his Zen ritual program.[12] However influential the *Chanyuan qinggui* was for Eisai's reform program, it is important to note that the *Kōzen gokokuron* was written with a different aim and set of concerns. For Eisai, knowledge of the *Chanyuan qinggui* was assumed. He was not inclined to repeat its contents *verbatim*. Moreover, Eisai wrote in a different context for an audience different from that for which the *Chanyuan qinggui* was intended. An examination of the general character of each work brings us closer to their implicit aims.

Broadly speaking, the two works have much in common, and one can understand many of the intentions of each in reference to the other. The *Chanyuan qinggui* was compiled as a manual for monastic organization. As such, it was primarily an internal document, a manual stipulating proper behavior and conduct during the routines that characterized Chan (and Zen) monastic life. Eisai's aim in the *Kōzen gokokuron* was different. While Eisai undoubtedly took the content of the *Chanyuan qinggui* for granted, his purpose in the *Kōzen gokokuron* demanded a different approach to the subject of monastic organization and discipline from the one the *Chanyuan qinggui* provided.

Large sections of the *Chanyuan qinggui* are unmentioned by Eisai, at least in the context for which he was writing in the *Kōzen gokokuron*. For example, there are numerous sections in the *Chanyuan qinggui* devoted to the incidentals of monastic life and behavior, sections on such things as the "preparation of personal effects" (*bian daoju*), "packing one's belongings" (*zhuang bao*), "taking up residence" (*guada*), "attendance at meals" (*fu zhoufan*), "attending the tea ceremony" (*fu chatang*), "entering the abbot's quarters" (*ru shi*), and so on.[13] The point of the *Chanyuan qinggui* is to regulate the behavior of monastics and the administrative functions at Chan monasteries.[14] The focus is on the conduct expected by denizens of the monastery as they encounter the specific situations of their monastic career, whether it be feasts sponsored by donors, procedures for burning incense or using the latrine, or fulfilling one of the numerous administrative offices of the monastery, from abbot down to street fund raiser or mill master.

This is not to say that Eisai was uninterested in the internal operation of the Zen monastery. He clearly was. Eisai's personal experiences with the Song Chan monastic institution clearly made a lasting impression on him. Eisai's proposed reforms for the monastic institution in Japan were the product of his experience at Song Chan monasteries. What Eisai wrote was not a document, like the *Chanyuan qinggui*, intended for the internal organization of the monastic institution. This document already existed, and Eisai took its existence for granted. The *Kōzen gokokuron* was written as an external document aimed at the cultural elite, both secular and religious, to adopt Zen as a means to achieve monastic, and thus moral and spiritual, reform.

However much the *Chanyuan qinggui* is influenced by procedures and protocols stemming from the larger Chinese cultural context, it is essentially an internal document designed for the organization and administration of the sangha community. Eisai is largely interested in outlining how this program of rituals is maintained at monasteries, in general terms, and why such a program is conducive to national well-being. In this context, the *Kōzen goko-kuron* provides the public rationale for encouraging and supporting secluded communities of Zen monastics. While it is specific to the medieval Japanese context, the rationale Eisai provides is not restricted by its temporal and geographical distinctness but resonates widely throughout the Chan and Zen world as public, political justification for its spiritual enterprise. Herein lies the value of Eisai's treatise. While Chan and Zen produced many monastic codes,[15] and evocative meditations on the value of monastic discipline (e.g., Dōgen), there are few explicit public arguments outlining the rationale for Chan and Zen's spiritual function on behalf of state and society. In this manner, Eisai's *Kōzen gokokuron* augments and enhances our understanding of the *Chanyuan qinggui* and other Chan monastic codes by making explicit their implicit rationale.

Eisai's "Regulations of the Zen School"

According to Eisai, the program of rituals at Zen monasteries is maintained through ten provisions and sixteen types of ceremonies.[16] Since Eisai does not attempt to provide a comprehensive description but is interested in demonstrating how each item contributes to the aim of protecting the country and enhancing its spiritual welfare, the emphasis given provides an opportunity to deduce something of Eisai's actual intention.

As noted above, Eisai's ten stipulated provisions constitute simply an outline of the rituals for protecting the country. The details are contained in the formal stipulations of texts such as the *Chanyuan qinggui*.

The first provision is for the monastic compound itself (*ji'en*, C. *siyuan*). According to Eisai, all monasteries are modeled after the plan of the Jetavana vihara (*Gion shōja*), reputedly the first monastery of the Buddhist order built by the wealthy merchant and Buddhist patron Sudatta. What Eisai emphasizes is not some allegedly unique architectural plan attributed to Zen monasteries, suggesting the priority of meditation in the monks' hall (*sōdō*, C. *sengtang*) or the Zen master's teaching in the Dharma Hall (*hōdō*, C. *fatang*), but the congruence of all Buddhist monasteries, including the Zen monastic compound. While this may not concur with the pattern imagined by ideologues of "pure"

Zen, it is actually consistent with the plans of Song Chan monastic compounds, which deviated little from their non-Chan counterparts.[17]

In addition to the plan for the monastery, Eisai stresses that the monastery compound is bounded on four sides with one main gate only and no side entrances. This main gate, moreover, is carefully monitored by a gatekeeper, who allows visitors to enter only during daylight hours (i.e., from dawn to dusk) and closes the gate at dusk. He especially prohibits nuns, women, and outlaws from spending the night inside the temple. The reason stipulated by Eisai echoes the logic reiterated throughout Buddhist monastic codes attributing the moral depravity of monks and the disappearance of Buddhist teaching to illicit affairs with women and fraternizing with unsavory characters. Although unstated, Eisai also implicitly invokes the criticism of sangha institutions by secular leaders as refuges for outlaws escaping civil prosecution. In either case, Eisai is affirming the moral integrity of the Zen monastery, which strictly guards against the circumstances leading to moral lapse or civil violation.

The second provision of the Zen monastery mentioned by Eisai is receiving the precepts (*jukai*, C. *shoujie*), the ritual associated with formal renunciation of lay life and entrance into the monastic order. According to Eisai, different sets of precepts, those of the greater vehicle and those of the lesser vehicle, exist on account of emotional differences (i.e., different aptitudes) in people. The point, however, is that regardless of which set of rules is followed, in either case they nourish feelings of great compassion to benefit sentient beings. As a result, the Zen school, according to Eisai, favors the precepts of neither the greater nor lesser vehicles but cherishes exclusively upholding the life of purity. While "exclusively upholding the life of purity" vaguely invokes the memory of Baizhang Huaihai,[18] the alleged architect of a separate set of rules governing the lives of Chan monks, Eisai is more concerned with how Zen monastic practice conforms to the established monastic regulations espoused by the greater and lesser vehicles than with some hypothetical notion of uniquely Zen monastic behavior.

Zongze, compiler of the *Chanyuan qinggui*, openly acknowledged the existence of a separate tradition of Chan monastic regulations stemming from Baizhang,[19] and this tradition was widely heralded as a trademark of Chan's alleged independence in Song China. It is inconceivable that Eisai did not know of it. The climate of moral decline and laxity that characterized monastic life in Japan did not lend itself to innovations, like those suggested by Baizhang's alleged suspension of the rules, that might further jeopardize the moral basis of monastic authority.

In China, moreover, when a novice was inducted into the precepts, he first received the precepts of the lesser vehicle (*sravaka*), followed by the greater vehicle (*bodhisattva*) precepts.[20] This deviated from the standard practice of Tendai-trained monks in Japan, like Eisai, who were required to follow only the bodhisattva precepts and forego the more rigorous rules prescribed by the lesser vehicle.[21] Eisai's third provision, guarding or upholding the precepts (*gokai*, C. *hujie*), specifically calls for Zen monks to follow the 250 precepts of bhiksus as well as the 10 grave and 48 minor precepts of bodhisattvas. Guarding the precepts, moreover, is not presented as an option but as concomitant with the responsibility of maintaining the precious pearl obtained. This marks the radical conservatism of Eisai's message—his aim to reinvigorate monastic discipline by invoking a stricter regimen and a more rigorous set of rules. Rather than the flaunting of rules and conventions associated with Zen rhetoric, Eisai demands a moral purification of the monastic clergy through a toughening of discipline. Rather than the breaking down of religious conventions, Eisai seeks to rigidify them by making monastic discipline stricter and harder.[22] An essential component of guarding the precepts, according to Eisai, also includes the twice-monthly uposatha recitation, as prescribed in the vinaya, where violations are disclosed, cleansing the sangha of any residue of impropriety.

The fourth provision for Eisai is study and inquiry, with particular focus on the precepts. Study should encompass the entire corpus of Buddhist scriptures and treatises. To this end, medieval Zen monasteries, whether in China or Japan, featured reading rooms (*shuryō*), literally "community halls," that by the late Song dynasty, at least, had become primarily used as places for scripture study.[23] The focus for Eisai on the precepts is not intended as a narrow explication of the precept rules themselves. Eisai envisions a study of the precepts that encompasses the texts of all Buddhist scriptures and doctrines, a kind of comprehensive understanding of Buddhism in its entirety. Eisai makes no reference to the texts studied in the reading room, but Dōgen's rules for Eiheiji monastery mention that Mahayana scriptures and the sayings of Zen ancestors "naturally accord with the instructions of our tradition to illuminate the mind with the ancient teachings."[24] Dōgen, too, gives special emphasis to precept texts, both of the greater and lesser vehicles, as the focus of students' study. The fact that the precepts would serve as the focal point rather than, say, some soteriological or doctrinal nexus underscores Eisai's commitment to the moral rejuvenation of the sangha. For Eisai, moral rectitude, as provided by strict adherence to the precepts, is the key: "Equipped externally with the rules for the correct behavior of monks (i.e., the precepts of the lesser vehicle), one creates a field of blessings for humans and gods. Nourished internally by the great compassion of bodhisattvas (i.e., the precepts of the greater vehicle), one acts as the sympathetic father of sentient beings."[25] The stakes, according to Eisai, could not be higher: "the valuable treasure of the emperor, and the effective medicine [for alleviating the ills] of the nation, consist entirely in [the blessings and compassion these precepts] generate."[26] Japan's renewal as a country is based on the revival of true precept practice.

The fifth provision outlines the actual daily routine, the ritual conduct (*gyōgi*, C. *xingyi*) of the monastery. For Eisai, this routine is tied directly to pure conduct resulting from upholding the precept rules (*jikai bongyō*), as preached by the Buddha. Again, monastic ritual is determined by general Buddhist teaching rather than any particular Zen formulation of it. The daily and nightly rituals are given in table 3.1.[27]

Of the thirteen periods that the day is divided into, seven are devoted to dharma activities: four periods are devoted to meditation (*zazen*), two periods involve worship activities, and one period is for reading and study. Of the remaining six periods, two are for sleeping, two for meals (note, no evening

TABLE 3.1. Daily Routine at Zen Monasteries

Dusk	Lighting lamps [in front of the image of the Buddha]
	At dusk, all the monks visit the Buddha Hall, burn incense, and prostrate themselves in front of the Buddha.
8 P.M.	People retire for the night
	Seated meditation (*zazen*)
12 P.M.	Third watch
	Sleep
2 A.M.	Fourth watch
	Sleep
4 A.M.	Fifth watch
	Seated meditation
6 A.M.	*Hōji* (Dawn)
	Morning rituals
Daylight	Congee breakfast
8 A.M.	*Shinji*
	Scripture reading, study, lectures by elders monks
10 A.M.	*Gūji*
	Seated meditation
12 A.M.	*Goji*
	Lunch
2 P.M.	*Miji*
	Bathing, etc.
4 P.M.	*Hoji*
	Seated meditation
6 P.M.	*Yuji*
	Free time for relaxation

meal, as stipulated in the vinaya rules), and two are for relaxation, including bathing. As Eisai specifically notes, there is no laxity in the routine, and the rationale for this intense regimen is clearly provided.

> Through their constant mindfulness (*nennen*), the monks repay the debt they owe to the country; through their every activity (*gyōgyō*), they pray for the longevity of the emperor.[28] Their efforts are in truth for the everlasting glory of the emperor's rule and the perpetual splendor of the Dharma-lamp.[29]

Eisai invokes here the *ōbō buppō* logic common in medieval Japan, where secular law, the rule of the emperor (*ōbō*), is paired with religious doctrine, the Buddha-dharma (*buppō*) as the basis of civilized culture. Noteworthy, however, is the hierarchy of authority presumed in Eisai's rationale: the monks are clearly subordinate; their activities are designed to foster the greater purpose of imperial (and by implication national) glory. While this rationale worked well for Eisai in the Japanese context, it should also be noted that Eisai was also inspired by the Song Chan context, where imperial sponsorship of Chan monasteries was the norm, and the function of Chan monasteries was rationalized by this context.

The sixth provision refers to appropriate conduct (*igi*, C. *weiyi*). Appropriate conduct for Eisai includes specifications on proper attire in public, specifically that monks always wear a large outer robe, or *samghati*, and that monks perform the proper rituals when they encounter each other as a sign of respect. More importantly, Eisai stipulates that monks not perform any activity—whether drinking or eating, walking in a row, sitting in meditation, studying, reading scriptures, or sleeping—independently, apart from the assembly. All rituals are to be conducted collectively. The absence of any individual is to be duly noted and investigated by the Rector (*inō*, C. *weina*) of the monastery.[30]

The seventh provision pertains to clothing (*efuku*, C. *yifu*). Eisai stipulates that the upper and lower garments of a monk, in addition to the outer robe mentioned above, should conform completely to vinaya specifications as followed in other great Buddhist countries (i.e., China).[31] Eisai here also reminds readers of the vinaya regulation for monks to reduce their desires to bare necessities and eliminate the need for luxurious items. Again, this is simply a reminder of common monastic practice and not unique to Eisai or Zen.

The eighth provision pertains to the community or assembly of disciples (*toshū*, C. *tuzhong*). For Eisai, entrance to the assembly is restricted to those committed to the spiritual life (i.e., to people who conceive the intention of attaining the state of nonretrogression). For these people, access is granted to both the precepts and the wisdom that the Zen monastic environment provides.

The ninth provision is associated with the benefits resulting from providing support to the monastic community (*riyō*, C. *liyang*). According to Eisai, Zen monks refrain from tilling the fields or rice cultivation because they have no time to spare from seated meditation (*zazen*). This contradicts the idealized view of the Zen monastery as a self-sufficient enterprise, with monks engaged in manual labor conceived alternatively in terms of its economic viability or as an integral part of a spiritual regimen. This idealized view has been challenged by T. Griffith Foulk, who argues that the term used to indicate manual labor in Chan monastic codes, *puching* (literally, "all invited"), actually covered a wider range of activities and should be understood as requiring "mandatory attendance" at a number of functions, services, ceremonies, etc., sponsored at Chan monasteries. The rhetorical emphasis on manual labor at Chan monasteries, according to Foulk, is probably best understood in association with Chan's quest to define itself as a distinctive entity. Foulk also contends that manual labor was not unique to Chan monasteries but was a common feature of monastic practice at Tiantai establishments as well.[32] If there is anything unique about Eisai's insistence against manual labor, it is probably the degree to which he rejects it. Generally speaking, Eisai describes the role of the Zen monastery in society in terms compatible with other Buddhist monastic establishments—as a place where monks simultaneously acquire stocks of merit through their spiritual exercises, namely, *zazen*, and where the acquired merit may be dispensed throughout the lay community on the basis of support provided. Engaging in the kind of manual labor required to make the monastery self-sufficient would, in effect, deny the lay community of supporters and society as a whole access to their share of the merit whose accumulation is the monastery's function. This is the implicit assumption behind Eisai's prohibition of manual labor for monks in a section extolling the virtues of providing support for the monastic community.

The tenth, and final, provision is for the summer and winter retreats. According to Eisai, observance of the two three-month-long retreat periods in Japan had long since perished, except perhaps in name alone, devoid of any actual practice. As periods designed around intense meditation practice, it makes sense that Eisai would be keen to revive them as a way to reinvigorate an ailing monastic system. He also takes care to point out how each of the two retreat periods was established by no less than Sakyamuni himself. Invoking Sakyamuni's authority, rather than, say, Bodhidharma's, again attests to the intrinsically Buddhist, rather than Zen, character of Eisai's reform program.

In addition to the ten provisions described above, Eisai also outlines sixteen types of ceremonies to be observed at Zen monasteries. As I have commented elsewhere,[33] these annual ritual observances at Zen monasteries helped insure that Zen fulfilled its social obligations as the official religion of the state. The premise for such annual ceremonies is a sociopolitical order maintained through moral virtue. Moral virtue, following the rationale employed in this context, is cultivated through specific ritual observances. In keeping with the nationalistic aims the Zen monastic institution was designed to serve, several of these observances are directed expressly toward the preservation of the emperor and the country. It is no accident, moreover, that these observances head the list.

The first are ceremonies conducted in the ritual hall (*dōjō*, C. *daochang*), commemorating the emperor's birthday (*shōsetsu*). Daily readings are made for thirty days leading to the birthday of the reigning emperor, from scriptures such as the *Large Sutra on the Perfection of Wisdom*, *Sutra on Benevolent Kings Protecting Their Countries*, *Lotus Sutra*, and *Golden Light Sutra*,[34] offering prayers on the emperor's behalf.

The second refers to a set of rituals associated with Buddha invocation and sutra chanting (*nenju*, C. *niansong*).[35] These rituals have various aims, with precedence given to spreading imperial virtue (*ōfu*) and enhancing imperial rule (*teidō*), but also to the propagation of the buddha-dharma (*buppō*) and the benefit of sentient beings. These aims concisely remind us of the *ōbō buppō* formula upon which state sanction of Buddhism in Japan was based. The rituals were conducted as a regular, formal ceremony (*gishiki*) throughout each month—on the third, thirteenth, and twenty-third, and the eighth, eighteenth, and twenty-eighth (six days in total). As a subsidiary aim, the rituals also served to repay kindnesses provided by donors.

The third are ceremonies involving local native deities (*tochi-kami*), which differ according to locale. Conducted on two days each month, the second and sixteenth, the ceremonies (the nature of which is unspecified) are designed to enlist the support of local guardian deities to protect the area that the Zen monastery occupies. In accordance with the theory of *honji-suijaku*, which reached maturity during the Heian period, Shinto kami (as *suijaku*) were incorporated into the Buddhist scheme as manifestations of the absolute and eternal Buddha (as *honji*).[36] As such, kami were regularly enlisted to serve the Buddhist cause. This accommodation of kami should not be deemed simply a concession by Eisai to native Shinto beliefs. The ground plans of Chan monasteries in Song China make clear that veneration of local protector deities (*tudi gong*) was a regular feature of Chan practice.[37]

The fourth are ceremonies, like those seen in the first and second set, aimed at repaying the kindness of the emperors (*hō'on*). In this regard, lectures are arranged on two days each month. Recitation of sutras on these days and for this purpose was also a feature of Song Chan monastic practice.[38] For

TABLE 3.2. Annual Monthly Observances at Zen Monasteries

Month	Observance
1	Arhat Assembly service
2	Ceremony commemorating the Buddha's Relics
3	Grand Assembly service
4	Celebration of the Buddha's Birthday; commencement of Summer Retreat
5	Recitation of the *Golden Light Sutra*
6	Recitation of the *Golden Light Sutra*
7	Recitation of the *Perfection of Wisdom Sutra*
8	Recitation of the *Perfection of Wisdom Sutra*
9	Recitation of the *Perfection of Wisdom Sutra*
10	Ordination Ceremony; commencement of Winter Retreat
11	Mid-winter Festival
12	Recitation of the *Sutra of Names of the Buddha*

the reigning emperor, lectures on the *Perfection of Wisdom Sutra* are offered on the last day of each month. For the previous emperor, lectures on the *Sutra of the Great Decease* are offered on the fifteenth day of each month. Both sutras, Eisai reminds us, contain passages urging the Buddhas to assist rulers.

The fifth refers not to rituals held on specified days through each month but to formal ceremonies (*gishiki*) held annually throughout the year (see table 3.2): the Arhat Assembly service in the first month,[39] the Ceremony commemorating the Buddha's Relics in the second month,[40] the Grand Assembly service in the third month,[41] the Celebration of the Buddha's Birthday and the commencement of the Summer Retreat in the fourth month, Recitation of the *Golden Light Sutra* in the fifth and sixth months, Recitation of the *Perfection of Wisdom Sutra* in the seventh, eighth, and ninth months, Ordination Ceremony (*jukai*) conducted at the commencement of the Winter Retreat in the tenth month, Mid-winter Festival in the eleventh month, and the Grand Assembly for the Recitation of the *Sutra of Names of the Buddha* in the twelfth month.[42] This also coincides, undoubtedly, with the cycle of observances conducted at Song Chan monasteries witnessed by Eisai.

The sixth ceremony is conducted specifically during retreat periods, the daily recitation of scriptures like the *Sutra of Heroic Deeds*.[43] According to Yanagida Seizan, the sutra is recited so that the retreat will pass safely and without incident.[44]

The seventh ceremony is daily scripture reading. Every day, one fascicle from the scriptures is read by each monk. According to Eisai's tabulation, a temple of a hundred monks in the span of a year will finish reading the equivalent of six canons worth of scriptures through this practice. He adds that in some cases, scriptures are read for the merit-earning intentions or prayers of donors. While scripture reading is disdained in the hagiographies of Chan patriarchs, this is far from the reality of actual monastic practice. The *Chanyuan qinggui*, for example, provides for the specific protocols to be followed by the Director of the Library (*zangzhu*) to facilitate scripture reading, as well as the procedures for proper scripture reading in the sutra-reading hall.[45] Ground plans of Song Chan monasteries also record the existence of a "community hall" (*shuryō*), which later functioned primarily as a room for reading and studying the scriptures.[46]

The eighth are ceremonies held in Shingon Halls erected within the compound of the Zen monastery. While specifically for providing offerings for the living beings of the water and land, according to Mikkyō (i.e., Shingon) teaching the offerings are designated for beings living in the world of the dead.[47] In practice, donors request these ceremonies to pray for blessings and earn merit for the deceased. The existence of water-land ritual halls (*suilu tang*) at Chan monasteries is confirmed by the *Chanyuan qinggui*.[48] The rituals themselves pre-date the Song and are not exclusive to Chan. They serve as the most important ritual for offering food to the deceased or to spirits.

The ninth are rituals held in Cessation and Contemplation (*shikan*) Halls also erected within the compound of the Zen monastery. These Tendai based rituals, originating with the Tiantai prelate Zunshi (964–1032), are based on the *Lotus Sutra*, *Amitayur dhyana Sutra* (*Kammuryōju kyō*, C. *Guan wuliang-shou jing*), and the *Sutra of Guanyin* (*Kannon gyō*, C. *Guanyin ching*), excerpted from a chapter (fascicle 25) of the *Lotus Sutra*.[49] There seems to be no precedent for the performance of such rites at Song Chan monasteries, nor any mention of the existence of a Cessation and Contemplation Hall in Chan monastic compounds. The types of devotions associated with the rites are clearly of Tiantai provenance. Zunshi's Guanyin repentance rite derived from one of the traditional rites of Tiantai's four samadhis, the *Invocation of Gua-nyin Repentance*, amended and recodified as the *Samadhi Rite for the Dharani that Eliminates Poison and Harm by Invoking Guanyin*.[50] Zunshi also produced two manuals advocating Pure Land practices: the *Rite for Repentance and Vows for Rebirth in the Pure Land* and *Two Teachings for Resolving Doubts and Establishing the Practice and Vow to be Reborn in the Pure Land*.[51] The erection of Cessation and Contemplation Halls for the specific implementation of these rituals was highly attractive to a Zen advocate like Eisai, trained on Mt. Hiei and aiming to supplant an indolent Tendai monasticism.

The tenth is the ritual of entering the master's quarters for personal interviews (*nisshitsu*, C. *rushi*). According to Eisai, this is the most important ritual of the Zen school. The procedures for this ritual are set forth in the *Chanyuan qinggui*.[52] The ritual protocols stipulated there concentrate almost exclusively on the minutia of proper behavior associated with entering and exiting the abbot's quarters, bowing, lighting incense, etc. Little is said in the text proper about the subjects discussed, other than the caution that petitioners should not be long-winded or speak of worldly or trivial matters. An interliner note, however, suggests three potential topics: kōan instruction, conversation between master and disciples, and further instruction requested by the monk. In some monasteries, separate times are allocated for each of these three methods; in others, the three methods are used simultaneously.[53] In any case, this is deemed as the defining ritual of the Zen monastery, where private dialogues between the master and his disciples are carried out and the progress of individual practitioners is determined. It is likely that the ritual itself is a reenactment of the hypothetical encounters between Chan masters and disciples in Chan hagiographies. The brief expositions of Chan truths in the lamp records (*tōroku*, C. *denglu*) served as models for ritual reenactment in the master's quarters, ultimately culminating in the disciple's awakening and the ceremony of dharma-transmission.[54]

Evidence that Eisai engaged in kōan style introspection is largely absent in the pages of the *Kōzen gokokuron*. He does, however, cite kōan like anecdotes in section seven, "Outlining Zen Doctrines and Encouraging Zen Practice," stating: "If one clarifies the cardinal principle [of the Buddha-dharma] through what is pointed to outside [the scriptures], one will never measure [the Buddha-dharma] in terms of words (i.e., scriptural accounts)."[55] Eisai cites the example of Elder Fu of Taiyuan, who after being ridiculed for his attachment to the *Nirvana Sutra*, reportedly said: "Up until now, I have been lecturing on this particular [*Nirvana*] sutra, content to sniff at an amorphous approximation [of the Truth] with the physically limited body born of my father and mother. Henceforth, I will never again [be content to] act like this."[56] In this connection, Eisai also cites the words of Muzhou Daoming, the disciple of Huangbo Xiyun, "When one does not understand the great event [of enlightenment], it is like mourning deceased parents."[57] Eisai's understanding of the importance of this "great event," in Zen terms, is illustrated by him as follows:

Let me try to present evidence from the awakening experiences of the ancients. We should consider it carefully.

For example, Leshan one day asked Shishuang:[58] "What should I do about rising and perishing [thoughts] that do not stop?"

Shishuang said: "You should straightaway rid yourself of [the lifeless state of] cold ashes and withered branches, rid yourself of [the effects of temporality by] imagining ten-thousand years in a single thought, and rid yourself of any cleavage separating the internal and external [aspects of rising and perishing thoughts]."

Leshan did not understand. He left to go visit Yantou,[59] and put the same question to him. Yantou then yelled: "Who is it in charge of this rising and perishing?" As soon as he uttered these words, Leshan achieved sudden awakening.[60]

Eisai explained the meaning of this story:

> The question to be considered here is what is this awakening? The ancient sage [Leshan] concentrated on this question and inhabited it. He exerted himself throughout the twelve periods of the day and night,[61] exclusively considering awakening as the goal. It was only through uttering this one question concerning mental disturbances and confusion—rising and perishing [thoughts] not stopping—that he resolved this matter. The venerable elder [Yantou] provided the remedy appropriate to the disease. In some cases, a single medicine will effect a cure. In some cases, several medicines are mixed together, as acupuncture and moxibustion are deemed appropriate. Only when the malady has lifted and the remedy is no longer necessary, the entire body reinvigorated, is the cure successful. Later students, without having penetrated the original source [from which awakening arises], are compelled to divide [the responses of Shishuang and Yantou] into superior and inferior. They claim in this context that Shishuang's explanation killed Leshan, and Yantou's explanation revived him. Viewed form this perspective, [Leshan's awakening] was first initiated when he bought sandals and set out on foot (i.e., left Shishuang to visit Yantou). They are like fish taking the bait while unaware of the hook; they mistakenly perceive [awakening] in terms of gradations on a measuring device. This is what is meant by [the saying]: "When a lion eats someone, wild dogs compete for the leftover corpse."[62]

From this passage it is evident that even though Eisai did not refer to the kōan introspection technique directly, he was certainly aware of it and its significance for Zen instruction. As a result, even in the absence of an actual description of kōan introspection practice in the *Kōzen gokokuron*, kōan practice was undoubtedly a feature of Eisai's Zen monastery. Even though kōan introspection was practiced, this does not mean that it was overly emphasized, as in later Rinzai practice. Far from the case, the lack of emphasis that Eisai gives to kōan introspection is indicative of its place in the medieval Zen monastery as one practice among many, albeit an important and defining one.

The eleventh is the fortnightly confessional ceremony (Skt. *posadha,* Pali *uposatha*) involving the recitation of the precepts and confession of violations that is the common practice among Buddhist monks, regardless of sectarian affiliation. Like many of the ritual observances on Eisai's list, there is nothing distinctly Zen about it. What distinguished Eisai's approach, as mentioned above, was his insistence that the detailed rules governing monastic behavior in the *Four Part Vinaya* be included along with the Mahayana precepts.

The twelfth ritual emphasized by Eisai is the inspection of the monks' quarters by the abbot (*junryō*). Every five days, the abbot inspects the monks' quarters following the lecture to instruct and admonish the assembly. The fact that Eisai emphasizes the inspection aspect of the ceremony rather than the lecture is significant to the extent that it focuses on the disciplinary function of the abbot and monastery, rather than the teaching function, making clear the order of priority with which Eisai regards each. The occurrence of the inspections every five days is suggested by Eisai for spurious reasons, as deriving from the fact that the Buddha himself instructed his disciples on five matters, as stipulated in the vinaya texts. The five matters refer to the aspects of monastic life stressed upon new initiates: mental state, health, vitality, sleep, and sustenance.[63] The routine suggested by these inspections calls attention to a monthly cycle of activities at Zen monasteries (see table 3.3), in addition to the daily and annual observances.

The thirteenth activity specifies bathing (*kaiyoku*) frequency, normally once every five days but daily in summer. Provisions for bathing are sponsored either by the government or lay donors.

The fourteenth type of ceremony regards vegetarian banquets sponsored on memorial days (*kishinsai*) to seek merit either for departed emperors, for departed abbots, or for the abbot's parents. While Eisai specifies that there are rules (*hōsoku*) to be complied with in sponsoring these banquets, he provides no indication of what these rules might be. Presumably they cover stipulations for proper conduct on such occasions.

The fifteenth are vegetarian banquets for the monastic community sponsored by government officials (*kanke sasai*) and include formal ceremonies, such as incense offering, held upon the occasion of official government visits. The rationale for such ceremonies as incense offering is discussed in detail below.

TABLE 3.3. Monthly Observances at Zen Monasteries*

Day	Activity
1	Lecture and inspection of monks' quarters
2	Ceremonies for local deities
3	Buddha invocation/sutra chanting
4	Bathing
5	
6	Lecture and inspection of monks' quarters
7	
8	Buddha invocation/sutra chanting
9	Bathing
10	
11	Lecture and inspection of monks' quarters
12	
13	Buddha invocation/sutra chanting
14	Bathing
15	*Sutra of Great Decease* lecture (for departed emperor)
16	Ceremonies for local deities; lecture and inspection of monks'quarters
17	
18	Buddha invocation/sutra chanting
19	Bathing
20	
21	Lecture and inspection of monks' quarters
22	
23	Buddha invocation/sutra chanting
24	Bathing
25	
26	Lecture and inspection of monks' quarters
27	
28	Buddha invocation/sutra chanting
29	Bathing
30	*Perfection of Wisdom* lecture (for current emperor)

*For some activities (such as bathing and lectures/inspections), the day specified is hypothetical only. Other activities (e.g., scripture readings, bathing during summer months) occur daily and are not included. In addition, some activities occur as warranted (e.g., water and land rituals, cessation and contemplation rituals, entering the abbot's quarters for personal interviews, memorial services for deceased emperors and abbots, etc.) and do not appear as regular monthly activities.

The sixteenth are turning the tripitaka rituals (*tenzō*), referring to occasions when the members of the monastic assembly gather to play music and spin the octagonal bookcase the tripitaka is placed on, a ritual reenactment of the turning of the wheel of the law and the symbolic spread of Buddhist beneficence throughout the world.

Against the objection that monks lack the aptitude for such observances (*gyōgi*) in the period of the decline of the Law (*masse*), Eisai stipulates that the Buddha-dharma is exceedingly simple to practice and exceedingly simple to accomplish. The Buddha, Eisai contends, spoke of "pleasurable approaches to the Dharma" (*anraku hōmon*),"[64] citing a verse in the *Abhidharmakosa Treatise* (*Kusharon*) that speaks of "the pleasure (*raku*) of accord in the community of monks, and the pleasure of their fearless progress when they practice together."[65]

Becoming a monk, argues Eisai, is no different from becoming a father or mother, or acquiring the skills of any common livelihood (Eisai specifically mentions metal work, tile making, weaving, sorcery, and farming). Through determination to acquire the necessary skills, monks master the techniques to successfully carry out their craft. In this they are no different from their counterparts in other professions and livelihoods. The regimen of conduct, rituals, and observances, in other words, serves as the basic training for Zen monks learning their "craft." What distinguishes them, according to Eisai, is their temperaments, which dispose them to become Buddhist monks rather than engage in other professions.

The above discussion reveals Eisai's plan for the program of observances at Zen monasteries. I now turn to the question of the theoretical basis for such activity. As mentioned above, I previously linked Eisai's *Kōzen gokokuron* to widely held assumptions regarding the role of Buddhism in Japan as the spiritual arm of the Japanese state. In the following discussion, I explore widely held assumptions throughout East Asia regarding the role and function of ritual as a means to sustain and nourish a prosperous state, an assumption upon which Eisai's program ultimately rests.

Ritual and Civilization: Confucian Pretexts for Buddhist Rites

Rites and ceremonies performed at Buddhist monasteries, like those promoted by Eisai at Zen monasteries in medieval Japan, were predicated on specific notions regarding the function of ritual in maintaining moral and social order. The social and political aims of Buddhist ritual were exemplified by official support for the monastic institution. The goal of such support was not so much spiritual enlightenment, at least not in the grand sense, as it was the creation and preservation of a moral society and stable political order. One of the chief ways for government officials to express support for Buddhism was through sponsorship and participation at incense rites. In addition to the vegetarian banquets for the monastic community sponsored by government officials that included formal ceremonies such as incense offering, many other ceremonies that occurred at Zen monasteries featured incense offering. Indeed, incense was a ubiquitous feature at ceremonies where prayers were offered, particularly at memorial services honoring the deceased. While the use and function of incense at services and ceremonies is well known, the rationale for the use of incense at Buddhist services resonates deeply throughout East Asia. One cannot fathom Eisai's appeal to ritual protocol as the basis for moral, social, and political renewal without acknowledging the structural function that ritual is believed to have in East Asian thought. In the analysis that follows, I look at the incense rite not only as one observance among the many that occurred at Zen monasteries but also as a symbol of the importance that ritual played in the socio-religious nexus of medieval Japan. To achieve this requires an excursus deep into the theoretical pretexts regarding the nature of civilization in East Asia and the role of ritual in maintaining it.

It is well known that communication with specific spirits or "heaven" in general constituted the motivation for ancient Chinese ritual practice. The esteem placed on ritual by Confucian scholars derives from the emphasis it was given by Confucius, and the central role of rites for proper conduct in affairs of state is clearly exhibited in the *Lun yu*. The welfare of the state ultimately rested on the reverent execution of the rites, a practical concern of grave significance to a ruler. The rites were thus intricately connected to the model ruler, the sage-king, and the Confucian ideal of how the state operated. The rites also played a leading role in the education of the *junzi*, the model Confucian gentleman.[66]

The Confucian emphasis on the importance of ritual for the proper conduct of the state is particularly evident in the thought of Xunzi. Xunzi fully exploited the implications for ritual implied in the *Lun yu* when he proclaimed: "a man without ritual cannot live; an undertaking without ritual cannot come to completion; a state without ritual cannot attain peace."[67] In this formulation, the meaning of human existence, the achievement of success, and the welfare of the state are all unfathomable apart from the employment of ritual.

At the basis of the Confucian emphasis on ritual is a belief in a moral order pervading the universe. In a world sympathetic to human goodness exhibited through moral behavior, ritual takes on a special meaning. The aim of ritual is to order human activity in a way that parallels the moral order of the universe. Rites are more than a mere reflection of the natural order. They are a positive affirmation of the moral nature of the universe. The order of the universe and human welfare are said to depend on the proper execution of the rites.[68]

Xunzi's depiction of a universe governed by moral principles, susceptible to human virtue or lack thereof, resulted in a belief in strict laws governing moral phenomena. These laws were believed to determine proper behavior in human relations in the same way that natural laws determined relations among physical bodies.[69] This belief had important consequences for codifying behavior in specific contexts.

Further determination of the model governing ritual behavior, including guidelines for proper observances on specific occasions, were recorded in three classical texts on ritual, the *Li ji* (Ritual Records), *Zhou li* (Rituals of Zhou), and *Yi li* (Propriety and Ritual). Together, these three texts were designated as one of the five classics of ancient Chinese civilization, the *Classics of Ritual*. Knowledge of their content was esteemed by Confucians as one of the cornerstones of civilization. Generally speaking, the contribution of these ritual texts lay in their ability to join the rationalistic tendencies of Confucian theorists with ancient Chinese custom. In the process, ritual conduct at sacrifices, etc., became aligned with Confucian theories regarding the moral nature of the universe.

The *Li ji* provides further elaboration on the function of ritual in the context of the ancient Chinese world view according to Confucian theory. According to the *Li ji*, "Music is the harmony of heaven and earth; ritual is the order of heaven and earth. Through harmony all things are transformed; through order all things are distinguished."[70] More specifically, music and ritual are modeled upon heaven and earth, respectively. Music and ritual can be properly instituted only after the relationship between them and heaven and earth is understood. When the relationship is misunderstood and music and ritual are improperly instituted, music is said to be excessive and ritual norms unheeded, resulting in violence and chaos.

This explains why, according to the *Li ji*, the greatest music preserves the same harmony that prevails between heaven and earth, and the greatest ritual preserves the same gradations that prevail between heaven and earth. Sacrifices to heaven and earth derive from this need to preserve the harmony and gradations prevailing between heaven and earth. The ritual and music performed at sacrifices are appropriate human responses based on the pattern of heaven and earth. They are designed to influence and appease the invisible forces that permeate the universe and determine human fate.

> In heaven on high and earth below, the myriad things are distributed
> distinctly; ritual patterns were distributed accordingly. Flowing
> forth unceasingly, [the myriad things] act in concord and are trans-
> formed; music arose therein. In spring [the myriad things] sprout
> forth, and in summer they grow; this is [the manifestation of] be-
> nevolence (*ren*). In autumn, [the myriad things] are consummated,
> and in winter they are stored up; this is [the manifestation of]

righteousness (*yi*). Benevolence is akin to music, and righteousness is akin to ritual.

Music establishes union and harmony, and so it accords with *shen* and follows the pattern of heaven. Rituals maintain difference and distinction, and so they accord with *gui* and follow the pattern of the earth. Therefore, the sages created music in response to heaven, and instituted ritual to correspond to earth. When ritual and music are arranged clearly, they function as organs of heaven and earth.[71]

The theory governing the use of aromatic fragrances in Chinese sacrifices was established in the classical period and was closely connected to beliefs regarding the nature of the human soul.[72] The use of fragrances was designed to help influence the *shen* and *gui* spirits for whom the sacrifice was offered, and this became a ubiquitous feature of memorial services. The *Li ji* clearly stipulates the use of different aromatic substances in specific ritual contexts.[73] For Confucians, the most important aspect of the ritual was the attitude of reverence and solemnity that it produced in the participant. These were perceived as outward signs of the participant's inner virtue. In short, the rite itself was of primary importance not for its external form but for the effect it produced. This meant changes in ritual etiquette could be considered so long as they met the Confucian criterion of fostering a reverential and solemn attitude. Consideration for such changes was already suggested in the *Li ji*, when it described different customs at sacrifices in ancient China according to the historical period they occurred in. The result was that the model existed and continued to be influential, but it was not a fixed one and could be adapted to changing historical exigencies. Such changes and adaptations were the subject of frequent debates among ritual specialists in the imperial bureaucracy.

From the perspective of the ruler, the importance of the rites was specifically associated with the preservation of his rule. The function of sacrifices generally was alternately to seek good fortune or avoid calamity, and it was to this end that *shen* and *gui* spirits were summoned in the first place. The performance of sacrifices was the prerogative of all ranking male heads of households, but the significance of these rites reached its apex in sacrifices conducted (or commissioned) by the head of state on behalf of the welfare of the entire country. The impact that these rites potentially had thus extended to the ruler's own mandate. In the classical model, this was rationalized in a typically Confucian manner, exemplified in the *Shu jing* when the Duke of Zhou proclaims: "Perfect virtue is like piercing fragrance (*xiang*); it influences the bright intelligence of the *shen* spirits. It is not the millet which has the piercing fragrance; bright virtue alone has it."[74] This underscores further the point made above: the effectiveness of the rites stems from inner virtue rather than external form. The aroma of the sacrifice cannot suffice where virtue is lacking. The fragrance is meaningful only to the extent that it mirrors the actual virtue of the ruler.

The Chinese character for incense (*xiang*) originally depicted the savory odor of millet spirits.[75] Etymologically, the meaning of the character is clearly associated with the ancient Chinese rites honoring ancestors and other spirits described above. Later, the meaning of the character came to include pleasant aromas from other substances. Incense became foremost among these substances.[76] Over time, the meaning of the character also naturally became associated with incense used in Buddhist rites.[77]

In Buddhism, incense was linked to divine fragrances and evoked visions of Buddhist utopias and personal salvation. These visions grew out of the way that incense was depicted in Buddhist scriptures. The *Vimalakirti-nirdesa Sutra* (*The Holy Teaching of Vimalakirti*), for example, reveals a Buddhist paradise known as the land of multitudinous fragrances (*zhongxiang*), inhabited by a Buddha whose name literally means "Fragrance Accumulated" (*xiangji*). The fragrance emitted from this land is said to surpass that of all others; everything existing in this land is said to be the product of this unsurpassable fragrance.[78] Fragrance (*xiang*) is a common feature of all Buddhist paradises, where it is counted among the conditions especially conducive to spiritual advancement that prevail there.

Given this association between fragrance, paradise, and enlightenment, the use of incense in Buddhist funeral and memorial rites is no surprise. The most authoritative precedent for this practice is the description of the death of the Buddha himself in *The Sutra of the Great Decease* (*Maha-parinibbana sutta*). In the events leading up to the cremation ceremony, garlands and perfumes frequently appear with song, music, and dance as means for honoring, reverencing, and paying homage to the Buddha's remains. The funeral pyre is also said to be made with "all kinds of perfumes" (using the character *xiang* in Chinese translations) and the fire extinguished with perfume-scented water after the corpse is consumed.[79]

The symbolism associated with the use of incense in Buddhism naturally stemmed from the Indian cultural environment. In India, as in China, the worship of ancestors formed the basis for all funeral rites. According to official Brahmanism, rites for the dead, known as *sraddha* rites, were incumbent upon the living relatives of the deceased. The object of these rites was to provide for the intermediate body assumed by the deceased after departing the gross corporeal body and before assuming a new form. Once the intermediate body was assumed, it had to be provided for. Failure to do so not only constituted an act of negligence on the part of the relatives of the deceased but was also believed to result in the deceased turning into a *preta*, a malevolent spirit driven to terrorize the living because of its unrequited desires. Sacrifice was conceived as a means of appeasing these desires and preventing this from happening. The *sraddha* rites thus served the dual function of insuring passage through the intermediate existence without incident, and that the deceased would not become a disruptive force to the living. Buddhism adopted many of the mythological elements associated with Brahmanical accounts of the fate of the deceased, including the notions of an intermediate body and of *preta*, but rejected as reprehensible sacrifice involving the slaughter of any living creature. From the Buddhist perspective, blood sacrifice was an act of particular barbarity. It amounted to a heinous crime for which no justification was possible.

While disagreeing over the aims of ritual, Confucians and Buddhists both concurred that its purpose was to effect a certain state of mind in the participant. In Buddhism, ritual worship was linked to the purification of the mind. It was designed to help people who were not inclined to engage in meditation formally. The symbolic associations of fragrant aroma played an important role in this regard. Incense was commonly used as a means of sending petitions to the Buddhas and Buddhist saints. The petitions were believed to rise heavenward, to the realms of the Buddhas, in the smoke that the burning incense produced.[80] As a result, offering incense was included as one of the chief means of worship in Chinese Buddhism, and incense came to have a ubiquitous presence in Buddhist worship.

It is not difficult to understand why incense offering was attractive to Buddhists. On the one hand, there was the practical benefit of using incense to mask unpleasant odors, thus contributing an air of purity and gravity to an occasion. There was also the symbolism that incense evoked as a fragrant aroma, suggesting the presence of the divine. The fact that incense offering was able to serve as a substitute for sacrifice, however, proved its most attractive quality. No matter how accepting the Buddhist approach toward public ritual became, strict taboos remained against blood sacrifice as a violation of cardinal Buddhist precepts. The use of incense as a means of worship offered the possibility of "pure sacrifice" (sacrifice that did not violate Buddhist prohibitions) in place of its vulgar counterpart that depended on the spilled blood of sacrificial victims.

A definite advantage that incense had as a substitute for conventional sacrifice was that it also produced smoke. The production of smoke, as we have seen, was symbolically important to the ceremony. In conventional sacrificial rites, the ascending smoke was believed to convey the petitions and aspirations of the participants to the realms inhabited by deities and spirits.

We noted above how incense smoke was believed to serve the same function, while eliminating the need for sacrificial victims.

One aspect of conventional sacrifice that the incense rite seemed ill equipped for was the ceremonial feast that followed. In conventional sacrifice, the victims offered served as the basis for a communal meal. From a sociological perspective, the affirmation of kinship bonds among the living provided a strong impetus for performing sacrifices. Combined with religious justifications, these sociological factors compelled participants to affirm their relationship with the departed and their status among the living. Incense ceremonies provided no victims to serve as a basis for the communal meal.

The Buddhist response to this dilemma was suggested in the early canonical literature. The *Kutadanta-sutta* provided a way that the communal aspects of the sacrificial meal could be met in accordance with Buddhist culinary restrictions. At such a sacrifice, "neither were any oxen slain, neither goats, nor fowls, nor fatted pigs, nor were any kinds of living creatures put to death.... With ghee, and oil, and butter, and milk, and honey, and sugar only was that sacrifice accomplished."[81] This suggests how the vegetarian banquet served as a substitute for the sacrificial feast in Buddhist incense offering ceremonies. When the incense rite was used in the context of a communal worship honoring spirits, etc., one typically found it followed by a vegetarian banquet. This combination of incense rite and vegetarian banquet had great appeal in China and throughout East Asia at memorial services honoring the spirits of deceased ancestors.[82]

In Buddhist legend, the rationale for sponsoring the incense rite and vegetarian banquet was directly related to concerns about the fate of departed ancestors. The rationale was predicated on the Buddhist belief in the "transfer of merit," the possibility of the living to accumulate merit on behalf of the departed by way of assisting the course of the departed in the afterlife.[83]

The requirement that Buddhist rites be performed to execute Confucian obligations at funerals and memorial services permeated Chinese and East Asian societies. Nowhere is this reflected more clearly than in the official ceremonies conducted by states, where Buddhist incense rites and vegetarian banquets were performed as memorial services for deceased members of the imperial family.

Concluding Remarks

The purpose of this study has been twofold. In the first place, my aim has been to detach Zen ritual from its modern rationale, where Zen practice is understood primarily as a regimen targeted at individual seekers in their quest for enlightenment. However appealing this prospect may be, whether in the past or at present, the function of the Zen monastery in medieval Japan throughout its history has been to serve the communal needs of society, from practical concerns, such as caring for the repose of the souls of the deceased, to loftier ambitions, such as bolstering a regime's political legitimacy. The primary role of the Zen monastery as a social institution was as a collective enterprise, not an individual concern. Individual activities counted to the extent that they served the collective purposes for which the monastery was designed. Zen's success as a social institution was predicated on the favor it received from the cultural elite of medieval Japan, both samurai and aristocrats, to serve these communal needs. Symbolic among these were rituals designed specifically to enhance the emperor and the glory of the Japanese nation. To this end, participation at Zen rituals like these was a patriotic service with wide appeal throughout Japanese society.

In the second place, the Buddhist rites like those performed at Zen monasteries fulfilled widely held assumptions in East Asian societies regarding the nature and function of ritual. Based on Confucian notions of how ritual preserved and maintained harmony throughout the visible and invisible realms of natural forces, Buddhist rites acquired specific functions in the East Asian worldview. Incense offering rites, particularly those performed to execute Confucian obligations at funerals and memorial services, permeated Chinese and East Asian societies. This is manifested clearly in official ceremonies like those conducted at medieval Zen monasteries, where Buddhist incense rites and vegetarian banquets were performed as memorial services for deceased members of the imperial family.

4

Is Dōgen's Eiheiji Temple "Mt. T'ien-t'ung East"?: Geo-Ritual Perspectives on the Transition from Chinese Ch'an to Japanese Zen

Steven Heine

The Question of Affinity between Temples

One of the main elements that appear in traditional records of Dōgen's career is the notion that he established Eiheiji temple in the mid-1240s in the remote, snowy mountains of Echizen (currently Fukui) province based on the model he experienced while training at Mt. T'ien-t'ung in China two decades before. According to the records of Dōgen's life in the autobiographical musings of the *Hōkyōki* and the main Sōtō sectarian biography from 1472, the *Kenzeiki*, he was admonished by his Chinese mentor Ju-ching to remain withdrawn from the corruption of mainstream society in a secluded natural setting. In the *Shōbōgenzō* "Shohō jissō" fascicle composed during the fall of 1243 shortly after Dōgen moved to Echizen in the seventh month, there is an extended account of one of Ju-ching's spontaneous midnight sermons accompanied by a detailed description of the halls and platforms of Mt. T'ien-t'ung. Following this, Dōgen refers to his "having crossed innumerable mountains and rivers" to reach the locale where Eiheiji was established.[1]

These and additional passages in a variety of sources including the *Shōbōgenzō zuimonki* and *Eihei kōroku* are frequently cited by the

Sōtō Zen tradition as examples of how Dōgen fulfilled the goal of patterning the Kamakura era Japanese temple after the Sung dynasty Chinese model. From this standpoint, Dōgen's pivotal move at the midpoint of his career from his first temple, Kōshōji in Fukakusa near Kyoto, to Echizen was not a matter of defensively running away from obstacles and rivals among the Tendai and Rinzai Zen schools in the capital, as it has often been portrayed by some critics. Rather, the move was a genuine effort to find the appropriate locale to introduce and implement Chinese-style rites and practices.

Reinforcing the image of intimate connections between the Chinese model and Eiheiji is the recent construction at Mt. T'ien-t'ung of a shrine to the memory of Dōgen's experiences in China. Figure 4.1 below is a diagram showing the layout of the Mt. T'ien-t'ung compound, which indicates the location of the Dōgen shrine to the center right, and figure 4.2 shows the shrine's memorial tablet, which contains Chinese writing on one side and Japanese on the other side of the stele. In addition, near the port of Ning-po another tablet commemorates the site of Dōgen's entry into China. There are four meditation halls at Mt T'ien-t'ung, including the one believed to be the site of Dōgen's enlightenment. The shrine was built in the post-Mao period of liberalization in 1980, primarily to accommodate the influx of tourists from Japan wishing to see the origins of the Sōtō sect, despite the irony that except for Ju-ching and several other prominent Ts'ao-tung abbots, the leadership of the Chinese temple through most of history has been primarily from the Lin-chi school. Therefore, it is only Japanese parishioners (danka-sha), not well aware of the details of the early history of the Chinese temple and the formation of the sect in Japan, who have come to think of Mt. T'ien-t'ung as the exclusive home temple of Ts'ao-tung Ch'an/Sōtō Zen Buddhism.[2]

This basic historical misconception raises the question, How closely related were the practices at the Chinese and Japanese temples? Was Mt. T'ien-t'ung the chosen model that Eiheiji emulated, such that the latter temple can best be understood in terms of how it set in motion the practices conducted at the former, or are there conflicts and contrasts between the ritual centers that are more relevant for us to consider? The primary aim of this chapter is to compare key elements of religious practice at the temples in the thirteenth century, the time that was so crucial for the process of transmitting Zen from China to Japan. The comparison is examined in terms of geo-ritual perspectives, that is, how the geographical settings of the respective sites seen in light of the overall social environment and cultural context affected the implementation of ritual activities. Such a comparative study must recognize that the thirteenth century needs to be viewed through the filter of the pres-

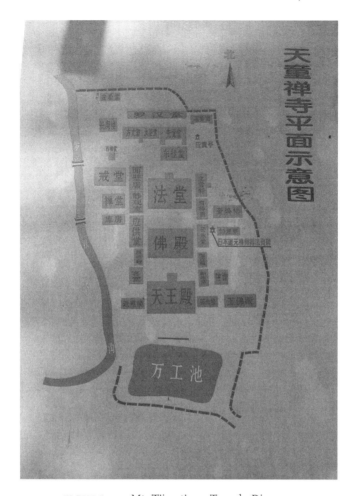

FIGURE 4.1. Mt. T'ien-t'ung Temple Diagram

ent and recent past, since the temples have been rebuilt numerous times, and the records of historical activity and exchanges, aside from Dōgen's own works, which have been questioned in recent studies, are sparse or nonexistent.[3]

On the one hand, it seems clear, as T. Griffith Foulk points out, that "Dōgen's mission in life was to establish in Japan the true buddha-dharma that he believed he had encountered in the great monastic centers of Sung China, and especially in the person of his teacher, Ju-ching."[4] He viewed himself and his dharmic mission as pioneering Sung Chinese rituals for the first

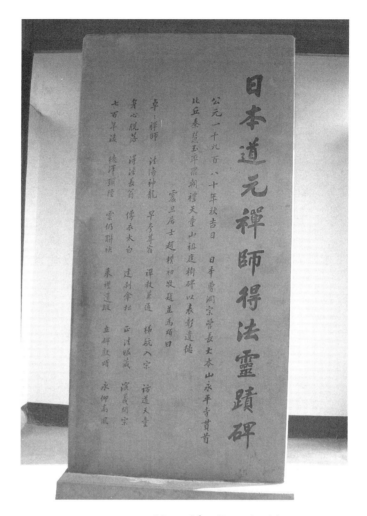

FIGURE 4.2. Memorial to Dōgen's visit

time in the Japanese setting. In addition to a rigorous approach to zazen meditation, which he experienced while training under Ju-ching, the elements of
practice Dōgen introduced cover many of the features of monastic rules contained in the 1103 text, *Ch'an-yüan ch'ing-kuei* (J. *Zen'en shingi*). These include
the summer (*ango*) and winter retreats, the delivery of formal (*jōdō*) and informal (*shōsan*)[5] sermons on a regular basis often in relation to seasonal and
other ceremonies such as Sakyamuni's birthday, and the role of the chief cook
(*tenzo*) plus other administrative positions (*chiji*). To illustrate his approach to
ritual practice, Dōgen sprinkled his sermons with generous helpings of kōan

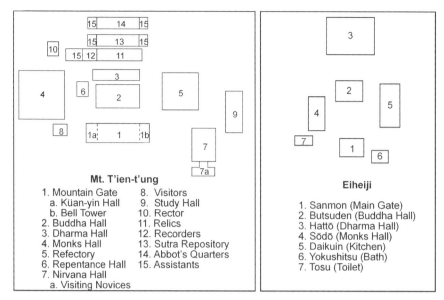

FIGURE 4.3. This diagram shows the key buildings in the temple compound of Mt. T'ien-t'ung juxtaposed with a diagram of Eiheiji, where the compound layout has probably been altered from the Tokugawa era. There are additional buildings on both compounds that are not listed.

citations and commentaries culled from the classic collections that he had apparently learned while studying and attending lectures at Mt. Tien-t'ung and other Chinese temples.

Furthermore, Eiheiji was built according to the seven-hall monastic compound construction (*shichidō garan*) initiated in China, highlighting the function of the Monks Hall for communal meditation and sleeping and the Dharma Hall for public sermons, as well as the Abbot's Quarters (not included in the list of seven) for private instruction.[6] The seven main halls were more or less required, but the temple complexes were generally much more developed with dozens of buildings spread out over a large compound. The site for T'ien-t'ung is a green uninhabited area at the base of a small mountain, and each hall, positioned right behind the previous hall, is a little higher than the hall in front of it, with about 750 halls and rooms in all.

In many instances, Dōgen claimed to be the first to introduce various Ch'an ritual practices, first at Kōshōji and then at Eiheiji, including the construction of the Monks Hall and the role of the cook, the use of *jōdō* and *shōsan* sermons, and celebration of the Buddha's birthday on the fourth month/eighth day and enlightenment (Rohatsu, 12/8) anniversaries. Yet we know in large part from Dōgen's own accounts that some of these practices, such as those of the cook, were already established by Eisai at Kenninji temple founded in Kyoto in 1202.[7] Some rituals may have also been in operation at Sennyūji temple founded in Kyoto in 1218 by Shunjō, a Tendai monk who traveled to China and returned to Japan in 1211.[8]

In addition to how the question of whether or not Dōgen was the very first to implement key ritual practices affects an understanding of the extent to which he was influenced by or borrowed from Chinese models, there is the question of how faithful he was to Ch'an sources. Dōgen maintained, for example, that he brought to Japan a unique approach to the *vinaya* (precepts) based on administering the simplified sixteen-article precepts, but his claim to have derived this system directly from Ju-ching is dubious since Chinese Ch'an monasteries uniformly required the full precepts (a combination of the 250 Pratimoksha and 58 Bodhisattva precepts). It seems that since Dōgen himself never received the Pratimoksha precepts, he sought to come up with a rationale for dismissing the need for these. Dōgen also claimed to bring back a ceremony for folding the robe (*kesa*) that he says he had observed at Chinese temples, although it is not clear that this was ever followed the way he describes it in either China or Japan.[9] Also, Dōgen's comments of both praise and criticism of Mt. T'ien-t'ung and Kenninji, especially in the *Shōbōgenzō zuimonki*, are interesting for historical purposes. Yet it seems clear that some of the remarks in which he eulogizes Ju-ching are exaggerated and made primarily for sectarian purposes in legitimizing his new movement in Japan and disputing rival forces aligned with the Lin-chi school.

Further contradicting the argument for a fundamental underlying affinity between temples is the observation that the geographical locations as well as the cultural landscapes they occupied are quite different. Mt. T'ien-t'ung is situated on a relatively small hill in close proximity to a major cosmopolitan port, Ming-chou (currently Ning-po), which is near the then-capital city of Hang-chou. In Ch'an/Zen discourse, the term "mountain" is often a conceit for a site of spiritual retreat, even if not actually occupying such a geographical setting. Not aligned with the Ch'an school until 1007, or about seven hundred years after its founding, Mt. T'ien-t'ung never was isolated but rather was a part of a conglomeration of Buddhist sites, including other major urban and ex-urban temples in the region. Eiheiji, on the other hand, was set in the deep, reclusive mountains (although not too distant from other important Echizen religious institutions, including the Tendai temple, Heisenji).

More significant than the matter of location are discrepancies concerning ritual activities conducted at the respective temples, especially involving the connection between lineage affiliation and transmission rites, moral precepts and behavioral etiquette reflected in disciplinary regulations and codes, and clerical and lay assembly convocations. Furthermore, as Ishii Seijun shows, to appreciate the significance of the discrepancies, it is necessary to compare not just specific rites but rather the overall institutional approaches at Eiheiji with the Five Mountains (Wu-shan) network of Chinese Ch'an. The main difference is that the Wu-shan system was a vertical, top-down model supervised and assigned by a government regulatory agency and with strong participation in temple rituals and affairs by a landed gentry from the capital. Eiheiji, on the other hand, was autonomous and unregulated by the government, although based on the patronage of the powerful samurai clan of Hatano Yoshishige, a Kyoto-based retainer who held land in Echizen province, and it involved the inclusion of uneducated lay believers from the countryside. It is also important to see both of these systems in the context of the Kenmitsu system prevalent in Japanese temples at the beginning of the Kamakura era, as well as two Japanese Zen models developed subsequent to Dōgen, the Five Mountains (Gozan) and Rinka styles.[10]

Chinese Ch'an Temples at the Time of Dōgen's Arrival

Dōgen was the second in a series of Japanese monks who went to China in pursuit of discovering true Buddhism and returned to found Zen temples. His travels from 1223–1227 were sandwiched between the two trips taken by Eisai at the end of the twelfth century, the first for six months in 1168 and the next from 1187–1191, and Enni Benen's pilgrimage, which began in the mid-1230s.[11] Whereas Eisai and Enni became leaders of the Rinzai school based in Kyoto, Dōgen at the height of his career departed from the capital in the mid-1240s to form a movement in the mountains of northwest Japan that eventually became known as the Sōtō school largely through the evangelical efforts of fourth patriarch Keizan and his long list of followers.

Like Eisai before him, as well as Enni and Shinichi Kakushin among other subsequent Kamakura era pilgrims, Dōgen was first trained as a Tendai novice but forsook this path to study at the Five Mountains temples located near Ming-chou (which can refer either to a larger provincial area or to the port traditionally known as Ching-yüan). Ching-yüan was a port city just east of the Southern Sung capital of Hang-chou (with another important city, Shao-hsing, located in between) in Chekiang province on the eastern seaboard of China.[12] Hang-chou with its multistorey houses was chosen as the capital after Kai-feng, the Northern Sung capital, more for its charm and culture as a site for the imperial court to perform ritual sacrifices and also for some geographical advantages than because it was considered politically or militarily significant.

Nevertheless, it was the biggest urban center in the world at the time with one million residents, and it earned a reputation for grandeur, according to Patricia Buckley Ebrey and the thirteenth-century traveler from the West she cites:

> After the north was lost, the new capital at Hangzhou quickly grew to match or even surpass Kaifeng in population and economic development. Marco Polo described it as without doubt the finest and most splendid city in the world: "Anyone seeing such a multitude would believe it impossible that food could be found to feed them all, and yet on every market day all the market squares are filled with people and with merchants who bring food on carts and boats."[13]

From Dōgen's writings, we find that monks and pilgrims from all over China and from Korea and Japan were thronging to the Hang-Ming area, which was connected in turn by canals and waterways as well as overland trade routes to the northwest and southeast of China.

The ancient history of Ming-chou dates back to Hemudu settlements in the fifth millennium BCE, making it one of the oldest continuous cultural locations in China. Marked by a confluence of three rivers merging into a bay near the ocean, Ning-po has been a seaport for two thousand years, although full-fledged urbanization came hundreds of years later, and it remains one of the largest in the world but is now overshadowed by the megalopolis of Shanghai across the bay. By the early centuries CE, Ming-chou was the primary entry to the "Silk Road of the Sea" (Marco Polo embarked from there on his return journey to Italy via the Indian Ocean, just about seventy years after Dōgen's visit). It was also a place where several early Buddhist temples had been established with styles of practice imported perhaps directly from India, or at least greatly influenced by Indian Buddhism, including the oldest center, Wu-lei temple.

In the late twelfth and early thirteenth centuries, Ming-chou was a cosmopolitan, dynamic port of call with a rich history of diverse cultural and religious developments as well connections with Japan and Japanese Buddhism in addition to countries throughout the Asia-Pacific region.[14] Because of its close proximity to Japan, there were early interactions during the T'ang, including those by Chinese monks who persisted in making the difficult journey to visit and to bring geomancy and other elements of Chinese society, as well as absorb cultural affinities with the Japanese.

The two main temples Dōgen visited, Mt. T'ien-t'ung and Mt. A-yü-wang located in the foothills of the sub-tropical T'ai-pai Mountains with evergreen foliage, were established by the end of the third century, in 300 and 283, respectively. The latter, named for King Asoka, is said to house one of three main relics of Sakyamuni Buddha found in China, a *sarira* (crystalline relic found in cremation pyre) maintained on the second floor of the Relics Hall. Both temples did not become considered Public monasteries and assigned to the Ch'an Five Mountains network until the eleventh century (in 1007 and 1008, respectively), the same decade that produced the seminal transmission of the lamp text, the *Ching-te chuan-teng lu* (J. *Keitoku dentōroku*), after over seven hundred years of being affiliated with various other schools and lineages.[15]

Although ranked one notch higher in the Five Mountains system than Mt. T'ien-t'ung, Mt. A-yü-wang—supposedly, it appeared suddenly out of the ground when a monk looking for a harmonious place discovered the miracle—has been better known for its relic and Indian style of practice than for dedication to Ch'an practice. This evaluation, which can imply a deficiency in Ch'an practice, is suggested in a key passage in the "Busshō" fascicle where Dōgen is quite critical of the temple's leading monks, who do not seem to exhibit typical Ch'an insight.[16]

Furthermore, Mt. T'ien-t'ung was not primarily known as a Ts'ao-tung temple, in that abbacies of Ch'an Public monasteries had a rotation of abbots assigned by a central government agency and were not distinguished by subsect, for example, Ts'ao-tung or Lin-chi. Therefore, while a prominent monk might have an exclusive affiliation or loyalty to a particular school, the temples never did, so that even when Hung-chih put great effort into refurbishing Mt. T'ien-t'ung in the twelfth century, the institution itself did not remain in Ts'ao-tung hands. Its sectarian reputation is primarily directed from a retrospective outlook based on Dōgen's status in Japan and recent shrines and memorials to Dōgen established at the temple and elsewhere in Ning-po largely to accommodate the Japanese tourist trade and pilgrimages.

The spread of Buddhism in the Hang-Ming area was not based on official government dissemination policies (unlike the T'ang emperor sending Hsüan-tsang to India, for example). Yet, by the time of the Sung, this area had become the center of the Chinese Buddhist world, encompassing such venerable institutions as the Five Mountains temples, another important Ch'an center at Mt. Hsüeh-t'ou, the sacred island of Mt. P'u-t'o considered the earthly abode of Küan-yin, and the massif of Mt. T'ien-t'ai along with dozens or even hundreds of temples of the T'ien-t'ai school.

Although located on what seems to have been a significant trade route between Fujien and the Hang-Ming area, Mt. T'ien-t'ai today remains an isolated, sprawling mountain region marked by literally hundreds of peaks and valleys with numerous monasteries strewn all over its slopes. Unlike Mt. T'ien-t'ung located in the hills in close proximity to an urban environment, Mt. T'ien-t'ai, several hours drive to the south, was genuinely remote and pastoral. By the Southern Sung, however, it had lost prominence and its place as the center of the school except as a site of pilgrimage and history. One of the main temples of the massif, Wan-nien ssu, had officially become a major Ch'an temple and was considered a part of the Five Mountain system.

At this stage of their development, the two schools, the T'ien-t'ai (also known as the Teaching or Doctrinal school) and Ch'an (also known as the Meditation school), both supervised by the government and with priests regulated by official ordinations, were quite similar in terms of religious rituals, doctrinal study, and meditation practices. For the elite clergy within these state institutions, the study of T'ien-t'ai doctrine generally required the practice of Ch'an meditation, and to practice Ch'an one needed to have studied T'ien-t'ai. Nevertheless, while both schools were considered Public monasteries, from the end of the eleventh century on, the Ch'an monasteries also referred to as Ten Directions monasteries superseded those of T'ien-t'ai and other movements in terms of prestige and the vigor of institutional growth based on government support and donations.

In addition to the five main temples, the Five Mountains system included ten highly ranked and at least thirty-five regular temples. Furthermore, there were literally dozens or even hundreds of temples located in the proximity of Ming-chou. When Dōgen got off the ship, even though Mt. A-yü-wang is located only about a dozen miles from the port and Mt. T'ien-t'ung about two dozen miles, it may have taken him several weeks to reach T'ien-t'ung because he probably would have stopped one-by-one at some of the temples along the way that had a custom of hosting itinerant monks or "clouds." Again, this does not indicate considerable distance from the temple. In fact, the cook from nearby Mt. A-yü-wang (admittedly closer to the harbor than Mt. T'ien-t'ung), whom Dōgen met on ship as cited in *Tenzokyōkun*, planned to return to the temple the evening of their conversation, suggesting that it was within a modest walking distance (for a well-trained monk). Mt. T'ien-t'ung at its peak is said to have housed a community of over a thousand monks, all fed from a single wok supervised by the temple's chief cook.

A full discussion of Dōgen's experiences in China have been covered elsewhere and are beyond the scope of this chapter, although the traditional narrative accounts have been increasingly questioned as reliable historiographical sources.[17] One very interesting though often overlooked episode that high-

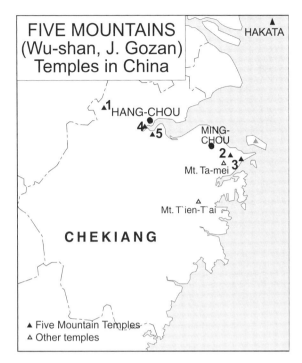

FIGURE 4. 4. Locations of Ch'an Five Mountain temples: (1) Mt. Ching-shan Wan-shou Ch'an ssu, of Hang-chou; (2) Mt. A-yu-wang-shan Kuang li Ch'an ssu, of Ming-chou; (3) Mt. T'ai-pai-shan T'ien-t'ung Ching-te Ch'an ssu, of Ming-chou; (4) Mt. Pei-shan Ch'ing-te ling-yin Ch'an ssu, of Hang-chou; (5) Mt. Nan-shan Ch'ing tz'u pao en kuang hsiao Ch'an ssu, of Hang-chou. These are the five main temples in the Zen monastic system of Sung China, but there were dozens of additional temples that constituted the entire network.

lights the way Dōgen's approach to Ch'an rituals has been portrayed in traditional narratives with supernatural implications is the account in the *Shō-bōgenzō* "Busshō" fascicle of a vision of the round full moon at Mt. A-yü-wang temple that appeared while Dōgen was looking at portraits of the thirty-three Ch'an patriarchs. This section of the fascicle follows a lengthy philosophical discussion of an anecdote in the *Ching-te ch'uan-teng lu* volume 1, in which Nagarjuna manifests as the moon. Dōgen says that "in former days, while traveling as a cloud [or itinerant novice]," he went to Mt. A-yü-wang in the first year of his journey to China (1223); but when he saw the paintings, he did not understand the meaning and nobody was available to explain it.[18] Then he

FIGURE 4.5. Said to be original temple wok now used to cast good-luck coins

returned to this site about two years later, during the summer retreat of 1225, apparently a short time after attaining his enlightenment experience under the tutelage of Ju-ching.

One question concerns why Dōgen would have returned to Mt. A-yü-wang during the retreat when it was expected that monks dedicated to an intensive and sacred period of meditation (*geango*) would not depart their home temple, especially given Dōgen's struggles in not being allowed to participate in the retreat until the third year of his stay in China. Surely, once Dōgen had taken up training under Ju-ching, he would not be looking to explore other alternatives. A possibility is that the two temples at Mt. T'ien-t'ung and Mt. A-yü-wang located in close proximity would have shared resources, or that the relic was so prominent—Dōgen refers to visiting the "six beautiful sites" of the compound—that he took time to see this for what was probably a second time.[19] In any case, according to "Busshō," this time he alone among the monks understood the vision, whereas the others either took it too literally or did not see it at all. Dōgen sensed the deficiency of Chinese Ch'an Buddhists, including the temple abbot, Ta-kuang, a relatively unknown figure from the Lin-chi school, for whom there is "no nostrils in their complexion" and "no sword in their laughter." This episode marks the moment in the traditional account when Dōgen is clear and confident of his spiritual authority and superiority. It also serves his partisan agenda a decade and a half after the trip by putting down members of a rival lineage from the vantage point of what he endorsed, retrospectively, in terms of what was relevant to his struggles at the time in Japan.

This account of what transpired in the mid-1220s was written in the early 1240s, around the time Dōgen received from China a copy of Ju-ching's recorded sayings and began citing his master more extensively while also disparaging rival lineages. A common theory is that Dōgen apparently felt that this version gave an inadequate picture of Ju-ching's teaching, and he wanted to enhance and revise the image of his mentor. It is interesting to note, however, that a few months before the arrival of the text of the recorded sayings of the teacher, Ju-ching was evoked by Dōgen to reinforce sectarian perspectives. For example, in "Gyōji" (part 2) from 4.5.1242, Dōgen quotes his mentor in a passage that is not found in his recorded sayings as severely criticizing the Lin-chi master Te-kuang in the lineage of the famous Ta-hui, whom Dōgen frequently excoriates:

> In former days, I hung my traveling staff at Mt. Ching when the head monk was Fo-chao Te-kuang. In the lecture hall, he said to his disciples, "About Zen Buddhism you should not seek another's views, but try to realize it for yourselves." So saying, he paid no attention whatsoever to what happened in the Monks Hall. The junior and senior monks were also unconcerned, and busied themselves with the reception of government officials. He was quite ignorant of the Buddha Dharma, and was instead attached to fame and fortune. If we could, as he says, grasp the Buddha Dharma by ourselves, then why have the sharpest monks gone searching for a true teacher? Really, Te-kuang has never even experienced Zen. Now, in every area we find those who have not awakened their bodhi-seeking mind who are followers of Te-kuang. It is regrettable that the Buddha Dharma is not found among them.[20]

Dōgen's Return to Japan and Establishment of Eiheiji

Once again, an extensive discussion of Dōgen's return to Japan and years of ritual practice before his eventual move to Eiheiji will not be covered here, but suffice it to say that the nearly two decades were divided into several cycles. These include about two years (1227–1229) of practice in Kenninji temple in

Kyoto and four years (1229–1233) at hermitages in the ex-urban town of Fukakusa. Six years after the return, Dōgen was able to establish his own temple
in Fukakusa, Kōshōji, which after a fundraising drive opened a Monks Hall in
1236 derived from the style of Sung Ch'an monasteries. Following a decade
(1233–1243) in which he led this temple, or about sixteen years after returning
from China, Dōgen and a small band of followers left in the seventh month of
1243 for Echizen province. There is no specific reference, let alone an attempt
to explain the reasons for the move in Dōgen's corpus of writings. Thus, all
discussions are speculative and based on piecing together threads of evidence
and ideas from pseudo-historical sources that are often unreliable.

A longstanding argument about the reasons behind the move is that
Dōgen, as the leader of a new movement, was embroiled in a political conflict
with the Tendai establishment on Mt. Hiei and may, in fact, have been driven
away from Kyoto or chose to flee rather than stand up to forces beyond his
control. The advent of the construction of the impressive compound at Tōfukuji temple, just down the road from Kōshōji, with abbacy awarded to Rinzai
priest Enni in 1243, may have forced Dōgen to flee the capital the same year.
Sectarian scholars have tried to give this argument a positive spin by portray-
ing Dōgen sympathetically as a heroic victim who eventually rose above his
opponents through a withdrawal to a reclusive retreat, in part with the assistance of Hatano's patronage.

The traditional Sōtō explanation is that the move was motivated by Dōgen's pure longing to uphold Ju-ching's injunction to escape the confusion
and turmoil of the capital (which is so eloquently described in Chōmei's
Hōjōki of 1212) and remain free from secular corruption by establishing an
ideal monastic community in the natural splendor of Echizen. There, he discovered what has been referred to as a mystical *axis mundi* in the remote
mountain forests.[21] In support of the emphasis on renunciation from worldly
connections, there are several prominent examples of teacher Ju-ching and
disciple Dōgen expressing disdain for false-hearted monks, even within the
upper echelons of the Buddhist hierarchy, who are prone to give in to temp-
tation, greed, or longing for power rather than a supreme dedication to pursue
the Dharma. For instance, both Ju-ching and Dōgen declined the offer to wear
the purple robe proffered by imperial authorities at key turning points in their
careers. In texts written in Kyoto, Dōgen exhorts Zen practitioners to dwell
among the crags and white rocks found only in secluded mountain landscapes
in *Bendōwa*, and in *Shōbōgenzō* "Sansuikyō," he suggests that mountain abo-
des are the natural setting for Zen masters.

According to *Hokyoki* no. 10, Ju-ching admonishes, "You must first make
your dwelling in steep mountains and dark valleys."[22] In a similar passage

recorded in *Kenzeiki*, he instructs, "Do not live near the capital or by rich and powerful persons. Avoid emperors, ministers and generals. Stay in the deep mountains far removed from worldly affairs and devote yourself to the education of young monks, even if you have only one disciple. Do not terminate the transmission I have given you."[23] Apparently following this advice, in *jōdō* sermon 7.498 delivered near the end of his career in 1252, Dōgen asserts:

> Those who are truly endowed with both practice and discernment are called patriarchal teachers. What is called practice is the intimate practice of the patriarchal school. What is called discernment is the discerning understanding of the patriarchal school. The practice and discernment of buddha patriarchs is simply to discern what should be discerned and to practice what should be practiced. The first thing to practice is to cut away all attachments and have no family ties, to abandon social obligations and enter the realm of the unconditioned. Without sojourning in towns, and without being familiar with rulers, enter the mountains and seek the way. From ancient times, noble people who yearn for the way all enter the deep mountains and calmly abide in quiet serenity. [24]
>
> The patriarch Nagarjuna said, "All zazen practitioners reside in the deep mountains." You should know that for leaving behind the bustle and turmoil while attaining quiet serenity, there is nothing like the deep mountains. Even if you are foolish, you should abide in the deep mountains, because the foolish abiding in towns will increase their mistakes. Even if you are wise, you should abide in the deep mountains, because the wise abiding in towns will damage their virtue.
>
> I [Eihei] in my vigorous years searched for the way west of the western ocean [in China], and now in my older years I abide north of the northern mountains. Although I am unworthy, I yearn for the ancient pathways. Without discussing our wisdom or unworthiness, and without discriminating between sharp or dull functioning, we should all abide in the deep mountains and dark valleys. [25]

The affinity shared by Ju-ching, who was not known so much as a philosopher or poet as a strict disciplinarian and charismatic leader, and Dōgen regarding a strict adherence to the teaching is reflected in the calligraphy below, "Uphold nothing beyond the Dharma," which is held in the Abbot's Quarters at Mt. T'ien-t'ung:

In his effort to gain a place for contemplation that was free of secular distractions, Dōgen may also have been inspired by the poetic tradition he had

FIGURE 4.6. "Uphold nothing beyond the Dharma," at Mt. T'ien-t'ung

studied as a child who was brought up with a late-Heian style aristocratic education. Japanese poetry, which was in part derived from Chinese aesthetics grounded in eremitic and reclusive traditions, celebrated the intense sense of privacy and solitude (*sabi*) that can only be experienced in secluded, natural areas. This was a theme well expressed in Dōgen's own verse composed in both Japanese and Chinese, as well as in *Shōbōgenzō* fascicles that evoke the serenity of the natural environment as the ideal backdrop for undisturbed ascetic meditation, including "Keisei sanshoku" and "Baika" (the latter written at Kippōji).

It is possible to imagine that Dōgen felt that only mountain seclusion would provide the unadorned simplicity needed to foster the path to enlightenment. According to one of Dōgen's Japanese *waka* poems, he never gave up a sense of longing for the refinement of the capital, whose beauty had an appeal that rivaled Echizen's:

> Miyako ni wa   All last night and
> Momiji shinuran   This morning still,
> Okuyama no   Snow falling the deepest mountains;
> Koyoi mo kesa mo Ah, to the see autumn leaves
> Arare furi keri.   Scattering in my home.[26]

Ienaga Saburō explains the Japanese view of nature as a mirror and a model for humans, an experience attained "in a secluded grass-thatched hut in the mountains (*yamazato*) where secular dust of worldly life does not reach," and nature has a supremely soteric (*kyūsai*) value. [27] Similar sentiments are expressed in a *kanbun* verse from this phase:

> For so long here without worldly attachments,
> I have renounced literature and writing;
> I may be a monk in a mountain temple,
> Yet still, I am moved in seeing gorgeous blossoms
> Scattered by the spring breeze,
> And hearing the warbler's lovely song—
> Let others judge my meager efforts. [28]

Dōgen's Claims for Transmitting Ch'an Rituals

The argument for withdrawal based largely on romantic and visionary imagery inspired by the teachings of Ju-ching at the Mt. T'ien-t'ung location is buttressed by the writings from the Eiheiji period, which indicate that Dōgen saw himself fulfilling his hope of opening a legitimate Sung-style Monks Hall and Dharma Hall in the mountains. There, he was able to carry out the genuine Ch'an approach to monastic leadership, as reflected in formal *jōdō* sermons delivered in *kanbun* (Sino-Japanese). Numerous passages from sermons collected in *Eihei kōroku* proclaim how Dōgen brought ritual elements and patterns from China for the first time in the history of Japanese Buddhism. These include:

> no. 2.138, on introducing the post of chief cook,
> no. 4.319, "On Mt. Kichijō there is a Monks Hall available for the first time for all Japanese to hear of its name, see its shape, enter and sit in it," [29]
> no. 5.406 (on 12.8.1251), "Japanese ancestors have been holding ceremonies to celebrate the birth of Sakyamuni Buddha and commemorate his death since an earlier era. However, they have not yet received transmission of the annual ceremony to celebrate his enlightenment. I [Eihei] imported Rohatsu (12.8 ritual) twenty years ago and maintained it. It must be transmitted in the future," [30]
> and no. 8.shōsan.10, "I first transmitted *shōsan* sermons twenty years ago."[31]

TABLE 4.1. Jōdō Sermons on Administrative Positions

1245
2.137—appreciation for the director
2.138—appreciation for the chief cook
2.139—appointment of a new director and chief cook
1246
2.157—appointment of a new receptionist
2.190—appreciation for and appointment of a new rector
3.214—appreciation/appointment of a new director and chief cook
1247
(none—period of Kamakura mission)
1248
4.298—appreciation for the rector
4.299—appreciation for the director
4.300—appointment of a new director
4.315—Monks Hall at Eiheiji
1249
4.336—appointment of a new secretary
5.357—appointment of a new chief cook
5.358—on introducing jōdō sermons
1250
5.385—appreciation for the rector
5.398—appointment of a new head monk
5.401—appointment of another new chief cook
1251
5.406—Rohatsu introduced
6.416—appointment of a chief cook
6.460—appointment of a new secretary
6.467—appointment of a new librarian

Furthermore, nearly a dozen sermons over the last few years of delivery are examples of administrative appointments or declarations, as listed in table 4.1 above.

The significance of the role of the delivery of *jōdō* sermons, first expressed in *Eihei kōroku* no. 2.128 based on Ju-ching's model, is particularly emphasized in no. 5.358, which declares, "Japanese people are curious about the meaning of the word *jōdō*. I [Eihei] am the first to transmit *jōdō* sermons to this country." [32] Further evidence of the regard with which Dōgen held the role of sermons is indicated in that he refers five times in his writings to the Pai-chang kōan also cited by Ju-ching about the query, "What is the most remarkable thing [in the world]?" In no. 5.378,33[33] five years after the original citation in the *Shōbōgenzō* "Kokū" fascicle, Dōgen returns to this case by responding, "I [Eihei] will go to the lecture hall today."

The following year, 1251, in no. 6.443 Dōgen revises the conclusion once more, this time by saying, "If someone asks me this question, I [Eihei] will respond, 'It is attending *jōdō* sermons on Mt. Kichijōzan [the name of the mountain where Eiheiji was built].' "[34] This demands a rethinking of conventional assumptions about Eiheiji religiosity in that Dōgen, unlike Paichang, is generally known for his emphasis on zazen rather than sermons. In no. 3.244, Dōgen remarks ironically, though without necessarily complaining, that despite his giving the first authentic Zen-style sermons in Japan at Eiheiji in the Echizen mountains, many onlookers denounce him by saying, "Just take a look at that preposterous rube on the mountain whose preaching is merely the talk of a 'wild fox Zen.' "[35]

In addition to following the Chinese Ch'an rituals described in the *Ch'an-yüan ch'ing-kuei*, Dōgen also emulated Ju-ching's style of ritual with supernatural implications for invoking clear weather by stopping the rains during an extremely wet season, as in *Eihei kōroku* no. 5.379, "Sermon in Supplication for Clear Skies on 10.6.1250," quoted at length below.

Last year and this year, through spring, summer, autumn, and winter, below the heavens the rains have fallen without cease. The whole populace laments as the five grains do not ripen. Now elder Eihei, for the sake of saving our land from lamentation, will again make supplications by lifting up this sermon praying for clear skies that was given by his late teacher T'ien-t'ung [Ju-ching] when he resided at Ch'ing-liang temple. What is the reason? What can we do if the Buddha Dharma does not relieve the suffering of human and heavenly beings? Great assembly, do you clearly understand Eihei's intention?

When my late teacher had not yet given a sermon, all buddhas and patriarchs had not yet given a sermon. When my late teacher gave a sermon, all buddhas of the three times, the patriarchs of the six generations, and all nostrils and the ten thousand eyeballs [of all teachers], at the same time all gave a sermon. They could not have been an hour earlier, or half an hour later. Today's sermon by Eihei is also like this.

After a pause Dōgen said: Without ceasing, one, two, three raindrops, drop after drop, fall continuously morning to night, transformed into torrents, so that we can do nothing. [36] The winds and waves overflow throughout the mountains, rivers, and the great earth.

[T'ien-t'ung Ju-ching] sneezed once and said, "Before one sneeze of this patch-robed monk is finished, the clouds part and the sun appears." He raised his whisk and said, "Great assembly, look here. The bright clear sky swallows the eight directions. If the waters continue to fall as before, all the houses will float away to the country of demons. Make prostrations to Sakyamuni; take refuge in Maitreya. Capable of saving the world from its sufferings, wondrous wisdom power of Avalokitesvara, I call on you."

Questioning Traditional Accounts

From both the traditional narrative account and the records of Dōgen's claims for importing and implementing rituals, it would seem fair and appropriate to imagine that Mt. T'ien-t'ung was the model for a remote, reclusive site for Eiheiji, which could be considered an eastward version of the Chinese Ch'an temple. However, considerations of geo-ritual perspectives, that is, how the geographical settings of the respective sites seen in light of social environment and cultural context affect the implementation of ritual activities indicates that although the temples have some common features, the differences and discrepancies in style, over and beyond basic cultural distinctions, are significant and even glaring. The following is a brief discussion of location, institutional history, and styles of practice at the thirteenth-century temples.

A. Location, Location, Location

Mt. T'ien-t'ung is not situated in the secluded mountain forests, as was the case with many Buddhist temples in China. Rather it is, first of all, close to the large cosmopolitan port area of Ning-po, which is in turn in close proximity to then-capital Hang-chou. Second, it is not in the deep, reclusive mountains but at the base of a small hill in the expanse of the T'ai-pai mountain forests. Mt. A-yü-wang is on completely flat ground, so that the term "mountain" in this case is used more as a literary conceit to evoke an atmosphere rather than a description. Both monasteries at that time were surrounded by dozens of other temples throughout the Hang-chou and Ming-chou provinces populated by full-time and part-time residents, who were among the literati and civil servantry. Furthermore, the climate in the area south of Shanghai is considerably warmer and more mild than the Echizen mountains, which is such a challenging environment—according to Dōgen's prose and poetic writings, the severity of the deep snowfalls was daunting for him at times (yet inspiring)—that it demands a high degree of austerity and commitment to Spartan ideals of training and self-discipline.

B. Sect and Inter-Sect

Whereas Eiheiji has always been a head temple of the Japanese Sōtō sect since its inception and continuing without any slight variance ever since, the situation is quite different in the case of Mt. T'ien-t'ung. The Chinese temple, which had a seven-hundred-year history before becoming affiliated with the Ch'an school in the first decade of the eleventh century, veered back and forth from Lin-chi and Ts'ao-tung connections, depending on who was appointed abbot by the authorities responsible for religious administration. For most of its thousand-year Ch'an history, it has been associated with the Lin-chi stream, though today it is known primarily for Dōgen's role there, which lends an impression that it is primarily of Ts'ao-tung affiliation. Ju-ching himself is "trans-sectual" in that he had trained at and was abbot of Lin-chi temples and was by no means a strict adherent to one school of thought and refuter of another. It appears that "bad blood" in the Hung-chih versus Ta-hui rivalry just a couple of generations before did not affect the time of Ju-ching's abbacy. Dōgen's affection and connection to him was based on his particular style of preaching rather than a sectarian standpoint. Lin-chi abbots served before and after Ju-ching's leadership.

C. Institutional Structure

Despite differences of instructional structure involving lineage affiliation and of instructional style involving training methods and transmission rites, both temples adhered to the seven-hall monastic compound construction emphasizing the function of the Monks Hall, Dharma Hall (and Abbot's Quarters), as well as the delivery of formal and informal sermons in relation to seasonal and other ceremonies. However, this was not a simple, uniform style since Mt. T'ien-t'ung had hundreds of buildings, and Mt. A-yü-wang has some of the main buildings on the central axis but dozens of other structures laid out in seemingly random fashion, as in Figure 4.7.[37] Furthermore, there were significant differences in religious practice, with Mt. T'ien-t'ung stressing zazen and precepts more than the use of kōan cases or regimented discipline and chores as found at Eiheiji. The Chinese temple also incorporated relics and esoteric ritual elements, in addition to a different approach to lay rituals, repentance, and ordination ceremonies. However, it was in subsequent generations that the assimilation of indigenous and folklore elements of religiosity made many Sōtō prayer temples (kitō jiin) in Japan even further removed— and for different reasons than in Dōgen's case—from the ritual style at Mt. T'ien-t'ung.

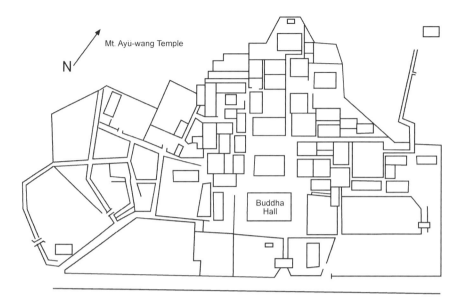

FIGURE 4.7. Ground plan at Mt. A-yü-wang

Comparing Monastic Systems

According to Ishii Seijun, who stresses a systems approach in evaluating the relation between temples, the key is to understand how Dōgen's temple was distinct from the two established monastic institutional systems at the time. One is the Five Mountains system of Chinese Ch'an in which the appointment and supervision of administrative officers in the monastery was handled by a centralized government agency, the Religious Administrative Office. The other was the Tendai—or, rather, the Kenmitsu (Tendai/Shingon, combining exoteric, or *kenjū*, and esoteric, or *mikkyō* elements)—temple system of the late Heian/early Kamakura era, as discussed by Kuroda Toshio and other scholars, in which the Imperial Court supervised and regulated the appointment of the abbot as well as the superior monks. [38] In addition to focusing on the issue of supervision, Ishii emphasizes the relation between the monks who lead the monastery and the lay community that helps support and benefits from their activities. For Ishii, Eiheiji was a "community-based" system following democratic principles, with the self-appointed abbot creating a rotation of administrative functionaries who were very much interactive and attuned to the needs of laypersons.

A main feature of Ishii's methodology is that Dōgen did not simply try to duplicate the Chinese model, which would have been impossible in any case,

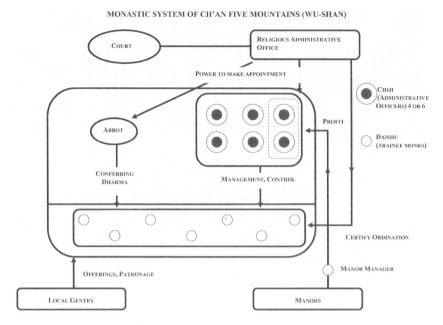

FIGURE 4.8. Monastic system of Ch'an Five Mountains

but adjusted it to the Japanese context. Whereas Ch'an Five Mountains was a highly politicized system with economic implications in terms of government control of ordinations and administration, as shown in figure 8, the Kenmitsu system had political implications based on an increasingly outdated economic structure involving fundraising monks (*kanjin hijiri*), who appealed to lords of manors for financial support. Seeking to avoid the pitfalls of these approaches, Dōgen developed a monastic unit based on the principles of autonomy from government regulation, democracy as well as a noncommercial work ethic in the role of monks and monastic leaders, and lay inclusion, as illustrated in Figure 4.9 showing Ishii's conception of the intertwining of elements of support and labor at Eiheiji.

There are several main implications of the systems approach. One is that Dōgen apparently did not want to control his administrative appointees, and in his *Chiji shingi* text on the role of various monastic administrators, he says that they should have their own autonomous council system to deal with any issue that would affect the monastery. When Dōgen visited Sung China, all the monastic administrators were appointed by the Religious Administrative Office, which was a political institution, and he apparently rejected this practice in kōan cases of antistructural monks who lived in the T'ang dynasty,

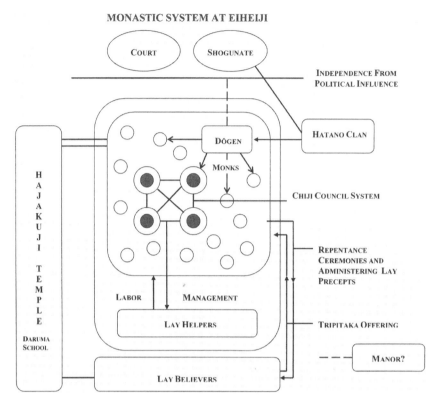

FIGURE 4.9. Dōgen's Eiheiji Approach

which marks a different attitude from longstanding custom at Mt. T'ien-t'ung. In *Chiji shingi*, Dōgen makes the highly innovative move, not found in Chinese Ch'an counterpart texts, of using kōans known for emphasizing antistructure in the context of instructing on the quality of monastic structure. This seems to be his way of asserting that the monks appointed to a role as administrator do not occupy a kind of political position or are not appointed for such reasons, but are selected because they represent the very best of Zen spiritual insight into human nature. In contrast to the way Mt. T'ien-t'ung appointees were regulated by the Religious Administrative Office, which also had the power to certify ordinations, Dōgen held this authority but apparently did not regard his own role as abbot as overwhelmingly important and intended to create a horizontal rather than hierarchical relationship among monks, abbot, administrators, and trainees in the monastery.

A second characteristic of Eiheiji as an independent monastery is that Dōgen tried to differ from the *Ch'an-yüan ch'ing-kuei*, in which the supervisor is considered to lead not only all the monastic work but also matters of the monastic farm and manor (*shoen*) located outside of the temple. In an effort to be faithful to Pai-chang's original injunctions about self-sustaining monastic compounds, Dōgen does not refer to work outside temple grounds, such as manor maintenance, but instructs the supervisor only to manage lay helpers for the upkeep of the temple yard and buildings. That is, all reference to external work is eliminated in Dōgen's commentary, although we have to consider that in actual practice there may have been a manor owned and maintained as a source of income by Eiheiji in Okayama prefecture, as was the case with large Ch'an temples in China.

The third implication of the systems approach is that, while Dōgen's late period is often seen as a time of cloistered monasticism either because it shows a diminishing of talents or an emphasis on his pursuit of purity, it actually marks a shift away from a clergy for clergy's sake approach that is characteristic of the *Shōbōgenzō*, largely completed during the pre-Eiheiji phase of Dōgen's career. In featuring the role of repentance meetings in which laypersons could make offerings to the *Tripitaka*, the Buddhist canon collection which Dōgen received from a donation by Hatano, Dōgen tended to equalize their role in relation to clergy, perhaps out of democratic as well as fundraising inclinations. [39] Dōgen reached out beyond the landed gentry and manor lords who were involved with Chinese Ch'an to encompass a much broader base of support. Nevertheless, the participation of laypersons, while gaining merit, could not actually lead to enlightenment or transmission, which was only available to full-fledged monks (who, in Dōgen's system, received the sixteen-article precepts).

Conclusions

Mt. T'ien-t'ung or Ju-ching as Model

Ishii's systems approach highlights complex features of Dōgen's texts and contexts often overlooked by other methods, but it seems necessary to evaluate Dōgen's standpoint in broader perspectives. The Eiheiji system needs to be contrasted not only with the then-current systems of Ch'an Five Mountains in China and the Kenmitsu temples in Japan but also with two crucial subsequent developments of Japanese Zen during the Ashikaga shogunate of the Muromachi era. The first is the Japanese Five Mountains system, which had eleven main temples and over three hundred branch or minor temples supervised by the shogunate, or *bakufu*—as in China, the role of civil authorities was paramount. The other is the Rinka system, including Rinzai and Sōtō

TABLE 4.2. Comparison of Eiheiji with Four Other Monastic Systems

Monastic System	Style of Supervision
Ch'an Five Mountains (Wu-shan)	Religious Administrative Office
Kenmitsu	Imperial Court
Eiheiji	Daimyō—community (precepts)
Japanese Five Mountains (Gozan)	Bakufu
Rinka Monasteries	Abbot—community (evangelical)

temples often based on a charismatic abbot, who stressed either evangelical, cultural, pedagogical or political functions. [40]

From a long-range historical vantage point, it appears that Dōgen, like other representatives of the new Kamakura Buddhist schools, had severed from the Court, but this meant that the accomplishments of his temple were based on two main factors. One was an affiliation with a *daimyō* (Hatano) beholden to the Hōjō shogunate, which resembled the later Japanese Five Mountains approach, and the other was the power of his teaching as a charismatic abbot resembling predecessors in the Tendai school as well as successors in the Rinka temple ranks. The fact that his independence was based largely on the support of the Hatano clan is acknowledged yet not fully taken into account in Ishii's evaluation. It must also be pointed out that the Rinka abbots of Sōtō monasteries generally integrated Dōgen-style sermons on seminal Chinese Ch'an texts with teaching methods that incorporated *mikkyō* elements. This included an instructional use of kōans based on the transmission of "slips of paper" known as *kirigami* replete with esoteric diagrams and instructions that were a major part of the *shōmono* style of *commentary*. [41]

Therefore, while Dōgen's writings indicate that he seemed to be aspiring to achieve a community-based approach based on precepts ceremonies, we have no indication one way or the other whether this was actually accomplished in his life, as his time of leadership at Eiheiji was cut short by an early demise. Nevertheless, Ishii's method shows that in the final analysis of geo-ritual elements, Mt. T'ien-t'ung and Eiheiji temples are quite distinct ritual environments in that they represent distinct monastic institutional systems. Furthermore, an understanding of the ritualism of Eiheiji must take into account a broader comparison involving at least three systems in Japan than with the Chinese model alone.

We can also raise the question of whether the best way of understanding the transition of Zen rituals from China to Japan is by examining the temples. Perhaps the examination should focus on the masters themselves. However, what we know about Ju-ching, as well as the practice at Mt. T'ien-t'ung, almost all derives from Dōgen and his somewhat biased position in using both Chinese teacher and temple as devices to promote his movement in Japan. Yet, an overly deconstructivist tendency that sees the relativity of perspectives and unreliability of sources does not obscure the fact that Dōgen crossed mountains and rivers to fulfill the goal of importing Zen ritualism.

5

Zazen as an Enactment Ritual

Taigen Dan Leighton

Buddhist meditation has commonly been considered an instrumental technique aimed at obtaining a heightened mental or spiritual state, or even as a method for inducing some dramatic "enlightenment" experience. But in some branches of the Zen tradition, zazen (Zen seated meditation) has been seen not as a means to attaining some result, but as a ritual enactment and expression of awakened awareness. This alternate, historically significant approach to Zen meditation and practice has been a ceremonial, ritual expression whose transformative quality is not based on stages of attainment or meditative prowess.

The Zen ritual enactment approach is most apparent and developed in writings about zazen by the Japanese Sōtō Zen founder Eihei Dōgen (1200–1253). After beginning with his ritual instructions for meditation practice, especially in his monastic regulations for the monks' hall in *Eihei shingi*, I will explore relevant teachings about meditation in a selection of his extended essays in *Shōbōgenzō* (*True Dharma Eye Treasury*), as well as in his direct teachings to his monks in *Eihei kōroku* (*Dōgen's Extensive Record*). This will be followed with a sampling of a few other Zen sources with analogous approaches.

Zazen as Tantra

Before focusing on teachings by Dōgen, we may briefly note that such enact-ment practice is usually associated with the Vajrayana branch of Buddhism, in which practitioners are initiated into ritual practices of identification with specific buddha or bodhisattva figures. Although Vajrayana is often consid-ered the province of Tibetan Buddhism, increasing attention is being given to the crucial role of the Japanese forms of Vajrayana (J. *mikkyō*).[1] In the Heian period, this *mikkyō*, also known as "esoteric" or tantric practice, was prevalent not only in Shingon (True Word), the main Japanese Vajrayana school, but also in the comprehensive Tendai school in which were first trained not only Japanese Zen founders like Dōgen and Eisai (1141–1215) but also Pure Land founders Hōnen (1133–1212) and Shinran (1173–1262), as well as Nichiren (1222–1282). Thanks to this *mikkyō* heritage that permeated all of medieval Japanese Buddhism, in many inexplicit ways *mikkyō* or tantric practice can be seen as underlying all subsequent forms of Japanese Buddhism. Further stud-ies exploring the direct and indirect influences of *mikkyō* on Japanese Zen promise to be especially instructive.

For Dōgen and others, Zen shares with the Vajrayana tradition the heart of spiritual activity and praxis as the enactment of buddha awareness and physical presence, rather than aiming at developing a perfected, formulated understanding. In the context of Tibetan Buddhism, Robert Thurman speaks of the main thrust of Vajrayana practice as physical rather than solely mental. "When we think of the goal of Buddhism as enlightenment, we think of it mainly as an attainment of some kind of higher understanding. But Buddha-hood is a physical transformation as much as a mental transcendence."[2]

The Japanese Vajrayana teacher Kūkai (774–835), the founder of Shingon, emphasized the effects of teachings over their literal meaning. As explicated by Thomas Kasulis, "Kūkai was more interested in the teachings' *aims* than in their content, or perhaps better stated, he saw the aims as inseparable from their content. He saw no sharp distinction between theory and practice."[3] The understanding of a teaching was not privileged independently from its prac-tical effects. "The truth of a statement depends not on the status of its referent, but on how it affects us."[4] For Kūkai, physical postures, utterances, and mental imagery are expressions of ultimate reality, and by intentionally engaging in them, practitioners are led to realization of that reality. The performance of the ritual practice helps effect an expressive realization deeper than mere cognition.

The Physical Expression of Practice-Realization

Both the Vajrayana and Zen emphasis on fully expressed performance of reality reflects the valuing of actual bodhisattvic workings and the realization of a teaching's enactment over theoretical dictums or attainments. In his early 1231 writing on the meaning of meditation, "Bendōwa" (Talk on Whole-hearted Engagement of the Way), now considered part of Shōbōgenzō, Dōgen directly emphasizes the priority of the actualization of practice expression over doctrinal theory. "Buddhist practitioners should know not to argue about the superiority or inferiority of teachings and not to discriminate between super-ficial or profound dharma, but should only know whether the practice is gen-uine or false."[5] This priority of a teaching's actual performance is reflected, for example, in the somewhat later Japanese Sōtō Zen prescription, "Dignified manner is Buddha Dharma; decorum is the essential teaching."[6] The point is to enact the meaning of the teachings in actualized practice, and the whole praxis, including meditation, may thus be viewed as ritual, ceremonial ex-pressions of the teaching, rather than as means to discover and attain some understanding of it. Therefore, the strong emphasis in much of this approach to Zen training is the mindful and dedicated expression of meditative aware-ness in everyday activities.

In perhaps his most foundational essay on zazen, "Fukanzazengi" (Uni-versally Recommended Instructions for Zazen), Dōgen gives detailed postural instructions for sitting meditation, largely patterned after Chinese Chan med-itation manuals. The earliest version of this essay, no longer extant, is from 1227, written shortly after Dōgen's return to Japan from four years of studies in China. Later revisions are from 1233 and 1242, the latter cited here from his Eihei kōroku.[7] This essay was aimed at a general audience of laypeople but still describes the practice in ritual terms. Dōgen specifies in detail preparation of the meditation space, suggesting a quiet room, and also grounding of the mental space, including to put aside involvements and affairs and not to think in terms of good or bad. He adds, "Have no designs on becoming a buddha," emphasizing the noninstrumental and instead ritual nature of this activity. He then describes postural arrangements, including details of full lotus and half lotus leg positions, how to hold the hand position, and physical guides for upright alignment, such as ears in line above shoulders and nose above navel. All these are provided so that the practitioner can "settle into steady, immov-able sitting."[8]

After the procedural descriptions, which were patterned closely after the Chan sources, Dōgen then comments, "The zazen I speak of is not [learning] meditation practice. It is simply the Dharma gate of peace and bliss, the practice-realization of totally culminated awakening."[9] Here Dōgen clarifies that the zazen praxis he espouses is not one of the traditional meditation programs that one can study and learn, step-by step. "Meditation" is a translation for Zen in Japanese, Chan in Chinese, or Dhyana in Sanskrit, which can be understood in terms of the four stages of the technical *dhyana* practices (often translated as "trances"), which pre-date the historical Buddha in India. But in China this term was used generally to refer to a variety of meditation curricula, the sense indicated here by Dōgen. He goes on to clarify that his zazen praxis bears no relationship to mental acuity, "Make no distinction between the dull and the sharp witted." Then he adds, "If you concentrate your effort single-mindedly, that in itself is wholeheartedly engaging the way. Practice-realization is naturally undefiled."[10] In many of his writings, Dōgen emphasizes the oneness of "practice-realization," that meditation practice is not a means toward some future realization or enlightenment but is its inseparable expression, as will be discussed further below.

The ritual context of Dōgen's zazen is highlighted at the beginning of his essay, "Bendōhō" (The Model for Engaging the Way), a manual for the proper procedures for practice in the monks' hall, within which the monks sit zazen, take meals, and sleep, each at their assigned places. This is the traditional mode of Chan practice in China, which Dōgen established at Eiheiji, the monastery he founded after moving in 1243 from the capital of Kyoto to the remote mountains of Echizen (now Fukui), and which remains one of the two head-quarter temples of Sōtō Zen. "Bendōhō" is one of the essays in *Eihei shingi* (*Dōgen's Pure Standards for the Zen Community*), the seventeenth-century collection of all of Dōgen's writings in Chinese about monastic standards and regulations. "Bendōhō" follows in this text after the more celebrated essay "Tenzokyōkun" (Instructions for the Chief Cook), which propounds the appropriate attitudes and responsibility of the *tenzo*, as well as rituals and procedures to be followed in preparing food in the monastery kitchen.

In "Bendōhō," Dōgen states that all monks should sit zazen together, "when the assembly is sitting," and stop together when it is time for all to lie down for the night. He states that "Standing out has no benefit; being different from others is not our conduct."[11] Clearly Dōgen sees zazen as a communal ritual, rather than an individual spiritual exercise. Commencing with the evening schedule, Dōgen imparts the proper ritual conduct for daily activities in the monks' hall throughout the day, including comprehensive ritual procedures for such activities as serving tea, teeth brushing, face cleaning, and using the toilet (in the lavatory located in back of the monks' hall). He speaks of zazen as one of such ritual activities and describes in detail the manner and route in which the abbot should enter the hall to lead the assembly's evening zazen.[12] Later, after describing less formal early morning sitting, Dōgen gives further instructions for zazen that copy in many particulars the detailed postural instructions in "Fukanzazengi." It is clear in context that Dōgen considers zazen the core ritual but still simply one of the many ritual activities in the everyday life of the monks' hall.

The Practice and Training of Buddhas

One of the *Shōbōgenzō* essays that focuses on zazen practice is the 1242 "Zazenshin" (The Acupuncture Needle [or Point] of Zazen). In it Dōgen says, "For studying the way, the established [means of] investigation is pursuit of the way in seated meditation. The essential point that marks this [investigation] is [the understanding] that there is a practice of a Buddha that does not seek to make a Buddha. Since the practice of a Buddha is not to make a Buddha, it is the realization of the *kōan*."[13] Here, as in many places in his writings, Dōgen emphasizes as the "essential point" that zazen specifically and practice generally are not about seeking some future buddhahood. Rather, they are already the practice of buddhas, realizing with awakened awareness what is crucial in this present situation.

As "Zazenshin" proceeds, it centers on Dōgen's commentary about a story about the great Chan master Mazu Daoyi (709–788; J. Baso Dōitsu), when he was studying under Nanyue Huairang (677–744; J. Nangaku Ejō). Mazu was sitting and his teacher Nanyue asked him about his intention in zazen. Mazu replied that he intended to make a Buddha. Nanyue took a tile and began polishing it with a rock. When Mazu asked what he was doing, Nanyue replied that he was polishing a tile to make a mirror. When Mazu perplexedly asked how this was possible, Nanyue responded, "How can you make a Buddha through zazen?"

This story is frequently referenced by Dōgen, for example, as case thirty-eight in his collection of ninety kōans with verse comments in volume nine of *Eihei kōroku*.[14] In one of his two verse comments, Dōgen inverts Nanyue's action by saying, "How can people plan to take a mirror and make it a tile?"[15] implying that such effort denigrates the Buddha already present. In "Zazenshin," commenting after Nanyue says, "How can you make a Buddha through zazen?" Dōgen declares, "There is a principle that seated meditation does not await making a Buddha; there is nothing obscure about the essential message that making a Buddha is not connected with seated meditation."[16] For Dōgen, zazen is adamantly not merely a means to achieve buddhahood. But after commenting in detail on this story, Dōgen says, "It is the seated Buddha that Buddha after Buddha and Patriarch after Patriarch have taken as their essential activity. Those who are Buddhas and Patriarchs have employed this essential activity...for it is the essential function."[17] Although it is not an instrumental activity for gaining awakening, zazen is still the fundamental activity of buddhas for Dōgen.

"Zazenshin" concludes with Dōgen commenting on and writing his own version of a poem about the function of zazen by Chinese master Hongzhi Zhengjue (1091–1157; J. Wanshi Shōgaku), the most important Sōtō (Ch. Caodong) teacher in the century before Dōgen, who was a primary source and inspiration for Dōgen. For the purpose of this article, the main point in Dōgen's discussion is that both verses begin with the proposition that zazen is "the essential function of all the Buddhas." Dōgen comments that "the essential function that is realized [by buddhas] is seated meditation."[18] Again, he sees zazen as the expression and function of buddhas, rather than buddhahood being a function, or consequence, of zazen.

Along with the playful, elaborate essays in Dōgen's *Shōbōgenzō*, noted for their poetic wordplay and intricate philosophical expressions, Dōgen's other major and massive work is *Eihei kōroku*. The first seven of the ten volumes of *Eihei kōroku* consist of usually brief *jōdō* (literally "ascending the hall"), which I will call dharma hall discourses. These short, formal talks are given traditionally in the dharma hall with the monks standing. (The development of the *jōdō* as a Chan ritual form is discussed elsewhere in this volume in the article by Mario Poceski.) Except for the first volume of *Eihei kōroku* from prior to his departure from Kyoto in 1243, the dharma hall discourses in *Eihei kōroku* are our primary source for Dōgen's mature teaching at Eiheiji, after he had finished writing the vast majority of the longer essays included in *Shōbōgenzō*. These talks to his cadre of disciples at Eiheiji reveal his personality qualities and style of training. This training apparently was effective, as Dōgen's seven major disciples present at Eiheiji, together with their disciples over the next few generations, managed to spread his Sōtō lineage and teaching widely in the Japanese countryside.[19]

In a great many of the *jōdō*, Dōgen discusses zazen as a ritual activity for enactment of Buddha awareness. For example, in dharma hall discourse 319 from 1249, just before celebrating the institution of the first Japanese monks' hall at Eiheiji, Dōgen says, "We should know that zazen is the decorous activity of practice after realization. Realization is simply just sitting zazen."[20] Dōgen again emphasizes that his zazen is not an activity prior to realization of enlightenment but its natural expression, comparable to the ongoing daily meditation by Sakyamuni Buddha after his awakening to buddhahood.

However, this ritual zazen expressing realization is not a pointless or dull, routinized activity, inertly enshrining some prior experience. In dharma hall discourse 449 from 1251, Dōgen says, "What is called zazen is to sit, cutting through the smoke and clouds without seeking merit. Just become unified, never reaching the end.... Already such, how can we penetrate it?"[21] Behind these zazen instructions and encouragements to actively enact awareness in practice is a strong attitude of persistent inquiry that permeates Dōgen's teachings and his challenges to his disciples. Dōgen's zazen can even be seen as a ritualized mode of silent inquiry, and this attitude of inquiry is reinforced in many of his mentions of zazen.

The ninth day of the ninth month was the traditional date in the Chan monastic schedule when the relaxed summer schedule ended and increased zazen practice began. Although Dōgen did not follow the relaxed schedule in his training set-up, he did honor the traditional date for renewed zazen with talks encouraging revitalized practice.[22] Dōgen's dharma hall discourse 523 from 1252 is the last such talk given on that date to encourage zazen. In that talk he says, "Body and mind that is dropped off is steadfast and immovable. Although the sitting cushions are old, they show new impressions." Here he refers to the importance of sustaining zazen as a practice ritual and its renewal with fresh impressions (on cushions as well as minds), ritually celebrated on this occasion. He then adds, "It is not that there is no practice-realization, but who could defile it?"[23] This refers again to the oneness of practice and realization and the story about it from the sixth ancestor and Nanyue, which will be discussed below.

In dharma hall discourse 531, his very last *jōdō* in 1252, during which he was succumbing to the illness that would take his life in the following year, Dōgen says in a verse, "A flower blooming on a monk's staff has merit. Smiling on our sitting cushions, there's nothing lacking."[24] In this, one of his very last teachings, he describes zazen as a joyful event that celebrates the full expression and blossoming of awakening.

There are many other such examples in Dōgen's writings. But one of the most revealing dharma hall discourses is 266 from 1248, truly astonishing in disclosing Dōgen's self-awareness of the subtlety of his training approaches. He states four aspects of his practice teaching and their intended impact on his students.[25] He begins with, "Sometimes I enter the ultimate state and offer profound discussion, simply wishing for you all to be steadily intimate in your mind field." This may refer to the impact of his talks, either from *Shō-bōgenzō* or *Eihei kōroku*. Then he adds, "Sometimes within the gates and gardens of the monastery, I offer my own style of practical instruction, simply wishing you all to disport and play freely with spiritual penetration." This refers to his teaching about engaging with everyday monastic activities, as in *Eihei shingi*. But in both of the first two instances, the desired impact is not about the students' acquiring some new state of being or understanding, but rather about their fostering steady intimacy in their awareness, or for them to disport and play freely, that is, to respond and engage with spontaneity, in their daily activities. In the third approach, "I spring quickly leaving no trace, simply wishing you all to drop off body and mind." This may refer to abrupt exclamations or startling demonstrations in Dōgen's teaching. But dropping off body and mind, his stated aim, is an expression Dōgen uses both for complete enlightenment and as a synonym for zazen. This dropping off, letting go of physical and conceptual attachments, is the activity of zazen that is enacted in the zazen ritual.

The fourth mode refers most directly to zazen. He says, "Sometimes I enter the samadhi of self-fulfillment, simply wishing you all to trust what your hands can hold." This samadhi of self-fulfillment (J. *jijuyū zanmai*) is another of Dōgen's synonyms for zazen, described fully in Dōgen's early 1231 essay "Bendōwa" (Talk on Wholehearted Engagement of the Way), in which he calls it the "criterion" for zazen.[26] In his excellent introductory book on Dōgen, Hee-Jin Kim says that this samadhi of self-fulfillment is "a total freedom of self-realization without any dualism of antitheses, [which are] not so much transcended as realized. [This freedom is] realized itself in duality, not apart from it."[27] In this dharma hall discourse 266, Dōgen describes the intention of the samadhi of self-fulfillment as supporting his students simply to "trust what your hands can hold." This implies that zazen supports the practitioner's confidence in their ability to respond aptly to the present situation, or to engage and abide fully in the circumstances of their own "Dharma position," another phrase used often by Dōgen.

In the conclusion of this dharma hall discourse 266, after describing these four teaching modes, Dōgen rhetorically asks, "What would go beyond these [teachings]?" He responds with a poetic capping verse, "Scrubbed clean by the dawn wind, the night mist clears. Dimly seen, the blue mountains form a single line."[28] Here Dōgen points to the suchness of reality, which is for him the object of attention in the enactment of zazen, in which is clearly seen the total interconnectedness of all particulars as in the image of the many peaks coalescing into a single horizon. The image "blue mountains form a single line" also implies Dōgen's appreciation of the single-minded lineage of Zen buddha ancestors, each teaching at their mountain temple, who have kept alive through the generations the practice-realization teaching of zazen as the practice of buddhas, rather than as a practice aimed at attaining buddhahood.

Awesome Presence Cannot Be Defiled

Dōgen provides what might be seen as an extended description of the content of the enactment in the ritual of zazen in a 1241 *Shōbōgenzō* essay, "Gyōbutsu igi" (The Awesome Presence [or Dignified Manner] of Active [or Practicing] Buddhas). Near the beginning of this long essay, Dōgen says directly, "Know that buddhas in the Buddha way do not wait for awakening."[29] Awakening for Dōgen is not some event that will occur some other time in the future, after doing the appropriate meditative exercises. He continues, "Active buddhas alone fully experience the vital process on the path of going beyond buddha.... They bring forth awesome presence with their body. Thus, their transformative function flows out in their speech, reaching throughout time, space, buddhas, and activities."[30] This zazen ritual does indeed involve transformation for Dōgen. We can see in all Zen rituals that, at least ideally, ritual activity does have some impact, or liberative effect, for the participants. And on the other hand, attachment to the mere procedural forms of ritual, in which the forms are followed in a routinized, rote manner, is traditionally considered a hindrance to practice.

This passage of "Gyōbutsu igi," with its description of the active process involved, gives a clear account of Dōgen's view of the workings of zazen. "Fully experiencing the vital process on the path of going beyond buddha" highlights the dynamic aspect of the ritual act of zazen. Its ongoing practice is a lively "vital process," open to the shiftings and complexities of life, and yet one engaging it is already "on the path," committed to awakening and support of universal liberation. "Going beyond Buddha" is a common phrase in Dōgen's writings, indicating the ongoing nature of awakening and of the active or practicing buddhas' conduct. For Dōgen, buddhahood is not some one-time attainment to be cherished thereafter but an ongoing vital process, requiring continued reawakening.

A little further in "Gyōbutsu igi," Dōgen says, "Practice-Realization is not defiled. Although there are hundreds, thousands, and myriad [of practice-realizations] in a place where there is no Buddha and no person, practice-realization does not defile active buddhas."[31] This key phrase, "Practice-Realization is not defiled," is frequently repeated by Dōgen from a story about Nanyue Huairang, who was featured in the later story of his polishing a tile to make a mirror, discussed previously. This earlier story of Nanyue as a student visiting the Chan sixth ancestor Dajian Huineng (638–713; J. Daikan Enō) is recounted fully in several places by Dōgen, including the 1250 dharma hall discourse 374 in *Eihei kōroku*.[32]

In the story, Nanyue appeared before the sixth ancestor, who asked, "What is this that thus comes?" This is a curious, probing manner of asking, "Who are you?" without assuming some fixed "self" or "you," which of course is antithetical to Buddhist teachings of nonself and emptiness.

Nanyue was speechless, but the story says, he "never put this question aside" for eight years of intensive practice thereafter. Finally, he returned to the sixth ancestor and responded, "To explain or demonstrate anything would miss the mark."

The sixth ancestor asked whether, if so, there is practice and realization or not. Nanyue validated his eight years of study by responding, "It is not that there is no practice-realization, but only that it cannot be defiled." The sixth ancestor affirmed that "this nondefilement" is exactly what all the buddhas and ancestors "protect and care for."[33] Part of the possibility of defilement warned against here is exactly that of meditation practice engaged as a mere means and enlightenment as a remote abstraction separate from our activity and awareness.

As we have already seen, Dōgen often cites this story in the context of his important teaching of the unity of practice and realization (shushō-ittō). He proclaims this clearly in his early 1231 writing "Bendōwa." In response to one of the questions posed, Dōgen states:

> In buddha-dharma, practice and enlightenment are one and the same. Because it is the practice of enlightenment, a beginner's whole-hearted practice of the Way is exactly the totality of original enlightenment. For this reason, in conveying the essential attitude for practice, it is taught not to wait for enlightenment outside practice.... Since it is already the enlightenment of practice, enlightenment is endless; since it is the practice of enlightenment, practice is beginningless.[34]

For Dōgen, true practice of buddha-dharma can only be a response to some present awareness of enlightenment or realization. And enlightenment is not realized, or meaningful, unless it is engaged in practice. Dōgen says that because of this unity, he urges all to engage in zazen, and then he cites Nanyue's, "It is not that there is no practice and enlightenment, but only that it cannot be defiled."[35]

Enactments of Unified Practice, Enlightenment, and Expounding

In the writing hōgo (dharma words) 11 from volume eight of Eihei kōroku, Dōgen goes beyond the unity of practice and enlightenment to discuss the unity of practice and enlightenment with the expounding or expression of the teaching.[36] These *hōgo* are probably from before he moved away from Kyoto in 1243 and are mostly from letters to individual students, although this *hōgo* 11 is one of the few in which a recipient is not specified. Dōgen says, "Within this [true Dharma] there is practice, teaching, and verification [enlightenment]. This practice is the effort of zazen."[37] It does require some effort to arrive at the monastery, to enter the meditation hall, to sit upright, to keep eyes open, to breathe, and to return to being present and upright in one's body and mind. This is the effort of zazen practice. Dōgen adds, "It is customary that such practice is not abandoned even after reaching buddhahood, so that it is [still] practiced by a buddha." Dōgen here points out that even after he became the Buddha, roughly 2500 years ago now in northern India, the historical Śākyamuni Buddha continued to do this meditation practice. When the Buddha became enlightened, that was not the end of Buddhism but just its beginning.

Dōgen goes on to say:

> Teaching and verification [enlightenment] should be examined in the same way. This zazen was transmitted from Buddha to Buddha, directly pointed out by ancestors, and only transmitted by legitimate successors. Even when others hear of its name, it is not the same as the zazen of buddha ancestors. This is because the principle of zazen in other schools is to wait for enlightenment.[38]

As in "Bendōwa," "Gyōbutsu igi," and elsewhere, Dōgen emphasizes that his ritual zazen praxis is not passively waiting for some future event or experience, and he notes critically that "[t]he principle of zazen in other schools is to wait for enlightenment." In many traditional branches of Buddhism, meditation practice may eventually lead to enlightenment. Dōgen states that some people even practice "like having crossed over a great ocean on a raft, thinking that upon crossing the ocean one should discard the raft. The zazen of our Buddha ancestors is not like this, but is simply Buddha's practice."[39] In this common Buddhist simile of the raft, once one reaches the other shore of liberation, the raft (e.g., of meditative practice) is no longer needed. But Dōgen implies that the practitioner should continue to carry the raft, even while trudging up into the mountains or down into the marketplace.

For Dōgen, zazen is not waiting for enlightenment, but simply the practice of buddhas. This practice is not to acquire something in some other time or in another state of consciousness or being. It is actually the practice of enlightenment or realization right now. And this enlightenment or realization for Dōgen is naturally expressed in practice. Enlightenment that was not actually put into practice would just be some abstracted idea of enlightenment and would not be actual, verified enlightenment. There could be no true enlightenment that is not expressed in practice.

This unity of practice and awakening expressed fully in this *hōgo* 11 is discussed elsewhere by Dōgen. But here he continues further:

> We could say that the situation of Buddha's house is the oneness in which the essence, practice, and expounding are one and the same. The essence is enlightenment; expounding is the teaching; and practice is cultivation. Even up to now, these have been studied together. We should know that practice is the practice of essence and expounding.[40]

The conventional view of spiritual practice and of a buddha's career would be that one first engages in meditative practice, then, after many years or, more likely, a great many lifetimes, one might experience awakening or enlightenment. Only thereafter would one "turn the wheel of dharma," or expound the teaching. But in the above passage and as *hōgo* 11 continues, Dōgen insists that the ritual meditative praxis of the buddha ancestors is completely one with "the essence" of enlightenment but also with its expounding. The Chinese character for "expounding" also means simply "to express." So from the first thought of practice and awakening, the practice completely expresses the enlightenment at hand. The zazen ritual is not only not separate from the verification of enlightenment but also completely expresses, expounds, and enacts that enlightenment. Buddha dharma "never comes from the forceful activity of people, but from the beginning is the expression and activity of Dharma."[41] In some sense, people's postures are always inevitably expressing their current realization. But also the effort and enactment of the practice ritual derives from the responsibility to more thoroughly enact that expression.

This expounding of awakening need not be offered only through verbal dharma talks. It may also be fully expounded and enacted simply through the physical, ritual expression of upright sitting, or zazen. Moreover, for Dōgen, the awakening of buddhas is expounded by buddhas listening to the teaching equally with those who give the teaching. In a later section of "Gyōbutsu igi" (The Awesome Presence of Active Buddhas), Dōgen describes buddhas listening to as well as speaking dharma. "Do not regard the capacity to expound the dharma as superior, and the capacity to listen to the dharma as inferior. If those who speak are venerable, those who listen are venerable as well."[42] The ritual enactment of a dharma talk is performed by the listeners as well as by the speaker. Dōgen clarifies, "Know that it is equally difficult to listen to and accept this sutra. Expounding and listening are not a matter of superior and inferior.... As the fruit of buddhahood is already present, they do not listen to dharma to achieve buddhahood; as indicated, they are already buddhas."[43] As with zazen itself, for Dōgen, the ritual of listening to the teaching is not undertaken as a means to the goal of awakening or understanding but simply as an enactment of the buddhahood already present.

Some of Dōgen's *jōdō* (dharma hall discourses) in his *Eihei kōroku* pose a further analogy to his approach to zazen as an enactment ritual. He uses his own expounding of the dharma as an enactment ritual rather than as a mere technique to communicate philosophical doctrines or practice instructions. This mode of enactment ritual represents a primary aspect of Dōgen's Zen expression. For example, in dharma hall discourse 70, given in 1241, Dōgen proclaims:

> As this mountain monk [Dōgen] today gives a dharma hall discourse, all buddhas in the three times also today give a dharma hall discourse. The ancestral teachers in all generations also today give a dharma hall discourse.... Already together having given a dharma hall discourse, what Dharma has been expounded? No other Dharma is expressed; but this very Dharma is expressed. What is this Dharma?... It is upheld within the monks' hall; it is upheld within the buddha hall.[44]

Dōgen never states the content of the dharma hall discourse, except to say that he is giving it, together with all buddhas and ancestors, and that it is upheld in the ritual activity of the monks in the monks' hall and buddha hall. This is a ritual discourse that celebrates the ritual itself and its enactment, beyond any other content signified by the ritual. As such, it provides a mirror to the ritual enactment of zazen that Dōgen proclaims as itself the essential realization or enlightenment. And, as in *hōgo* 11 discussed above, this also reflects zazen as itself the expounding or expression of zazen practice and realization.

Dōgen provides a further turn to his mode of ritual enactment in a remark near the end of *hōgo* 4, one of three of the fourteen *hōgo* or dharma words in *Eihei kōroku* volume eight that are addressed to the nun Ryōnen. Ryōnen was one of Dōgen's women disciples, whom he praises lavishly, saying that she has long had "seeds of prajñā," and "strong, robust aspiration." He continues:

> Without begrudging any effort in nurturing the way, for you I will demonstrate the precise meaning of coming from the west [of Bodhidharma]. That is, if you do not hold onto a single phrase or half a verse, a bit of talk or a small expression, in this lump of red flesh you will have some accord with the clear, cool ground. If you hold onto a single word or half a phrase of the buddha ancestors' sayings or of

the kōans from the ancestral gate, they will become dangerous poisons. If you want to understand this mountain monk's activity, do not remember these comments.[45]

In effect, Dōgen is saying not to remember the content of what he is telling her. And yet, he is clearly praising and encouraging her practice. The enactment here seems more important than the particular meaning enacted. But what he goes so far as to call the "precise meaning" of the ultimate teaching (commonly represented in Zen by Bodhidharma's coming from the West) is exactly that in order to understand his activity, then the content of that activity, his comments, should not be remembered. The ritual enactment itself is given primal meaning by Dōgen.

Nonattachment or not clinging is a primary feature of Dōgen's practice-realization as expression. Such clinging would be to neglect rather than to "protect and care for" the nondefilement of practice-realization proclaimed by Nanyue and Huineng. Practice marked by pursuit or attainment of enlightenment can become a form of spiritual materialism or greed and even an unwitting attempt to defile enlightenment. Radical nonattachment through not even remembering the teaching, as suggested by Dōgen to Ryōnen, may actually fully demonstrate appreciation and enactment of the meaning of practice-realization. Dōgen's zazen celebrates and enacts Buddha's practice of inquiry, rather than some practice of acquisition, and takes refuge in the actuality of Buddha's practice, rather than aspiring to some external imagined ideal.

Ritual Enactment Meditation in Chinese Chan

This approach to zazen as a ritual of enactment, which is clearly articulated throughout Dōgen's writings, is not unique to Dōgen. As mentioned at the outset, in Japanese Zen it may derive in part from the significant influence throughout Japanese Buddhism of *mikkyō*, in which the practitioner identifies with and takes refuge in a particular buddha or bodhisattva. The bulk of the Chinese Chan kōan or encounter dialogue literature does not deal directly with meditation as a ritual. But in Chinese Chan, we indeed can see signs and intimations of this practice approach of zazen as an enactment ritual, evident in the following brief sampling of sources, all later mentioned by Dōgen.

We have already seen how the eighth-century Chan master Nanyue explored the enactment meaning of zazen in declaring to the sixth ancestor that "practice-realization cannot be defiled" and later used a rock and tile to demonstrate to his student Mazu that zazen is not about "becoming a buddha."

When Mazu himself became a prominent Chan teacher, he later taught that "[t]his very mind is Buddha." Although not directly about ritual zazen, this implies an enactment rather than attainment approach to practice. And Mazu's disciple Damei Fachang (752–839; J. Daibai Hōjō), whom Mazu and Dōgen both praised, spent thirty years on his mountain practicing zazen based on this teaching.[46]

Another prominent disciple of Mazu, Nanquan Puyuan (748–834; J. Nansen Fugan) was asked about the Way by his student, the renowned adept Zhaozhou Congshen (778–897; J. Joshu Jushin). Nanquan responded, "Ordinary mind is the Way."[47] When asked by Zhaozhou how to approach this, as if it were something to be attained, Nanquan replied, "If you try to direct yourself toward it, you will move away from it." Again, this implies an enactment approach to practice, rather than seeking some attainment, which Nanquan clarifies as counterproductive. Nanquan continues that "[w]hen you reach the true Way beyond doubt, it is vast and open as space."

One of Mazu's major contemporaries was Shitou Xiqian (700–790; J. Sekitō Kisen). Progenitor of the Caodong (Sōtō) lineage that Dōgen inherited, Shitou is noted for his teaching poem, "Harmony of Difference and Sameness" (C. Cantonqi, J. Sandōkai), which originates the fundamental philosophical dialectic of Caodong.[48]

Shitou also wrote a teaching poem that metaphorically describes his hermitage as a ritual space of meditative practice expression, "The Song of the Grass Hut" (C. Caoanke, J. Soanka). Therein Shitou says, "Just sitting with head covered all things are at rest. Thus, this mountain monk doesn't understand at all. Living here he no longer works to get free."[49] He is modeling a praxis not involved in the effort to gain some understanding or insight but simply intended to allow all things to be "at rest," just as they are. Shitou further adds, "Let go of hundreds of years and relax completely. Open your hands and walk, innocent."[50] He is recommending practice that expresses just simply letting go whether in sitting or everyday conduct, reminiscent of what Dōgen would later call "dropping body and mind." In such aware and responsive presence, the practitioner may be able to act effectively, innocent of grasping and attachment. The stories of Nanyue, Mazu, and Nanquan and the writings of Shitou indicate a classic Chan background for zazen as an enactment ritual.

A major predecessor for Dōgen's teachings on meditation is the important twelfth-century Caodong (Sōtō) master Hongzhi Zhengjue, a prolific writer already mentioned for his poem on the acupuncture needle of zazen, discussed in Dōgen's *Shōbōgenzō* essay, "Zazenshin." Hongzhi's meditation teaching, sometimes referred to as silent or serene illumination, was a model for Dōgen's just sitting zazen. Here is one sample of Hongzhi's clear, evocative articulation of his meditative praxis:

> The practice of true reality is simply to sit serenely in silent introspection. When you have fathomed this you cannot be turned around by external causes or conditions. This empty, wide open mind is subtly and correctly illuminating.... Here you can rest and become clean, pure, and lucid. Bright and penetrating, you can immediately return, accord, and respond to deal with events.[51]

In a later section of this volume of his *Extensive Record*, Hongzhi says, "Sit empty of worldly anxiety, silent and bright, clear and illuminating, blank and accepting, far-reaching and responsive."[52] As Dōgen would do in his own way a century later, Hongzhi elaborates the workings of a meditation of open, responsive presence in which subtle awakened awareness is enacted.

Zazen as Ritual Enactment in Sōtō after Dōgen

Teachings on meditation as enactment ritual continued among Dōgen's successors in Japan. Keizan Jōkin (1264–1325), a third-generation successor of Dōgen, is considered the second founder of Sōtō Zen after Dōgen. Keizan's manual on Zen meditation, "Zazen Yōjinki" (Writing on the Function of Mind in Zazen), begins, "Zazen just lets people illumine the mind and rest easy in their fundamental endowment. This is called showing the original face and revealing the scenery of the basic ground."[53] This resting in and revealing of the fundamental ground certainly continues Dōgen's enactment practice. As this text proceeds, Keizan gives extensive ritual instructions on when, where, and how to perform zazen, incorporating much of the procedural recommendations of Dōgen's "Fukanzazengi" while adding much more detail.

In the midst of these ritual instructions, Keizan also provides detail on how he sees zazen's relationship to and enactment of teaching, practice, and realization:

> Zazen is not concerned with teaching, practice, or realization, yet it contains these three aspects.... Although teaching is established within zen, it is not ordinary teaching; it is direct pointing, simply communicating the way, speaking with the whole body.... Although we speak of practice, it is practice without any doing. That is to say, the body doesn't do anything, the mouth does not recite anything, the mind does not think anything over.... Though we may speak of

realization, this is realization without realization, . . . the gate of illumination through which the wisdom of the realized ones opens up, produced by the method of practice of great ease.[54]

Here clearly Keizan is not espousing zazen as some technique to gain enlightenment, or some perfected practice or expounding, but simply is affirming the full endowment of realization already expressed in zazen.

This approach continues in much of later Sōtō Zen. The Sōtō scholarmonk Menzan Zuihō (1682–1769) significantly influenced the development of modern Sōtō Zen. Among his many writings is a long essay called "Jijuyūzanmai" (The Samadhi of Self-fulfillment), in which he includes excerpts from many of Dōgen's writings about meditation, including "Bendōwa" and "Zazenshin," discussed above.[55] Before the Dōgen selections, Menzan comments briefly on many other Buddhist meditation teachings. Menzan critiques the dualistic meditation of those who "aspire to rid themselves of delusion and to gain enlightenment. . . . This is nothing but creating the karma of acceptance and rejection."[56] For Menzan, on the other hand, "zazen is not a practice for getting rid of delusions and gaining enlightenment."[57] Commenting on a teaching attributed to the third ancestor, Menzan adds, "If you do not make mental struggle, the darkness itself becomes the Self illumination of the light."[58] Later he says, "This is the culmination of the Buddha-Way and the unsurpassable samadhi which is continuously going beyond. For this reason all Buddhas in the world of the ten directions . . . always dwell in zazen."[59]

In closing, it is important to note that the approach to zazen as an enactment ritual described in this article is far from the only approach to zazen in the Zen tradition or in modern Zen. For example, the modern Rinzai Zen incorporation of kōan introspection into zazen has its own set of associated rituals, many related to private interviews with the teacher. This praxis dates back to the great Japanese Rinzai master Hakuin (1686–1769), contemporary with Menzan, and has roots back to Dahui Zonggao (1089–1163; J. Daie Sōkō) in Song China. This version of the kōan introspection approach includes a curriculum that at least has the appearance of fostering attainment of stages of mastery of kōans and seeking impactful experiences of *kenshō*, or "seeing into [Buddha] nature."

The kōan curriculum tradition from Hakuin, while contrary to much of Dōgen's approach to zazen addressed in this article, seems to have been successful and effective for many of its followers, historically and today. It is probably the approach most usually assumed in modern academic general discussions of "Zen practice" and remains popular among some Western practice groups. It is not accurate, however, to stereotype Dōgen's enactment ritual zazen as only in Sōtō, since it can also be found used by a number of historical Rinzai teachers and has not necessarily been followed by all Sōtō teachers. We should remember that Zen is far from monolithic; there is a pluralism of Zen traditions and ritual systems derived from Japan, and even more so when we include the developments in Korean Son, in Vietnam, and in Chan as it has evolved in China.

In the West, Zen meditation traditions continue to be influential among a range of spiritual practitioners and contemplatives. And recently, along with its philosophical insights, Buddhist ritual practices are being studied more closely by religious and historical scholars. The enactment ritual approach to zazen expounded by Dōgen may serve as a helpful antidote and be particularly illuminating in Western cultures dominated by materialist and consumerist orientations, where a bias toward acquisitiveness often can color even spiritual activities.

6

Women and Dōgen: Rituals Actualizing Empowerment and Healing

Paula K. R. Arai

This chapter is a revised and amplified version of a paper I delivered at Zen Mountain Monastery Conference "The Many Faces of Dōgen" in July 2004. I benefited from the feedback generated during the discussion.

Anan Kōshiki and *Jizō Nagashi* are two distinctive rituals led by Sōtō Zen Buddhist nuns of Aichi Senmon Nisōdō, a women's monastery in Nagoya, Japan. They reveal a piece of Sōtō Zen ritual life currently exclusive to this community. Analysis of these rituals provides suggestions about ritual dynamics in a Zen-based mode. In particular, the *Anan Kōshiki* illustrates an aspect of a Buddhist approach to social change through nonconfrontational methods. The *Jizō Nagashi* highlights how an ancestral memorial rite, or *senzo kuyō*, ritual functions as part of a larger healing process. Together, the rituals indicate the creative ways in which Sōtō Zen Buddhist women incorporate ritual into their lives and, in turn, how rituals are an actualization of their concerns. These rituals are an important aspect of their practice of purportedly living in accord with the teachings of Dōgen (1200–1253)—the recognized founder of the sect—even though there is no evidence that he practiced, encouraged, or even knew about these rituals.

An ethnographic and qualitative approach is required for this study because the rituals are not well documented, if at all. Moreover, my interest in ritual is to examine and understand the lived dynamics and how people create, express, and change themselves through ritualized behavior. Therefore, the primary sources for this study are ethnographic data gathered in the greater Nagoya region of Japan beginning in 1988. Primary textual sources were consulted as pertinent and available. Secondary sources were consulted in fleshing out theoretical issues. Accessing the primary data required first establishing relationships with the nuns who lead the rituals. Since the women are leading monastic lives, it was imperative that the research methods be respectful and nonobtrusive. Linguistic and cultural fluency were the foundation upon which appropriate connections were based. It necessitated time to build trust through first adhering to the rigors of their monastic schedule for a period of being cloistered for four months as dictated by the abbess, Aoyama Shundō. I had to demonstrate my commitment clearly, for most nuns, including the abbess, did not see value in academic pursuits that are not directly in support of the person's own spiritual discipline. Since then, maintaining respectful relationships has resulted in permission for me to be a participant-observer in dozens and dozens of rituals, in addition to receiving information and gaining access to relevant textual documents not available elsewhere. The abbess also supported the research on healing that I began in 1998, which focuses more on the experience of laywomen in their community. Her endorsement provided the basis for me to establish consulting relationships with laywomen ranging in ages from fifties to eighties.

It is unlikely that these critical contacts would have been possible were it not for the abbess's trust in the way I conducted myself and my scholarship during the prior decade. I am also doubtful that the consultants would have been so forthcoming with intimate information and insights gained through painful experiences were it not for my being recognized by the seriously committed Nisōdō community as a trustworthy person and scholar.[1] It has become famous for being dedicated to Buddhist practice and committed to training women how to live out the teachings of wisdom and compassion in the face of sociological, economic, educational, and personal trials and tribulations. It was founded by women who established their own monastic training facility and educational curriculum before the sect recognized or supported them, and they went on to win equal regulations for monks and nuns from the sect. It is in this context that I interpret and analyze the *Anan Kōshiki* and *Jizō Nagashi*.

The *Anan Kōshiki* is over an hour long ritual performed by the nuns with laity in attendance. I participated as a laywoman in a shortened version of this ritual on three occasions. I also was a participant-observer of the day-long *Jizō Nagashi* on three separate occasions, always held on the seventh day of the seventh month, or July 7. I was given a copy of a taping of the full *Anan Kōshiki* ritual. I relied on my own footage for the *Jizō Nagashi* ritual. Viewing the video footage of both rituals has enabled me to carefully consider and analyze the details of each ritual. This has tremendously enhanced the observations I made while participating in the rituals.

This study examines these rituals in their broader contexts. The greater historical and personal contexts of the nuns and laywomen in this community provided critical information that helps to explain the significance of the rituals. The historical context is particularly illuminating in the case of the *Anan Kōshiki* ritual. I investigated the particulars of that history in my volume *Women Living Zen.*[2] The history and the aims of the nuns working toward egalitarian status within the sect brings into focus the importance of the ritual for establishing their concerns as central, in that these date back to the origins of the Buddhist tradition. In the case of the *Jizō Nagashi* ritual, it was only after hundreds of hours of in-depth consultation with eleven laywomen and one nun that the import of this ritual became evident. The personal experiences of the participants of the *Jizō Nagashi* became the sources for insight into the importance and dynamics of this ritual.

A self-reflexive process is an integral dimension of my ethnographic research and analysis, for I am aware that my presence in their community has an influence upon them as I also change through my interactions with them.[3] Careful field notes and journal entries enable me to revisit experiences in the field to gain a clearer perspective and contextualization of the data collected through in-depth consultations and participant-observation of rituals. The self-reflexive process extends to examining root concepts embedded in historical, textual, and spiritual perspectives I bring with me as a person and a scholar *vis-à-vis* the women I am seeking to understand. Engaging in this process uncovers the assumptions, contours, and dynamics of the material sought: how rituals help empower and heal Zen Buddhist women.[4] I amplify this process in the following section.

Hermeneutical Sleuthing

The first sleuthing required involves finding out what a "ritual" is in this context. There is no evidence that Dōgen thought in terms of the category "ritual"; nor do the women who served as consultants for this study, for the English term "ritual" finds no easy translation into Japanese. There are terms like *hōyō* (Buddhist service), *gishiki* (ceremony), *girei* (etiquette), and a generic suffix, *shiki*, added to a wide range of activities, as in *seijinshiki* (Coming of Age), *sotsugyōshiki* (graduation), *kekkonshiki* (wedding), and *sōshiki* (funeral). Notably, there is no abstract category with the overarching sense that accompanies the current usage of the English word "ritual." In fact, I had a great deal of difficulty communicating with the women who served as consultants for this study that I was interested in understanding their use of "ritual." Even those with advanced academic training were not clear what I meant. Therefore, it is with acute awareness that I am projecting a Western academic category onto the material in the interests of communicating to a Western academic audience. In *Ritual Perspectives and Dimensions*,[5] Catherine Bell cautions about the dynamics of this phenomenon: "While such developments may foster easier communication and shared values, they may do so by means of political subordination and substantive diminution of the diversity of human experience."[6] It is my every intention to fully respect the experiences of the women who are examined in this study, and I make every attempt to understand them in their larger cultural, historical, and personal context. I have not found a thoroughly satisfactory way to communicate the activities highlighted in this study in English without using the term "ritual." I am cognizant, however, that as Bell states:

> Western scholarship *is* very powerful. Its explanative power rests not only on tools of abstraction that make some things into concepts and other things into data but also on many social activities, simultaneously economic and political, that construct a plausibility system of global proportions. Hence, it is quite possible that categories of ritual and nonritual will influence people who would define their activities differently.[7]

I have not entirely found my way out of this dilemma yet, so reader beware that my delineating these two "rituals" does not accurately capture how the women understand themselves, nor does it communicate the understanding I have of the topic in colloquial (nonacademic) Japanese. In Japanese we talked in amorphous ways that communicated volumes with such phrases as *kō iu yō na koto* ("Events like this"). Even after hundreds of hours over years conversing with dozens of Japanese nuns and laywomen, no clearer terminology emerged. This confirmed to me that the concept "ritual" does not quite explain their experience or represent their worldview. To leave it at this amorphous level, however, would make it difficult to discuss the material in an academic context in English. Therefore, I choose to enlist the term "ritual," for I agree with Bell who argues that "[t]he form and scope of interpretation differ, and that should not be lightly dismissed, but it cannot be amiss to see in all of these instances practices that illuminate our shared humanity."[8] I maintain that explaining the material within the context of ritual studies offers a view of important activities that play a significant part in their lives, which is worthy of even such a partial understanding as I can convey here.

The study of "ritual" will continue to complicate matters as increased crosscultural and interdisciplinary investigations proceed. For now, it raises interesting questions that bring into focus some important points and exploratory speculation. My first speculation is that back in the thirteenth century, Dōgen might have thought of activities that today scholars, including myself, are tempted to apply the term "ritual" to as *sahō* or, rendered in my own translation, as "method of actualizing." I take my translation/interpretation cues from Dōgen's teachings, especially *shushō ittō*, "practice and enlightenment are one,"[9] and such articulations as found in his "Genjōkōan" fascicle of the *Shōbōgenzō*.[10] The root assumptions are: (1) there is no dichotomy between subject and object, (2) a holistic understanding of body/mind, and (3) the present moment is all there is. Contemporary Zen monastic women demonstrate with their actions that they agree with Dōgen's concern to manifest certain events, including clean floors, a nourished body/mind, and footwear kept in respectful order.[11] To manifest these specific events requires exacting activity, as anyone knows who has tried to eat properly with an *ōryōki* set of bowls in a Japanese Zen meditation hall, where even which angle you rest your chopsticks down is prescribed and differs depending on whether you are about to eat, in the middle of eating, or finished eating. To extend this line of analysis to the two "rituals" under consideration in this study, a fruitful question to ask might be: What are the "rituals"/*sahō* actualizing?

Japanese lay and monastic women[12] employ Dōgen's practices and teachings to guide, empower, and heal themselves.[13] Through ethnographic data, it becomes apparent that many Sōtō Zen Buddhist women are steeped in Dōgen's distinctive teaching on Buddha nature. Viewing these women through the avenues they created to work within the context of an imperfect institutional structure, the influence of Dōgen's teachings is revealed in the assumptions the women make in achieving their goals. Dōgen's teaching that we are all Buddha nature is not directly invoked during the rituals women perform that empower and heal them, but the rituals bear out the teaching. The rituals are in no way dependent on male permission, authority, or recognition. The rituals begin with assuming everyone's Buddha nature and proceed from there. In this way, they empower women to actualize their Buddha nature and heal them from delusions of male domination, despair, and loneliness.

From a perspective that is trained upon historical currents, sociological dynamics, cultural impulses, philosophical analysis, and ethnographic data, the critical role of rituals in these Japanese Zen Buddhist women's notable accomplishments and effectiveness becomes visible. Central to the efficacy of their practices is how their constructions of self shape their experiences. Their concept of self is part of a Buddhist cosmology that Dōgen brilliantly articulated. He made a paradigm shift when he translated a Chinese translation of the *Nirvana Sutra* phrase, "All sentient beings have Buddha nature" to "All existents are Buddha nature."[14] Although Dōgen did use all the *kanji* from the original Chinese, he made a striking grammatical move. He interpreted the Chinese verb "to have" as part of a noun, coming up with "existents." The profound implications of this subtle grammatical shift continue to reverberate. Some could interpret this move as the logical conclusion of a nondualistic philosophy. Others might note how it resonates with the seamless worldview of indigenous Japan. Whatever the case, this teaching is one of Dōgen's most important, perhaps especially when we examine the activities of his female followers.

Noting that Buddha nature is not something "to have," or not have, underscores that no institution, no person, no natural phenomenon can control it, take it away, or even give it away. The women in this study indicate that Dōgen is implicitly recognizing and acknowledging the agency of each woman. Many of his female followers have evidently been empowered by this, because they have acted accordingly. When beginning with the assumption that all people are agents, particularly when examining issues involving women, many questions arise. When I read or hear about matters involving women, I actively seek out from whose perspective the statement is made and analyze the assumptions latent in the statement. Doing this reveals when androcentric views and values are represented as the norm. Such questions illuminate when women are not assumed to be agents, in other words, when the line of thinking is not in accord with Dōgen's teaching that all are Buddha nature.

In order to see the women more clearly, I had to learn how to see the dynamics of representation and interpretation of them in scholarly and popular sources. When one begins to sleuth around, what looks on the surface like women having little power becomes more fully contextualized. What becomes exposed is an entirely different scenario. The process is akin to when Dorothy and her cohorts discover the Wizard of Oz behind his impressive machinations. Suddenly, what looked so powerful is not so, and those who were fearful and intimidated are no longer. Although the Wizard of Oz was deliberate, the illusion of women's powerlessness comes primarily from not having peeked behind the curtain of unexamined assumptions. Applying the finely honed sleuthing device of critical reasoning uncovers important pieces of the puzzle. An example of how I conduct my investigation is when I see a statement such as "women were (or are) viewed as...," I always ask "by whom?" Often this is not explicit in the statement. Although increasingly less so, sometimes the statement means "viewed from an androcentric perspective, women appear...." It is important to make this clear, because keeping the perspective of the statement vague makes it look like it is a general statement of fact. The net effect is that women's agency and power are hidden or denied. Other types of statements that I pause to examine include the following: "Women did not [insert a verb, such as 'study']." I ask, "Where?" Or, I make a mental note that "the act does not seem to have occurred under the purview of male institutions; nor has it appeared in any publicly known extant documents." In other words, it is not necessarily the case that no proof is negative proof. When I see a sentence that asserts, "Women could not...," I quickly want to know, "according to whose authority and what sources?"

In addition to these types of sentences, there are certain words—whether explicitly stated or implied—at which I pause. They include any variation of the words "official," "authority," "acknowledge," and "recognize." If a statement is that "women do not have an official capacity," I want to know by whose authority is something deemed "official." I also want to know what the women did in that context. I assume that women did something. Nobody can do nothing. I also assume that women have their own authority. Moreover, when women are or are not being acknowledged, I want to know by whom. Are they even seeking acknowledgment? Is someone actively denying acknowledgment of them? Is it because no one actually recognizes the women? Or, is it that those who are doing the recognizing are not even being recognized? These are the types of questions and concerns that I bring to my study of Zen women. They are informed by Dōgen's articulation of Buddha nature, which derives from a worldview oriented to emptiness, rather than a subject/object dichotomy.

Dōgen's teaching has also helped me see more clearly the multifarious ways people express their Buddha nature. Just because something is not written down or recorded in "official" documents that are catalogued in accessible and organized places does not mean that an expression of Buddha nature did not occur. Assumptions to the contrary look for a particular expression of Buddha nature, forgetting—or not taking into consideration—the basic teachings of impermanence and interrelatedness. Valuable expressions of Buddha nature are not necessarily available in a form accessible to others, particularly those in different time periods or locations. This must be kept in mind when trying to ascertain the contributions of women.

In seeking insight into the nature of Zen Buddhist women's rituals, ethnographic research reveals important ways their sundry practices offer guidance as well as demonstrate the complexity of their lived tradition. Data collected for this study suggest that several ritual practices done within the context of Zen offer ways to address the noncognitive, nonintellectual, emotional, and psychological needs people have to cope with the problems of human existence—love, loss, birth and death, longing for belonging.

A focus on these women's lives and practices brings to the fore complex dynamics and concerns that shape what values and strategies women use to negotiate their lives. The project is based on the assumption that each person is an active agent and that each person has the authority to define her religious tradition. Therefore, the scope of practices examined in this study extends beyond Zen rituals recognized by the Sōtō Zen sect's voluminous documentation on what purports to be all its rituals.[15] Through surveys and interviews I conducted and participant-observation of Japanese Buddhist activities over an extended period, I discovered that many Buddhist women who choose Zen practice in Japan seem to weave agilely together these diverse elements in their practice.

Indeed, exploring ritual practices followed by Sōtō Zen women today reveals a broad spectrum of activities and ceremonies, including functional, "sacramental," daily, annual, private, public, expensive, inexpensive, and even esoteric rites. These practices are not outlined or advocated in any text. It is through ethnographic research methods and analysis that the range and significance these practices have for women become clear. Such investigation expands our understanding of the contours of Zen experience and helps clarify what it means to be a Zen Buddhist woman.

Despite the distinctly ritual-based practices of these women, the iconoclastic image and antiritual rhetoric generated about the Zen Buddhist tradition has deflected attention away from the roles of ritual practices in Zen Buddhist lives. Compounding this antiritual rhetoric is what I would call the "Protestant Undercurrent" that has dominated most Western practice of Zen, which until recently placed a premium on zazen and philosophical understanding with few of the ceremonial practices of Japan having been imported. This volume is a significant effort to rectify this myopic and ethnocentric view of Zen.

With ethnographic data, we can see that women weave various practices that are distinctive and tailored to their needs. To see the dynamics of the rituals in terms of how they assist women, it is important to view the ethnographic data from the concept of self of the women. It is critical to be clear about the assumptions of the concept of self that are at work in a description or an analysis of people because oftentimes the concept of self explains why interpretations follow a certain course.[16] In teaching courses on Buddhist women to Western men and women, it has become apparent that the differences in concept of self that are brought to the table are significant. Although I am about to make vast generalizations, some of which might not hold up under close scrutiny, I think it is worth offering some observations that help clarify differences in understanding and interpretation of Buddhist women.

A modern Western concept of self emerges out of a sense of reifying the individual. This individual has rights. Implicit in the concept of rights is the notion of the discrete self that is inherently valuable. I describe the Japanese concept of self as relational or explicitly contextualized. That is, there is no self that is even conventionally isolatable from the people around oneself. For example, one is the daughter or son of a particular mother and father, perhaps a niece or nephew, older sister, younger brother, teacher of, student of, classmate of, from a particular town or region, etc. In this relational concept of self, power is understood to take many forms. Ideally, different people take on specific responsibilities in a cultural context where each role is valued because of respect for each niche that is required for harmony of the whole. Concepts and uses of power differ when one begins with an individual versus a relational concept of self. With an individualistic concept of self, the expectation of equality is that each person receives the same amount and type of power. With equality as a goal, differences in power can be the source of tension between people. With a relational concept of self, however, even when there are tensions between people, differences in type and amount of power are expected. This does not mean, however, that oppression is validated. On the contrary, respect for the whole relational network necessitates that respect be accorded to all.

These women have found that various rituals facilitate the changes in perspective needed to experience their interrelatedness and know deep in their body/minds that their contributions are important to the whole—even when surface appearances would suggest otherwise. In other words, even though interrelatedness is assumed, immediate conflicts and direct difficulties can make it difficult to maintain focus on that expansive context. Because they involve the body, rituals are effective in reminding one who is engulfed in an unjust or painful situation of the context of interrelatedness. The mind can comprehend interrelatedness, but this knowledge alone does not bring about healing. A visceral experience of interrelatedness is required for the healing to occur. This observation based on ethnographic data seems to be corroborated in neurophysiological research. Three medical doctors and professors of psychiatry, Thomas Lewis, Fari Amini, and Richard Lannon, collaborated on a volume that explores the relationship between emotions and mechanisms of the brain. They assert that "comprehension proves impotent to effect emotional change."[17] Their conclusion is based on the structure of the brain, which has three major sections known as the reptilian, limbic, and neocortical brains. "The primordial purpose of the limbic brain was to monitor the external world and the internal bodily environment, and to orchestrate their congruence."[18] One of the limbic brain's functions is to assess what response is appropriate given the input received. "Once the limbic brain has settled on an emotional state, it sends outputs to the neocortical brain, spawning a conscious thought."[19] Neurophysiological research that focuses on the relationship between input through ritual experience and healing is required for any direct conclusions to be drawn, but the circumstantial evidence is enticing.[20]

The women in this study have found that some rituals are especially effective in facilitating visceral experience because they help generate heightened awareness of the greater whole. I should quickly add, though, the women are not necessarily cognizant of this process. They experience the results, but they do not do the rituals *in order to* experience interrelatedness. They do the rituals in order to remember deceased loved ones or express their gratitude. That is the power of rituals. They accomplish some things that are not intentionally sought but are deeply wanted. Some things that are helpful are elusive when directly pursued. Indeed, by its infinitely expansive nature, experiencing interrelatedness is a target that dissolves in the mere effort to aim at it. Through certain rituals, however, it is possible. Rituals affect the body, even if the mind is not conscious of what is going on. That is the key to their healing power.

Rituals shape, stretch, define, and redefine the identity of their participants. As one engages in a ritual, one's consciousness changes. The power of ritual lies not in the ability to communicate conscious knowledge, but to frame experience in such a way that it may be apprehended meaningfully.[21] Ritual can have the impact of lived experience because the body performs it. In this way, people can learn about what is important through experiencing "fresh" what those before have experienced. Real life is very messy and organic whereas discourse about life tends to be tidier and more linear. Ritual is in-between. Being in a ritual with a long tradition can make a person feel connected and that they belong. A ritual can affirm a person's identity.

Rituals work through the senses to cultivate wisdom in the bones. Unlike discourses on wisdom that focus on understanding the empty nature of ultimate reality—and hence are sometimes too abstract and cold to comfort someone who is experiencing excruciating pain—rituals can help one feel the sense of connectedness bodily. People can really experience certain feelings that shift one's view of life through the guidance of rituals.[22] For example, it is not just a matter of intellectually knowing that by virtue of DNA you are still connected to your family members after they die. A ritual that welcomes them home can make someone feel, as in the case of the summertime memorial rites of O-bon, that they are really there enjoying a meal together.[23]

My anthropological and historical research bore this out. It revealed that Sōtō nuns entered the twentieth century with a strong sense of confidence and less of a sense of frustration than I had expected to find. I began an inquiry of women's contributions and accomplishments in the religious history of Japan to understand why twentieth-century Zen nuns were not debilitated by unfair practices. I found a history of women in Japanese religion that reveals many women maintained a positive understanding of themselves and their capabilities.

When Japanese Sōtō Zen nuns look at the history of their sect, they see women seriously engaged with Buddhist practice. When they read Dōgen's writings, they see women being affirmed. All evidence indicates that they take seriously Dōgen's teaching that all existents, which includes themselves, could actualize their Buddha nature. Despite the historical circumstances that included structural oppression of women, they did not just listen to the men. Just like men did not need to be told that they are valuable, women did not either.

Nuns embrace the views of women found in Dōgen's writings as positive, and empowered by these views, the nuns have influenced the course of Sōtō history in the twentieth century. They began the century encumbered by misogynous regulations that had developed like an insidious disease in a sect administration that did not acknowledge nuns' abilities, contributions, commitments, and certainly not their Buddha nature. A significant core of Sōtō nuns were determined to rectify these inequities. To achieve their goal to be treated with respect would require a creative mix of established practices and novel methods, and most of all penetrating awareness of their own worth and Buddha nature.

The nuns' actions tell us a lot about what they thought of themselves. They did not act like women who were just discovering liberation. They acted like women who knew their Buddha nature. So, they acted with deliberate and well-reasoned conduct. They knew that nuns were supposed to be full members of the sect, and they were tired of men not recognizing that. They understood Buddhism to be a tradition that was respectful of women, and they acted with confidence. We will see how the rituals these women practice are dynamic aspects of their culture, both shaping it and being shaped by it. They embody strategic actions that use culturally specific tactics to achieve particular ends.

Anan Kōshiki

Through the mode of ceremonial ritual, nuns have found a powerful way to express their emotional and political concerns. Focusing upon one particular

ritual, the *Anan Kōshiki*,[24] I will illustrate how the ritual functions to legiti-
mize and empower the nuns yet remains cloaked in the noncontentious expression of gratitude. It helps them manifest a quality they respect—the
quality of water—to be flexible and soft as one moves with a power that stands
the test of time.

The contours of the *Anan Kōshiki* ceremony are as follows. The ceremony
begins with the lead celebrant entering the worship hall with dignity and solemnity, marking the seriousness of the events about to transpire. This is known
as the *Shikishijōden*. Then, incense is offered at the main altar followed by all
the nuns doing three formal prostrations. This is known as the *Jōkōfudōsanpai*.
Next comes the *Sangedōjō*, which involves three nuns who make a circle
starting from the front of the altar, around the center of the worship hall, and
back to the altar. The first one carries an incense burner, the second one sprinkles purified water with a pine branch, and the third nun scatters lotus petals
(made of colored cardboard).

A *Santōhatsu*, playing of cymbals, is done both before and after the
chanting of the Four Wisdoms or *Shichisan* (Skt. *catvārijñāna*). The four
wisdoms are as follows: (1) Great perfect mirror wisdom (J. *daienkyōchi*, Skt.
ādarsajñāna) is that which reflects all phenomena in the three worlds in their
true state, with no distortions; (2) Wisdom of equality (J. *byōdōshōchi*, Skt.
samatājñāna) is that which perceives the underlying identity of all *dharmas*, to
overcome separating oneself and others. Bodhisattva compassion draws on this
wisdom; (3) Wisdom of wondrous perception (J. *myōkan zacchi*, Skt. *pratya-
veksanajñāna*) is that which enables one to see the truth/Dharma clearly, so
one can preach free from error and doubt; (4) Wisdom of accomplishing
metamorphoses (J. *jōshosachi*, Skt. *krytyānusthānajñāna*) is that which takes on
various forms to act in the world for the benefit of others' advancement toward
enlightenment.

After this is complete, elaborate offerings of incense, cakes, and tea are
made at the main altar. This is known as the *Jōkōkenkasa*. It is completed with
three full prostrations done by the lead celebrant. Next, the *Saimon* is recited
by a head nun. Here the background and purpose of the ceremony is articulated, highlighting the activities and merits of Ananda, especially how he
interceded on behalf of the women, resulting in Sakyamuni accepting women
into the group of wandering ascetics committed to his path. Then two nuns
chant a complicated chant called the *Bonon no ge*. The text to be chanted is
brought in with a flair on a red stand, setting the stage for the dramatic chant:
"The miraculous form, body, and world of the Thus Come One." The *Sange no
ge* and *Shakujō no ge* comes next. It involves three nuns standing together in
front of the altar and chanting. Each carries a tray filled with lotus blossom

petals. One also carries a *shakujō* staff; striking the floor with each step jangles the rings. They throw lotus petals as they chant. After these nuns are finished, the lead celebrant returns to the center. She does three prostrations and then begins the *Shikimon*. This is the most substantive aspect of the ceremony. It includes five distinct subsections of chanting headed by the lead celebrant. The first section praises Ananda for practicing hard and renouncing the world. The second section expresses the nuns' gratitude to him for facilitating their renunciation. The third section highlights some of Ananda's merits. Section four expresses the nuns' gratitude to Sakyamuni. Section five is an *ekō*, or offering of prayers, to transfer the merit accrued through the ceremony to all sentient beings. Everyone then does three prostrations. The ceremony ends with a ceremony often done independently called the *Anantange*. It is a concise series of chants in praise of Ananda that is done with an Indianesque melody and timbre.

Applying Catherine Bell's approach to understanding ritualized activity as practice illuminates the dynamics of the *Anan Kōshiki*. She explains the four aspects. "Practice is (1) situational; (2) strategic; (3) embedded in a misrecognition of what it is in fact doing; and (4) able to reproduce or reconfigure a vision of the order of power in the world, or what I will call "'redemptive hegemony.'"[25] Analysis of the ritual follows these four aspects of practice. It is significant that the original analysis was done prior to applying Bell's theory, suggesting that this ritual and her theory on the parameters of "practice" correspond.

Situation: With the advantage of historical perspective, we can see that the revitalization of this nuns' ritual occurred on the eve of nuns launching into a public and institutionalized effort to bring egalitarian practices to bear on twentieth-century Sōtō regulations. Not only was the timing in sequence, but the actors were also directly related. The teacher (Kankō-ni) of the nun (Mizuno Jōrin) who led the movement to establish an official Sōtō Zen monastery for women is the one who revived this ceremony. This relationship of events and people strongly suggests that doing a ritual that acknowledges the legitimacy and importance of being Buddhist monastic women helped cultivate a community of women who were not dissuaded by the male-dominated institutional attempt to treat nuns as though they were subordinate to monks.

Sōtō nuns perform the *Anan Kōshiki* ceremony to thank Ananda for what they maintain was his act of wisdom in entreating Sakyamuni to allow women to enter the path of the renunciants. Performing the *Anan Kōshiki* can be seen as an act that started the wave that led to Sōtō nuns fighting for and, by the 1960s, winning equal regulations in the institutional records of the Sōtō Sect administration. The *Anan Kōshiki's* power lies in its affirmation of nuns. The ritual ends with a declaration that all women can attain enlightenment. From this vantage point, the erroneous ways of the male-dominated institution are glaring, yet imminently surmountable. In effect, the *Anan Kōshiki* authorizes nuns to demand Buddhist virtue be practiced over sexism.

Strategy: The fundamental strategy employed by this ritual is the use of a ceremonial format that is firmly established in the Japanese Buddhist repertoire of ceremonial rituals. This genre of ceremonial ritual is fundamentally an act of gratitude to exalt a highly revered figure. Other *Kōshiki* are for Daruma, Jizō, and Sakyamuni. Doing such a ceremony puts the nuns ritually on the same plane as men who also perform *Kōshiki*. They did not have to fight for the right to do this ritual. Doing it, though, implies to monks and laity that nuns and monks are not fundamentally different, because both can perform this type of ritual. It is a nonconfrontational method that the act of doing is itself an actualization of the nuns' goal to be fully respected by monks and the laity. When laity attend the ritual, it confirms that nuns' acts are authoritative. In attending, they are brought into this drama, thereby being witness to the nuns of today being legitimate heirs.

Misrecognition: A number of things are accomplished in this ritual precisely because they are not immediately obvious in the performance of the ritual itself. Since a *Kōshiki* is a ceremony of gratitude, it humbles the performers before the exalted figure being singled out for appreciation. However, the act of exalting the central figure, in this case Ananda, also exalts the nuns. The ritual posture of the nuns, however, is profound gratitude, literally bowed with head to the floor facing Ananda ('s picture) on the altar. To praise Ananda for having served Sakyamuni for twenty-five years also establishes that Ananda knew Sakyamuni intimately, thereby contextualizing his act of beseeching the Buddha on behalf of the women who wanted to become Buddhist renunciants. By praising Ananda for his vast knowledge of the Buddha's teachings, it establishes Ananda as one who has the authority to recognize when an act is in accord with those teachings. This legitimates the women's request to become nuns, thereby validating the women themselves. To praise Ananda serves to exalt the nuns doing the praising.

The actual practice of being grateful is one of the ways nuns are empowered through this ritual. Being a grateful person, especially in the Japanese reciprocal gift-giving culture, facilitates one's access to the power of other members in the community. Having strong reciprocal relationships, then, makes one a more effective actor in society. A public display of the nuns' gratitude to a person who lived nearly 2,500 years earlier on another side of the globe effectively convinces the people in attendance that these nuns are people with whom you would want to have close relationships because you can be assured that you will be respected and appreciated. They will not forget their indebtedness to you. In order for the nuns to build their monastery facilities, large donations from laity were required. Indeed, these nuns found and continue to receive support from donors large and small.

More is going on than meets the eye in the nuns' process of thanking Ananda for all he has done. The nuns performing the ritual today also establish their link to the first nuns who were direct disciples of the Buddha. So, not only are the nuns depicted in the story of Ananda, but the nuns performing the ritual are exalted. This is all accomplished without a nun ever saying she deserves to be respected as a legitimate heir of Buddhism or requesting others to recognize nuns' deep commitment to Buddhist teachings and practice. They just sing praises and verses of gratitude. In so doing, nuns are empowered through their expression of gratitude as they establish—indirectly and (therefore) effectively—that then and now women can attain enlightenment.

Redemptive Hegemony: The specifics of a *Kōshiki* format are an effective way to accomplish their goal of establishing legitimization for themselves without having to prove this in any direct way and, thereby, not setting up an offense that can be retaliated. In the ritual, they receive formal acknowledgment of their claims by no less than Sakyamuni Buddha, Ananda, and Mahāprajāpatī. The act of jointly praising and offering gratitude to Ananda makes the nuns a distinct group. First, it identifies the nuns to themselves. They are women in a few millennia-long line of women committed to fully living their lives according to the Buddha's teachings. Without the nuns having to explain it themselves, the elements of the ritual inform the laity in attendance about the monastic women in their community. The ritual also highlights the merits of the monastic life, making it explicitly clear that those who enter this path are dedicated people. Therefore, the women who have chosen to become nuns today are validated as serious disciples of the Buddha. It dispels the misinformed image that they are merely trying to escape to the nunnery because they could not succeed at anything else.

When interpreted in a social and historical context, the power of the ritual is best understood. Examining the socio-historical context of the *Anan Kōshiki* brings into high relief the many goals of the ceremony. The goals include praising and thanking Ananda, Sakyamuni, and Mahāprajāpatī and cultivating virtues such as respect and gratitude, affirming the women's self-identity as legitimate Buddhist nuns, confirming that being a Buddhist nun is a positive thing, receiving recognition by the community as disciples of the Buddha, gathering donations, verifying the nuns' ability to attain Buddhahood, and winning full status in the Sōtō Zen sect's regulations.

The situation of the *Anan Kōshiki* at the time it was revived in Japan was that Sōtō nuns were beginning to work toward receiving the treatment they deemed was appropriate and in accord with Dōgen's teachings. The nun who went on to teach the ritual to many others was the same nun who led in the establishment of officially sanctioned training facilities for nuns. Her disciples were the ones who fought for and won equal regulations in monastic training and teaching ranks. In this context, it is no little thing that the ritual climaxes at the point where it is exclaimed that women are able to attain Buddhahood. Through expressions of gratitude, these nuns actualized their empowerment as they accomplished their numerous goals. In so doing, they changed the face of the Sōtō Zen institution, bringing about a major change through the nonconfrontational mode of ritual practice.

Jizō Nagashi

No document even intimates that Dōgen performed a ritual that resembles anything like the *Jizō Nagashi*. The historical context for the origins of this ritual conducted only by Sōtō Zen nuns is unknown even to the abbess of the main Sōtō Zen nunnery, Aichi Senmon Nisōdō, who leads the ritual. Historical origins are not the focus of concern for the women who lead and participate in this ritual. What matters is that people can experience this unique form of memorial rite, which takes place partially in a boat in the middle of a large lake. They have woven it into the array of ceremonies that help people live with loss, a critical dimension of the nuns' practice and of vital interest to lay participants. Refining the art of living with loss is not a uniquely Zen concern, for such concerns cannot be contained within conceptual and institutional sectarian boundaries. Life—and surely death—defy such categorization. Many laywomen who engage in this ritual every July 7 do not indicate a loyalty to Sōtō Zen; many I interviewed are actually formally affiliated with another Buddhist sect. Why do they join in this extensive day-long ritual? Is there anything Zen about it other than the fact that Zen nuns lead and organize the ritual? Although I cannot provide a full response to these intriguing questions here, I view this ritual in the context of a larger ethnographic project on healing in Zen.[26] Viewed from this perspective, the *Jizō Nagashi* is a ritual that gets at the heart of the Zen mode of healing I have found in the lives of Japanese Buddhist women.

A key feature of healing in this context is experiencing interrelatedness. Rituals can be effective conduits for such experiences. The aspects of the *Jizō Nagashi* that facilitate such an experience are in accord with Dōgen's teaching on "All existents are Buddha nature." From this perspective, the profound wisdom of conducting the climax of the ritual in the center of a body of water comes to the surface. In order for the dynamics of this to be clear, an explication of the contours of the ritual is warranted.

The *Jizō Nagashi* ritual assumes the authority and leadership of Sōtō Zen nuns. In this ritual, the nuns begin with an understanding of their worth—their Buddha nature—as is demonstrated by the fact that they lead a singular ritual which regularly attracts 450–500 lay people, mostly women. The ritual falls into the "ancestor/memorial" ritual category, which, when taken into a larger context, functions as a healing ritual. In a Sōtō Zen context, healing equals awareness of one's Buddha nature. In short, what one needs to heal from is the delusion that we are separate entities. The medical analogy of the Four Noble Truths implies this (diagnosis, cause, prognosis, treatment). The specific *Jizō Nagashi* ritual focuses on helping lay people integrate the loss of loved ones into their lives. It responds to psychological needs of people as they suffer from loneliness and regret. Jizō Bosatsu is a bodhisattva who guides people in the different realms of existence, and *nagashi* means to "let flow." It is not a common ritual, and currently only Sōtō Zen nuns lead this ritual annually on the seventh of July. Fourteen chartered buses are typically needed for transporting. Buses numbered four and nine are not included, however, for these numbers are homonyms for "death" and "suffering," respectively. People from the greater Nagoya area ride in these luxury buses that are impeccably timed to arrive simultaneously at the designated temple and lake where the formal parts of the ritual occur. Some years they go to Lake Biwa and others to Lake Hamana. It is a one-day mini-pilgrimage where people bond together in laughter and pain. "Communitas" is fostered by the treats that are passed around the bus along with stories of new aches and pains, new babies, and new deaths.

The formal ritual involves two main parts. The first part is held in a Sōtō Zen temple. The focus of this aspect of the ritual is the reciting of posthumous Buddhist names, or *kaimyō*. When one registers to participate in the ritual, the names of the dead that one would like to be remembered during the ritual are requested. The nuns then write each name with brush and ink onto a wooden tablet. In July, it is always hot and humid, yet the laity sit in tight formation around the center of the worship hall. The silence as abbess Aoyama Shundō makes the incense offering conceals the presence of more than 450 people. After chanting and ceremonial music of cymbals and bells, each nun receives a stack of the tablets. Raising one tablet at a time to her forehead in a gesture of respect for the Buddha represented, they intone each name, some voices loud, others soft, all overlapping.

Although it is a group activity, as the nuns chant each individual deceased's name, the women with whom I collaborated expressed that they heard the calling of the name in their hearts in a way that made the dead feel present. Furthermore, in the context of hearing the name of your loved one chanted among hundreds of others, the connection between your loss and others' loss makes one feel that one is not alone but in a community of people living with loss. Being part of a community of grievers is healing because it makes it clear that you are not singled out in your pain. Death is a condition of life.

The second part of the ritual takes place at a lake with all participants riding on a large boat chanting and singing Buddhist hymns (go-eika). Jizō Bosatsu's shingon, or darani, is chanted quietly, "onkakakabisanmanesowaka" over and over. The chant is like the musical ground over which the melancholic melodies of the pilgrimage songs ride. The beauty of the natural setting and the mixing of the sounds of chanting, singing, and the wind are conducive to experiencing a blurring of the realms of living and dead.[27] This is a grieving ritual where people feel the connections between themselves, lost loved ones, and the natural world. Upon boarding the boat, each person is handed seven slips of rice paper, washi, about 3 x 1.5 inches with an image of Jizō Bosatsu stamped in vermillion. After the boat has reached the center of the lake, each person finds a place—whether among close friends or off to a quiet corner— to send off the slips. With the mournful melodies as accompaniment, each slip is raised to the forehead before it is let go on its journey to flutter in the breeze and swirl into the lake. When the rice-paper Jizōs that symbolize a lost loved one dissolve into the water, the women speak of experiencing a visceral sense of interrelatedness. In other words, in death one is transformed and liberated into the universe that supports all. In this moment, many people experience a keen awareness that one and all are what constitute the universe. This experience—which Sōtō women implicitly connect with Dōgen's insight into the primacy of Buddha nature—is a conduit for people to experience their own Buddha nature as they recognize the rice-paper Jizō image as an expression of universal Buddha nature, which in turn dissolves into the water, another expression of Buddha nature, as a poignant expression of their deceased loved one: a Buddha unencumbered by a form body as it swirls, floats, and dissolves in the beautiful interrelated expanse of the universe. Even though there is no evidence that Dōgen did this ritual, the nuns perform it because they know intuitively that it helps people experience his teachings, especially to know viscerally that all existents—oneself, one's deceased loved ones, the deceased loved ones of others, and those living all around—are all Buddha nature. Such an experience is the pinnacle of healing in the Sōtō Zen Buddhist context.

The *Jizō Nagashi* memorial rite brings those living with loss together as a community. It affirms the lives of the living as it honors the lives of the dead, who have been recognized as Buddhas at their funeral. In affirming that a deceased loved one is a Buddha, the rite can be experienced as a healing rite for the survivors (we cannot speak for the deceased[28]). Publicly honoring one's "personal Buddha" in a community ritual is part of the healing process of many of these women. Again, "misrecognition" occurs in this ritual. Healing or experiencing one's Buddha nature is not the purported purpose for the ritual. It is formally a memorial ritual. Yet, in honoring the deceased, the living can experience their interrelatedness with all things, in other words, their Buddha nature. They are not usually cognizant of this in a cerebral manner, but their bodies know. Intellectual understanding of interrelatedness does not heal. It is only when interrelatedness is experienced that it can heal.

This is one of many rituals that offer a glimpse of the way in which the living interact with the dead in a manner that helps the living heal. The "redemptive hegemony" is in becoming aware that the most intimate healers are the dead loved ones, their "personal Buddhas" who know them best and who are with them everywhere all the time, no longer restricted by the forces of gravity or the limitations of space and time. What enables healing is to cut out the delusion that one is an isolated, independent entity. This healing is actualized in the *Jizō Nagashi*.

Concluding Reflections

Expressing gratitude and experiencing interrelatedness are key aspects that empower and heal these women. A transformation of one's perspective is vital to this process. To do this requires focusing on the larger picture. The fundamental assumption is that the women think that they are not living independent lives based solely upon their own power and effort. They see that they are alive because the myriad interconnections in the universe work together to generate and support life.

The rituals of *Anan Kōshiki* and *Jizō Nagashi* facilitate a direct experience of interrelatedness that gives rise to gratitude—a place where women can feel at peace and intimately connected—to Sakyamuni, Mahāprajāpatī, Ananda, family, friends, both living and dead, and to the cosmos. This experience is an actualization of their Buddha nature.

What comes into focus when viewing Zen through this ethnographic lens is a complex picture in which constellations of practices defy sectarian boundaries, blurring the definition of Zen. In the reports of these women who are oriented to Zen practice, we see that they are engaging in rituals that are not traditionally recognized as Zen. These women's practices are oriented in a Zen worldview, but their interest is rarely philosophical or sectarian. Indeed, for these women, the definition of Zen is not much of a concern. Their concerns focus upon what is effective in helping them care for themselves and others in the vicissitudes of daily life. Their concern is practical. It reveals their wisdom that cognitive knowledge alone does not have the power to heal; rather, bodily experiences are the conduit for healing.

This study offers four avenues of inquiry into Zen Studies. First, this research demonstrates that an ethnographic approach is essential to learn about the ritual practices that are employed by women and to gain insight into the meaning the rituals hold for them. Second, this study illustrates how a tradition famous for strictly disciplined monasticism and nondualistic philosophy can simultaneously offer a venue for people to find meaningful symbolic and ritual resources for navigating life's problems and opportunities. Third, this close analysis of ritual practices in Zen Buddhism facilitates discourse with ritual studies and gender studies crossculturally, suggesting that "method of actualization" might be an appropriate way to think of "ritual" in a Sōtō Zen context. Fourth, this ethnographic research provides points for comparison and contrast with text-based historical and philosophical views of Zen, working in a complementary way expanding the purview of Zen Studies.

Alhough Dōgen did not specify empowerment and healing rituals in his panoply of guidelines on body/mind practice, his acute insight into the kinesthetics of actualizing specific experiences suggests that he would not see conflict in the nuns' practice of these rituals. These rituals require women to do specific motions with their bodies—bowing, chanting, letting slips of paper fly—which in turn activate the empowering and healing awareness of interrelatedness. The innovation of women including both the *Anan Kōshiki* and *Jizō Nagashi* rituals in their Zen practice is a manifestation of their insight into Dōgen's teaching on the "total body." These women do not draw sectarian lines around their practice. They do not bifurcate the whole and relegate themselves into an "inferior" or "powerless" category. They are creative in their responses to daunting situations such as a powerful and pervasive male-dominated institutional structure and male chauvinistic impulses in the culture. They even show no fear in the face of death. They have found ways to experience themselves as the "total body," where Dōgen, too, realizes, "there is no obstruction for it, it is graciously smooth and tumbles freely."[29] Invoking his metaphor, these innovative and powerful not-specifically-Zen rituals are all part of that "one bright pearl" manifesting beauty as it tosses around in the currents of human life.

7

Invocation of the Sage:
The Ritual to Glorify
the Emperor

Michel Mohr

The ritual of "Invoking the Sage," *Shukushin* (C. *Zhusheng*),[1] is still
regularly performed in most Japanese Zen monasteries[2] and in
some temples, regardless of their affiliation to the Sōtō, Rinzai, or
Ōbaku denominations. This ritual, sometimes translated as "prayers
for the emperor" or "prayer service," outwardly entails benefits
for both the emperor and the country he represents, but merits supposedly also reach the clergy and all beings. Moreover, the word
"sage" implies a saint whose virtue extends beyond that of a human
ruler. The Daoist classic from which this expression derives
employs subtle irony to depict the true "sage" as a person without
title, breaking up common ideas of rank and nobility. Translating this
ritual as "the invocation of the sage" is an attempt to remain literal
while conveying some of the irony in the Daoist term.

Prelude

Reasons for Choosing This Topic

At first sight, the scope of this study seems circumscribed to a peculiar ritual little known outside monasteries. But this ritual will
serve as a prism through which to view various images provided
by Zen institutions in the past and in the present, to connect
different periods of history, and to bridge concepts and practices.
It also gives us a way to glimpse the complex relations between the

clergy and political power. In modern Japan, the ritual immediately suggests the controversial links between religion and the State, a sensitive subject that explains the dearth of research on this topic.[3]

Although the word "emperor" suggests a kind of monolithic function continued through the different phases of Japanese history, it is a fluid concept, as can be seen in the two most dramatic changes that affected the imperial role and its signification. First, the young Meiji emperor was thrust into being head of the State by the 1868 coup known as the Meiji "Restoration," a move implying that his authority had been usurped for centuries. Second, the Shōwa emperor publicly affirmed his mortality in his radio broadcast of 15 August 1945 announcing Japan's surrender. Subsequently, the Japanese Constitution has recast the emperor's function as that of a "symbol." Such creation of a symbolic role for the former monarch was a choice made by the American General Headquarters within the context of the Cold War, which avoided cutting the Japanese citizens off from their past beliefs too abruptly.

It is even more important to recognize that the institution of the *Tennō* (emperor) comes from the Japanese adaptation of the Daoist deity *Tianhuang dadi,* the deification of the Pole Star, the ruler of the universe.[4] This deity was also identified with the Great Emperor of the Sacred Mountain of the East (*Dongyue dadi*), the one who rules over life, death, and longevity.[5] This, in my opinion, lies at the root of the ambiguity of all things associated with the emperor even today. Scholarly research into connections between Buddhism and the emperor needs to look beyond the modern era links between the emperor and militarism, without any sympathy for revisionist theories. The present chapter will examine one aspect of the ancient mutual support system between Buddhism and the emperor.

Approach and Sources

It is especially important to let the people who practice rituals express their understanding, their feelings about the *raison d'être* of such traditions, before any attempt at interpretation. I follow the approach of a historian of religion, but I have sometimes adopted the guise of an anthropologist, making field trips, scrutinizing the ritual and those who performed it, before resorting to textual evidence. I attended Shukushin ceremonies, sometimes using video when allowed, and interviewed monks who had performed the ritual. At a certain stage, I was tempted to adopt a more sociological approach and to make a survey that could have revealed general trends. However, most replies to my questions were so similar that I chose instead to clarify the classical context from which this ritual emerged.

Most textual evidence for this ritual goes back to Song China and belongs to the genre known as "Rules of Purity," whose compilation coincides with the reorganization of Chan during the Song period. There is also a wealth of Daoist sources, which I will only briefly mention and suggest that they deserve further exploration. I will then move to Japanese developments, focusing on the Tokugawa period, before examining the way this ritual is understood in contemporary Japan.

Despite the interest of recent studies that attempt to apply the "performance theory" to the study of Buddhist rituals,[6] I find that this approach fails to do justice to the complex aspects involved in ritual behavior, especially in intricate cases such as the Shukushin. The division into "experientialists" versus "textualists," whose limitations could be transcended by the "third standpoint" of the performance theory, neglects the standpoint of the very actors who perform these rituals. In other words, it lacks concern for the perspective and motivation of those who display religious behavior.

An important distinction must be made between the "perspective" of the practitioner and the interpretation of the ritual in terms of "meaning," often recast to carry a "symbolic" significance. Richard Payne has made this point clear: "While they are performing rituals, practitioners are not concerned with the symbolic meaning of the ritual elements, but rather with properly following the rules of the ritual performance."[7] This is precisely what my informants said about their state of mind while performing Shukushin.

Outline of the Ritual

In the monastic context, the ritual itself most often consists of two phases. The first phase is led by the head abbot (*dōchō*) in the main building, usually the Dharma-hall, and consists of prostrations followed by recitation of sutras. Texts recited on this occasion slightly differ depending on each denomination and monastic tradition. When it is performed on the New Year, bows are made in the four directions, either from a standing position or kneeling, depending on the school. Then, all participants go around the buildings of the monastery or temple, reciting sutras and *dhāraṇīs*, which are dedicated to the well-being and long life of the emperor and to the stability of the country. Performance of the ritual usually requires at least one hour and involves both clerics and laypeople wishing to join the event. Shukushin usually occurs on the beginning and mid-month day of each month (the first and the fifteenth), the emperor's birthday, and the New Year, that is, at least twenty-six times per year. The nomination of a new abbot as head of a monastery, a ritual called even today "the opening of the hall" (*kaidō*),[8] is also centered on the same ceremony and is alternatively named *Shukkoku kaidō* ("invoking the country and opening the hall") or *Shukushin jōdō* ("invoking the sage and ascending the hall").[9]

The Chinese Origins of the Invocation

Traceable Origins

Buddhist expressions of allegiance to the emperor can be found in early, pre-Chan records. The chronological anthology *Fozu tongji* published in 1271 includes a section on the celebrations of emperors' birthdays by famous clerics.[10] According to this document, on the occasion of his birthday in 425, the ruler of the North Wei Dynasty "ordered all Buddhist temples to construct a practice place to pray for [his] longevity (*zhushou daochang*)."[11] We see here the typical combination of birthday celebration and the ritual for longevity.

This was an imperial edict (*zhao*), but there was some reluctance to abide with such obligations toward the ruler, and for a while polemics raged about whether or not clerics should pay homage (*jingli*) to the monarch. The *Hongmingji* attributed to Sengyou (445–518) includes the correspondence left by Huiyuan (334–416) of Mount Lu on this topic.[12] Huiyuan's position, known as "the view that monks do not pay respect to sovereigns" (*Shamen bujing wangzhe lun*), defends the preeminence of the Dharma over secular power.[13] Yet, Huiyuan also points out that "emperors of the past expected respect (*li*) [from Buddhist monks], but never requested them to make prostrations (*bai*) [in front of them]."[14]

By the Tang Dynasty, such sparks of resistance had apparently vanished. For instance, the above-mentioned *Fozu tongji* records that emperor Dezong requested the Huayan patriarch Chengguan (738–839) to come to his palace to celebrate his birthday and give a lecture on the sutras, but there is no record that Chengguan felt any hesitation.[15] This is the beginning of celebrations during which a cleric "ascends the seat and invokes the sage" (*shengzuo zhusheng*) on auspicious occasions.[16] The tendency to accommodate the court seems common to most Buddhist lineages, since the Pure Land patriarch Shandao (613–681) also goes to great pains wishing that "the merits benefit the great emperor of the Tang, [making] the foundation of his fortune long and stable, and the sage's leadership (*shenghua*) inexhaustible."[17]

Within the Chan monastic context, the emergence of Shukushin coincides with the growing success of this lineage during the Northern Song dynasty (960–1127). One of the earliest traces appears in the *Tiansheng Extensive Record of the Lamp* (*Tiansheng guangdenglu*) completed in 1036. A passage describes an exchange that took place when Fuyan Liangya (n.d.) took his function of new abbot at Fuyansi, a famous temple in present Hunan. A monk asked him about the distinctive feature of his lineage, and Liangya replied:

> In past years, [I] intimately received the [flow of the] Han River.[18]
> Today, in this very place *I invoke His Majesty.*[19]

Liangya was a successor of Dongshan Shoushu (910–990), himself the spiritual heir of Yunmen Wenyan (864–949). The meaning of his "invocation" here is not explicit, and it does not necessarily reflect an established ritual. For a more precise dating and context, we have to wait until the publication of the *Rules of Purity for the Chan Monastery* (*Chanyuan qinggui*) printed in 1103. This compilation contains a section called "The Role of the Venerable," which includes this ritual as one of his duties:

> [When] an official asks to burn [incense] and to practice [rituals], it is definitely for the purpose of *making an invocation to extend the longevity of the sage* (*zhuyan shengshou*). Therefore the venerable should do his best and wield the great mind, exposing the great Dharma, accumulating great virtues, promoting the great practice, expanding the great compassion, making the great deeds of a Buddha, and realizing great [spiritual] benefits.[20]

The venerable, that is the "abbot," is thus encouraged to accept such official requests and to exercise the best of his abilities while taking them as opportunities to spread the Dharma. The incorporation of Chan monasteries within the religious network of the Song government gave rise to a ceremony that would embody the relation of mutual dependence between clerics and the court. On one hand it served to acknowledge official sponsorship and to express gratitude for it, and on the other it functioned as a performative utterance,[21] whose effect would contribute to protecting the health of the sovereign and the stability of the country.

The classical study of Yanagida Seizan has shown that the increasing proximity of the Chan clergy to imperial power originated within the "East Mountain lineage" (*Dongshang famen*).[22] This is further demonstrated by the recorded sayings of a series of teachers of the Linji school during the same period, who invariably began their sermons by offering "one piece of petal-like incense" in front of the altar, saying this is "for the present emperor" (*wei jinshang huangdi*).[23] The addition of the exclamation "ten thousand years, ten thousand times ten thousand years!" (*wansui wanwansui*) can probably be credited to Yuanwu Keqin (1063–1135).[24] This way of wishing "long life" ("eternity" is in principle alien to Buddhism) constitutes the prototype for the exclamation *Banzai* revived during the Meiji period and still used in present-day Japan, for instance, when dissolving the Parliament.[25]

Respect for the sovereign is also seen in ancient Buddhist literature, in, for example, the idea of having to repay four debts of gratitude (C. *sien,* J. *shion*) toward one's parents, sentient beings, the sovereign, and the three jewels (Buddha, Dharma, Sangha).[26] Until the Tang dynasty, rituals of enthronement and spells to protect the emperor were associated with Daoist lineages and the Tiantai and Tantric schools. Chan monks needed to provide some new ritual that would please their sponsors and valorize their own role. The "invocation of the sage" apparently represents such an innovative device. They created this ritual by building on the ancient Buddhist ceremonies and gave it a new name enhanced with the prestige of a venerable Daoist classic. The link between this Daoist classic and the new ritual sheds some light on the spirit that might have inspired the Chan literati.

Mythological Origins

In pre-Buddhist China, various religious cults served to legitimate the ruler, and rituals aimed at extending the longevity of the emperor have existed since antiquity. The character *zhu,* the first word of Shukushin translated here as "invoking," is made of two elements: on the right we see a shaman-like figure kneeling in front of the altar on the left, either praying or communicating with the deity.[27] Originally, *zhu* denoted both the *invocation* of a god and the *wish* addressed to it, as in the expression *zhufu,* "the invocation of Heaven's favors." The closely related character *zhou* means "a spell" and serves to translate the word *dhāraṇī,* the Buddhist magic formula.[28]

The text that seems to have inspired the "invocation of the sage" ritual is the twelfth chapter of the *Zhuangzi,* the famous Daoist philosophical text. The Japanese monk-scholar Mujaku Dōchū (1653–1745)[29] identifies the expression used in the *Zhuangzi* as the source for the ritual performed in Chan monasteries. In his *Zenrin shōkisen,* Mujaku says: "According to me, the words *Shukushin* and *Shukuju* come from this source."[30] Mujaku's assertion demands that we examine the fascicle "Heaven and Earth," the twelfth chapter of the *Zhuangzi.* This chapter provides nine tales that illustrate the virtue of non-action and emphasize the necessity for the emperor to be completely "natural." The story related to our ritual unfolds in the setting of a remote area, where the following dialogue takes place between the legendary emperor Yao and a border guard:

Yao was seeing the sights at Hua when the border guard of Hua said, "Aha—a sage! I beg to *offer up prayers for the sage* (*zhu shengren*). They will bring the sage long life!"

Yao said, "No, thanks."

"They will bring the sage riches!"

Yao said, "No, thanks."

"They will bring the sage many sons!"

Yao said, "No, thanks."

"Long life, riches, many sons—these are what all men desire!" said the border guard. "How is it that you alone do not desire them?"

Yao said, "Many sons means many fears. Riches mean many troubles. Long life means many shames. These three are of no use in nourishing Virtue—therefore I decline them."

The border guard said, "At first I took you for a sage. Now I see you are a mere gentleman." ... The border guard turned and left.

Yao followed him, saying, "Please—I would like to ask you..."

"Go away!" said the border guard.[31]

The irony of this dialogue, which turns the "sage" into a fool, is striking. What did the Chan clerics have in mind when they coined the expression *zhusheng* much later? To clarify this point, let us reexamine the above *Zhuangzi* story.

It begins with an anonymous soldier, without rank or name, who appears at first to hold a naive idea of what a "sage" or a "Daoist saint" is. He seems to assume that the emperor Yao is one of them and puts him to the test. Yao keeps declining the three offers made to "invoke" (*zhu*) him and to provide him with long life, wealth, and descendants through this "miraculous invocation." Then, when the soldier inquires further about the reason for such refusal, Yao replies by giving only common sense justifications, revealing the paucity of his spiritual attainments. The tale ends with a reversal of the roles, the emperor realizing that the simple soldier was a sage in disguise and trying to ask him questions, but to no avail.

In the end, the guard who offered prayers is far from being naive and displays a superior understanding. The emperor's refusal is dismissed as inappropriate, a conclusion that may be interpreted in the sense that a clever ruler should accept sincere prayers directed at him, even if he has transcended the desire for worldly attainments. Such a literary context seems to provide a perfect background for the creation of a ritual implying that both sides (the clerics and the emperor) are aware of the relative value of such ceremonies and have reached such a deep insight that they are no longer affected by the mundane aspects of the ritual.[32]

Mujaku also mentions a Buddhist source for the ritual, the *Rules of Purity for the Huanzhu Hermitage* (*Huanzhu'an qinggui*), a set of codes composed by Zhongfeng Mingben (1263–1323) and published in 1643.[33] This text includes a description of the "Six good days for invocating the sage" (J. *roku kōnichi shukushin*):

> The birth of the emperor has six corresponding days in the branches and stems [of the Chinese calendar]; [on these occasions] sutras will be chanted and words of praise (*shukusan*) [will be said in his honor]. Since every year there are six auspicious days with the [same] configuration as his birthday, they are called the six good days."[34]

This means that since the combination of the 12 Earthly Branches with the 10 Heavenly Stems makes a total of 60 days, the same combination will be repeated six times a year. Thus, Mujaku explains the frequency of the ritual on the basis of the *Rules of Purity for the Huanzhu Hermitage,* but he clearly identifies the *Zhuangzi* as the original source for its inspiration. In the Chinese religious setting where Buddhists and Daoists had often been competing for official support, the recasting of this classic into a Chan ritual shows consummate rhetorical skills. Authorship of this transformation is not nominal, but rituals often result from the addition of different layers by several generations. What is now becoming clearer is how the Shukushin emerged from the Chinese monastic milieu during the twelfth century and how learned monks such as Mujaku still could identify the allusion to the *Zhuangzi* story.

Japanese Developments

The Song-style Chan practice of invocation of the emperor was imported to Japan along with the other Chan rituals. Before discussing this, a word must be said of an ancient imperial rite that bears striking resemblance with some aspects of the Shukushin ritual.

Bowing to the Four Directions

This *Shihōhai*, or "bows to the four directions," rite was originally performed by the emperor or the empress themselves, especially at dawn of the New Year's Day. The *Nihon shoki* records that empress Kōgyoku "knelt down and bowed to the four directions" in the eighth month of 642 as an intercession for rain in a period of severe drought, after Buddhist chanting of sutras had failed.[35] Despite the early date, this was a Daoist ritual that had been transmitted to the imperial household, like many so-called Shinto ceremonies that were based on Daoist rituals. This ritual is found in the archaic *Rites of the Zhou* (*Zhouli*), which contains an explicit description of how the Great Master of Sacrificial Rites should bow to heaven, to the earth, and to the four directions (*li tiandi sifang*), each of which is associated with a different color.[36]

The Shukushin is also similar to the Daoist Memorial-Presenting Rituals (*jinbiao keyi*).[37] Among the many benefits obtained from these rituals, the *Great Collection of Daoist Rituals* (*Daomen kefan daquan*) by Du Guangting (850–933)[38] lists "intercession for rain" and "prolonging life," items of perennial concern for Chinese as well as Japanese sovereigns. A thorough comparison of both rituals requires further research and is beyond the scope of this chapter, but these Daoist practices are just one more instance of the many common denominators between the Buddhist and Daoist rituals.

Medieval Japan

In the process of transmitting the Zen traditions to Japan, both Eisai and Dōgen relied on the *Rules of Purity for the Chan Monastery,* which is the source for the Shukushin ritual. In his *Promotion of Zen for the Protection of the Country,* Eisai presents the Zen temple as a "Practice Place [to Celebrate the] Sage's Birthday" (*Shōsetsu dōjō*).[39] He puts this celebration first among the sixteen cardinal observances (*gyōji*).[40]

In the *Kankin* ("Read Sutras") fascicle of the *Shōbōgenzō*, Dōgen recommends hanging a tablet (*hai*) in front of the Buddha hall saying, "Practice Place [for the] Invocation of the Sage."[41] The fascicle *Bendōwa* explicitly argues for the interdependence between Buddhism and political stability:

> When the true Buddha Dharma spreads throughout a nation, since all buddhas and deities give in permanence their protection, the ruler's leadership (*ōka*) is peaceful. When the sage's leadership (*sei-ka*)[42] is peaceful, the Buddha Dharma gains power from it.[43]

For the concrete ritual details, Dōgen heavily relied on the *Rules of Purity for the Chan Monastery.*[44] In his work to reorganize the Sōtō tradition and to build a stable institution, Keizan Jōkin (1268–1325) systematized rules, including prescriptions about how to invoke the longevity of the emperor.[45] The *Keizan Rules of Purity* (*Keizan shingi*) mentions the Shukushin on ten different occasions. For instance, the New Year rice gruel should be offered for "the boundless longevity of the present emperor" (*kinjō kōtei seiju mukyō*),[46] and "Shukushin, chanting of sutras and dedication" is to be accomplished on the first and fifteenth of every lunar month (*sakubō*).[47]

The Turning Point of the Kenmu Restoration

During the Kenmu Restoration (1333–1336), when two emperors pretended to the throne and religious leaders were asked to take sides, a subtle shift occurred. Kenneth Kraft observes that "the Kenmu Restoration marks the entry of the Zen institution into the religious and political mainstream of medieval Japan,"[48] and I would add that this was true for Buddhism in general. The case of emperor Godaigo personally performing elaborate Shingon rituals to subdue his adversaries certainly constitutes a landmark in the history of interactions between the court and the clergy.[49] In Keizan's replies to ten queries by Godaigo,[50] Godaigo confesses his long and unsuccessful practice of the kōan *Mu* and asks for advice. After reassuring the learned sovereign that diligent practice will necessarily bear fruits, Keizan concludes by wishing "the greatest blessings, the greatest longevity" (*shishuku shiju*).[51]

An illustration of the new type of relations established during the troubled times of the Northern and Southern Courts, which lasted until 1392, can be seen in the foundation of Eihōji in the present Gifu prefecture. The emperor Kōmyō, second generation of pretenders to the throne in the Northern Court, was an ardent follower of the Rinzai teacher Musō Soseki (1275–1351), who had once retired at Eihōji to escape the turmoil of Kyoto. In 1339, Kōmyō issued a decree to consecrate this temple as "a place [chosen] by imperial will" (*chokuganjo*) and appointed Musō as founder. Since that time Eihōji has performed Shukushin twice a month, invoking the name of its first patron, the emperor Kōmyō.[52]

This case shows how the Shukushin ritual could serve to seal a mutual relationship between an emperor and a regional temple. We can thus discern the specificity of Shukushin, which was used to establish links to the court, whereas memorial temples (*bodaiji*) could be dedicated to any powerful patron. The whole rhetoric behind Shukushin is that it invokes "a sage," in other words, "a saint," distinct from other men of high position. Clerics in Japan had to have appropriate relations with both the court and the Bakufu, dealing with each of them in a specific way. In the following section, we see how Chinese newcomers addressed this challenge during the Tokugawa period.

Competition with Ōbaku Monks for Imperial Support

When Yinyuan Longqi (J. Ingen Ryūki; 1592–1673) and his cohort of Chinese monks arrived in Nagasaki in 1654, the Tokugawa regime had consolidated its grip on the whole country, although tensions remained in the Kyushu area where the eradication of Christianity was continuing.[53] The Japanese clergy wavered for a while between rejection and support of the newcomers, who claimed to represent the authentic Rinzai tradition. But eventually Yinyuan managed to obtain official recognition, and in 1661 Manpukuji opened on land bestowed by the Bakufu.[54] In 1672, one year before his death, Yinyuan and his successor Muan Xingtong (J. Mokuan Shōtō, 1611–1684) put together the *Ōbaku Rules of Purity* (*Ōbaku shingi*), the rules they wanted future generations to observe at Manpukuji.

Yinyuan puts unusual stress on the need to adapt to new circumstances, saying that "depending on the time and the place, the established rules are not identical."[55] An example of this adaptation appears in the beginning section about "Invoking Blessings" (C. *zhuli*, J. *shukuri*),[56] where he takes great care to emphasize the weight of secular power:

> The Buddha Dharma [transmitted by Śākyamuni on] the Vulture
> Peak has been entrusted to the country's ruler and [his] ministers.
> [Since] many rulers and ministers come from a high level of reali-
> zation,[57] the freedom of their authority and virtue [allows] them to
> skillfully support the Buddha Dharma. [It] takes the form of protec-
> tive screens, writing brushes, gold, or warm water. For us who have
> left the world, [being able] to obtain a place to settle down and
> practice the Way without external aggression truly makes us indebted
> to the favors and power of the ruler and [his] ministers. This is why,
> when we get every year occasions to perform the ceremony of "In-
> vocating Blessings," how could we not do our best [to express] this
> [grateful] mind.[58]

One could hardly be more explicit. The reader will have no difficulty in identifying the "country's ruler and [his] ministers" as the emperor and the Bakufu, which constitute the situation specific to Japan. Manpukuji still commemorates the death of the fourth Shogun Tokugawa Ietsuna on the eighth of May and the death of emperor Gomizunoo on the nineteenth of September.

The *Ōbaku Rules of Purity* also explains how to perform the New Year ceremony including the Invocation of the Sage. In the case of the Ōbaku tradition, the celebration of Shukushin involves specific Chinese-like reading of sutras and dedications and distinctive posture. The ceremony also includes the recitation of an esoteric *dhāraṇī* supposed to prolong life,[59] which provides an interesting indication of the convergence with esoteric rituals.

The Impact of Ōbaku on Tokugawa Zen Rituals

The inauguration of Manpukuji and the presence of Chinese monks who had close connections to both the emperor and the Bakufu were an unprecedented challenge, especially for monks of the Rinzai denomination. They were facing a new competitor, who not only claimed to represent a more authentic tradition but also drew the authorities' attention.

As far as monastic rules are concerned, the reaction came from Myōshinji, where Mujaku Dōchū compiled the *Abbreviated Rules of Purity for Small Monasteries (Shōsōrin ryakushingi)*.[60] As the title suggests, one of the tendencies within Myōshinji was to value practice in small-size communities. These new rules also contain instructions regarding the frequency and procedure to observe for performing Shukushin. However, the ritual doesn't occupy the central position given to it by Eisai or by the Chinese newcomers. This may be because established institutions with a stable income such as Myōshinji didn't have as much need to appeal to new patrons. On the other hand, both Eisai and Yinyuan had to "sell their product," and as Helen Baroni has written, the early implantation of the Ōbaku tradition is similar to a new religious movement.[61] Apparently, the same kind of competition for imperial support occurred within China before and after Yinyuan's journey to Japan. At the old Wanfusi, Yinyuan's native temple in Fujian, the central building had a plaque saying, "Practice Place [for the] Invocation of the Sage" (*Zhusheng daochang*), which was still visible in the early twentieth century.[62]

In the upheaval produced by the growing importance of the Ōbaku lineage, there was a general trend toward reforms within both the Rinzai and Sōtō denominations.[63] The lines of Hakuin and Kogetsu merged to form a new current which, before becoming the mainstream, occupied a marginal position known as Rinka, literally "under the woods," in opposition to the more prestigious Gozan lineages. Here, we should not be taken in by the stereotype of Hakuin spending his whole life in his small countryside temple Shōinji, surrounded by disciples who sometimes died of starvation.

While it is true that he chose to refuse appointments in large temples, his strategy was not one of complete indifference to secular power. Hakuin's writings do include mentions of Shukushin, in particular his commentary of the *Recorded Sayings of Daitō Kokushi*, where he emphasizes without any perceptible irony the ceremony accomplished for the opening of Daitokuji on January 1, 1327.[64] During this ritual, Shūhō Myōchō (1282–1338) followed the tradition of wishing the emperor long life by shouting *Banzai Banbanzai*.[65] Furthermore, in 1768, the Ryūtakuji monastery founded by Hakuin and Tōrei became the repository for the funerary tablets of emperor Reigen (1654–1732, reign 1663–1687), a mark of deep trust from the imperial family.[66] However, emperor-related rituals do not constitute a central aspect in the work of either of the two teachers, who tend to stress other priorities.

The Present Context of Shukushin and Concluding Remarks

Actually, the above distinction between the Gozan and the Hakuin lineage reflects a contemporary perspective. Yokota Kōgaku rōshi, the present teacher at the Engakuji monastery whom I asked about his perception of Shukushin, proposed seeing the tradition from a twofold perspective, using a word suggesting "ambiguity" (*nimensei*). Presenting his perspective and discussing it may serve to highlight convergences and divergences between traditional and contemporary interpretations of Shukushin and similar rituals.

The Twofold Characteristic of Rinzai Zen

The reasoning proposed here is especially relevant to the Rinzai tradition because of my informant. Other analytical schemes may be appropriate for other denominations, but I believe this discussion hints at broader implications. Yokota rōshi suggested that the present monastic system is the blend of two traditions, one coming from the Gozan and the other from the Hakuin-Kogetsu line. Kogetsu, who is still utterly neglected in Zen studies, is important to Engakuji since the Kogetsu-line teacher Seisetsu Shūcho (1745–1820) founded the monastery.[67] Yokota rōshi says that rituals such as the Shukushin and other formal public ceremonies are the product of the Gozan legacy, whereas the Hakuin-Kogetsu line emphasized *dokusan* (individual consultation) and *teishō* (lectures by the teacher) as the two main occasions to deepen one's practice. He acknowledges that the former Gozan-type rituals have become formalized (*keigaika*) and ritualized (*gishikika*).

Because of this, some teachers in the postwar period have chosen to omit all mention of "the present emperor" (*kinjō tennō*) when performing Shukushin or to replace it with the stock expression "the ultimate reality of Suchness (Tathatā)" (*shinnyo jissai*). Kōno Taitsū rōshi, the former abbot of Shōfukuji, who supported the apology of the Myōshinji Branch for its war collaboration,[68] was mentioned as an example. Another shift in attitudes that appeared at Engakuji in the postwar period was the addition of several new expressions to the Shukushin phrasing, including "world peace" (*sekai heiwa*). Interestingly, there is no document to justify this change in the temple rules, and it has been passed on by word of mouth (*kuchizutae*) only in this lineage. Yokota rōshi's opinion is that Beppō Sōgen (Asahina, 1891–1979) is the likely candidate for this alteration.[69] This indicates that some degree of flexibility regarding the Shukushin ritual is left to individual lineages.

The above distinction between the Gozan legacy, held responsible for all the formalistic aspects of monastic rules, and the Hakuin-Kogetsu legacy, representing the essentially "spiritual" dimension, can be seen as an apologetic device to defend the authenticity of the present monastic system and its founder Hakuin.[70] Yet, Yokota rōshi's schema also represents a testimony from inside the living tradition that expresses some of its inherent contradictions, or "tensions," some of them going back to early phases of the importation of Chan/Zen to Japan. Transmitting a religion that was already fully institutionalized and codified in Song China necessarily meant that the "indigenization" process would be limited by textual constraints. The periodic rewriting of the "Rules of Purity" arose from this necessity, but even so-called reforms have not gone to the point of rejecting rituals that had been performed for centuries in China and Japan.

Even now, when the Japanese imperial system itself is being questioned, clerics said they could not imagine reciting Shukushin with the name of the acting Prime Minister. But they also could not imagine dropping the Shukushin ritual altogether, perhaps because they felt that with such an old tradition, if one starts choosing and removing bits according to contemporary dislikes, the whole framework would collapse. This attitude is in sharp contrast to Zen centers abroad, which, as far as I know, do not perform the Shukushin or an equivalent ritual.

Concluding Remarks

As stated at the beginning of this chapter, it is beside the point to search for a "hidden meaning" in the way the ritual itself is performed. Most monks interviewed said they are just "trying to do their best" when performing Shukushin—and since its execution can easily last more than one hour, this task requires concentration. In fact, the *Ōbaku Rules of Purity* advises that at the beginning of Shukushin once the monks are aligned, they should "bate their breath and cut off [all] thoughts" (C. *bingxi juelü*, J. *heisoku zetsuryo*).[71]

Reading various Buddhist and non-Buddhist sources for this ritual has shown how its focus on the "sage" implies more than simple prayers for a monarch and cannot be reduced to a "birthday celebration." This ritual invokes the archaic understanding that the sage embodies the macrocosm and that dedicating the merits to him will bring universal concord. To borrow Sharf's poetic description, "Through the choreography of the rites, the sage-king participates in the cosmic dance that both enacts and engenders the harmony of all under heaven. The sage needs only perfect his ritual comportment to bring the whole into balance."[72]

During the Song period, the archaic rites were incorporated into a Chan ritual that served as a practical means to seal the relationship between the court and the Chan community. The earliest mention of the ritual in the *Rules of Purity for the Chan Monastery* still presents this ceremony as the result of a request made by officials ("[When] an official asks to burn [incense] and to practice [rituals]..."). In this context, it justifies the performance of the ritual as an occasion for the venerable to "expose the great Dharma." However, Chan institutions gradually incorporated this invocation in their annual schedule, making it into a periodical reminder of the crucial symbiosis between official support and the very existence of the clergy. In Japan, the need to perform Shukushin was reasserted in new monastic rules or in texts aimed at legitimizing the tradition. Two outstanding examples are Eisai's *Promotion of Zen for the Protection of the Country* and Yinyuan's *Ōbaku Rules of Purity* that gave it central importance. The whole monastic structure in the present Japanese Sōtō, Rinzai, or Ōbaku denominations is based on rules established during the Tokugawa period, so this ritual is regularly performed, although with little attention to its origins or possible significance, not to speak of political implications in the modern context.

We briefly saw how a contemporary teacher envisions the distinction between formal ritual and personal practice aspects of monastic life. The Shukushin disappeared in the process of transmitting Zen lineages abroad, but the ritual continues to be performed in the Japanese tradition. The ability of the Zen denominations to adapt to twenty-first-century conditions is constrained by the very wealth of their textual legacy. We are far from the slogan "not relying on written words," and daily life in Japanese monasteries remains largely governed by rituals such as Shukushin. Perhaps rediscovering the original spirit of the "invocation of the sage" in the *Zhuangzi* would remind the Zen community of a richer understanding of the relationships between monks and emperors.

REFERENCES

References in Japanese

Amino Yoshihiko. 1986. *Igyō no ōken*. Tokyo: Heibonsha.
Cheng Sa-wen. 2003. "Sōdai zenrin ni okeru 'Shukushin jōdō' no igi" (English title in the original: The Meaning of Ritual Preaching in Honor of the Emperor in Song Period Chan Monasteries). *Indogaku Bukkyōgaku kenkyū* 102 (51/2): 77–80.
Fukunaga Mitsuji. 1978. *Sōshi*. Chūgoku kotensen 12–17. 5 vols. Tokyo: Asahi shinbunsha.

Kagamishima Genryū, Satō Tatsugen, and Kosaka Kiyū, eds. 1972. *Yakuchū Zen'en shingi.* Tokyo: Sōtōshū shūmuchō.

Katō Jōken et al., ed. 1983. *Kadokawa jigen jiten.* Tokyo: Kadokawa shoten.

Kimura Tokugen. 2005. *Ōbakushū no rekishi, jinbutsu, bunka.* Tokyo: Shunjūsha.

Masuda Hidemitsu, ed. 1998. *Tennō no hon: Nihon no reiteki kongen to fūin no hishi o saguru.* Tokyo: Gakushū kenkyūsha.

Miura Katsuo. 1985. "Engakuji no rekishi." *Zuirokuzan Engakuji.* Kamakura, Daihonzan Engakuji, pp. 51–76.

Mujaku Dōchū. 1698. *Zenrin shōkisen.* Facsimile in Yanagida Seizan, ed. 1979. Zengaku sōsho, vol. 9. Kyoto: Chūbun shuppan.

Nakamura Hajime. 2001. *Kōsetsu bukkyōgo daijiten.* 4 vols. Tokyo: Tōkyō shoseki.

Nakano Jūsai. 1989. "Shūmon fukyōjō ni okeru sabetsu jishō (4): Tennōsei kō Uchiyama Gudō ni manabu." *Kyōke kenshū* (Sōtōshū kyōke kenshūsho) 32: 209–16 (English title in the original: The Discriminating Phenomenon in Sōtō-shū Propagation: In Relation to Emperor System[73]).

Nishimura Eshin. 1982. *Tōrei oshō nenpu.* Kinsei zensōden 8. Kyoto: Shibunkaku.

Nishio Kenryū. 1977. "Sōdai nitchū Bukkyō kōryūshi: Zen'en shingi to Eihei shingi." *Bukkyō shigaku kenkyū* 19/2: 1–32.

———. 1986. Entry on "Shukushin" in the *Kokushi daijiten*, vol. 7, pp. 332d–333a. Tokyo: Yoshikawa kōbunkan.

Ogawa Tamaki, ed. 1994. *Kadokawa shinjigen kaiteiban.* Tokyo: Kadokawa shoten.

Ōtsuki Mikio, Katō Shōshun, and Hayashi Sekkō, eds. 1988. *Ōbaku bunka jinmei jiten.* Tokyo: Shibunkaku.

Suzuki Kakuzen, Kawamura Kōdō, et al., ed. 1988–1993. *Dōgen zenji zenshū,* 7 vols. Tokyo: Shunjūsha.

Takahashi Tōru, and Senda Minoru. 1991. *Nihonshi o irodoru dōkyō no nazo: Nihon no shūzoku, shinkō ni hisomu Chūgoku dōkyō no konseki.* Tokyo: Nihon bungeisha.

Tsukamoto Zenryū, ed. 1973. *Mochizuki Bukkyō daijiten,* 10 vols. Tokyo: Sekai seiten kankō kyōkai.

Yamada Gyokuden. 1926. *Shina soseki junpai ki.* Uji: Uji Ōbaku Shinkōin.

Yanagida Seizan. 1967. *Shoki zenshūshi no kenkyū.* Kyoto: Zenbunka kenkyūsho [Reprinted in Yanagida Seizan. 2000. *Yanagida Seizan shū dai rokkan.* Tokyo: Hōzōkan].

Zengaku daijiten hensansho, ed. 1978. *Zengaku daijiten.* Tokyo: Taishūkan.

References in Western Languages

Baroni, Helen Josephine. 2000. *Obaku Zen: The Emergence of the Third Sect of Zen in Tokugawa Japan.* Honolulu: University of Hawaii Press.

Chen, Jinhua. 2005. "Fazang (643–712): The Holy Man." *Journal of the International Association of Buddhist Studies* 28/1: 11–84.

Collcutt, Martin. 1981. *Five Mountains: The Rinzai Zen Monastic Institution in Medieval Japan.* Vol. 85, *Harvard East Asian Monograph.* Cambridge, MA: Harvard University Press.

Faure, Bernard. 1996. *Visions of Power: Imagining Medieval Japanese Buddhism.* Translated by P. Brooks. Princeton, NJ: Princeton University Press.

Foulk, T. Griffith. 1993. "Myth, Ritual, and Monastic Practice in Sung Ch'an Buddhism." In Patricia Buckley Ebrey and Peter N. Gregory, eds., *Religion and Society in T'ang and Sung China.* Honolulu: University of Hawaii Press, pp. 147–208 [see especially p. 178].

———. 1999. "Sung Controversies Concerning the 'Separate Transmission' of Ch'an." In Peter N. Gregory and Daniel A. Getz Jr., eds., *Buddhism in the Sung.* Honolulu: University of Hawaii Press, pp. 220–94.

———. 2004. "*Changyuan qinggui* and Other 'Rules of Purity' in Chinese Buddhism." In Steven Heine and Dale S. Wright, eds., *The Zen Canon: Understanding the Classic Texts.* New York: Oxford University Press, pp. 275–312.

———. 2006. " 'Rules of Purity' in Japanese Zen." In Steven Heine and Dale S. Wright, eds., *Zen Classics: Formative Texts in the History of Zen Buddhism.* New York: Oxford University Press, pp. 137–69.

Gregory, Peter N., and Daniel A. Getz Jr., eds. 1999. *Buddhism in the Sung.* Honolulu: University of Hawaii Press.

Heine, Steven. 2000. *Opening a Mountain: Kōans of the Zen Masters.* New York: Oxford University Press.

Kraft, Kenneth. 1992. *Eloquent Zen: Daitō and Early Japanese Zen.* Honolulu: University of Hawaii Press.

McBride, Richard D. 2005. "Dhāraṇī and Spells in Medieval Sinitic Buddhism." *Journal of the International Association of Buddhist Studies* 28/1: 85–114.

Mohr, Michel. 1994. "Zen Buddhism during the Tokugawa Period: The Challenge to Go beyond Sectarian Consciousness." *Japanese Journal of Religious Studies* 21/4: 341–72.

———. 1999. "Hakuin." In Yoshinori Takeuchi, James W. Heisig, Paul L. Swanson, and Joseph S. O'Leary, eds., *Buddhist Spirituality: Later China, Korea, Japan, and the Modern World.* New York: A Herder & Herder Book, The Crossroad Publishing Company, pp. 307–28.

———. 2000. "Emerging from Non-duality: Kōan Practice in the Rinzai Tradition since Hakuin." In Steven Heine and Dale S. Wright, eds., *The Kōan: Texts and Contexts in Zen Buddhism.* New York: Oxford University Press, pp. 244–79.

———. 2002. "L'héritage contesté de Dokuan Genkō: Traditions et conflits dans le bouddhisme Zen du XVIIᵉ siècle." In F. Girard, A. Horiuchi, and M. Macé, eds., *Repenser l'ordre, repenser l'héritage: paysage intellectuel du Japon (XVIIᵉ–XIXᵉ siècles).* Paris-Genève: Droz, pp. 209–63.

———. 2005. "Imagining Indian Zen: Tōrei's Commentary on the *Ta-mo-to-lo ch'an ching* and the Rediscovery of Early Meditation Techniques during the Tokugawa." In Steven Heine and Dale S. Wright, eds., *Zen Classics: Formative Texts in the History of Zen Buddhism.* New York: Oxford University Press, pp. 215–46.

Payne, Richard K. 2004. "Ritual Syntax and Cognitive Theory." *Pacific World: Journal of the Institute of Buddhist Studies* Third Series Number 6: 195–227.

Robinson, Richard H. 1967. *Early Mādhyamika in India and China*. New Delhi: Motilal Banarsidass.

Sawada, Janine Anderson. 1998. "Political Waves in the Zen Sea: The Engaku-ji Circle in Early Meiji Japan." *Japanese Journal of Religious Studies* 25/1–2: 117–50.

Sharf, Robert H. 2001. *Coming to Terms with Chinese Buddhism: A Reading of the Treasure Store Treatise*. Honolulu: University of Hawaii Press.

Stephenson, B. 2005. "The Kōan as Ritual Performance." *Journal of the American Academy of Religion* 73/2: 475–96.

Victoria, Brian. 1997. *Zen at War*. New York: Weatherhill.

———. 2003. *Zen War Stories*. London: Routledge Curzon.

Yifa. 2002. *The Origins of Buddhist Monastic Codes in China: An Annotated Translation and Study of the Chanyuan qinggui*. Honolulu: University of Hawaii Press.

8

Meditation in Motion: Textual Exegesis in the Creation of Ritual

David E. Riggs

Zen Buddhism has come to be so identified with seated meditation (*zazen*) that it is easy to overlook the fact that zazen is but one of the many ritual activities that form the core of traditional Zen monastic life. This article concerns one such ritual that has become a mark of modern Japanese Sōtō Zen: the slow walking (*kinhin*) that is done between periods of seated meditation. The super-slow style is unique to Sōtō and can now be seen in places around the world that have been influenced by Sōtō Zen. The precise ritual is thought of as having been passed down in an unbroken transmission from Dōgen (1200–1253), the founding figure who is taken as the source of all Sōtō orthodoxy. If, however, one reads the texts that the lineage has so meticulously preserved, it is clear that the details of this practice were in fact put together about 250 years ago, based on textual scholarship. The way that pieces were carefully assembled to make the rule was never secret, but the ritual was presented in such a way as to divert attention from how it was made and focus the light onto the founding figure of Dōgen. The acceptance of this way of kinhin as being simply Dōgen's teaching is a tribute to both the rhetorical skill and the textual scholarship of the person who was single-hand-edly responsible, Menzan Zuihō (1683–1769). The newly packaged but allegedly old way of kinhin did not gradually evolve from a community of Zen practitioners. Rather, it came from Menzan's *Kinhin-ki*.[1] After an introduction to the historical situation and a survey of the textual background, I present a translation of this short and well-known text, followed by a translation of the *Kinhinkimonge*, Menzan's own commentary, which includes very detailed arguments for his position. These translations are followed by a discussion of their contents and some concluding remarks.[2]

Although it may be translated "walking meditation," in order to distinguish it from seated meditation, kinhin as practiced today is closer to standing still than it is to normal walking. The prescribed procedure is that one should coordinate one's walking with one's breathing so that each tiny half step takes the time for a complete in and out breath. At a casual glance, the walker seems to be standing still, or frozen in mid-step. The practice is taken very seriously among mainstream Sōtō monasteries, and popular Japanese books about Sōtō include diagrams and precise instructions about how to do both seated and walking meditation.[3] As a measure of the influence of Sōtō Zen on the practices of Buddhism in the West, the word "kinhin" and the emphasis on slowness is in widespread use in English language popular books about Zen and about meditation in general. "Kinhin" seems to have broken free of its Japanese roots in the same way as the words "Zen" or "zazen" did earlier and is now used in popular books to mean mindful quiet walking in a circumstance and manner to be freely chosen.[4] This usage is apparently due to the widening ripples of influence from Japanese Sōtō Zen teachers in America, and especially from Shunryū Suzuki and his descendants at the San Francisco Zen Center, which includes an orthodox Sōtō style of slow kinhin as part of its meditation hall practice. The new use of "kinhin" to mean any kind of quiet walking is a recent Western innovation, but this popular usage is much closer to the general Buddhist usage, wherein the same word (which is pronounced *kyōgō* in other Japanese Buddhist schools) simply refers to one of the four possible postures of the Buddha and his followers: sitting, standing, walking, or lying down. Of course, the walking posture should be dignified and collected, but there is nothing in the mainstream texts prescribing the slow creep of Sōtō Zen.

Dōgen does not give kinhin the same detailed treatment he gives to seated meditation, and it is scarcely mentioned in standard writings about monastic ritual. Menzan pieced together the prescription for the ritual described in the *Kinhinki* by picking up phrases here and there out of writings attributed to Dōgen. The bulk of this short text, however, is taken up with his attempt to forge associations between the walking meditation style glimpsed in Dōgen's writings and mainstream Buddhist texts, including two of the most well-known and widely accepted texts of Buddhism: the *Buddhāvataṁsaka Sutra* and the *Lotus Sutra*.

In addition to the *Kinhinki* itself, which is only a page long in the modern edition, Menzan also wrote the *Kinhinki monge* (hereafter *Monge*), a thirteen-page record of his own informal explanations and comments, including long quotes from the texts that he used. In 1739, these two were published by a Kyoto bookstore as a small book, printed from carved wooden blocks. In the *Monge*, Menzan added his own instructions about crucial details and defended these additions with quotes from Chinese and Indian sources. There are also asides that give us a glimpse of what problems Menzan was most concerned about in the practices of Sōtō monks of the day. The *Kinhinki* has continued to be popularly available and can still be purchased in Kyoto from the Baiyōshoin, in the same form as originally published. It was included in such Sōtō compendiums as the 1930 *Zenmon Sōtōshū ten*, as well as in a 1910 compendium of Zen texts called the *Zengaku hōten*, which was used for teaching young students of both Rinzai and Sōtō Zen lineages.[5] The *Zengaku hōten* contains a variety of Zen texts ranging from parts of standard *kōan* collections to pieces by Dōgen (including his *Fukan zazengi* and *Zazen shin*) and Hakuin's *Zazen no wasan*. It is surprising to find a text like the *Kinhinki* in such company, and it bears witness to the lack of other sources for instruction in the ritual of kinhin.

There is even evidence that the influence of the *Kinhinki* spread beyond the confines of Buddhist practice places to a more popular audience. Sekimon Shingaku, a syncretic popular religion, uses rules for seated meditation that appear to have been lifted from Dōgen, and their rules for walking meditation follow almost exactly the wording of the *Kinhinki*. Janine Anderson Sawada comments that the content of the *Kinhinki* "is largely based on Dōgen's writings, which in turn draw on earlier Ch'an sources."[6] This is certainly the impression Menzan intends to make and the way that it is accepted in modern Sōtō. As I argue below, however, there is really nothing except Dōgen's report of the words of his Chinese teacher Ju-ching upon which to base the characteristic Sōtō style, and there is apparently nothing whatsoever in earlier Ch'an sources. Indeed, the whole project of the *Kinhinki* is remarkable because it is an extended textual exegesis of a ritual that Dōgen knew of only because he received the instruction directly from Ju-ching, who claimed that he was the only one left who knew about it. For Menzan, it is quite the opposite. Although he does not say so explicitly, apparently there was no living model for him to refer to, so Menzan was obliged to rely on texts and texts alone to put together the details of kinhin.

The reform of the ritual of walking was just one very small part of Menzan's lifelong efforts to change Sōtō practice and doctrine by rooting out undesirable practices that Menzan saw as not Dōgen's teaching.[7] Menzan was especially concerned about the influence of Ōbaku Zen, a recent import from China that had become very popular and had affected Japanese Zen in many ways.[8] But Menzan went beyond opposing Ōbaku practices and ideas. He also opposed many practices that, although long established as normative in Sōtō training halls, did not follow the teachings that Menzan was discovering in the newly available writings of Dōgen. Dōgen is now so closely identified with Sōtō that it is hard to realize how little was known about him in Menzan's time. Although acknowledged as the first patriarch of Sōtō Zen in Japan, his writings had been practically unread for centuries, and his life story was not well known. In the view of Menzan and other Sōtō reformers, Sōtō monks were not following the way of Dōgen and had become corrupted by later accretions and influences such as Ōbaku Zen. Reformers had the difficult task of rejecting much of what had been passed down to them by their teachers. Menzan revered his teacher Sonnō Sōeki (1645–1705) for his respect for Dōgen, and Sonnō was also the first person to call attention to the differences between Dōgen and Ōbaku, a position that became so important to Menzan.[9] Presumably, Menzan learned something about walking meditation from Sonnō and other contemporary teachers, but whatever this may have been is simply passed over in silence in his explanations in the *Monge*. Sonnō's death when Menzan was only twenty-two years old was a great loss, but Sonnō's absence may have freed Menzan to make reforms that entailed discarding much of the customary lore he had learned from his teacher.

The Sōtō reform movement began in 1700 when a group of Sōtō leaders made appeals to the government about dharma transmission, the ceremonial authentication of the status of a Zen teacher. They drew the government's attention to the 1615 government ruling that Sōtō must follow the house rules of the head temple, Eiheiji. The ruling was much like similar decrees that had been issued to other Buddhist schools, but since there was no written set of house rules for Eiheiji, the reformers now made the claim that Dōgen's writings, all of them, should be taken as the house rules. They mined Dōgen's writings for selections to support their claim that the current customs of the Sōtō school were not following the house rules, that is, the texts of Dōgen. The contemporary residents of Eiheiji, on the other hand, claimed the authority of being the direct lineal descendants of Dōgen and the protectors of his monastery, which had preserved details of his practice. They resisted having their long-established customs overturned with textual evidence, even if the texts were those of Dōgen. The government eventually agreed to support the group that proposed dharma transmission reforms based on textual evidence, despite the heavy opposition from many leaders of the Sōtō school.[10]

Once the writings of Dōgen had been recognized as Eiheiji house rules, the reformers had a tremendous reservoir of textual material to use, and the conservative side was in turn obliged to look for textual support for their position. The arguments by opposing sides in the many disputes of this era were the beginning of the trend toward making the words of Dōgen the anchor point of any Sōtō doctrinal dispute. Nowadays, the Sōtō school, when referring to itself, usually uses the term *Dōgen Zen*, by which it means the real thing, the undiluted direct teaching of the great ancestor Dōgen that has been transmitted person to person down to the present. As can be seen in the history of the reforms, however, many of the concrete details of the rituals of *Dōgen Zen* were constructed in the eighteenth century, some five hundred years after Dōgen lived. The authority for the new (but presented as old) rituals was the newly edited and studied texts of Dōgen, rather than a contin- uous lineage of teachings passed down from teacher to student. Ironically, the initial campaign to promote the importance of face-to-face transmission of the dharma was based entirely on those long-unread texts. The texts had the authority of being written by Dōgen, but as there was no living tradition of their study and interpretation, their charisma as the teaching of Dōgen came from the historical and textual research of Menzan and others. There is a similar irony in much of Menzan's reforms, including the case of kinhin, as we shall see below.

Menzan became one of the leading figures in this spreading reform movement, especially in the area of monastic life. His interpretations were eventually put into practice at Eiheiji and were widely influential in the Sōtō school. Menzan saw himself in the role of a reactionary innovator. He wanted to thoroughly change the way things were done by taking monastic practice back to doing things the old true way of the Sung dynasty era Buddhism that Dōgen had witnessed and transmitted to Japan. Menzan rejected the teaching of recent Chinese masters, however much others might have respected them. Menzan's writings about rituals of monastic life need to be understood in the context of this campaign to return to the early ways of Dōgen and the texts of his times, and to counter the recent reforms based on Ōbaku models. For Menzan, the standard for monastic life was Dōgen's writings and especially the *Ch'an-yüan ch'ing-kuei* (1103), the rule book for Zen monastic life that was in use in China when Dōgen was there. Dōgen frequently refers to the text and indeed defers to it for the many monastic specifics that he did not write about.[11] Similarly, Menzan relied on it in his other writings about monastic practice; but in the case of kinhin, the *Ch'an-yüan ch'ing-kuei* has almost nothing to say. Furthermore, there are only scattered and incomplete refer- ences to kinhin to be found in Dōgen's works. As is discussed below, Menzan was forced to widen his scope quite significantly and to go far afield to

construct the instructions for a ritual that has come to be a hallmark of
Sōtō Zen.

Sources for the Meaning of the Term "Kinhin"

After discussing the meaning of the term "kinhin," I will survey the sources
that were important to Menzan's project, including quotes of relevant passages
given in their entirety. Menzan refers to most of these, but he does so by
plucking phrases from here and there, which obscures the original context. In
this section, I have used existing translations when they are available; but
when Menzan uses these same passages, I translate them again myself, following his interpretation.

The first character of "kinhin" (*kin*) means to pass through (in either time
or space) and also indicates the warp of cloth, the upright thread as opposed to
the horizontal (the woof). The second character (*hin*) also means to go and
often refers to Buddhist practice. As a non-Buddhist compound, the two together mean correct activity, or to pass by or through a place. The mainstream
Buddhist technical meaning is correct walking demeanor, one of the four positions of standing, walking, sitting, or lying down. Mochizuki's *Bukkyō daijiten*, a standard Buddhist encyclopedia, provides quotations from early Buddhist
texts like the Āgamas and Four Part Vinaya.[12] In these quotations, the term
indicates walking that is done in a variety of places outside. Menzan provides
extended quotations from most of these same early sources and many others,
and he also relies heavily on another text quoted by the *Bukkyō daijiten*, the *Nan-
hai chi-kuei nei-fa chuan*. This is a record of the travels of the Chinese pilgrim
I-ching to India in the seventh century. The following translation of the relevant
section is by Jung-hsi:

> In the five parts of India, both monks and laymen are in the habit of
> taking a walk, going straight forward and coming back along the
> same route at proper times when they feel like it, but they do not take
> walks in noisy places. First it cures diseases, and second it helps
> digestion. When noontime is approaching, or when the sun is to the
> west, it is time to take a walk. They may either go out of the mon-
> astery for a long walk, or just stroll slowly in the corridor. If one does
> not do so, one is liable to suffer from illness, being often troubled by
> swelling of the legs and of the stomach, or pain in the elbows or in
> the shoulders, or with phlegmatic symptoms which will not dissolve.
> All these ailments are caused by our sedentary posture. If one can

take this exercise, one will have a healthy body and increase one's spiritual cultivation.

The most detailed description in the early texts is found in the *Hsiu-ch'an yao-chüeh*. Menzan makes extensive use of this text, which purports to be a T'ang era record of questions and answer sessions with Buddhapālita, an Indian monk:

> He asked what do you call the manner of going? He replied: "Going is kinhin. It is good for it to be a level place, about fourteen or fifteen paces to twenty-two paces. Do kinhin inside this length. When you do kinhin, cover the left hand. Fold the thumb into the palm, and with the remaining four fingers grasp the thumb making a fist. Next cover it with the right hand, grasping the left arm. Then stand straight for a short time and collect the mind and concentrate. (That is, for example, concentrate on the tip of the nose.) Then walk. Go back and forth, neither very fast nor very slow. When you walk, just collect your mind and walk. When you get to the boundary (of the measured area), turn around following the sun (turn your body properly), face where you came from, and stand still for a short time. Then return, walking just like before. When walking keep the eyes open, when stopped the eyes should be closed. If you tire from walking a long time in this way then rest for a bit from kinhin. Do it only during the day, do not do it at night."... Someone asked, "What is the difference between walking around a stupa and kinhin?" He replied, "Kinhin is going directly forward, and directly returning. How could it be the same as going around a stupa?"[13]

In the texts of the Zen tradition, there is practically nothing about kinhin to be found before Dōgen. In the *Ch'an-yüan ch'ing-kuei*, there are two passing references: "When you do kinhin in the corridor, do not talk or laugh aloud," and "When doing kinhin be silent."[14] The *Ju-chung jih-yung* of 1209 merely mentions in passing that one of the things one can do if there is free time is to do kinhin in the tea hall.[15] The *Zenrin shōkisen*, a Zen dictionary by the Tokugawa era scholar-monk Mujaku Dōchū, refers to most of the same sources as Mochizuki and adds nothing further for early sources except the above notice of the *Ju-chung jih-yung*.[16]

From the monastic rules sources that were available to Dōgen, it is impossible to conclude much beyond that kinhin was walking done inside or under the eaves during free time. Furthermore, there is little to support my translation of "do kinhin," which follows modern Japanese Sōtō usage.

Simply "walking" is a better translation for these texts, since there is no evidence that anything besides walking in a way appropriate to the monastic setting is implied. There is a real gap between the kinhin of contemporary Sōtō and these pre-Dōgen descriptions of walking.

For Menzan, Dōgen's words about kinhin are the primary authority, but as he laments in the opening passage of the *Monge*, there is no systematic description of kinhin to be found in Dōgen's writings. The *Kinhinki* is intended to address that unfortunate gap and is explicitly modeled on Dōgen's work devoted to a description of seated meditation, the *Fukan zazengi*.[17] Menzan builds the core of his text from the scattered and not always consistent passages that appear in various places in Dōgen's works.

In the "Gyōji 1" chapter of Dōgen's *Shōbōgenzō*, the word "kinhin" first appears in the story of Bodhidharma walking (kinhin) to Mt. Sung in a passage that Dōgen is quoting from the *Lin-chien lu*, printed in 1107.[18] This passage is also quoted at the beginning of the "Butsudō" chapter and is used by Menzan in order to assert that the practice of kinhin was done by Bodhidharma. Dōgen never makes that kind of claim, and it seems highly unlikely that Bodhidharma walked across China at the pace of a tiny half-step for every in and out breath. The word "kinhin" also appears in the sense of walking in a monastic setting (not just walking to somewhere) near the end of the same "Butsudō" chapter after a series of stories about the high level of practice under Ju-ching. Dōgen relates the story of the visiting Taoists, who vowed to not return home until they had attained the Buddha way:

> Ju-ching was extremely pleased, and had them do the practice of kinhin along with the assembly. He had them line up separately after the nuns.[19]

This passage suggests that kinhin was a separate activity suitable for outsiders like Taoists and foreigners, including Dōgen. Perhaps the reason that Ju-ching placed so much emphasis on it when teaching Dōgen was because it was something Dōgen could do by himself, being an outsider like the Taoists.

In the *Bendōhō*, which is one of the texts later collected in the *Eihei shingi*, there are two brief descriptions of how to walk when leaving one's meditation seat. The word "kinhin" does not appear; rather, slow walk (*kanpo*) is used. It appears that kinhin and *kanpo*, here and elsewhere, are used interchangeably. I translate only the first passage since the second adds nothing further. Dōgen describes the procedure for leaving one's place in the monks hall to go to the washroom during morning meditation. After getting down from the seat:

Do not let the feet get ahead and the body behind. Move body and feet together. Look directly ahead at the ground one fathom ahead. The measure of the pace is equal to the instep of the foot. Be as though standing in one place, as though not moving forward. It is splendid to move slowly, walking in magnificent ease and quiet. Do not make noise with your slippers and rudely distract the assembly. When you are walking, clasp both hands together, putting them inside the sleeves. Do not let the sleeves dangle down to the right and left near your feet.[20]

Note that the walk described is for leaving the hall, not for taking a break from zazen, which is the contemporary usage. The *Fushuku hanpō*, also collected in the *Eihei shingi*, says that after the meal is finished: "They leave the hall in the same manner that they entered it: one breath for each half step (this is in the *Hōkyōki*). This is the way to leave meditation and begin walking."[21]

Based on these passages from Dōgen, kinhin is to be done with the hands held together inside the sleeves, and one should walk slowly, half a step at a time, almost as if standing still. This is the prescribed way of leaving one's place, but it would surely be an incredibly slow way to move about in a large training monastery. There is nothing about matching the speed of the walk to the breath.

By far the most important source is the *Hōkyōki*, a text discovered after Dōgen's death that purports to be the record of Dōgen's time in China. Menzan accepted it as an authentic record of Dōgen's trip and of Ju-ching's teaching, and I will ignore modern doubts about its authenticity, which are not relevant to the task at hand. There are three brief passages about walking meditation that contain instructions similar to what is seen in the *Bendōhō* but provide more detail, apparently using the terms "*kanpo*" and "*kinhin*" interchangeably. The translation here is by James Kodera, using his section numbers for reference:

#12. The slow walk consists of one step per breath. Take a step without looking at your feet, without bending over or looking up. Viewed from the side, it would seem that you are standing in one spot, [for] you must not move nor shake your shoulders or chest. Ju-ching often walked back and forth between the east and the west in the Ta-kuang-ming-tsang Hall to demonstrate this to Dōgen. He then remarked: "Nowadays, I am the only one who knows [the importance of] this slow walk meditation. If you should ask the abbots of all corners of the world, you will surely discover that others do not yet know it."

#28. Ju-ching taught with compassion: "When you get up from the sitting posture and walk, you must practice the method of one breath per half a step. This means: as you move your foot, let it not exceed half a step, and be sure to pace yourself to the length of one breath."

#46. Ju-ching taught: "If you wish to rise from the sitting posture and walk [in meditation], do not walk in circles [nyōho], but in a straight line. If you wish to turn around after twenty or thirty steps, make sure to turn right and not left. And when you move your feet, move the right foot first, then the left."[22]

These passages clearly describe the slow and seemingly motionless walk and the use of the breath to regulate the speed that has become a Sōtō trademark. The Hōkyōki indicates that kinhin can be done for its own sake, not just to leave the hall, apparently whenever one needs to take a break from sitting. Ju-ching also emphasizes that this is not a circular walk. The term that is used here for the prohibited circular walk, nyōho, is not a standard Buddhist term, but as we shall see, Menzan reads it as equivalent to the standard term nyōgyō, which means to circumambulate a Buddha image or stupa.

Although not by Dōgen, there is a relevant passage in the Zazen yōjinki by Keizan (1268–1325), a towering figure of early Sōtō history. It was first published in 1680 with a preface by Manzan Dōhaku, soon after the first compilation of the Eihei shingi. "After only a hundred paces or less, you will certainly get rid of sleepiness. The way to do kinhin is one breath per half step. Walk as though not walking, silently and without motion. This is kinhin."[23] This seems to describe an individual choice to be done when necessary to wake up during seated meditation, not part of a group routine. Although Menzan quotes this passage at the beginning of the Monge, he does not further refer to it, nor does he incorporate it into his instructions, which have nothing to do with warding off sleep.

From these quotations it is clear that Dōgen and Ju-ching are teaching something that is not attested elsewhere: a very slow walk strictly coordinated with the breath. There is no prescribed time for kinhin, just that it is the way to leave the hall. The level of detail about posture and ritual movements is not comparable to the precise ritual instructions available from Dōgen and others concerning zazen. Although it is possible to find some of the missing details from the much earlier Nan-hai chi-kuei nei-fa chuan and the Hsiu-ch'an yao-chüeh, these texts also directly contradict the super slow walk and say nothing about the coordination with breathing. Menzan's task was to find a way to put together this jumble of disconnected comments and asides into a coherent and inspiring description of the ritual of kinhin. He needed to write a text that was sufficiently similar to the writing style of Dōgen to be accepted and to provide enough textual evidence in his commentary to claim that the details were authentic.

The Text of the *Kinhinki*

The following translation is based on the woodblock edition of 1739, using a recently printed copy from the bookstore Baiyōshoin in Kyoto. This modern "reprint" was pressed from the same woodblocks that were carved for the original edition. The bracketed page numbers in the text, however, are to the standard modern printed version in the *Sōtōshū zensho*, which is identical to the woodblock in all but the most trivial details.[24] The *Kinhinki* was originally published along with Menzan's own commentary, the *Kinhinkimonge*. The commentary first quotes a section of the *Kinhinki* (in boldface type in my translation) and then discusses the sources and meaning of that passage. Thus, for example, the first section of the commentary is an explanation of the title. The comments in parentheses are Menzan's own interlinear notes, and the passages in square brackets are my additions to make the English read more naturally. The citations for the forty-two texts that Menzan uses are listed with the endnotes.

Kinhinki

The Buddha said, "First I sit in the practice place, contemplate the tree, and do kinhin." This is definitely the origin of kinhin, as a part of seated meditation. This way of kinhin was passed down from the time of T'ien-t'ung Ju-ching to our First Ancestor, face to face, nearly half a thousand years ago. But the standards of our house have collapsed and these latter descendants are benighted. Many of them have dashed off into unorthodox dead ends. Alas, how can this be anything but a disaster? This has persisted even until the present day. Therefore, taking the intention of our Ancestor as my basis, I searched widely in the ancient traces. I have taught a little of this to students, with the hope that we do not drift into the bustle of the practices of another family.

The way of kinhin that is to be wished for is to clasp both hands in front of the chest [*isshu*] (it should be just like this), putting them inside the sleeves, and not letting the sleeves fall down near the feet to the right and left. Look directly one fathom ahead (about six or seven feet). When walking properly, use the breath as measure: a half step is taken in the time of one breath (in and out). The measure of the pace is equal to the instep of the foot (the back of the foot). Do not let the feet get ahead and the body behind. Move body and feet together. Do not look around right and left or gaze up and down. Do not move your chest and shoulders. Do not make noise by dragging your slippers. Be as though standing in one place, as though not moving forward. It is splendid to move slowly, walking in magnificent ease and quiet. This is the meaning of what we call slow walking. If you high step or take big strides, if you run quickly or gallop, that is improper and you may be censured.

Of old, Koṭi Putara did kinhin and did not tire. Blood from his feet sprinkled the earth. The Buddha said, "If Putara does kinhin so vigorously, such as to grind Mt. Sumeru to dust, he will not be able to attain the way. And furthermore it will harm the feet. Truly this is to be carefully avoided." You should know about selecting the place. You should know that the place has its measure. And you should know the time for it. Know that it is different from going around in a circle. Go straight ahead and return straight, following just one path. It is like the warp [kin] of the cloth. That is why it is called kinhin. When you get to the boundary (of the measured area), turn around following the sun (turn your body properly), face where you came from, and stand still for a short time.

In the Ch'u yao ching it says there are five virtues. In the Ta-pi-ch'iu san-ch'ien wei-i ching it explains five things. You must not fail to know that if you vigorously work on this, it will greatly benefit your physical constitution and bring your practice to fulfilment. Of old it was said that the original locations for the kinhin of the World Honored One are at the foot of Vulture Peak and below the tree of awakening, in the deer park and Rājagṛha, and in other places where there are traces of the sage. And it also says that Bodhidharma did kinhin at the foot of Mt. Sung. How can we fail to honor the excellent example of the Buddhas and Ancestors?

In the Buddhāvataṁsaka Sutra it says, Sudhana saw Sudarśana Bhikṣu, in the grove going straight forward [kinhin], stopping, and returning. His wisdom vision is expansively broad like the great sea. His mind is unmoved by any of the objects of experience. He goes beyond them all, whether the state of being subdued or excited, with or without knowing, turning and moving, or being caught up in words. He has attained the realm of the nondual which the Buddha realized, and ceaselessly converts sentient beings with great compassion and remains without thoughts. From the wish to benefit and comfort all sentient beings, from the wish to teach the eye of the teaching of the Tathāgata, to tread the path taken by the Tathāgata, he does the true kinhin, neither fast nor slow. Sudhana explained saying, "When I do kinhin, in one thought moment, all the four quarters, each and every one is before me because of the purity of my wisdom. In one thought all the realms, each and every one is before me. It passes beyond the ineffable, and the realm of the ineffable." He also said, "Good man, I know only this teaching of liberation, the flame upon which the Bodhisattvas rely." If you see it this way, this is what our first patriarch passed down face to face.

This meaning fits the teaching of the sage like two lips coming together, without the slightest deviation, and thus it is the true transmission of the Buddhas and Ancestors. Ah me, the people of this degenerate latter age truly can rejoice that due to causes from past lives they can receive this teaching. Just preserve the breathing in and breathing out, clearly observe the forward step and the trailing step. Without pursuing conditions, and not abiding in dismal emptiness, the empty [mind] is bright and self-illuminating, and the power of the mind is not impeded. He is named the Tathāgata of the Boundless Tranquil Slow Walk. Ah, how could he be far away? If you turn away from this, you have slipped off the true path before you have even taken a step. You certainly should fully master in detail what is practiced in my assembly.

Kinhinkimonge

Kinhinki

This title indicates an addition to the *Zazengi*. The great teaching is that seated meditation and kinhin, moving and quiet, are not two. However, we have only the *Fukan zazengi* [*General Rule for Seated Meditation*] of our Ancestor [Dōgen], and the manner of kinhin has not been described in detail. So I have composed this *Kinhinki* [*Standard for Walking Meditation*] to supplement it. Just as these two words, "rule" and "standard," follow close together, I have written this *Standard* to go with the *Rule*. In the dictionary it says the pronunciation is "ki" and the meaning is rut. When the cart goes back and forth, there are tracks. The first cart goes, and if the following cart does not follow the tracks, then the way will be difficult. However, if the first track is taken as the rule, then the others can proceed without hindrance. The dictionary says it means the law or the rule. There is also the meaning that this kinhin is to be respected as the trace of the Buddhas and Ancestors, and we should not fall into the unlawful evil ways.

The Buddha said, "First I sit in the practice place, contemplate the tree, and do kinhin."

This is two stanzas from the "Expedient Means" chapter of the *Lotus Sutra*. In the commentary [*Miao-fa liang-hua wen-chü* of Chih-I], it says,

The main reason for the "First I sit in the practice place," is that it was an informal event, not a particular time, and it was at first for teaching people. "Practice place" is translated that way because the first time he practiced in this place he attained the way. He sat under this tree and attained awakening, so it is called the tree of awakening. He recognized the influence of the tree and so he mindfully gazed at the tree. He was aware of the virtue of the location, and so he did kinhin. There is fundamentally no separation between the tree and the location, but one must respect their origins. As it says in the marvelous teachings, "Respecting the origins is just teaching the people and transmitting the dharma." Regarding the mind is like the great tree trunk of the twelve conditions of the tree. If you deeply regard conditioned arising, then you will naturally attain awakening. It is called contemplating the tree because he wished to benefit people with the doctrine of awakening, like the shade of the tree. Kinhin is among the practices of the Great Vehicle, it is the walking practice, and one naturally takes on this way of practice. The place to do it is where the Buddha way is attained. This practice is done from the desire to save people.

This is the explanation of the commentator on the truth of the text. I understand what he is saying, but it is mincing of words by a scholastic. Where it says, "When I first sit in the practice place," this means to just sit in correct posture. And "contemplate the tree" means to see without entangling oneself. "Kinhin" means the slow walk, the normative practice of all the Buddhas of the three times, the Buddha wisdom vision that reveals the entry to awakening.

This is definitely the origin of kinhin, as a part of seated meditation.

"This" refers to the prior quotation, which says that in the teaching of the Buddha, kinhin definitely goes along with seated meditation, which is how the Tathāgata himself did it.

This way of kinhin was passed down from the time of T'ien-t'ung Ju-ching to our First Ancestor, face to face, nearly half a thousand years ago. But the standards of our house have collapsed and these latter descendants are benighted.

[626] "This" means the kinhin of the Buddha. "Way" is the proper method for kinhin. The character for "First" means the very first bud of a plant, so it means here the First Ancestor. In the *Book of Documents* it says, "It goes right back to the First Ancestor." "Face to face" is not a matter of seeing and hearing as in books. It means one face and another face, mutually illuminating, and passing down. The authenticity is attested in the Hōkyōki, in the following passages.

The Master of the Hall taught, "If you wish to get up after seated meditation to do kinhin, you must not walk in a circle, but in a straight line. If you wish to turn around after twenty to thirty paces, you must turn to the right, not to the left. When you begin to walk, the right foot is first, then the left foot."

The traces of the kinhin of the Tathāgata after he arose from seated meditation can now be seen in India in Udyāna.

When you arise from seated meditation and walk, you should use the method of one breath to one half pace. That is to say you should not have your pace more than the length of half a foot, and the time you are moving your foot should span the time of a breath.

For monks living in the monks hall, kinhin is a most important technique. Among the teachers of recent times, there are many who do not know about this, indeed few know about it. Walk slowly, using the breath as the measure of the movement of the feet. Do not look at your feet. Move without bending over or looking up. Looked at from the side, it is as if you were standing in one place. Do not move or shake your chest nor your shoulders and so forth.

Ju-ching walked from east to west in the Ta-kuang-ming-tsang time after time to show this to Dōgen. He said, "Nowadays I am the only one who knows about this slow walk. If you were to enquire of the Zen teachers everywhere, you will certainly find that no one else knows it."

"Walk" means slow walking, and all these expressions mean kinhin. "Ta-kuang-ming-tsang" is the honorific name referring to Ju-ching's quarters. You can see here the expression "walked from east to west," which means to go from east to west and from west to east, doing kinhin back and forth. This is the standard. And when entering and leaving the monks hall also kinhin is to be done. The *Eihei shingi* has the following passages.[25]

The proper demeanor for leaving the hall is the same as when entering: one breath to half a step, as in the *Hōkyōki* description of how people should walk after meditation.

If you wish to arise from sitting, move slowly and slowly get down from your seat. Do not lift your feet high, nor take big steps and walk fast. And do not make noise dragging your slippers.

When you are leaving or entering, do not look at the back of the heads of those who are doing seated meditation. Just keep your head down and go. Do not put the foot first and the body after, but move body and feet together. Walk with your gaze directly ahead about six feet, with a pace the length of your instep. To proceed so very slowly and quietly is magnificent. It is just like standing still, like walking without moving. Do not drag your slippers and make noise, which would lack respect for the assembly. While walking, you should clasp both hands together and put them inside the sleeves, but you must not let the sleeves dangle to the left and right near your feet.

This is the face-to-face detailed teaching that we have received. In addition to this, in Teacher Keizan's *Zazen yōjinki*, he explains a number of expedient methods.

If you are still not awakened, get up and do kinhin. After only a hundred paces or less, you will certainly get rid of sleepiness. The way to do kinhin is one breath per half step, walking as if not walking.

"T'ien-t'ung" [Heavenly Child] is the name of a mountain. During the Ch'ing era, the monk I-hsing lived there, and the spirit of the Venus Star in the guise of a child came to serve him. So it came to be called Heavenly Child Mountain or Venus Mountain, as can be seen in *Ta-ming I-t'ung-chih* gazetteer. "From the time of" is understood in that way by Lu in the *Wen-hsüan*, who says "From the time of that elegant poetry." [627] "Nearly" means approximately. "Half of one thousand years" means five hundred. It has been about four hundred and eighty years since the passing of our Ancestor, so it is "nearly." "The standards of our house" means the teachings that are used only for our house, not in some other, like the *Yen-shih chia-hsün* or the *Chu-hsi chia-hsün*. And in the *Eihei kōroku* it says, "The small assembly is an excellent part of our house standards." The way of kinhin that has been passed down face to face from Ju-ching is the house standard of the Eihei school. "Collapsed" means that what was high has now been leveled, it has been knocked down to flatness, it is worn out and disused. "Latter descendants" is defined in the dictionary as grandchild or great grandchild and so forth until there is a cloud of descendants. The descendants in the present age have discarded the teachings of the ancestors and are in the dark about kinhin.

Many of them have dashed off into unorthodox dead ends. Alas, how can this be anything but a disaster?

The slow walk that was the true and direct transmission has been forgotten and the great way has been thrown into darkness. The assembly of monks laments that we are dashing around in the bad ways of heterodoxy.

This has persisted even until the present day. Therefore, taking the intention of our Ancestor as my basis, I searched widely in the ancient traces. I have taught a little of this to students, with the hope that we do not drift into the bustle of the practices of another family.

The lamenting continued, but nothing was done to stop the practice. My vow was simply to make known the original intention of the Ancestor, and to show in various ways the correct understanding of the standards of our house. I took the intention of our Ancestor as the basis, and excerpted and collected widely from the teachings of former sages for supplementary detail. I explained some of this and have written this *Kinhinki* and taught it to the students who came to me for advice. The word "bustle" is used in the Blissful Practices Chapter [of the *Lotus Sutra*]: "Gently, modestly, and not bustling." The dictionary explains that it means quickly and in a frenzy, or going in circles. It means to run back and forth like dogs and horses, in an unruly way. And now the house standard of the serene, hidden way of our ancestors has declined and become like the uncouth ways of the other schools. "My hope" implies that we should put our sincere effort toward preserving the teaching lest in the future we will bustle around like dogs and horses.

The way of kinhin that is to be wished for is to clasp both hands in front of the chest [isshu] *(it should be just like this), putting them inside the sleeves, and not letting the sleeves fall down near the feet to the right and left.*

These eighteen characters are the words of Dōgen as seen earlier. The interlineal note, "You should do it this proper way," means that pressing the palms together, whether bowing, or with hands in *isshu*, or *shashu* are all done in the same way with hands at the chest. To have them lower at the waist is not correct. In the *Shuo-wen* it says, "Hands coming together at the chest is called *isshu*." Nowadays, one faction of clerics do *shashu* with the hands at the waist. People of Nagasaki say that Chinese whores walk swinging to right and left so this is not the correct style. [628] Concerning the hand position of kinhin, the *Hsiu-ch'an yao-chüeh* of Buddhapālita says:

> When you do kinhin, cover the left hand. Fold the thumb into
> the palm, and with the remaining four fingers grasp the thumb
> making a fist. Next cover [it with] the right hand, grasping the left
> arm. Then stand straight for a short time and collect the mind
> and concentrate (for example, concentrate on the tip of the nose).
> Then walk.

This is the correct way. The truth of this hand position [*mudra*] is an oral transmission.

Look directly one fathom ahead (about six or seven feet).

These eight characters are also the words of the Founder, as seen before. The dictionary says that a fathom is six or eight feet. The number of feet in a fathom is not fixed. In the *Ch'an-yao* of Śubhākarasiṃha it says to look ahead six feet. So it is good to look ahead about six to seven feet. Look with eyes half open, half shut, and level, that is the standard. "Look directly" means to look straight ahead, not to the side.

When walking properly, use the breath as measure: a half step is taken in the time of one breath (in and out). The measure of the pace is equal to the instep of the foot (the back of the foot).

In the dictionary it says that a step is one foot, and twice that is a pace. And in the *Tzu-hui*, "Two feet is called a pace." Combining the front pace and the following pace together makes one pace. In the previous quotations there was: "use the breath as measure," and "a half step is taken in the time of one breath," and also, "the measure of the pace is equal to the instep of the foot." All of these are the words of the Ancestor. The interlinear note of "One inhale and one exhale makes one breath" is the entry about breath from the *Wan-ping wei-ch'un.* "The back of the foot is the sole," is the entry about "sole" from the *Hung-wu Cheng-yün.* The Japanese reading is "ashi no kō." This means that in the interval of one in and one out breath, you move one foot, this is one pace. The measure of this pace is the length of the sole of the foot. In the *Sarvastivadavinaya* it says, "When there is discomfort get up and go, the way a goose walks." This is kinhin.[26]

Do not let the feet get ahead and the body behind. Move body and feet together.

These twelve characters, as we saw before, are the words of the Patriarch. They are easy to understand.

Do not look around right and left or gaze up and down.

The first verse means to look straight ahead, and the second is from the Founder's words, "You must not look up and down as you walk."

Do not move your chest and shoulders. Do not make noise by dragging your slippers.

In the words of the Patriarch, "Shoulders, chest, and so forth, must not move with a wobble and shake." He also said, "You should not make a noise with your toilet slippers."

Be as though standing in one place, as though not moving forward. It is splendid to move slowly, walking in magnificent ease and quiet.

Of these ten characters, eight were seen earlier in two places. They are the easily understood words of our Ancestor.

This is the meaning of what we call slow walking.

The eight characters are based on the words of our Ancestor seen above. The meaning is seen in the name itself. [629]

If you high step or take big strides, if you run quickly or gallop, that is improper and you may be censured.

This is following the words of our Ancestor seen earlier. "High Step" means to lift the foot up high and walk. "Big step" means to stride widely.

"Quickly" means to walk in a busy way. "Gallop" means to run like a horse. These are all improper and so you should be careful about them.

Of old, Koṭi Putara did kinhin and did not tire. Blood from his feet sprinkled the earth. The Buddha said, "If Putara does kinhin so vigorously, such as to grind Mt. Sumeru to dust, he will not be able to attain the way. And furthermore it will harm the feet. Truly this is to be carefully avoided."

This is from the *Mahāsāṅghikavinaya*, chapter thirty-one.

> He had recently left home, and did kinhin in the graveyard tirelessly, such that the soles of his feet were lacerated, and blood flowed onto the ground. The Buddha saw this and understanding what had happened, he asked a bhikṣu, "Who is it that has done kinhin here such that blood has flowed out like this?" The bhikṣu replied, "This is the place where Koṭi Putara did kinhin." Buddha instructed the bhikṣu, "If Koṭi Putara or anyone does kinhin with vigor as if to pulverize Mt. Sumeru into dust, he will not be able to attain the way. Moreover alas, he will harm his skin."

The end of this long passage is omitted. The name is read as Koṭi Putara because the Chinese translation uses the number one hundred times a hundred million. The Sanskrit word *koṭi* [means a large number, but is used as a name] in Vinaya texts and also in the *Ch'an-lin lei-chu*. The Tathāgata warned Koṭi Putara against doing kinhin so much that blood dripped from his feet to the ground, and against walking fast, galloping like a horse. Improper kinhin is to be carefully avoided.

You should know about selecting the place.

In the *Mahāsāṅghikavinaya*, chapter thirty-five, it says:

> "You should not do kinhin in front of bhikṣus who are doing seated meditation, or in front of the assembly of monks, teachers and preceptors or elders." And it also says, "When you walk, you should not walk behind [the elders] when you return, but keep the face to the right and return. If you are doing kinhin together with teachers and preceptors, you should not be in front of them or lined up beside them, but follow behind. When you return, you should not return in front, but rather face towardthe right and turn behind them. You should not do kinhin in front of prostitutes, in front of gamblers, sellers of alcohol, sellers of meat from animals slaughtered for sale, jailers, or murderers."

This text is the evidence for selecting the place.

You should know that the place has its measure.

In the *Hsiu-ch'an yao-chüeh* it says: "He asked what do you call the manner of going? He replied, 'Going is kinhin. It is good for it to be a level place, about fourteen or fifteen paces to twenty-two paces. Do kinhin inside this length.'" A pace means to pick up the feet twice, so the length of a pace for an average man is about one foot five inches, and twenty-two paces comes to about three fathoms and three feet. Also, in the *Ch'an-yao* of Śubhākara-siṁha: "You people doing meditation, you should also know about how to do kinhin. In a quiet place, make a level and clean surface. The length is twenty-five cubits." Cubit means one foot eight inches. In the *Fan-i ming-i-chi* it says four cubits is about five feet. Also in the *Nan-hai chi-kuei nei-fa chuan* [630] it says, "The width is about two cubits, the length is about fourteen or fifteen cubits, and the height is two cubits or more. Make it by piling up paving tiles." This is about three fathoms. These three cases are roughly the same as the Japanese measurement of five *kan* to eight or nine *kan*. Now we do kinhin under the eaves of the monks hall, so of course the right way is to adapt to that dimension.

And you should know the time for it.

In the *Hsiu-ch'an yao-chüeh*, it says, "Kinhin is only to be done during the day, do not do it at night." The *Nan-hai chi-kuei nei-fa chuan* says, "Do kinhin in the forenoon and afternoon." This means to do it only during mid-day, not at night. This is the practice of monks and laypeople in India and China. In the *Lotus Sutra* it says, "Seeing that the disciples were still experiencing sleepiness, they did kinhin in the grove and vigorously pursued the Buddha Way." So the vigorously practicing disciples of the Buddha did kinhin at night. And in the *Ching-te ch'uan-teng lu* Chapter Fourteen, in the biography of Yüeh-shan, it says, "One night the Teacher climbed the mountain and did kinhin." According to this, it is not limited to midday. However, in the *Hsiu-ch'an yao-chüeh* and *Nan-hai chi-kuei nei-fa chuan* mentioned earlier, the time is fixed.

Know that it is different from going around in a circle.

In the *Shih-shih yao-lan* it says, "I say that circular walking is the highest form of showing respect." And again, in the *Shih-wei ching* it explains the five felicities of going around. Because this is to go around a Buddha or a stupa, it is called going around or walking in a circle or going in a path. It means to rely on and respect. And so it is called "highest form of showing respect." And in the *Nan-hai chi-kuei nei-fa chuan* it says, "In the case of circling with the Buddha Hall on the right, or going around a caitya, this is different. It is for making merit, and basically one desires to show respect. Kinhin on the other hand means to extinguish tension and to loosen up, which nourishes the body." Going around originally meant to revere and respect the three treasures. Three rounds, seven rounds, up to a hundred, a thousand rounds. All this is for the production of merit. Kinhin is to go straight, to get rid of stuffiness and revive one's spirits, to revitalize. There is a great difference between them.

The *Ta-pi-ch'iu san-ch'ien wei-i ching* explains twenty-five things about circumambulating a stupa, and then it has five things about kinhin, in two separate explanations. In the *Hsiu-ch'an yao-chüeh*, it says, "Someone asked, 'What is the difference between walking around a stupa and kinhin?' He replied, 'Kinhin is going directly forward, and directly returning. How could it be the same as going around a stupa?'" That is how you should understand the essence of this. Nonetheless, the Ming Zen monks mistakenly took up the practice of the preaching clerics, which was recalling the Buddha's name while circumambulating the Amida in the Hall of the Sixteen Reflections. They mistook this walking in circles for the kinhin of the old rules of our teaching. It was explained in this way when it was brought to Japan and now everyone says that kinhin is walking in a circle, a most unfortunate bad habit. We should establish the patriarchal practice, lest even people who can tell black from white become confused.

Go straight ahead and return straight, following just one path.

[631] These eight characters are from the *Nan-hai chi-kuei nei-fa chuan*. It says, "In India, both lay and clerics often do kinhin. They go straight ahead and return straight, following just one way." I extracted these characters, which mean to go straight and return on one path.

It is like the warp [kin] of the cloth. That is why it is called kinhin.

These eight characters are from the second chapter of the *Shih-shih yao-lan*. "He explained with compassion, 'In the countries to the West, they moisten the ground and they pile up tiles so it becomes a path. They go and come in the middle. Because it is like the warp of cloth, it is called 'warp-walk.'" The eight characters are excerpted and used here. The word "warp" goes along with "woof," and is pronounced "tatenuki" in Japanese. It is the up-and-down, left-and-right of the thread of the loom.

When you get to the boundary (of the measured area), turn around following the sun (turn your body properly), face where you came from, and stand still for a short time.

These sixteen characters are taken directly from the *Hsiu-ch'an yao-chüeh*. The phrase in the original interlineal note "of the measured area" refers to the length of the place of kinhin, which was quoted earlier. "Turn your body properly" means the correct way is to turn facing the south, like the sun. "Face where you came from" means to face the place where you started walking. "Stand for a short time" means that of the four postures of walking, stopping, sitting, and sleeping, it is the stopping. The mistake was in taking stopping for sitting.[27] The reason is that he did not understand the four postures, which are divided into either moving or being still, and divided again to become four postures. To rest from walking is stopping, and to rest from sitting is lying down. As spring to summer, and fall to winter, there are four positions in order. You should understand it like the two positions of yin and yang. One who does not understand kinhin is ignorant of what stopping means. The proper understanding of "stop and stand" means to stand still and not move for a "short time." Likewise, these words all mean for a little while... [list of synonyms]. For that amount of time, you should practice it, this is the standard explanation. Now to fix the duration of the "short while" [hsü-yü, the last of the synonyms], we turn to a quotation from the third chapter of the *Fa-yüan chu-lin*. One *kṣana* is translated as one thought moment. One hundred and twenty *kṣana* make one *tat-kṣana*, which is translated as one blink. Sixty *tat-kṣana* make one breath. One breath is one *lava*. Thirty *lava* make one *mara*, which is translated as a short while. Therefore this "short while" is thirty breaths duration. The practice that accords with the explanation of the sages is to stand in one place for this duration, for the measure of thirty breaths in and thirty breaths out.

In the Ch'u yao ching it says there are five virtues.

The *Ch'u yao ching* has twenty volumes, and was put together by Vasumitra Dharmatrāta and translated by Chu Fu-nien. In volume eighteen, it says:

> As explained by the Buddha in the Sutras, those who do kinhin will obtain five virtues. What are these five? The first is endurance for long walks. The second is increase of strength. The third is that food is naturally digested. The fourth is having no sickness. Fifth, the person who does kinhin quickly enters samādhi.

This is the text that is abbreviated for presentation here. Of these five, the first four are worldly virtues that preserve and nourish the bodily form. The last one is a virtue for those leaving the world, and it brings to fulfillment the dharma body. [632]

In the Ta-pi-ch'iu san-ch'ien wei-i ching it explains five things.

In the first chapter of the *San-ch'ien wei-i ching* it says:

> There are five things about kinhin. First, it should be in a quiet place. Second, it should be in front of the door. Third, it should be in front of the lecture hall. Fourth, it should be under the pagoda. Fifth, it should be beneath a large building. There are another five. First, do not sit in meditation in the upper story of a large building. Second, do

not walk holding a staff in the temple. Third, do not chant a sutra aloud while reclining. Fourth, do not wear clogs. Fifth, do not make a noise by lifting up your feet in big steps and stamping on the ground.

The first five are about the place for kinhin. Of the latter five, the first and the third have nothing to do with kinhin. The second means not to do kinhin while holding a staff. In the fourth, the word "shoes" is explained to mean wooden shoes. Now we call them high wooden clogs (geta). These are forbidden because they make so much noise. The fifth one is the same as our Patriarch's explanation about "high step or take big strides, if you run quickly or gallop."

You must not fail to know that if you vigorously work on this, it will greatly benefit your physical constitution and bring your practice to fulfillment.

This teaching of the sages has two aspects [of body and mind]. The phrase "You must not fail to know" is from chapter three of the *Nan-hai chi-kuei nei-fa chuan*:

> You may go outside the temple for extended walking, or you may walk slowly under the eaves. If you do not do this you will have much illness and suffering. Eventually your feet will become swollen, your belly will become swollen, you will have pain in the elbows and in the knees [po] (po in the *Shih-ming* is defined as "knee cap") and there will be a condition of congestion that will not go away.[28] These are all what usually happens. Certainly if one does this practice then one will be able to help the body and bring the way to fulfillment.

I selected the last four characters to represent the meaning of this passage.

Of old it was said that the original locations for the kinhin of the World Honored One are at the foot of Vulture Peak and below the tree of awakening, in the Deer Park and Rājagṙha, and in other places where there are traces of the sage.

"Of old" refers to the *Nan-hai chi-kuei nei-fa chuan*. Vulture Peak is Mt. Gṙdhrakūṭa, in Magadha, and the tree of awakening is the bodhi tree, which is also in Magadha. Bodhi is translated as awakening, and so it is called the tree of awakening. The Deer Park is the Deer Field Park in Vārāṇaśī, and Rājagṙha is the palace of the king in Magadha. These four places are where the Tathāgata lived and therefore are sites of kinhin. As for the other places that have traces of the sages, in the *Hōkyōki*, it says, "The traces of the kinhin of the Tathāgata can now be seen in India in Udyāna." In the biography of Hsüan-tsang in the *Hsü kao-seng chuan*, Hsüan-tsang goes to Ujāna and sees the old traces. Also we read that Hsüan-tsang saw the stone foundations of kinhin of the Four Buddhas of the Great Kalpa in the countries of Mathurā and Kapitha. The Four Buddhas of the Great Kalpa are Krakucchanda Buddha, Kanakamuni Buddha, Kāśapa Buddha, and Śākyamuni Buddha. I-ching also saw these traces, so they all exist. The "foundations" refers to the remains of the foundations, or the ruins of an estate and so forth. In the *Nan-hai chi-kuei nei-fa chuan* it says, "They made figures of blooming lotus flowers about two inches deep and one foot wide. Fourteen or fifteen of these mark the footprints of the Sage." In the biography of Hsüan-tsang it also says, "Everywhere that there were footprints, the mark of the lotus flower appeared."

And it also says that Bodhidharma did kinhin at the foot of Mt. Sung.

[633] "It also says" refers to the words of the *Lin-chien lu*. This text is recommended in the *Hōkyōki* and there is a long quote from it in Chapter Seven of the *Eihei kōroku*. In regard to the name "Bodhidharma," in the *Ching-te ch'uan-teng lu*, "dharma" is explained as "penetrating the great." In translation "bodhi" means to wake up, and "dharma" means the law, so "bodhidharma" means the law of awakening. Thus the poem of Hung-chih says, "The law of awakening is the location of my greatest good." Now I will put this all together into an explanation. To "penetrate" means to go through without obstruction. "Great" means the great teaching. So it means to penetrate the great teaching. Penetrate completely means awakening, which is the same as to awaken to the teaching. Mt. Sung is the common name for the middle peak of the Five Mountains. At the foot of this mountain is Shao-lin Temple, the location of the nine years of wall gazing. There were nine years of seated meditation but not without interruption. At intervals there was also kinhin and reading. Bodhidharma said to the second patriarch, "I see that of all the scriptures that are in China, only the four-chapter *Laṅkāvatāra Sutra* has the mind seal." So the Patriarch had read all the texts of the Old Translations into Chinese. Furthermore, in the *Erh-chung-ju* he quotes from the *Vimalakīrtinirdeśa Sutra* and the *Vajrasamādhi Sutra*. This is different from the idea of "Not relying on words and letters," and so we should revise our understanding.

How can we fail to honor the excellent example of the Buddhas and Ancestors?

The World Honored One and Bodhidharma are mentioned to affirm the kinhin of the Seven Buddhas and the succession of patriarchs. We should cherish the memory of that excellent example.

In the Buddhāvataṁsaka Sutra it says,

The *Buddhāvataṁsaka Sutra* was translated by Buddhabhadra in sixty chapters. It is called the new translation. The subsequent translation by Śikṣānanda in eighty chapters is called the T'ang translation. And there is a separate work of the activities and vows in forty chapters translated by Prajñā. The passage that is quoted here is chapter sixty-five from the eighty-chapter

T'ang translation called "Entering the Dharma Realm." This chapter concerns Sudhana's encounters with his fifty-three teachers. Sudarśana Bhikṣu is the eleventh, and the tenth is the young girl Maitreyaṇī whose teaching led to his meeting Sudarśana Bhikṣu. The following quotation excerpts portions that concern kinhin.

Sudhana saw Sudarśana Bhikṣu, saw him in the grove going straight forward [kinhin], stopping, and returning. His wisdom vision is expansively broad like the great sea.

Because he is both going and coming in one and the same path, it says "going and returning." Just as "the bright wisdom enlightens without dependence on conditions," the various conditions all become bright. Hundreds of rivers of different sources all return to the great ocean and become one flavor, and each and every drop completely penetrates throughout the great ocean. That is how expansively broad it is.

His mind is unmoved by any of the objects of experience.

He is unmoved by the eight things buffeting the human being: profit and loss, praise and slander, fame and infamy, pain and pleasure. [634]

He goes beyond them all, whether the state of being subdued or excited, with or without knowing, turning and moving, or being caught up in words.

"Subdued" means composed and quiet. "Excited" means being unsettled, scattered. "With or without knowing" means the relativism of two opposites. "Turning and moving" means confused and scattered. "Being caught up in words" means to be both with and without understanding. "All of them" means to include all of the following items in praise of the virtue of Sudhana for stopping these bad things. The following section [on the other hand], is in praise of his virtue of doing good.

He has attained the realm of the nondual which the Buddha realized, and ceaselessly converts sentient beings with great compassion and remains without thoughts.

This is the attainment of the Buddha realm of the three nondistinctions between mind, Buddha, and sentient beings, in which the vow of benefiting sentient beings with great compassion is upheld without stopping even for a moment.

From the wish to benefit and comfort all sentient beings,

Kinhin also benefits and comforts all sentient beings. "From the wish to" emphasizes the "kinhin" which comes later in the text.

from the wish to teach the eye of the teaching of the Tathāgata,

The "eye of the teaching" is the wisdom vision of the Buddha. "Teaching" is an abbreviation for teaching and bringing to the path of awakening. This "from the wish to" is also to emphasize the later "kinhin."

to tread the path taken by the Tathāgata, he does the true kinhin, neither fast nor slow.

Treading the splendid path taken by the Tathāgata, neither slow nor fast, this is a cardinal teaching. To know and enact the truth by doing the true kinhin is to complete the deed of a lifetime. The true and the mundane, forms and emptiness, being and nonbeing, good and bad, expedient and perfect, long and short, straight and biased, bright and dark. All pairs are like the forward step, the after step, breathing in and breathing out. The true kinhin is the unimaginable, the unattainable marvelous practice. One action is all actions, one phenomenon is all phenomena. And so the true teaching is that since all phenomena are one phenomenon and all actions are one action, there is not a single phenomenon nor a single action, neither are there all phenomena nor all actions. You should study this carefully.

Sudhana explained saying, "When I do kinhin, in one thought moment, all the four quarters, each and every one is before me because of the purity of my wisdom."

This is the shining of his brilliance, as he explains that which has no limits. "One thought moment" is an arising and a falling. This is the same as in *Chen-hsieh Ch'ing-lian Ch'an-shih yü-lu*: "Constant brightness before me, moment after moment without any darkness." And it includes the idea that the three times utterly penetrate everywhere in the ten directions.

"In one thought all the realms, each and every one is before me. It passes beyond the ineffable, and the realm of the ineffable."

Included here is the idea that the three times utterly penetrate everywhere in the ten directions. The "passes beyond" is a word that refers to going over space. Body and mind are one. Understanding is unhindered. Far and near are the same. Past and present are not two. The great and the small merge. This is the teaching of the freedom of movement and stillness, which defers to no other teaching. The phrase that marks the end of the quotation [yūyū] was used in old Chinese commentaries to mean "that what I have just said, it was indeed just like that." But here *yūyū* means that this is an abbreviation from a longer passage and thus refers the reader to the original text. [635]

He also said, "Good man, I know only this teaching of liberation, the flame upon which the Bodhisattvas rely."

"He also said" means it is the words of Sudarśana. "Good man" refers to Sudhana. The first phrase, "I know only," means that to know only this one practice, in this one practice are included all practices. "Flame" means that the wisdom of the Buddha dispels all ignorance, just like the lamp in the night is bright. In various sutra and commentary the flame of knowledge or wisdom is spoken of and this is explained as meaning the truth of Buddhism. The transmission of the flame has this meaning. In this sutra the expressions like

"Breadth of wisdom," "Eye of Wisdom of the Tathāgata," and "Pure Wisdom" and so forth all mean the great wisdom light of the Buddha's wisdom sight. The explanation is that he relies on this light, and "He goes beyond them all, whether the state of being subdued or excited, with or without knowing, turning and moving, or being caught up in words." "Bodhisattva" means the dharma body. "The flame upon which they rely" means *prajñā*. Because it means to be awakened in the three virtues of the Buddha, it is called the teaching of liberation.

If you see it this way, this is what our first patriarch passed down face to face.

"This" means the *Buddhāvataṁsaka Sutra*. "It" refers to kinhin, and generally to the transmitted teachings of our ancestors. "Face to Face" is from the *Hōkyōki*, as mentioned above.

This meaning fits the teaching of the sage like two lips coming together, without the slightest deviation, and thus it is the true transmission of the Buddhas and Ancestors.

The meaning is that the rule for kinhin passed down from our Ancestor is the same as the teaching of the *Buddhāvataṁsaka Sutra*. The character "opening" means lips, and "meeting lips" means that when the upper and lower come together they meet without a gap, and hence that there is not the slightest difference. From the Seven Buddhas down through the succession of Patriarchs to Ju-ching, this teaching has been passed down face-to-face, unchanged.

Ah me, the people of this degenerate latter age, truly can rejoice that due to causes from past lives they can receive this teaching.

"Ah me" is the sound of a sigh of lamentation. "Degenerate" means shallow. "Latter age" refers to the age of the extinction of the dharma, quite unlike the time of strictness of the ancients. Humans born in the degenerate latter age are exactly this way. When we appreciate that we were able to practice the unexcelled great teaching, to enter into this teaching of liberation, the flame upon which the ancients relied, we see that it is not just from the good roots of this life, it must be from the good causes of prior lives. Truly this is rejoicing. "Prior" refers to the past.

Just preserve the breathing in and breathing out, clearly observe the forward step and the trailing step.

[636] "Just" refers to the following characters. The six characters starting from "preserve" are borrowed from the words of Prajñātāra, "Breathing out without being entangled with objects, breathing in without dwelling in the world of appearances."[29] "Without being entangled, without dwelling" means to hold fast. The six characters after the "clearly observe" are an expression borrowed from *Ts'an-t'ung-ch'i*: "Light and darkness each has its corresponding place, like forward and afterward steps." To not oppose light and dark means to "clearly observe."

Without pursuing conditions, and not abiding in dismal emptiness, the empty [mind] is bright and self-illuminating, and the power of the mind is not impeded.

This is borrowed from the words of *Hsin-hsin ming.* "Without pursuing" and "not abiding" accentuate kinhin, in the same way the earlier phrase "neither slow nor fast" was used. The first four characters of the phrase, "the empty [mind] is bright and self-illuminating, and the power of the mind is not impeded," mean the flame which is relied upon, the pure wisdom. The second four characters mean putting an end to them all, whether it is turning and moving, or being caught up in words. This is the fundamental meaning of the Third Patriarch's explanation of the samādhi of the essential activity of the Buddhas and Patriarchs as seen in his *Hsin-hsin ming.*

He is named the Tathāgata of the Boundless Tranquil Slow Walk. Ah, how could he be far away?

If you attain this superb practice, "It is not different from attaining the [Buddha] position of full awakening in this very body which was born from your father and mother." These are the wise words of all the disciples of the Buddha. In the canon there is the eight-volume *Buddhanāmasahasrapañcaśatacatustripañcadaśa Sutra*, translated in the Sui Dynasty by Jñānaguptā. In the fifth volume, the one thousand eight hundred forty-third Buddha name is Tathāgata of the Boundless Tranquil Slow Walk. Many of the Buddhas take their Buddha name from the practices they did, and in this way he is named Tranquil Slow Walk. So you know that his practice to become a Buddha is kinhin, that which is relied upon, the teaching of awakening. Today as well, if you affirm this superb practice of marvelous cause and marvelous result, of neither before nor after, how can it be far away?

If you turn away from this, you have slipped off the true path before you have even taken a step. You certainly should fully master in detail what is practiced in my assembly.

If you turn your back on the excellent example of the Buddhas and Patriarchs and go into some other byway, you are outside the teaching, and without even taking a single step, you are quickly separated from the great way of the Buddhas and Ancestors. "What is practiced in my assembly" means that it is exclusively the traces of the Patriarch of Eihei which is to be relied on. The phrase "certainly should" indicates it is definitely so. The word "master" is explained in *Chao-lun hsin-shu yu-jen* as: "Master means to understand, to penetrate." This means to understand thoroughly, as used in the expressions to master or to make it your own. "In detail" is explained in the dictionary as utterly detailed or to know thoroughly. In other words, to understand thoroughly and in detail.

This way of kinhin is described in detail in the old records of the generations of ancestors and it begins with the seven Buddhas. Nonetheless, in the contemporary Tendai school and even in the Zen school it has fallen into disuse and error. Indeed, already in the Sung and Yuan era, there were few who knew about it. According to the teaching of our ancestor Ju-ching, "Nowadays, I am the only one who knows this slow walk. If you were to enquire of the Zen teachers everywhere, you will certainly find that no one else knows it." So one cannot expect that Zen people from the Yüan and Ming will understand. Without this face-to-face transmission we also would not have known of this "one breath to half a step," [637] but we could at least have understood that kinhin means to go straight ahead and come straight back, since that is what the characters mean. Furthermore, as is seen in the old texts, it is a grave error to confuse circular walking with kinhin. Despite all this, the followers of the teachings of Eihei have let the face-to-face teaching of their ancestors fall into disuse, and circular walking has usurped the place of kinhin. Furthermore, they give it the name of fast kinhin and gallop about like horses and dogs. It is not just another path, this is positively un-Buddhist, and it is not going too far to say that this shows a lack of respect to the Buddhas and Ancestors. The careful explanations of our Founder have been so forgotten that one could say, "Each and every one, spending the days of their life for naught."

This matter of kinhin appears in explanations scattered here and there in the old texts, so I collected them and became familiar with them, hoping to put them to good use. I took the intention of our Teacher as the foundation, and then gathered up the examples of the practice of the Buddhas and Ancestors of the past, and made this *Kinhinki*. I did this for practitioners like me who respect our Ancestor, and if one or two people come to do this marvelous practice in this final age, then it may be that the old ways of our Founder will be revived and the bad habits of today blow themselves out. My sincere wish is to repay my debt to our Ancestor, and if two or three students hear this talk about the standard and inscribe it on their hearts, then this teaching will not fall into neglect.

Delivered this twenty-eighth day of mid-autumn [eighth month] of the third year of Genbun [1738], in the Takuboku Room of Mt. Kenin, Kūin Zen Temple, of Wakasa Prefecture.

The Making of a Traditional Ritual Practice

Let us leave aside the philological details of the *Monge* for the moment and consider the impact of reading the *Kinhinki* by itself as intended: a guide to and inspiration for practice. The believer would presumably understand kinhin to be an old and orthodox practice of the Buddha himself that was preserved until the time of Ju-ching. Although Dōgen had learned it from Ju-ching, this correct practice had become neglected. By finding the texts that have the old instructions, Menzan has restored the true ritual practice of the Buddhas and Patriarchs.

This understanding of Menzan's writing has been widely accepted in Sōtō Zen, and the modern practice of kinhin follows the instructions of the *Kinhinki*. Part of the power of his work comes from the ritual detail of the one paragraph that is carefully mined from Dōgen. It is also important that the *Kinhinki* is explicitly modeled on Dōgen's *Fukan zazengi*. The rest of the work, however, has little to do with Dōgen or with any other aspect of Zen. The text begins with a quotation from the *Lotus Sutra* and ends with a long extract from the *Buddhāvataṁsaka Sutra*. These citations place the Sōtō ritual of walking meditation within the orthopraxis of the larger Buddhist world, using two of the most well-known and well-accepted texts. The remainder of the *Kinhinki* is a survey of passages in Buddhist literature where the term "kinhin" appears. Menzan borrows the authority of these texts to lend weight to his ritual instructions and to assert that kinhin is a central practice of the true way of the Buddha.

In the following paragraphs, I will look in some detail at a few examples of Menzan's careful and thorough, if not disinterested, scholarship. Menzan did much more than dust off a misplaced ritual rule; he crafted something new out of fragments of unrelated texts scattered across the continents and millenia of Buddhism.

Three quite different kinds of authority have a role to play in the structure of the *Kinhinki*. The first is Dōgen's written instructions. When Menzan quotes from Dōgen in the core second paragraph of the *Kinhinki*, he simply stitches together bits and pieces of these texts, making only the slightest alterations so they will fit together. The second kind of authority is the texts that contain additional ritual details. These are relatively minor works, which are used only in the *Monge* and are discussed in detail below. The bulk of the *Kinhinki* is taken up with the third kind: mainstream Buddhist texts and Zen texts that are not part of the monastic rules literature. Menzan borrows the charisma of these texts but ignores what few details they provide. He is typically very clear about his sources and exact in his transcription of them. However, if one reads the exerpts from the non-Dōgen texts in context, then a different impression emerges: kinhin simply means one of the four postures of standing, walking, sitting, and lying down. There is little in common with Dōgen's idea of kinhin except the shared term, and if anything, the few details mentioned often contradict Dōgen's instructions. For example, the kinhin of the oldest texts is outside and neither too fast nor too slow, which is quite different from Dōgen's snail-slow creep inside the hall.

One kind of authority is conspicuous by its absence. Menzan makes almost no reference to any positive example of living kinhin ritual; he never asks us to consider the good practice of a certain temple or lineage. In fact, he does not even tell us explicitly how kinhin was being done in contemporary Sōtō practice. The only time he uses anything except texts is the aside that the hand position as described by Buddhapālita is affirmed by an "oral transmission." All of his additional details come from texts, but rather than attempt to show some kind of evidence that the *Hsiu-ch'an yao-chüeh* was used by Dōgen, he simply juxtaposes the citations into his Dōgen-centric narrative.

Before looking in detail at an example of Menzan's techniques, I want to say a few words in general about his use of sources. First of all, he scrupulously limited himself to material that had been composed before Dōgen's time and ignored later material that would not have been available to Dōgen, including, of course, the Ming period monastic rules. Menzan almost always quotes accurately from his sources, and in the *Monge*, he clearly distinguishes between the original text and his own comments. He is particularly careful to distinguish Dōgen's words from material that Menzan himself is adding from various sources. His quotations from Dōgen are exactly the same as the modern standard edition, and when Menzan inserts some clarifying details, they appear as double column small characters (which are enclosed in parentheses in my translation). His additional ritual detail is taken from material that he regarded as a translation of an Indic text or as based on the authority of travelers to or from India. When he is handling this kind of material, he more freely interprets them to make his case. He also makes rather free use of material from other Zen sources. For example, he asserts that Bodhidharma did kinhin, when the text clearly says he walked (using the word "kinhin") across China to his practice place, surely not at the pace of a tiny half step for every in and out breath. In general, Menzan presents an accurate picture of the kinhin style taught by Ju-ching and then provides quotes from the mainstream Buddhist tradition where the same term is used. This is his evidence for claiming that this kinhin (of Dōgen) was practiced by the ancestors, indeed by Śākyamuni Buddha himself.

In a few crucial cases, Menzan ingeniously picks apart a connected narrative and arrives at a meaning that contradicts a straightforward reading. This process is apparent in his use of selective quotations from the *Hsiu-ch'an yao-chüeh* to provide precise instructions for matters missing from Dōgen's writings.[30] Of the forty-two texts Menzan quotes, this is his only source for crucial additional details of ritual deportment, and he is obliged to explain away or ignore parts that he does not want to follow. He does not, however, insert these crucial details (like the hand position discussed below) into the *Kinhinki* itself. They only appear in his commentary. Nonetheless, these details have become firmly established in the standard Sōtō practice.

The detailed ritual instructions in the *Kinhinki* begin with the following passage, which is a simple quote from Dōgen:

> The way of kinhin that is to be wished for is to clasp both hands in front of chest [*isshu*] (it should be just like this), putting them inside the sleeves, and not letting the sleeves fall down near the feet to the right and left.

In Dōgen's instructions about seated meditation, which is Menzan's model here, there are instructions about how to place the hands and feet, and so forth. In the case of kinhin, however, there is no further detail from Dōgen concerning how to clasp the hands together, so Menzan finds another source:

> Concerning the hand position of kinhin, the *Hsiu-ch'an yao-chüeh* of Buddhapālita says, "When you do kinhin, cover the left hand. Fold the thumb into the palm, and with the remaining four fingers grasp the thumb making a fist. Next cover [it with] the right hand, grasping the left arm. Then stand straight for a short time and collect the mind and concentrate. (That is, for example, concentrate on the tip of the nose.) Then walk." This is the correct way. The truth of this hand position (*mudra*) is an oral transmission.[31]

The *Hsiu-ch'an yao-chüeh* does contain a short and rather detailed description of kinhin, but Menzan only quotes part of it at this time and returns to other pieces of it at other places in his explanations. The following is the entire section, which was quoted above, but here I have added some critical apparatuses to make clear how he is using this text. The parts that Menzan did not quote are in square brackets, and each section he does quote is numbered, so that, for example, (1) indicates that the following passage (which is in the middle of the text) was the first part quoted in the *Monge*.

> (2) He asked what do you call the manner of going? He replied: "Going is kinhin. It is good for it to be a level place, about fourteen or fifteen paces to twenty-two paces. Do kinhin inside this length. (1) When you do kinhin, cover the left hand. Fold the thumb into the palm, and with the remaining four fingers grasp the thumb making a fist. Next cover [it with] the right hand, grasping the left arm. Then

stand straight for a short time and collect the mind and concentrate. (That is, for example, concentrate on the tip of the nose.) Then walk. [Go back and forth, neither very fast nor very slow. When you walk, just collect your mind and walk.] (5) When you get to the boundary (of the measured area), turn around following the sun (turn your body properly), face where you came from, and stand still for a short time. [Then return, walking just like before. When walking keep the eyes open, when stopped the eyes should be closed. If you tire from walking a long time in this way then rest for a bit from] (3) kinhin. Do it only during the day, do not do it at night."... (4) Someone asked, "What is the difference between walking around a stupa and kinhin?" He replied, "Kinhin is going directly forward, and directly returning. How could it be the same as going around a stupa?"[32]

The passage provides the needed details of the hand position, but the pace of the walk is not the very slow pace described by Dōgen, nor does Dōgen prescribe opening and closing the eyes. Menzan particularly needs this text because it is the only description he has of the proper hand position, but the text taken as a whole contradicts much of the Sōtō ritual style: kinhin is not slow; it is done only during the day; and when it is done for a long time, one should take a rest. Menzan uses most of the words from this paragraph of the *Hsiu-ch'an yao-chüeh*, but they are scattered over several pages of commentary and quoted out of order. He surely was aware that this style of walking meditation is not at all the same as that described by Dōgen, but by careful selection he has managed to extract needed details without making the jarring differences too obvious.

Menzan is usually very careful to distinguish between close meanings of different but similar words. When it suits his purpose, however, he sometimes forces an equivalence upon different but similar terms. He uses this technique to support his assertion that kinhin is altogether different from *gyōdō*, the circular walk about a Buddha statue or stupa. Menzan is not on very firm ground here, because all he has is an aside by Ju-ching (quoted above) that recommends not walking in circles. Ju-ching uses the unusual word *nyōhō*, which is not used for Buddhist circumambulation. When Menzan prohibits circular kinhin (on page 630 of the original), he says, "Know that it is different from going around in a circle (*sennyō*)." He uses the unusual word *sennyō*, which at least seems similar to Ju-ching's *nyōhō*, since they have one character in common. In the *Monge*, however, Menzan does not use this unusual word again: he uses either *nyōgō* or *gyōdō*, which are standard Buddhist terms for circumambulation (of a stupa, for example) in order to show respect and make merit. He concludes his quotations with the passage from the *Hsiu-ch'an yao-chüeh*, which asserts that kinhin is going back and forth and is completely different from *gyōdō*, which is walking around a stupa. Menzan has taken a single aside from Ju-ching about not going in a circle and made a tenuous chain of word associations linking that aside to the common practice of circumambulation. Having prepared the textual basis as best he can, Menzan makes his key point: the way that Ming monks applied the term kinhin to the activity of doing a circular walk while invoking the name of Buddha (*nenbutsu*) was a terrible error that they brought to Japan, and so now everyone refers to this circular walking as kinhin. Despite all this disparaging of circular walking, Menzan's textual support is quite thin and is almost entirely based on early sources that have nothing in particular to do with Dōgen.

Menzan discussed in detail the origins of the practice of applying the word "kinhin" to circumambulation in his *Tōjō sōdō shingi gyōhō shō*. He claims that the Ming monks modified their practice halls to accommodate the Chinese T'ien-t'ai practice of Buddha contemplations done during circumambulation.[33] Since the modification changed the layout of the seats and other details were different, the old rules used by Dōgen no longer suited the new building. Menzan mentions that he saw many practice halls in Japan that had been modified in this way. The distaste for Ming practices is also obliquely apparent in the explanation (on page 626 of the *Monge*) of Dōgen's injunction not to let the sleeves dangle down to the right and left. Apparently, he was unable to find any textual support to back up this directive, so he was reduced to commenting that according to the people of Nagasaki, swinging the sleeves to the right and left is the style of Chinese prostitutes. As might be expected, he made it clear that he was not claiming that he had seen any such thing himself.

Concluding Remarks

In the *Kinhinki* and his commentary, Menzan wove together scattered phrases from Dōgen into a paragraph of ritual instructions. To this he added bits and pieces of texts that either carry the authority of the Buddhist mainstream or are the reports of a traveler to or from India. He attempted to show that the way of walking meditation of Dōgen is both the true way and is different from the practice of walking in a circle around a Buddha statue. Apparently, another purpose of the text, though not explicitly admitted, was to put a stop to the practice of walking while reciting the Buddha's name, which Menzan believed was not the ritual of kinhin. Menzan refers at the beginning of the *Kinhinki* and other places to the so-called degenerate practice of kinhin, but in the *Monge* he tells us explicitly that the degenerate practice was walking while reciting the name of the Buddha.

It is not at all clear how many Sōtō monks were doing this kind of kinhin, and Menzan does not discuss how it was incorporated into the monastic routine. This style of kinhin was probably borrowed from Ōbaku, like many monastic practices in both Sōtō and Rinzai Zen. Menzan's prescription for kinhin is entirely different from this style and is very close to the posture and pace of present-day Sōtō ritual. There is, however, nothing at all in Menzan's writing about how to integrate it with seated meditation, and so the modern practice of a fixed period of walking between two consecutive periods of seated meditation cannot be attributed to Menzan. The striking feature of his prescription, pacing the slow walk with the breath, is a characteristic ritual in modern Sōtō, and as far as I have been able to determine, is unique to Japanese Sōtō Zen. It is apparently not found in any document prior to the *Hōkyōki*, where Ju-ching himself says that it is unknown to others. The other details such as how exactly to hold the hands and the length of time to stop after turning around are not found in Dōgen, nor any texts that Dōgen uses. Menzan is obliged to find textual evidence elsewhere, and he has to go very far afield from the usual Zen sources, but his ritual instructions have been faithfully preserved as if from Dōgen himself.

Ritual detail is one area where one would expect that personal, hands-on instruction would be paramount, but Menzan utterly ignores contemporary custom in the *Kinhinki* except to disparage it. He never refers to what he must have learned from his own teacher, and he even dares to point out that Bodhidharma had read all the available translated scriptures, and therefore, the Zen maxim of "Not relying on words and letters" needs to be reconsidered. The very texts that Menzan uses, however, stress the importance of personal teaching, or of face-to-face transmission, which is indeed a hallmark of the Zen mythos. This is especially clear in the *Hōkyōki*, which depicts Ju-ching as the only source for the proper style of kinhin, a fact that Menzan affirms: he finds no other authority for this practice. Menzan took this core, which was unknown outside of his lineage, and wove an impressive web of Buddhist textual authority around it. He added details where needed from these sources and situated the ritual in the context of mainstream Buddhist practice, while keeping its unique Sōtō elements. He took cold fragments of texts and brought a ritual to life from these unpromising phrases. As a result of Menzan's efforts, the *Kinhinki* became an accepted part of the ritual literature and the kinhin ritual became a living orthodoxy that has been passed on from master to disciple. Thanks to his textual research, his persuasion, and his self-effacement, there is now a traditional ritual of walking meditation that is a characteristic of Sōtō Zen, strictly preserved and transmitted to Buddhist practitioners around the world.

SOURCES QUOTED BY MENZAN

Bendōhō. D 2: 317.

Book of Documents.

Buddhanāmasahasrapañcaśatacatustripañcadaśa Sutra. T 14#0443: 339a16.

Buddhāvataṁsaka Sutra. T 10#279: 349c04–350b05.

Ch'an-lin lei-chu. ZZ 67#1299-11: 67a01.

Ch'an-yao. T 18#917: 946a08–a11.

Ch'u yao ching. T 4#212: 755a14.

Chao-lun hsin-shu yu-jen. ZZ 54#872: 284a05.

Chen-hsieh Ch'ing-lian Ch'an-shih yü-lu. ZZ 71#1426: 780c07.

Ching-te ch'uan-teng lu. T 51#2076: 217a14, 312b22.

Chu-hsi chia-hsün. House rules for Neo-Confucians, Ch'ing era.

Eihei kōroku. D 2: 129, 147 (ch. 7#491, ch. 8#12).

Eihei shingi. D: 357, 318, 317.

Erh-chung-ju. T 48#2009.

Fa-yüan chu-lin. T 53#2122: 273b22.

Fan-i ming-i-chi. T 54#2131: 1107c.

Fukan zazengi. D 2: 3-5.

Hsin-hsin ming. T 48#2010.

Hsiu-ch'an yao-chüeh. ZZ 63#1222: 15b23–c15.

Hsü kao-seng chuan. T 50#2070: 448c17.

Hung-wu Cheng-yün. Ming era pronunciation dictionary.

Hōkyōki. D 2: 376, 380, 386 (#12, 24, 40, 41).

Lin-chien lu. ZZ 87#1625: 247c21.

Lotus Sutra. T 9#262: 009c04.

Mahāsaṅghikavinaya. T 22#1425: 481c09–14.

Miao-fa liang-hua wen-chü. T 34#1718: 630c23.

Nan-hai chi-kuei nei-fa chuan. T 54#2125: 221b21–c09.

Sarvāstivādavinaya. T 23#1435.

Shih-ming. Latter Han list of definitions, p. 33.

Shih-shih yao-lan. T 54#2127: 288a06, 299a15.

Shih-wei ching. Lost Chinese compilation, known from surviving quotations.

Shuo-wen. Latter Han Chinese Dictionary.

Ta-ming I-t'ung-chih. National gazetteer of Ming era.

Ta-pi-ch'iu san-ch'ien wei-i ching. T 24#1470: 915c18.

Ts'an-t'ung-ch'i. T 51#2076: 459b.

Ts'ung-chung lu. T 48#2004: 229a12.

Tzu-hui. Ming era dictionary.

Wan-ping wei-ch'un. Ming era medical encyclopedia.

Wen-hsüan. Early Chinese encyclopedic collection.

Yen-shih chia-hsün. Regulations for Sixth–Century Dynasty.

Zazen yōjinki. S-Shūgen 2: 427a11.

9

Dharma Transmission in Theory and Practice

William M. Bodiford

In autumn 2004, a group of Zen priests from across North America gathered at the Great Vow Monastery in Clatskanie, Oregon, to perform a new ritual called the Dharma Heritage Ceremony. This ceremony concluded the first national conference of the Soto Zen Buddhist Association (hereafter SZBA), a new organization formed to facilitate communication and cooperation among Soto Zen priests active in North America.[1] There are at least two noteworthy features of this event. First, the SZBA limits its membership, in the words of the organizers, to "Soto Zen Buddhist priests active in North America who have received Dharma Transmission in a recognized Soto line."[2] Second, they performed the Dharma Heritage Ceremony in explicit recognition of "the need for an accessible Western ceremony" that will "express a common ground of acknowledgment and affirmation for Soto priests in North America." In other words, they want to provide a ritual forum for members of otherwise separate organizations to jointly recognize and confirm the dharma transmissions that have been granted by their peers. Both features highlight the continued importance of dharma transmission rituals for Zen Buddhists and, accordingly, raise questions relevant not just to the participants in this event but also to the larger field of Buddhist Studies: What exactly is dharma transmission? What have been its roles in Zen lore, Zen history, Zen ritual, and Zen institutions? To what extent is it strictly a private or even secret affair, involving only teacher and student, and in what ways does it involve rituals of public affirmation and institutional power? What issues arise when Zen teachers attempt to transplant these various aspects of dharma transmission into twenty-first-century North America?

These questions are too numerous and each one far too complex and multifaceted to address adequately in this short chapter. We can, however, place dharma transmission within a conceptual and historical context that will help us better understand the issues presented by these questions.[3] I will divide my presentation into three broad themes: (1) the familial ideal of the dharma transmission in East Asia; (2) the vicissitudes of dharma transmission in the history of Sōtō Zen in Japan; and (3) issues presented by dharma transmission in America.[4]

Familial Structure

My point of departure will be Dōgen (1200–1253), the Japanese Buddhist teacher regarded as the founder of the Sōtō Zen lineages that flourish in Japan and that recently have been transplanted to North America. In his essay "Butsudō," Book 44 of his *Shōbōgenzō* (True Dharma Eye Collection), Dōgen makes two key assertions. First, he identifies Buddhism or, rather, authentic Buddhism with the dharma transmission of the Zen lineage:

> From Sakyamuni Buddha to Caoxi Huineng there are 34
> ancestors.... Therefore, the True Dharma Eye Collection has
> been passed down from heir to heir to our own time. The authen-
> tic life of the Buddha dharma exists only in this authentic trans-
> mission. Because the Buddha dharma has been properly
> transmitted in this manner, it is bestowed on heir after heir.[5]

Scholars normally interpret this kind of assertion as an example of sectarian rhetoric, in which members of the Zen school declare their superiority over rival schools. Immediately after this assertion, however, Dōgen denies that Zen is a particular sect or school of Buddhism. He claims that real Buddhism is united. Only the enemies of Buddhism would attempt to divide it into sects. Dōgen says:

> People who have never understood this principle, irrationally and
> mistakenly talk about the True Dharma Eye Collection, Marvelous
> Heart of Nirvana. They irrationally refer to it as the "Zen
> School.".... In India and China, from ancient times to the present day,
> there has never existed anything called the "Zen School."[6]

Dōgen then goes on to say:

> Know that those fellows who would go so far as to refer to the great wisdom that is authentically transmitted from Buddha to Buddha as "the Zen School" are people who even in their dreams have never seen Buddha wisdom, never heard it, and never transmitted it. Do not permit yourselves to think that those who refer to themselves as "the Zen School" have any knowledge of the Buddha dharma. This name, "the Zen School": Who uses it? None of the Buddhas or ancestral teachers ever have. Know that the name "Zen School" is used by Māra, the Tempter (Ma Hajun; Māra Pāpiyas). Whoever uses the designations of Māra must be Māra's companions. They are not descendants of the Buddha.[7]

If we look past Dōgen's reference to Māra, his statements need not be interpreted as a pronouncement of religious doctrine. They might simply describe the facts on the ground that he had observed while in China. When Dōgen studied Buddhism in China, he was an outsider in a strange land. As an outsider, he noticed and wrote about many things that most likely would have seemed perfectly normal, and therefore beneath notice, to people raised in that culture. One of the things that Dōgen noticed was that all the major Buddhist monasteries in China during the early thirteenth century, the monasteries that had received government plaques designating them as Chan (Zen) monasteries, were simply officially recognized public monasteries. All the officially recognized members of the Buddhist clergy in China—the people whom we normally label as Chan (Zen) monks or nuns—were simply legally ordained members of the Buddhist sangha. Within these official public monasteries, people might engage in a wide variety of Buddhist practices, such as Tiantai (J. Tendai) or Huayan (J. Kegon) or Pure Land, but they also practiced sitting Zen (*zazen*), and all of them studied under teachers affiliated with what we would call the Zen lineage (*zenshū*). Outside of these elite public institutions, there also existed countless other private Buddhist or quasi-Buddhist establishments patronized by ordinary people and staffed by pseudo-members of the clergy (*weilan seng*) who lacked proper ordinations. In Dōgen's eyes, no doubt, the practices of common people and self-proclaimed priests could not be equated with authentic Buddhism. He identified authentic Buddhism with the official monasteries, which the state had designated as Chan/Zen. Therefore, Dōgen's assertions conflate sectarian rhetoric (only Zen is authentic) with the Chinese legal policy of labeling state-recognized monasteries as Chan/Zen.[8]

In Japan, Zen eventually came to be seen as one sect among many; but in China and in Korea (and nominally in Vietnam), the mainstream monastic elite identified themselves with Zen.[9] When viewed in terms of the clerical elite, in other words, Zen clearly constitutes the most successful form of Buddhism in East Asia. Why has it been so successful? In 1987, John Jorgensen suggested one answer. It is basically the same explanation that Dōgen gave. To wit: "The authentic life of the Buddha dharma exists only in this authentic transmission." In other words, Zen is the predominant form of Buddhism because of dharma transmission. Jorgensen gives the same explanation, but he uses different terminology. Jorgensen writes that Zen is the most prominent form of Buddhism because it is the most Chinese of any form of Buddhism. It is the most Chinese because it is the form of Buddhism that is closest to Confucianism. It is Confucian because it conforms to traditional Chinese family values. Like any good Confucian family, it has ancestors whom it honors. It honors those ancestors by transmitting their legacy to proper descendants, from generation to generation, who will maintain and carry on their family traditions. We can complete Jorgensen's explanation by saying that in Zen this process of transmitting a family legacy is given structural form through the ritual of dharma transmission. If we consider Zen dharma transmission as an expression of Chinese social norms for family structure and for the proper behavior of familial heirs, then several key features seem to apply equally to family relationships within secular society and within dharma lineages. These features span many different dimensions. Some of the more obvious ones are as follows:

(1) *Ancestral dimension*: Ancestors (*so*) constitute a fundamental source of power (both benevolent and malevolent) within East Asian kinship systems and religious life. People in positions of responsibility must devote much ritual effort (whether in the form of Confucian, Buddhist, or Daoist rites) to commemorate the ancestors of their clan, of their household, and of their immediate family to ensure that the ancestors will attain exaltation among the living and, equally, among the celestial realms populated by similar ancestors. The status of the living can be enhanced by high-status ancestors, even if the ancestors attain that higher status posthumously.[10] Because the Buddhist order (*sangha*) constitutes a pseudo-kinship group with its own dharma clans (*shū*), dharma households (*ka*), and dharma families, the members of that order must perform similar rites to commemorate their spiritual ancestors. Accordingly, Chinese Buddhist monasteries have ancestral halls (*sodō*; sometimes translated as "patriarch halls") that conform to traditional Confucian norms.[11]

(2) *Biological dimension*: The biological creation of new life is the great mystery. It cannot be explained in words. It cannot be defined by science. Everyone knows that this dimension lies at the core of the family, but it is

private. Outsiders normally have no right to talk about it. Outsiders can only see and talk about other dimensions. In Zen as well, the spiritual creation of a new Buddha is the great mystery. It cannot be explained in words. It cannot be explained by science or causality. In Zen, this is something that "only a Buddha together with a Buddha" (*yuibutsu yobutsu*) can "transmit mind-to-mind" (*isshin denshin*). Everyone knows that this dimension lies at the core of dharma transmission, but it is private. It takes place inside the room (*shitsunai*). Outsiders normally have no right to talk about it.[12] Outsiders can only see and talk about other dimensions. Nonetheless, some of the secrets are known. Medieval Zen dharma transmission documents abound with biological terminology. For example, failure to find a proper heir is called "the sin of cutting off the Buddha seed" (*dan busshu no tsumi*). This biological terminology is not just metaphorical. In some rituals, the teacher and heir write a portion of the transmission documents with ink that they make by mixing their own blood together. They get this blood by taking a small knife and cutting the underside of their tongues. The tongue is the organ by which a Buddha gives birth to a new Buddha by teaching the dharma.[13]

(3) *Linguistic dimension*: Parents give children their names, both their ancestral family names as well as their personal names. As children mature and move out into the world, the children can acquire other names and titles. Nonetheless, the name received from one's parents will remain the most personal one. Buddhist teachers likewise bestow names on their heirs. Historically, they bestowed the family name "Shaku" and a personal dharma name (*hōki*). The family name "Shaku" derives from Sakya, the family name of the Buddha Sakyamuni (Shakamuni). Buddhist monks and nuns can use many other names and titles (*gō*), but in important documents they always include the dharma name given by their teacher.[14] In modern Japan, the Japanese government restricted the scope of this linguistic dimension after 1872 when it began to regulate family names. Since that time, Buddhist clergy have retained their secular family names.

(4) *Ritual dimension*: There are proper ways that children bow to their ancestors, bow to their grandparents, and bow to their parents. Most important of all, there are proper ways that children should conduct funeral rites for their parents and memorial rituals for their ancestors. If they do not conduct any of these rituals properly, then they are not their parents' heirs. Conversely, even an illegitimate child—or a child who has been disowned—can assert (and, perhaps, even regain) his lineage by performing these rituals properly. These exact same rituals are practiced in Zen monasteries. The order of dharma succession also plays a role. The number-one heir should act as master of ceremonies, and the other heirs should be lined up in order: number two,

number three, and so forth. In addition, there are special Buddhist ceremonies for honoring one's teacher. In Zen temples, the most important one is the ritual offering of incense on behalf of one's teacher (*shikō* or *shijō kō*) that is performed as part of the ceremony when one is inaugurated (*kaidō*) as the abbot of a temple or monastery. Another one is the annual lectures that one performs to commemorate the death anniversary of a deceased teacher. There also exist private or secret rituals like the one mentioned above when the teacher and student write out dharma transmission documents.[15] The ceremonies themselves are secret, but the documents survive.[16] In premodern times, these kinds of documents had value not merely because of their contents but because of the process by which they were produced. They would be written by hand, over a period of many months, in the same handwriting as that of the person who possesses it. Therefore, they could serve as legal witnesses to demonstrate that the person who possessed them actually completed a course of training.

(5) *Legal dimension*: Parents have a legal obligation to discipline their children. If the children break the law, then the parents can be punished. Likewise, the parents have a moral obligation to feed, clothe, shelter, and educate their children. And the children must reciprocate. Children have a legal obligation to obey their parents. As they become older and able to earn a living, children have a moral obligation to feed, clothe, shelter, and care for their parents. Modern societies no longer recognize religious jurisdiction. In premodern times, though, Buddhist monasteries governed their own residents with full legal authority. Teachers had the legal right to discipline and beat their disciples. And monks and nuns had the legal obligation to obey their teachers. Secular courts could punish teachers if their disciples broke the law. There was one way in which the legal situation differed between Buddhists and secular families. In a secular family, the economic power of the family head to spend the family property was unchecked. Buddhists, on the other hand, always were trying to come up with new ways to ensure that abbots of temples would not misappropriate temple funds or property. Usually, the main patrons of the temple, the heads of locally important families, and local government officials would exercise some oversight on temple finances. Legal aspects also include the rights of inheritance. Certain children inherit personal property and have the right to dispose of it. Just as in secular families, dharma heirs inherit their teacher's personal property and have the right to dispose of it. This brings us to another dimension.

(6) *Institutional and financial dimension*: Certain children may inherit the family business. They learn the family craft, the traditional recipes, the secret

ingredients, and so forth, so that they maintain family traditions. Other children might go off and pursue employment somewhere else. Even these other children, however, have a financial obligation to their home. They should send financial contributions back to support the main household. They should physically return to the main household on important ritual occasions and contribute money for those rituals. Dharma heirs normally inherit something of their teacher's personality. This is what Dōgen refers to as home style or family style (*kajō*). Only dharma heirs can legitimately use the same vocabulary, the same teaching methods, and perform ceremonies in the same way as their teacher. But this is not a requirement. Dharma transmission can occur without the heirs having to master their teacher's style. In some cases, heirs might also inherit the same temple or monastery. In thirteenth-century China, the elite, state-recognized monasteries could not be passed down from one abbot to that abbot's own students. Other smaller, privately sponsored temples and monasteries, though, usually were handed down within one's own lineage.[17] By the twentieth century (if not earlier), the abbotship of both types of temples was reserved for the previous abbot's dharma heirs, each of whom would be identified as the inheritor of the True Dharma Eye Collection (*Zhengfayanzang*, J. *Shōbōgenzō*).[18] In all cases, though, when dharma heirs leave the monastery and become teachers in a different location, they nonetheless owe an economic obligation to their home temple. They must send alms back to support it. They should physically return to it on important ritual occasions, such as the inauguration of a new abbot.

(7) *Temporal dimension*: Finally, almost all of these dimensions presuppose that ancestors, parents, and children exist together at the same time. A long-term, continuous relationship is not strictly required, but the longer the relationship and the fewer interruptions, then the more strongly felt and deeply rooted these other dimensions are likely to be.

These seven dimensions (ancestral, biological, linguistic, ritual, legal, business and financial, temporal) lie at the heart of the Chinese family system. I think (as John Jorgensen suggests) that they also play indispensable roles in the social structure of Chan/Zen and of the Buddhist Sangha in East Asia. This family model is easier to see when using an East Asian language, like Chinese or Japanese, because the same terminology is used in both contexts. Chinese, especially, has a very highly developed vocabulary for ancestors, grandparents, parents, aunts, uncles, older and younger siblings, cousins, and so forth. The Buddhist clergy uses similar vocabulary to refer to dharma families, with dharma ancestors, dharma grandparents, dharma parents, dharma aunts, dharma uncles, dharma brothers and sisters, and so forth. To be ordained is to join a dharma family that functions exactly like any other family, with the same Confucian family values and the same Confucian family expectations and obligations.

Dharma transmission is inherently multidimensional. None of these seven dimensions always exists in every case. There are many historical examples where the Zen tradition has accepted a dharma transmission as legitimate even though one or more of these dimensions were missing. There are other cases where the lack of only one of these dimensions would cause a dharma transmission to be rejected and labeled illegitimate. Indeed, one of the reasons that dharma transmission has proved to be such a powerful source of Zen's success is because of its inherent flexibility. As T. Griffith Foulk points out, dharma transmission is both concrete and abstract.[19] Every link in the genealogy of dharma transmission occurs in documented historical circumstances: a specific place and time, identifiable individuals, and specific words and actions. At the same time, though, Zen texts also assert that true dharma transmission consists of no transmission. In other words, it occurs only mind-to-mind. Nothing is actually handed down from teacher to student. Each generation awakens to his or her own authentication of the Buddhas.

Therefore, Foulk notes that when the historical evidence is in one's favor, one can demonstrate the validity of dharma transmission by citing any number of the aforementioned seven dimensions. When the historical evidence is less favorable, then one can shift the argument to the religious realm by arguing that the only facts that really matter are the depths and quality of one's Buddha realization. This religious realm constitutes an eighth dimension. Every dharma transmission reenacts a mythological model, as illustrated by the fact that traditional Zen histories, such as the *Jingde Era Transmission of the Flame*,[20] locate the origin of the Zen lineage not with Sakyamuni (a.k.a. Gautama, the historical Buddha), but with the Seven Buddhas of the Past (*shichibutsu*). These mythological Buddhas place the origins of dharma transmission outside of time and outside of our world. They demonstrate its immutable validity for all times and all worlds.

The inherent flexibility of dharma transmission tells us that historical evidence alone can never legitimate nor invalidate any particular case of dharma transmission. Ultimately, it is a matter of religious faith, an expression of a sacred truth. This kind of truth lies beyond the reach of historical criticism. In medieval Japan, this religious truth was more powerful than any doctrinal argument. Consider, for example, the following episode in which the Japanese Zen priest Enni Ben'en (1202–1280) easily defeated a Confucian critic named Sugawara Tamenaga (1158–1246) merely by invoking the aura of dharma transmission:

The minister [Kujō Michiie (1193–1252)] said: "Lord Sugawara is the greatest Confucian in our kingdom. He always grumbles about Buddhist dominance over Confucianism. Now let the two advocates meet and resolve this matter in debate."

Enni said: "I have heard that Lord Sugawara is a student of Confucian policies. Is this correct?"

The councilor [Sugawara], in a very dignified manner, replied: "Correct."

Enni continued: "The Buddha dharma is handed down from buddha to buddha and transmitted from ancestor to ancestor. Anything not received from one's teacher is a false proposition. Accordingly, I am a fifty-fifth generation descendant of Sakyamuni Buddha and a twenty-seventh generation heir of Ancestor Bodhidharma. Although I cannot claim that deep arrows from their mighty bows have pierced my humble fabric, nonetheless based on this lineage I call myself a son of Sakya [i.e., a Buddhist]. Confucians no doubt conform to similar standards. Lord, do you not know what generation descendant of Confucius you are?"

The councilor, teeth clinched, withdrew. [Later] he told a bystander, "I wanted to contest Enni's doctrines, but when he spoke of genealogy I could not evade his stipulations."[21]

This incident tells us that the spiritual power of dharma transmission was recognized even by people, like this Confucian scholar, who opposed Zen teachings. It is this spiritual power that breathes life into the various other familial dimensions so that they might function more fully as social realities in the lives of Buddhist priests. The spiritual power of dharma transmission encapsulates these dimensions in a mythological framework, unites them in genealogical terminology, and reveals them through concrete ritual performances.[22] As a result, all properly ordained members of the priesthood could partially share in some of these familial dimensions whether they received dharma transmission or not.

Dharma Transmission in Japanese Sōtō Zen

My analysis of the vicissitudes of dharma transmission in the history of Sōtō Zen in Japan begins with three key points: dharma transmission replicates Chinese family values; it conveys great spiritual power and authority; and it is inherently flexible and multidimensional, so that no single criteria always exists in every case. We can see evidence for these three points repeatedly in the history of Sōtō Zen in Japan. Nonetheless, since 1703, official Sōtō doctrine has stipulated that dharma transmission must conform to two criteria, which supposedly describe the norms that Dōgen introduced from China. This Dōgen model demands exclusive authentication from no more than one teacher (*isshi inshō*) and face-to-face bestowal of succession (*menju shihō*). The first condition prohibits clerics from inheriting more than one lineage. The second condition prohibits conferral by proxy, conferral at a distance to strangers, or posthumous conferral. This is the official doctrine. The actual meaning of these terms and the historical evidence for them, however, is not completely clear. There are numerous examples in Japanese Sōtō history that deviate from these stipulations. Since I already have discussed this topic elsewhere,[23] below I will only briefly summarize a few well-known cases.

First, Dōgen's own community of disciples seems to have incorporated at least three separate dharma lineages. Thirty-five years before Dōgen traveled to China, a Japanese monk named Nōnin (fl. 1189) already was teaching Zen in Japan. Nōnin had never been to China, but he had received a mail-order (*yōfu*) dharma transmission from the Chinese teacher Fozhao Deguang (Busshō Tokkō; 1121–1203). Nōnin then bestowed dharma transmission on Ekan (d. 1251), who in turn bestowed dharma transmission on Gikai (1219–1309). Afterward, Ekan and Gikai (along with Ekan's other disciples) joined Dōgen's community in 1241. According to Gikai's writings, Dōgen told Gikai that his dharma lineage—from Deguang to Nōnin to Ekan to Gikai—was a legitimate lineage and that Gikai had been most fortunate to receive dharma transmission. Dōgen himself had two Zen teachers. First he studied under Myōzen (1184–1225), who had inherited a Zen lineage from Eisai (1141–1215). After Myōzen died, then Dōgen studied under Rujing (1163–1227). Modern biographies always note that Dōgen succeeded to Rujing's Sōtō lineage. Biographies written during the medieval period also state that Dōgen had inherited a dharma lineage from Myōzen. The actual facts of the matter are not clear. Nonetheless, it is certain that at least some members of the early Sōtō community believed that Dōgen had inherited two dharma lineages, one from Myōzen and a second one from Rujing. The history of Rujing's own dharma lineage is clear: it had been recreated by means of a posthumous transmission by proxy. Rujing traced his lineage back to Touzi Yiqing (Tōsu Gisei; 1032–1083) in the forty-fourth generation and through Touzi to Dayang Jingxuan (Taiyō Kyōgen; 942–1027) in the forty-third generation. Dayang Jingxuan died in 1027. Touzi Yiqing was born five years later, in 1032. These two generations are connected by a priest of another lineage named Fushan Fayuan (Fuzan

Hōon; 991–1067). Thus, Touzi Yiqing received his Sōtō dharma transmission from Dayang Jingxuan by the posthumous proxy (*daifu*) of an outsider.

Similar incidents occurred in Japan. The famous early Sōtō patriarch Keizan Jōkin (1264–1325) bestowed dharma transmission on Kohō Kakumyō (1271–1361). In 1325 when Keizan died, however, Kohō Kakumyō abandoned his Sōtō connections. He founded his own Zen temple, Unjuji, with the support of a patron who wanted to sponsor someone in the Rinzai lineage of Shinichi Kakushin (1207–1298). When Kohō Kakumyō performed his inauguration ceremony at Unjuji temple, therefore, he offered his succession incense in the name of Shinichi Kakushin, a teacher under whom he had studied briefly some twenty-eight years earlier. At the time when Kohō Kakumyō performed this ritual, Shinichi Kakushin had been deceased for some twenty-seven years. Kohō Kakumyō succeeded to his lineage posthumously. Thereafter, all of Kohō Kakumyō's disciples inherited the Rinzai Zen lineage of Shinichi Kakushin. Keizan's disciple Gasan Jōseki (1276–1366) was involved in a similar arrangement. Among Gasan's many dharma heirs were the two monks Mutei Ryōshō (1313–1361) and Gessen Ryōin (1319–1400). Mutei founded Shōbōji temple in northern Japan but died shortly thereafter. At the time of his death, Mutei did not have a disciple who was ready to become head of that temple. Therefore, Mutei's teacher Gasan Jōseki sent Gessen Ryōin to Shōbōji temple to become a posthumous dharma heir.

Today, in retrospect, these kinds of dharma transmission practices might seem irregular. Before condemning them, though, first we should remember the social conditions of the historical period during which they occurred. The thirteenth and fourteenth centuries were times of warfare and social unrest. Communications were difficult, and travel between regions of Japan could be dangerous. Most Sōtō Zen communities were isolated in rural areas. They did not know what was happening elsewhere. Zen itself was still relatively new in Japan. In most areas, the local Zen teacher was the first and only Zen teacher that anyone had ever seen. Thus, there were no established norms or social expectations.[24] These kinds of norms became established only after the Sōtō Zen had grown large enough to develop into regional networks of Zen temples.

As regional networks of Zen temples developed in Japan, dharma transmission became a central ritual in their organizational structure. Unlike the state-sponsored public monasteries of China, where the dharma heirs of the previous abbot were forbidden from succeeding their teacher to become the next abbot, in Japan abbotship succession and dharma transmission were tied together. It did not always work. As in the case of Shōbōji temple, mentioned previously, sometimes an abbot might die without having produced a dharma heir. In that case, an adopted heir would have to be brought in. Sometimes, the opposite situation existed. The previous abbot had produced a dharma heir and appointed him as his successor, but for whatever reason he did not become the new abbot. In early Sōtō history, a very famous case of this problem arose at Daijōji monastery. Daijōji was founded by Gikai (1219–1309). Gikai appointed Keizan Jōkin as his successor. Keizan Jōkin appointed Meihō Sotetsu (1277–1350) as his successor. Keizan then left Daijōji and founded a new monastery called Yōkōji. Shortly thereafter, something went wrong at Daijōji. We do not know the details, but Daijōji's main patrons became dissatisfied with Meihō Sotetsu and kicked him out of the monastery. In his writings, Keizan mentions the existence of a problem with the lay patrons of Daijōji, but he does not explain what it might have been.[25] This incident at Daijōji and the case of Kohō Kakumyō at Unjuji are the only two where the historical record specifically mentions the role of the patron in determining who could serve as abbot. Nonetheless, patrons always played a major role in the selection of abbots. Lay people form strong attachments to the Buddhist teachers whom they sponsor. They want to know that their previous teacher's legacy will continue under his successor. Moreover, throughout most of Buddhist history, people have always been taught that great karmic merit is generated by having a priest in the family. Thus, historically, whenever a very rich or very powerful family sponsored a Buddhist temple, almost invariably some of the offspring of that family became monks or nuns at that temple. As children of the main sponsors, they would be expected to receive dharma transmission and to be promoted to the abbotship. Thus, the patron's involvement in monastic succession goes without saying.

As a result of Meihō Sotetsu's setback at Daijōji, Keizan wrote guidelines for the appointments of abbots. These guidelines were not fully implemented until a couple of generations later, during the time of Tsūgen Jakurei (1322–1391), Baisan Monpon (d. 1417), and Jochū Tengin (1365–1440). These are the three people who developed the institutional structure of Sōtō Zen in medieval Japan. Tsūgen and Baisan established rotating abbotship (rinjū) at the major monasteries of Sōjiji (in Noto), Yōtakuji (in Settsu) and Ryūtakuji (in Echizen). From these three centers, rotating abbotships became the norm for other major monasteries.[26] Rotating abbotships link networks of temples together according to the dharma lineage of their abbots. There is a head temple at the center, surrounded by branch temples. The founders of the branch temples are dharma heirs of the founder of the head temple. The abbotship of the head temple is passed in regular sequence among candidates who are promoted by the branch temples. If there are four branch temples—branch A, branch B, branch C, and branch D, for example—then the abbotship of the head temple first goes to a candidate from A, then B, then C, then D, and then the cycle repeats by going back to A. So long as each new abbot represented a different branch temple, then the main temple would benefit from the political loyalty, the financial support, and the most able teachers of several affiliated temples. This system also helped to promote growth and stability by providing a surplus of retired abbots. These surplus retired abbots always could return to help when any difficulties or problems arose. And, when they were not needed, they could travel to new regions and found new branch temples.

A key element in this system of rotating abbotships was the requirement that anyone who received dharma transmission at any of the branch temples had to assume at least one rotating term as abbot of the main temple. Moreover, a rotating term as abbot required a major financial contribution. Usually, this financial contribution took the form of a donation in honor of the dharma ancestors enshrined at the main temple. Thus, receiving dharma transmission imposed a heavy institutional and financial responsibility. Anyone who received dharma transmission had to become an administrator and had to become a fundraiser. These were obligations that many people tried to avoid. Tsūgen, Baisan, and Jochū each demanded that future generations excommunicate any Zen teacher who failed to fulfill his obligation to serve as abbot of a head temple. Baisan decreed that the obedient Zen successors should seize defiant ones and then burn the offender's succession certificate (*shisho*) before his eyes.[27] Note the remarkable inversion that has occurred here. Instead of dharma transmission being a qualification for becoming an abbot, successful service as abbot has become a requirement for being allowed to retain one's dharma transmission. In other words, anyone who does not support the family and the ancestors will be disinherited and stripped of his or her religious status.

Being abbot also has its personal rewards. First, during the medieval period, the abbot's quarters (*hōjō*) of head temples were the only places where one could find copies of the writings of major Japanese Zen teachers, such as Dōgen and Keizan. Anyone who wanted unfettered access to their writings would have had to serve as abbot of a head temple. Second, over time, the title of "retired abbot" (*senjū*) of a head temple came to provide priests with special authority or certification as Zen teachers. Without this experience, priests might find it difficult to attract students. Finally, it opened doors. The more prestigious the head temple at which one had served a term as abbot, the more easily one could gain access to other temples and to the ears of people of power. Ambitious Zen priests, therefore, naturally wanted to acquire the title of "retired abbot" of a prestigious head temple. The most prestigious head temple was Sōjiji, which always has stood at the head of the largest networks of temples. During the medieval period, Sōjiji won recognition by the aristocratic court, so that anyone who served a rotating term as abbot at Sōjiji (even if only for a few days) became eligible for a purple robe. Purple is the royal color, which can be awarded only by the ruler. A purple robe was one of the most prestigious awards any Buddhist monk could receive. As such, it could be obtained only with substantial contributions to the court and to Sōjiji. These contributions were justified by the symbolic value (or capital) of the purple robe. Receiving it not only enhanced the personal status of the individual priest but also that of his local community of supporters and his peers within the same network of temples. By conferring royal authority on the individual priest, the robe also brought great prestige and honor to his home temple and generated great karmic merit for everyone who had contributed alms for its acquisition. Simultaneously, it also denoted a mark of recognition for the priest's dharma lineage, his teachers, and his peers. Without their support and cooperation, a priest could never achieve the honor of a temporary term as abbot at a major monastery like Sōjiji. Thus, the collective membership (priest, peers, and lay patrons) of the local Zen circle confer status on one of their members.

In this way, the temporary term as abbot represents a public confirmation of the legitimacy of one's dharma transmission. This expression of public confirmation eventually became ritualized as the *zuise* (literally, auspicious debut) ceremony of honorary abbotship.[28] Today in Japan, a Sōtō cleric cannot be officially installed as abbot of a dharma temple (*hōchi*; i.e., major temple) without first attaining certification from the Sōtō Headquarters (Sōtōshū shūmuchō).[29] One of the requirements for that certification is the performance of *zuise* ceremonies, during which a priest will act as honorary abbot for the duration of one full day (*ichiya jūshoku*) at the Sōtō School's two head temples: Sōjiji (the monastery founded by Keizan) and Eiheiji (the monastery founded by Dōgen). As honorary abbot, the most important ritual consists of honoring ancestors of each temple, generating ritual merit on their behalf, and presenting offerings (*hōon kin*) to them. At Sōjiji, the honorary abbot presents offerings to Sōjiji's first two abbots: Keizan and Gasan Jōseki. At Eiheiji, he presents offerings to its first two abbots: Dōgen and Ejō (1198–1280).[30] This requirement for honorary abbotship at both temples seems designed to foster unity. Regardless of temple network or dharma lineage, all senior priests should recognize the authority of both Sōjiji and Eiheiji. And, Sōjiji and Eiheiji should receive and welcome all Sōtō teachers irrespective of their affiliation.

Historically, though, *zuise* was developed not to unify but as a weapon to divide. The leaders of Eiheiji always sought to enhance its importance based on the idea that it is the true ancestral temple of the entire Sōtō school because it was founded by Dōgen. The leaders of Sōjiji always resisted Ei-heiji's assertions based on the fact that Sōjiji is the actual head of the largest network of temples in Japan. Throughout the course of this rivalry, Sōjiji has repeatedly issued proclamations asserting that anyone who received honors at Eiheiji would never be allowed back into a temple affiliated with Sōjiji.[31] The power of Sōjiji's threat rested on its authority over dharma transmission. Any-one who violated Sōjiji's policies could not become abbot at any temple af-filiated to Sōjiji's dharma lineage. Moreover, they could not become abbot at any temple outside of Sōjiji's temple network either, because their dharma transmission would be recognized only by temples affiliated to their own lin-eage. If a Zen teacher wanted to assume a position at a temple that belonged to another dharma faction, then that Zen teacher would have to renounce his or her previous dharma lineage and accept a new one based on the new temple. In Japanese Sōtō, this process is called changing (eki) one's lineage (shi) in accordance (in) with one's temple (in), or in'in ekishi.[32]

Today, there is a tendency to regard these kinds of sectarian rivalries as little more than petty squabbles that are beneath the dignity of great religious institutions. In reality, though, they might very well reflect the flip side of the Confucian family model found in Zen. On the one hand, traditional family values ensure cohesion and strength. Everyone pulls together and supports one another. Their loyalty to the family traditions and desire to maintain family honor help produce high standards of performance that can withstand public scrutiny. At the same time, though, all the other members of the family exert considerable influence and control over one another. They can place severe demands on other family members. When these demands are combined with institutional power, sectarian rivalries are almost inevitable. Family-run enterprises—regardless of their nature—exhibit these same kinds of conflicts. Some Western observers have suggested that one of the reasons that some Zen teachings seem to so strongly emphasize Western-sounding notions of liberation, freedom, spontaneity, and self-reliance is because they provide a self-critique of the very strong, group-oriented, social structures of traditional Japanese society and its Confucian family norms.[33] While consideration of that suggestion lies outside the scope of this paper, it does remind us that Zen teachings (like teachings of any religion) acquire their scope and significance from within specific contexts of belief.

Since the 1880s when the Sōtō School in Japan began to reorganize itself in response to the demands of modernization, Zen in Japan has gradually been turning away from the family structure and temple networks described above. As Japanese society moves away from traditional Confucian family values, it is only natural that the Sōtō School does likewise. Today, the Sōtō headquarters (Shūmuchō) relies on a variety of checks and balances—built around not just traditional monastic training but also bureaucratic committees and educational degrees—to maintain the standards of its clergy.[34] On paper, at least, there are four broad classes of temples, each one of which has different criteria for selection of abbots.[35] There are two levels of supervisory certification (*shike* and *jun shike*), without which one cannot serve as a Zen master in charge of the ninety-day retreats (*ango*) at a certified monastic training center (*ninka sanzen dōjō*).[36] There are eight ecclesiastical grades (*sōkai*) based on a combination of academic learning and dharma seniority as evaluated by review committees.[37] Finally, there are four levels of dharma seniority (*hōkai*) based on monastic training, age, and religious attainments.[38] These different types of certification, grade, and seniority overlap in a bewildering variety of ways.

What I find most significant about this system of ecclesiastical grades is that dharma transmission provides access to only a relatively low grade. It is listed as a requirement for the very lowest ecclesiastical status, that of an instructor third class (*santō kyōshi*). Thus, in present day Sōtō Zen, dharma transmission constitutes a preliminary step, after which one's real development begins. The relatively low status of dharma transmission means that in and of itself it does not qualify one to accept students or to train disciples. According to the regulations, Zen students should be supervised only by a teacher who has attained supervisory certification (i.e., *sanzen dōjō shike* status), that is, someone who in the popular literature might be called a Zen master. To attain supervisory certification requires not just high ecclesiastical grades and dharma seniority but also at least three years' experience as an assistant supervisor at a specially designated training hall (*tokubetsu sōdō*), during which time one undergoes an apprenticeship. This monastic apprenticeship agrees with the popular image of Zen Buddhism as a form of extreme asceticism. The popular image, however, reflects only a limited view of Zen life. These training halls are found at only about one hundred of the nearly 14,000 temples that constitute the modern Sōtō school. The vast majority of Sōtō Zen religious activities occur not at the training halls but at the local temples.

Today, the key authority conferred by dharma transmission is that it qualifies a priest to manage an ordinary (*jun hōchi*) local temple. These temples are not sites of ascetic training but of ceremonial services on behalf of lay patrons. Lay involvement in local temples typically includes the priests' own families. Since the government legalized clerical marriage in 1872, the family model of Buddhist relationships has gradually become actualized in biological form as more and more Zen priests have married and raised children.[39] As a result of this transformation to a married clergy, in modern Sōtō it is common for ordinary temples to be handed down from father to son. A son will enter the clergy, undergo a brief period of training under a certified supervisor at a training monastery, and then return home where he will eventually receive dharma transmission from his biological father and inherit his father's temple. Since this practice reflects individual family circumstances, it exhibits many variations. There is at least one notable variation that (to the best of my knowledge) has not been discussed in scholarly literature, namely, temple families with daughter(s) but no son. Here, as in secular society, the daughter assumes responsibility for continuing the family line. The daughter's husband can assume her family name, which will enable him to join the family, enter the priesthood, and eventually receive dharma transmission from her father. But what happens when the daughter divorces her husband? As likely as not (it seems), not only will the man lose his wife, but he also will lose his dharma transmission. He certainly will not be welcome to inherit his former father-in-law's temple. And it is very unlikely that another temple would accept him with his outside lineage. This atypical example illustrates how a bonding ritual of inclusion can—when circumstances change— become a ritual of exclusion.

Dharma Transmission Issues

No one can predict what future roles dharma transmission might play among the nascent Zen communities of North America. The communities are very diverse, too new, and many of them remain in a state of flux. It does seem clear, though, that North America presents a cultural environment that differs greatly from that of traditional East Asia. However much Zen rituals might be performed in a similar manner within this new culture, in so far as they must function within a different context of belief (where neither the world imagined nor the world lived is the same as that of East Asia) one must question whether the same kinds of ethos or religious meaning can be conveyed by those rituals.[40] This question applies not just to areas outside of East Asia, of course, but also among the various regions within it and across their respective historical developments. People around the world who were raised within modern urban environments might well share more cultural assumptions with one another than they would with their own ancestors of two or three generations previous who had lived in preindustrial rural societies. Nonetheless, if we focus simply on dharma transmission within North America, then even at this premature stage we can identify several areas of dissonance.

First, if, as suggested above, dharma transmission replicates the values of the Confucian family model, then how will that model fit into a society where families lack multigenerational cohesiveness or where family roles seem to be so much in flux that the definition of family itself has become subject to political debate? Can a religious practice continue to draw strength from a secular model that is foreign to its practitioners?[41] The traditional Asian ideals of honoring ancestors, filial piety, and hereditary privilege seem to directly conflict many celebrated American values, especially notions of personal freedom, individual autonomy, and egalitarian self (re-)invention. Second, what mythological framework will inspire North American interpretations of dharma transmission? Today the traditional Zen mythos—with its stories of the Seven Buddhas of the Past, of Sakyamuni Buddha holding up a flower before his assembled disciples on Vulture Peak, and of Bodhidharma's journey to China—lacks historical authority. In the eyes of skeptics, it seems to be at best quaint and at worst a blatant falsehood. Many North Americans approach Zen more as a form of self-realization therapy than as a religious faith.[42] It is impossible to imagine them citing their dharma lineage in public debate as did the Japanese Zen priest Enni Ben'en in the thirteenth century. Third, what religious distinction can dharma transmission convey in a society of fluid identities where even the traditional Buddhist distinction between priest and laity tends to disappear?

While dharma transmission has never been restricted exclusively to clergy, it always has been controlled by ordained members of the clergy, that is, by people who receive rites of ordination, shave their heads, and wear Buddhist robes. Within this group, dharma transmission always has been a matter of insider knowledge, discussed only by the clerical elite, who themselves have been initiated into a dharma lineage. For ordinary lay people, in contrast, the much more obvious public social distinction bestowed by ordination always has been of prime importance, since it is the people with shaved heads and Buddhist robes who can generate karmic merit for the laity by accepting their gifts. At Zen Centers in North America, however, a lay-clerical distinction based on gift giving (by laity) and generating merit (by priests) is all but meaningless. Most people see Zen (especially sitting Zen or *zazen*) as a form of self-realization or relaxation exercises that lay people can practice as well as (or better than) clerics.[43] Within this context, lay practitioners who might care nothing about priestly status can, nonetheless, become very concerned about dharma transmission, who has it and who does not. From conversations among practitioners at different Zen Centers, it seems each Center has developed its own individual culture of dharma transmission: here it might signify eligibility to join a Center's board of directors, there it might mark completion of a kōan curriculum, and somewhere else it might be seen as equivalent to clerical ordination, and so forth.

These variations in the social significance assigned to dharma transmission highlight the unsettled state of North American Zen communities. Differences in their respective histories, founders, economic circumstances, and facilities have imbued each Zen Center with its own distinctive culture and idiosyncrasies. The Dharma Heritage Ceremony serves to remind Soto priests from these dissimilar Centers of the collective tradition they share. It provides a common ritual in which all of them can participate simultaneously, jointly offer homage to the founders of one another's lineages, and formally acknowledge one another as religious peers.[44] Clearly, it is designed to help foster the development of a new shared culture of dharma transmission. Each of the individual elements within the ceremony (the setting, musical instruments, processions, prostrations, circumambulations, prostrations, chants, and so forth) consist of standard Zen ritual practices as performed at Buddhist temples in Japan. The ceremony as a whole, its format and sequence as well as its emphasis on mutual affirmation, however, presents something new and uniquely American. Significantly, it concludes with all the participants chanting the Zen hymn known as the *Harmony of Difference and Sameness*, a title that aptly expresses the goal of the ceremony itself and the task now faced by the SZBA.[45] Thus, the ceremony represents a development of traditional ritual forms for new purposes in a new land. It is a development that reflects both the growing maturity of Zen traditions in North America and their precarious, difficult quest to harmonize imported and native, old and new, similar and different.[46]

REFERENCES

Bellah, Robert N. 1985. "The Meaning of Dōgen Today." In William R. LaFleur, ed., *Dōgen Studies*. Honolulu: University of Hawaii Press, pp. 150–58.
Bodiford, William M. 1991. "Dharma Transmission in Sōtō Zen: Manzan Dōhaku's Reform Movement." *Monumenta Nipponica* 46/4: 423–51.
———. 1993. *Sōtō Zen in Medieval Japan*. Honolulu: University of Hawaii Press.
———. 1999. "Kokan Shiren's 'Zen Precept Procedures.'" In George J. Tanabe, Jr., ed., *Religions of Japan in Practice*. Princeton: Princeton University Press, pp. 98–108.
———. 2000. "Emptiness and Dust: Zen Dharma Transmission Rituals." In David Gordon White, ed., *Tantra in Practice*. Princeton: Princeton University Press, pp. 299–307.
———. 2005. "Bodhidharma's Precepts in Japan." In William M. Bodiford, ed., *Going Forth: Visions of Buddhist Vinaya*. Honolulu: University of Hawaii Press, pp. 185–209.

————. 2006. "Remembering Dōgen." *Journal of Japanese Studies* 32/1: 1–21.

Buswell, Robert E., Jr. 1992. *The Zen Monastic Experience: Buddhist Practice in Contemporary Korea*. Princeton: Princeton University Press.

Chappell, David W. 2005. "The Precious Scroll of the Liang Emperor: Buddhist and Daoist Repentance to Save the Dead." In William M. Bodiford, ed., *Going Forth: Visions of Buddhist Vinaya*. Honolulu: University of Hawaii Press, pp. 40–67.

DZZ (*Dōgen zenji zenshū*). Ed. Ōkubo Dōshū. 2 vols. Tokyo: Chikuma Shobō, 1969–1970.

Foulk, T. Griffith. 1993. "Myth, Ritual, and Monastic Practice in Sung Ch'an Buddhism." In Patricia B. Ebrey and Peter N. Gregory, eds., *Religion and Society in T'ang and Sung China*. Honolulu: University of Hawaii Press, pp. 147–208.

————. 2000. "The Form and Function of Kōan Literature: A Historical Overview." In Steven Heine and Dale S. Wright, eds., *The Kōan: Texts and Contexts in Zen Buddhism*. New York: Oxford University Press, pp. 15–45.

Geertz, Clifford. 1966. "Religion as a Cultural System." In Michael Banton, ed., *Anthropological Approaches to the Study of Religion*. London: Tavistock, pp. 1–46.

Genkō shakusho. 1322. By Kokan Shiren (1278–1346). 30 fascicles. (1) Reprint in *Dai Nihon Bukkyō zensho*. Vol. 1, pp. 1–137. Tokyo: Bussho kankōkai, 1912–1922. (2) Reprint as "Electronic Text of the Genko Shakusho by Kokan Shiren." Michel Mohr, ed. Kyoto: International Research Institute for Zen Buddhism, 2001.

Gernet, Jacques. 1995 (1956). *Buddhism in Chinese Society: An Economic History from the Fifth to the Tenth Centuries*. Trans. Franciscus Verellen. New York: Columbia University Press.

Heine, Steven, and Charles S. Prebish, eds. 2003. *Buddhism in the Modern World: Adaptations of an Ancient Tradition*. New York: Oxford University Press.

Hori, G. Victor Sōgen. 1994. "Sweet-and-sour Buddhism." *Tricycle: The Buddhist Review* 4/1: 48–52.

Ishikawa Rikizan. 2002. "Colloquial Transcriptions as Sources for Understanding Zen in Japan." Trans. and intro. by William M. Bodiford. *The Eastern Buddhist* (new series) 36/1: 120–42.

Jingde chuandeng lu. 30 fascicles. Published 1004. Reprint in *Taishō shinshū dai zōkyō*. Ed. Takakusu Junjirō, Watanabe Kaikyoku et al. Vol. 51. No. 2076. Tokyo: Taishō issaikyō kankōkai, 1924–1935.

Jorgensen, John. 1987. "The 'Imperial' Lineage of Ch'an Buddhism: The Role of Confucian Ritual and Ancestor Worship in Ch'an's Search for Legitimacy in the Mid-T'ang Dynasty." *Papers in Far Eastern History* 35: 89–131.

Kasulis, Thomas P. 1981. *Zen Action/Zen Person*. Honolulu: University of Hawaii Press.

Kuriyama Taion. 1980 (1938). *Sōjiji shi*. Reprint. Yokohama: Sōtōshū Daihonzan Sōjiji.

Lewis, I. M. 1986. *Religion in Context: Cults and Charisma*. Cambridge: Cambridge University Press.

Morreale, Don, ed. 1998. *The Complete Guide to Buddhist America*. Foreword by H. H. the Dalai Lama. Introductions by Jack Kornfield and Joseph Goldstein. Boston: Shambhala.

Nara Yasuaki and Nishimura Eshin, eds. 1979. *Zenshū*. Nihon Bukkyō kiso kōza. Vol. 6. Tokyo: Yūzankaku shuppan.

Nguyen, Cuong Tu. 1997. *Zen in Medieval Vietnam: A Study and Translation of the Thiền Uyển Tập Anh*. Honolulu: University of Hawaii Press.

Numrich, Paul D. 1996. *Old Wisdom in the New World: Americanization in Two Immigrant Theravada Buddhist Temples*. Knoxville: University of Tennessee Press.

Prebish, Charles S. 1999. *Luminous Passage: The Practice and Study of Buddhism in America*. Berkeley: University of California Press, 1999.

Prebish, Charles S., and Martin Baumann, eds. 2002. *Westward Dharma: Buddhism Beyond Asia*. Berkeley: University of California Press.

Prebish, Charles S., and Kenneth K. Tanaka, eds. 1998. *The Faces of Buddhism in America*. Berkeley: University of California Press.

Reichelt, Karl L. 1927. *Truth and Tradition in Chinese Buddhism: A Study of Chinese Mahayana Buddhism*. Trans. Kathrina V. W. Bugge. Shanghai: The Commercial Press.

Schlütter, Morten. 2005. "Vinaya Monasteries, Public Abbacies, and State Control of Buddhism under the Song Dynasty (960–1279)." In William M. Bodiford, ed., *Going Forth: Visions of Buddhist Vinaya*. Honolulu: University of Hawaii Press, pp. 136–60.

Shōwa shūtei Sōtōshū gyōji kihan. 1988. Ed. Sōtōshū shūmuchō kyōgakubu. Originally *Meiji kōtei Tōjō gyōji kihan*, 1889, revised 1918. Revised and enlarged 1950, 1952, and 1966 as *Shōwa kaitei zōho Sōtōshū gyōji kihan*. Tokyo: Sōtōshū shūmuchō.

Sōtōshū hōshiki sahō shashin kaisetsu. 1983. Ed. Hōshiki kenkyūkai Sōtō bukai. Tokyo: Meicho fukyūkai.

SZBA (Soto Zen Buddhist Association). 2004a. "Dharma Heritage Ceremony." Program. Privately Published.

———. 2004b. "First National Conference." Program folder. Privately Published.

Tamamura Takeji. 1981a (1937). "Zensō hōki ni tsuite." Reprinted in *Nihon Zenshūshi ronshū*. Vol. 1. Tokyo: Shibunkaku, pp. 3–20.

———. 1981b (1941). "Zensō shōgō kō." Reprinted in *Nihon Zenshūshi ronshū*. Vol. 1. Tokyo: Shibunkaku, pp. 21–94.

Tweed, Thomas A., and Stephen Prothero, eds. 1999. *Asian Religions in America: A Documentary History*. New York: Oxford University Press.

Watsuji Tetsurō. 1996. *Watsuji Tetsurō's Rinrigaku: Ethics in Japan*. (Originally: *Rinrigaku*, 1937–1949). Trans. Seisaku Yamamoto and Robert E. Carter. Albany: State University of New York Press.

Welch, Holmes. 1963. "Dharma Scrolls and the Succession of Abbots in Chinese Monasteries." *T'oung-pao* 50/1–3: 93–149.

———. 1967. *The Practice of Chinese Buddhism, 1900–1950*. Cambridge, MA: Harvard University Press.

Wetzel, Sylvia. 2002. "Neither Monk nor Nun: Western Buddhists as Full-time Practitioners." In Charles S. Prebish and Martin Baumann, eds., *Westward Dharma: Buddhism Beyond Asia*. Berkeley: University of California Press, pp. 275–84.

Williams, Duncan Ryūken, and Christopher S. Queen. 1999. *American Buddhism: Methods and Findings in Recent Scholarship.* Surrey, UK: Curzon.

Wright, Dale S. 1992. "Historical Understanding: The Ch'an Buddhist Transmission Narrative and Modern Historiography." *History and Theory* 31/1: 37–46.

Yifa. 2002. *The Origins of Buddhist Monastic Codes in China: An Annotated Translation and Study of the Chanyuan qinggui.* Honolulu: University of Hawaii Press.

Yoo, David K., ed. 1999. *New Spiritual Homes: Religion and Asian Americans.* Honolulu: University of Hawaii Press.

Pinyin–Wade-Giles Conversion Table

PINYIN	WADE-GILES	PINYIN	WADE-GILES
a	a	bou	pou
ai	ai	bu	pu
an	an		
ang	ang	ca	ts'a
ao	ao	cai	ts'ai
		can	ts'an
ba	pa	cang	ts'ang
bai	pai	cao	ts'ao
ban	pan	ce	ts'ê
bang	pang	ceng	ts'êng
bao	pao	cha	ch'a
bei	pei	chai	ch'ai
ben	pên	chan	ch'an
beng	pêng	chang	ch'ang
bi	pi	chao	ch'ao
bian	pien	che	ch'ê
biao	piao	chen	ch'ên
bie	pieh	cheng	ch'êng
bin	pin	chi	ch'ih
bing	ping	chong	ch'ung
bo	po	chou	ch'ou

PINYIN	WADE-GILES	PINYIN	WADE-GILES
chu	ch'u	e	ê, o
chua	ch'ua	en	ên
chuai	ch'uai	eng	êng
chuan	ch'uan	er	êrh
chuang	ch'uang		
chui	ch'ui	fa	fa
chun	ch'un	fan	fan
chuo	ch'o	fang	fang
ci	tz'ŭ	fei	fei
cong	ts'ung	fen	fen
cou	ts'ou	feng	feng
cu	ts'u	fo	fo
cuan	ts'uan	fou	fou
cui	ts'ui	fu	fu
cun	ts'un		
cuo	ts'o		
		ga	ka
da	ta	gai	kai
dai	tai	gan	kan
dan	tan	gang	kang
dang	tang	gao	kao
dao	tao	ge	kê, ko
de	tê	gei	kei
dei	tei	gen	kên
deng	têng	geng	kêng
di	ti	gong	kung
dian	tien	gou	kou
diao	tiao	gu	ku
die	tieh	gua	kua
ding	ting	guai	kuai
diu	tiu	guan	kuan
dong	tung	guang	kuang
dou	tou	giu	kuei
du	tu	gun	kun
duan	tuan	guo	kuo
dui	tui		
dun	tun	ha	ha
duo	to	hai	hai

PINYIN	WADE-GILES	PINYIN	WADE-GILES
han	han	ke	k'ê, k'o
hang	hang	ken	k'ên
hao	hao	keng	k'êng
he	ho	kong	k'ung
hei	hei	kou	k'ou
hen	hên	ku	k'u
heng	hêng	kua	k'ua
hong	hung	kuai	k'uai
hou	hou	kuan	k'uan
hu	hu	kuang	k'uang
hua	hua	kui	k'uei
huai	huai	kun	k'un
huan	huan	kuo	k'uo
huang	huang		
hui	hui	la	la
hun	hun	lai	lai
huo	huo	lan	lan
		lang	lang
ji	chi	lao	lao
jia	chia	le	lê
jian	chien	lei	lei
jiang	chiang	leng	lêng
jiao	chiao	li	li
jie	chieh	lia	lia
jin	chin	lian	lien
jing	ching	liang	liang
jiong	chiung	liao	liao
jiu	chiu	lie	lieh
ju	chü	lin	lin
juan	chüan	ling	ling
jue	chüeh	liu	liu
jun	chün	long	lung
		lou	lou
ka	k'a	lu	lu
kai	k'ai	luan	luan
kan	k'an	lun	lun
kang	k'ang	luo	lo
kao	k'ao	lü	lü

PINYIN	WADE-GILES		PINYIN	WADE-GILES
lüan	lüan		nin	nin
lüe	lüeh		ning	ning
lun	lun, lü		niu	niu
			nong	nung
ma	ma		nou	nou
mai	mai		nu	nu
man	man		nuan	nuan
mang	mang		nun	nun
mao	mao		nuo	no
me	mê		nü	nü
mei	mei		nüe	nüeh
men	mên			
meng	mêng		ou	ou
mi	mi			
mian	mien			
miao	miao		pa	p'a
mie	mieh		pai	p'ai
min	min		pan	p'an
ming	ming		pang	p'ang
miu	miu		pao	p'ao
mo	mo		pei	p'ei
mou	mou		pen	p'ên
mu	mu		peng	p'êng
			pi	p'i
na	na		pian	p'ien
nai	nai		piao	p'iao
nan	nan		pie	p'ieh
nang	nang		pin	p'in
nao	nao		ping	p'ing
ne	ne		po	p'o
nei	nei		pou	p'ou
nen	nên		pu	p'u
neng	nêng			
ni	ni		qi	ch'i
nian	nien		qia	ch'ia
niang	niang		qian	ch'ien
niao	niao		qiang	ch'iang
nie	nieh		qiao	ch'iao

PINYIN	WADE-GILES	PINYIN	WADE-GILES
qie	ch'ieh	she	shê
qin	ch'in	shei	shei
qing	ch'ing	shen	shên
qiong	ch'iung	sheng	shêng
qiu	ch'iu	shi	shih
qu	ch'ü	shou	shou
quan	ch'üan	shu	shu
que	ch'üeh	shua	shua
qun	ch'ün	shuai	shuai
		shuan	shuan
ran	jan	shuang	shuang
rang	jang	shui	shui
rao	jao	shun	shun
re	jê	shuo	shuo
ren	jên	si	ssŭ, szŭ
reng	jêng	song	sung
ri	jih	sou	sou
rong	jung	su	su
rou	jou	suan	suan
ru	ju	sui	sui
ruan	juan	sun	sun
rui	jui	suo	so
run	jun		
ruo	jo	ta	t'a
		tai	t'ai
sa	sa	tan	t'an
sai	sai	tang	t'ang
san	san	tao	t'ao
sang	sang	te	t'ê
sao	sao	teng	t'êng
se	sê	ti	t'i
sen	sên	tian	t'ien
seng	sêng	tiao	t'iao
sha	sha	tie	t'ieh
shai	shai	ting	t'ing
shan	shan	tong	t'ung
shang	shang	tou	t'ou
shao	shao	tu	t'u

PINYIN	WADE-GILES		PINYIN	WADE-GILES
tuan	t'uan		yi	i, yi
tui	t'ui		yin	yin
tun	t'un		ying	ying
tuo	t'o		yong	yung
			you	yu
wa	wa		yu	yü
wai	wai		yuan	yüan
wan	wan		yue	yüeh
wang	wang		yun	yün
wei	wei			
wen	wên		za	tsa
weng	wêng		zai	tsai
wo	wo		zan	tsan
wu	wu		zang	tsang
			zao	tsao
			ze	tsê
xi	hsi		zei	tsei
xia	hsia		zen	tsên
xian	hsien		zeng	tsêng
xiang	hsiang		zha	cha
xiao	hsiao		zhai	chai
xie	hsieh		zhan	chan
xin	hsin		zhang	chang
xing	hsing		zhao	chao
xiong	hsiung		zhe	chê
xiu	hsiu		zhei	chei
xu	hsü		zhen	chên
xuan	hsüan		zheng	chêng
xue	hsüeh		zhi	chih
xun	hsün		zhong	chung
			zhou	chou
ya	ya		zhu	chu
yai	yai		zhua	chua
yan	yen		zhuai	chai
yang	yang		zhuan	chuan
yao	yao		zhuang	chuang
ye	yeh		zhui	chui

PINYIN	WADE-GILES	PINYIN	WADE-GILES
zhun	chun	zu	tsu
zhuo	cho	zuan	tsuan
zi	tzǔ	zui	tsui
zong	tsung	zun	tsun
zou	tsou	zuo	tso

Notes

INTRODUCTION

1. T 48.397c.

2. T 47.497b; Ruth Fuller Sasaki, trans., *The Recorded Sayings of the Ch'an Master Lin-chi Hui-chao of Chen Prefecture* (Kyoto: The Institute for Zen Studies, 1975), p. 8.

3. T 47.498b; Sasaki, p. 13.

4. T 47.497c; Sasaki, p. 10.

5. T 47.499b; Sasaki, p. 18.

6. For interpretation and analysis of this film, see Dale S. Wright, "Human Responsibility and the Awakening of Character in the Buddhist Film *Mandala,*" *Literature and Theology: An International Journal of Religion, Theory, and Culture* 18/3 (2004); and David E. James and Kyung Hyun Kim, *Im Kwon-taek: The Making of a Korean National Cinema* (Detroit: Wayne State University Press, 2002).

7. This phrase is from Bernard Faure, *The Rhetoric of Immediacy* (Princeton: Princeton University Press, 1991), in chapter 13, appropriately entitled "Ritual Antiritualism." It is worth noting, however, that beyond the stylized narratives in Sung dynasty Chan texts, very few cases or examples of antiritual gestures are known in the historical records. Adherence to proper ritual form was clearly the norm of the period. It is perhaps ironic that this was nowhere more true than in modern Japanese Zen, where the image of the radical Zen iconoclast was so thoroughly valorized.

8. Faure, *The Rhetoric of Immediacy*, p. 286.

9. On Confucian ritual there are numerous excellent sources, but see especially: Philip J. Ivanhoe and T. C. Kline, eds., *Virtue, Nature, and Moral Agency in the Xunzi* (Indianapolis, IN: Hackett Publications, 2000);

Antonio Cua, *Human Nature, Ritual, and History: Studies in Xunzi and Chinese Philosophy* (Washington, D.C.: Catholic University of America Press, 2005); and Robert Eno, *The Confucian Creation of Heaven: Philosophy and the Defense of Ritual Mastery* (Albany: State University of New York Press, 1990).

10. It is worth noting that there is no word in Buddhist languages that corresponds precisely to our word "ritual." The Japanese *gyōji*, observances, is perhaps closest in connotations.

11. See Catherine Bell, *Ritual Theory, Ritual Practice* (New York: Oxford University Press, 1992); and Catherine Bell, *Ritual: Perspectives and Dimensions* (New York: Oxford University Press, 1997). Among other outstanding contemporary work on ritual, see the works of Roy Rappaport and Talal Asad.

12. While this is true of most Zen monasteries, it is not true of the much more numerous Zen temples in Japan today. Although trained in *zazen* in Zen monastic settings, the priests who oversee these temples serve primarily as ritualists for local communities. The connection drawn between these two—monastic meditation training and rituals such as funerals—is that the character and presence of mind developed in meditation provides the sanctity of character required to engage people in their matters of life and death.

13. T. Griffith Foulk, "The Zen Institution in Modern Japan," in Kenneth Kraft, ed., *Zen: Tradition and Transition* (New York: Grove Press, 1988).

14. Robert E. Buswell, Jr., *The Zen Monastic Experience* (Princeton: Princeton University Press, 1992), p. 168.

15. It is within this context of kōan study that we can consider Zen discourse as a ritualized activity. John McRae has shown how early Zen "discussions" between masters or between masters and disciples quickly took on the appearance of ritual. Although "encounter dialogue" was presumed to be the place in Zen where "spontaneity" was most pronounced, McRae shows how these "ritualized exchanges" followed a heavily "scripted recitation-and-response pattern." See John McRae, *The Northern School and the Formation of Early Ch'an Buddhism* (Honolulu: University of Hawaii Press, 1986), pp. 92–93.

16. On understanding gleaned from empathetic participation in traditions belonging to someone else, see Paul Ricoeur, *Symbolism of Evil* (Boston: Beacon Press, 1967).

17. Robert H. Sharf, "Ritual," in Donald S. Lopez, Jr., ed., *Critical Terms for the Study of Buddhism* (Chicago: University of Chicago Press, 2005), pp. 245–70.

18. On innate enlightenment, see Jacqueline I. Stone, *Original Enlightenment and the Transformation of Medieval Japanese Buddhism* (Honolulu: University of Hawaii Press, 2003).

19. Stanley Tambiah, *Magic, Science, and Religion and the Scope of Rationality* (Cambridge, MA: Cambridge University Press, 1990); and Stanley Tambiah, "A Performative Approach to Ritual," in *Culture, Thought, and Social Action: An Anthropological Perspective* (Cambridge, MA: Harvard University Press, 1985).

20. For example, notice how acts of ritual bowing in Zen embody various forms of understanding. My prostrations before the Zen master embody the deference that

I am learning through the act; they embody a respect for the enlightenment that he has achieved and the humility appropriate to my status. In every act of bowing I understand this in a very physical way, more deeply on each occasion. Similarly, in *zazen*, every time I sit as the Buddha once sat in enlightenment, I practice that state of existance, I perform enlightenment myself, in whatever preliminary and underdeveloped form I am now capable of.

21. On ritual change and the appearance of "invariance," see Bell, "Invariance," in *Ritual: Perspectives and Dimensions*, p. 150.

22. The subject of ritual change is taken up in chapter 9 of this volume, "Dharma Transmission in Theory and Practice."

CHAPTER I

1. T. Griffith Foulk, "Myth, Ritual, and Monastic Practice in Sung Ch'an Buddhism," in Patricia Buckley Ebrey and Peter N. Gregory, eds., *Religion and Society in T'ang and Sung China* (Honolulu: University of Hawaii Press, 1993), pp. 147–208; T. Griffith Foulk, "Sung Controversies Concerning the 'Separate Transmission' of Ch'an," in Peter N. Gregory and Daniel Getz, eds., *Buddhism in the Sung* (Honolulu: University of Hawaii Press, 1999), pp. 220–94; and T. Griffith Foulk, "*Chanyuan qinggui* and Other 'Rules of Purity' in Chinese Buddhism," in Steven Heine and Dale S. Wright, eds., *The Zen Canon: Understanding the Classic Texts* (New York: Oxford University Press, 2004), pp. 275–315.

2. T. Griffith Foulk, " 'Rules of Purity' in Japanese Zen," in Steven Heine and Dale S. Wright, eds., *Zen Classics: Formative Texts in the History of Zen Buddhism* (New York: Oxford University Press, 2006), pp. 137–49.

3. In the Meiji period, scholars generally accepted the historicity of the traditional (i.e., Song) account of the Chan lineage (*chanzong*), with its list of twenty-eight generations of Indian patriarchs who formed the trunk, as it were, of a Chan family tree that eventually produced five main branches in the late Tang. It was only in the 1930s, with the comparative study of various Dunhuang manuscripts that contained very different versions of the early lineage, that scholars began to realize that the "Zen lineage in India" was a myth invented by the Chinese.

4. The pioneers of the field were scholars such as Sakaino Satoshi (1861–1933), Nukariya Kaiten (1867–1934), Matsumoto Bunzaburō (1869–1944), Suzuki Daisetsu (1870–1966), Yabuki Keiki (1879–1939), Okada Gihō (1882–1961), and Ui Hakuju (1882–1963).

5. Martin Collcutt, "Buddhism: The Threat of Eradication," in Marius B. Jansen and Gilbert Rozman, eds., *Japan in Transition: From Tokugawa to Meiji* (Princeton: Princeton University Press, 1986), pp. 143–67.

6. T 51.250c28–251b3. The provenance of the *Regulations of the Chan School* (*Chanmen guishi*) is uncertain, but the earliest evidence for its existence is found in the *Song Biographies of Eminent Monks* (*Song gaoseng zhuan*), compiled in 988 (T 50.770c–771a). For an English translation, see T. Griffith Foulk, "The Legend of Baizhang, 'Founder' of Chan Monastic Discipline," in Wm. Theodore de Bary and

Irene Bloom, eds., *Sources of Chinese Tradition*, 2d ed., vol. 1 (New York: Columbia University Press, 1999), pp. 517–22. A summary of the contents of the text may also be found in Foulk, "*Chanyuan qinggui*," pp. 280–82.

7. See, for example, Ui Hakuju, *Zenshūshi kenkyū* no. 9 (Tokyo: Iwanami shoten, 1935), pp. 81–90; Yanagida Seizan, "Chūgoku Zenshūshi," in Nishitani Keiji, ed., *Kōza Zen*, vol. 3: *Zen no rekishi: Chūgoku* (Tokyo: Chikuma shobō, 1974), pp. 27–28; Imaeda Aishin, *Zenshū no rekishi* (Tokyo: Shibundō, 1966), p. 1; Kondō Ryōichi, "Hyakujō shingi no seiritsu to sono genkei," in *Hokkaidō Komazawa Daigaku kenkyū kiyō* 3 (1968): 19–48; and Heinrich Dumoulin, *A History of Zen Buddhism* (Boston: Beacon Press, 1969), pp. 77–79.

8. Kagamishima Genryū, *Dōgen zenji to sono monryū* (Tokyo: Seishin shobō, 1961), pp. 30–56; Ogisu Jundō, *Zenshū shi nyūmon* (Kyoto: Heirakuji shoten), p. 71.

9. Kagamishima Genryū, "Dōgen zenji to Hyakujō shingi," in *Dōgen zenji to sono in'yō kyōten, goroku no kenkyū* (Tokyo: Kijisha, 1965), pp. 181–92; Kagamishima Genryū, "Hyakujō ko shingi henka katei no ichi kōsatsu," in *Komazawa Daigaku Bukkyōgakubu kenkyū kiyō* 25 (1967): 1–13; Kagamishima Genryū, "Kaisetsu," in Kagamishima Genryū, Satō Tatsugen, and Kosaka Kiyū, eds. and trans., *Yakuchū zennen shingi* (Tokyo: Sōtōshū shūmuchō, 1972), pp. 1–25; Kagamishima Genryū, "Hyakujō shingi no seiritsu to sono igi," in *Aichi Gakuin Daigaku Zen kenkyūjo kiyō* 6 & 7 (1967): 117–34. Also see: Kondō Ryōichi, "Hyakujō shingi to Zennen shingi," in *Indogaku Bukkyōgaku kenkyū* 17/2 (1969): 773–75; Kondō, "Hyakujō shingi no seiritsu to sono genkei," pp. 31–39; Harada Kōdō, "Hyakujō shingi to Zennen shingi," in *Sōtōshū kenkyūin kenkyūsei kenkyū kiyō* 1 (1969): 5–14; and Kosaka Kiyū, "Shingi hensen no teiryū," in *Shūgaku kenkyū* 5 (1963): 126–28.

10. Hu Shih, "Ch'an (Zen) Buddhism in China: Its History and Method," in *Philosophy East and West* 3/1 (1953): 6–7; Yanagida Seizan, *Shoki Zenshū shisho no kenkyū* (Kyoto: Zen bunka kenkyūjo, 1967), p. 452; and Yanagida, "Chūgoku Zenshūshi," pp. 48–49.

11. For a survey of Song and Yuan rules of purity, see Foulk, "*Chanyuan qinggui*," pp. 297–306.

12. ZZ 2-17-1, 28–74.

13. ZZ 2-16-5.438a–471c. Sōtōshū Zensho kankōkai, ed., *Sōtōshū Zensho: Shingi* (Tokyo: Kōmeisha, 1931), pp. 867–934. For an annotated edition and Japanese translation, see Kagamishima, Satō and Kosaka, eds. and trans., *Yakuchū zennen shingi*. For an English translation, see Yifa, *The Origins of Buddhist Monastic Codes in China: An Annotated Translation and Study of the Chanyuan Qinggui* (Honolulu: University of Hawaii Press, 2002).

14. T 48.109c–160b.

15. Nukariya Kaiten, for example, categorized the Song as the "period of over-ripeness in the way of Zen" (*zendō jukuran no dai*). That was followed by the "period of fundamental reversal in the way of Zen" (*zendō henchū no dai*), by which he meant a degeneration into syncretism during the Yuan and Ming, and the complete eradication of true Zen by Lamaism in the Qing. See "Table of Contents" (*mokuji*) in Nukariya Kaiten, *Zengaku shisōshi*, 2 vols. (Tokyo: Genkōsha, 1923–1925). Also see Nukariya

Kaiten, *The Religion of the Samurai: A Study of Zen Philosophy and Discipline in China and Japan* London: Luzac, 1913. pp. 24–27, s.v. "Decline of Zen."

16. Sakaino Satoshi, *Shina Bukkyōshi kō* (Tokyo: Morie honten, 1907), p. 344.

17. D. T. Suzuki, for example, defended Mahāyāna Buddhism against the misjudgments of Western scholars in his *Outlines of Mahāyāna Buddhism* (London: Luzac and Co., 1907; rpt., Schocken Books, 1963), pp. 16–22.

18. For statistics on the size of the Chinese Buddhist sangha in the Republican period, see Holmes Welch, *The Practice of Chinese Buddhism: 1900–1950* (Cambridge: Harvard University Press, 1967), pp. 411–20.

19. See, for example, Kagamishima, *Dōgen zenji to sono monryū*, pp. 30–56; and Kagamishima Genryū, "Nihon Zenshūshi: Sōtōshū," in Nishitani Keiji, ed., *Kōza Zen*, vol. 4 (Tokyo: Chikuma shobō, 1974), pp. 91–93. For similar views, see Takeuchi Dōyū, "Shoki sōdan no tenkai: kyōdan," in Kagamishima Genryū and Tamaki Kōshirō, eds., *Dōgen Zen no rekishi, kōza Dōgen* 2 (Tokyo: Shunjūsha, 1980), pp. 2–5; and Martin Collcutt, *Five Mountains: The Rinzai Zen Monastic Institution in Medieval Japan* (Cambridge: Harvard University Press, 1981), pp. 50–51.

20. T 82.15c28–16a1. This passage is also found, with very slight variations, six times in Dōgen's subsequent writings. There are three occurrences in his *Shōbōgenzō: Gyōji* (T 82.143b4–5); *Bukkyō* (T 82.195b2–3); and *Zanmai ōzanmai* (T 82.243c20). The other three occurrences are in Dōgen's *Eihei kōroku* (vol. 1, nos. 33 and 432; vol. 9, no. 85).

21. See, for example: Kagamishima, "Nihon Zenshūshi: Sōtōshū," in Nishitani, ed., *Kōza Zen*, vol. 4, pp. 107–9; Suzuki Taizan, *Zenshū no chihō hatten* (1942; rpt., Tokyo: Yoshikawa kōbunkan, 1983), pp. 47–61; Imaeda Aishin, "Chūsei Bukkyō no tenkai," in Akamatsu Toshihide, ed., *Nihon Bukkyōshi* 2 (Kyoto: Hōzōkan, 1967), pp. 202–3; and Takeuchi Dōyū, *Nihon no Zen* (Tokyo: Shunjūsha, 1976), pp. 196–98.

22. Imaeda, "Chūsei Bukkyō no tenkai," pp. 153–221; and Imaeda, *Zenshū no rekishi*, pp. 13–71.

23. Takeuchi Michio, *Nihon no Zen* (Tokyo: Shunjūsha, 1976), pp. 121–81.

24. Collcutt, *Five Mountains*, p. 28.

25. Ibid.

26. Ibid., pp. 28–29.

27. The Ōtōkan line consists of Nanpo Jōmyō (1235–1308), a.k.a. National Teacher Daiō (Daiō Kokushi), his disciple Shūhō Myōchō (1282–1337), a.k.a National Teacher Daitō (Daitō Kokushi), and Kanzan Egen (1277–1360), who are collectively revered as founders of the Daiō branch of the Rinzai lineage.

28. See, for example, Yanagida Seizan, *Rinzai no kafū* (Tokyo: Chikuma shobō, 1967), pp. 144–51, 173–92; Hirata Takashi, "Musō," in Nishitani Keiji, ed., *Kōza Zen*, vol. 4, pp. 233–48; Ōmori Sōgen, "Nihon ni okeru Rinzai Zen no tenkai," in ibid., pp. 137–41; Ogisu Jundō, "Daitō," in ibid., pp. 214–15, 228, 232; and Collcutt, *Five Mountains*, pp. 127–29.

29. D. T. Suzuki, *An Introduction to Zen Buddhism* (1934; rpt., New York: Grove Press, 1964), p. 40. The articles collected in this book originally appeared in the journal *New East*, published in Japan between 1914 and 1918.

30. Suzuki, *An Introduction to Zen Buddhism*, p. 39.

31. Daisetz Teitaro Suzuki, *The Training of the Zen Buddhist Monk* (Kyoto: The Eastern Buddhist Society, 1934; rpt., Berkeley: Wingbow Press, 1974), p. 80.

32. Ibid.

33. Ibid., pp. 80–81.

34. Ibid., p. 77.

35. Ibid.

36. D. T. Suzuki, *Essays in Zen Buddhism*, Third Series (London: Rider & Co., 1953), p. 347.

37. G. B. Sansom, *Japan: A Short Cultural History* (1931; rpt., New York: Appleton-Century-Crofts, 1943), p. 337.

38. Philip Kapleau, *The Three Pillars of Zen* (Boston: Beacon Press, 1967), pp. 211–12.

39. An early example of such a work is Suzuki, *The Training of the Zen Buddhist Monk*. That book was subsequently translated into Japanese and published as Suzuki Teitarō, *Zendō no shugyō to seikatsu* (Tokyo: Morie shoten, 1935). A similar set of drawings of Zen monks in training, with detailed explanations, is found in Satō Giei, *Unsui nikki* (Tokyo: Shunjūsha, 1972). Sato's drawings, accompanied by brief remarks in English by Eshin Nishimura, are also published in Giei Sato and Eshin Nishimura, *Unsui: A Diary of Zen Monastic Life* (Honolulu: University of Hawaii Press, 1973). See also "Life at the Zen Training Center," in Daisetz T. Suzuki, *Zen and Japanese Buddhism* (Tokyo: Japanese Travel Bureau, 1958), pp. 5–16; The Japan Times, *Zen Buddhism* (Tokyo: Japan Times, 1970); Koji Sato and Sosei Kuzunishi, *The Zen Life* (New York: Weatherhill/Tankosha, 1972); Nishimura Eshin, *Zensō no seikatsu* (Tokyo: Yūzankaku, 1983); Murakoshi Eiyū, *Irasuto de yomu Zen no hon* (Tokyo: Suzuki shuppan, 1998); and Shinohara Hisao and Satō Tatsugen, *Zusetsu Zen no subete: ikiteiru Zen* (Tokyo: Zusetsu shuppan, 1999).

40. See, for example: Suzuki Daisetsu, *Zen no mikata, Zen no shugyō* (Tokyo: Shunjūsha, 1952); Sohaku Ogata, "Life in a Zen Monastery," in *Zen for the West* (London: Rider and Company, 1959), pp. 34–59; Nishitani Keiji, ed., *Kōza Zen*, vol. 2: *Zen no jissen* (Tokyo: Chikuma, 1974); and Akizuki Ryūmin, *Zendō seikatsu* (Tokyo: Hirakawa, 1983).

41. Ordinary temples are explained more fully in Part Three.

42. Suzuki, *The Training of the Zen Buddhist Monk*, p. 33.

43. Ibid., p. 3.

44. Inaba Meidō, "Shingi o chūshin to shite mitaru samu kō jōsetsu," Part 2, *Zengaku kenkyū* 10 (1929): 40–41, 44–45.

45. Inaba Meidō, "Samu kō jōsetsu," Part 1, *Zengaku kenkyū* 9 (1929), p. 90.

46. Fukuba Hoshū, "Zenshū kyōdan ni okeru keizai seikatsu jō no taido ni tsuite," *Zengaku kenkyū* 34 (1940): 133–35.

47. For details of these practices, see Daniel Stevenson, "The Four Kinds of Samādhi in Early T'ien-t'ai Buddhism," in Peter N. Gregory, ed., *Traditions of Meditation in Chinese Buddhism* (Honolulu: University of Hawaii Press, 1987), pp. 45–97.

48. Foulk, "'Rules of Purity' in Japanese Zen," pp. 145–46.

49. "Butsudō," in Ōkubo Dōshū, ed., *Dōgen zenji zenshū*, 2 vols. (Tokyo: Chikuma shobō, 1969, 1970), vol. 1, pp. 376–79.

50. Foulk, "'Rules of Purity' in Japanese Zen," pp. 144–45.

51. Ibid., pp. 142–43.

52. For information on these two texts, see Foulk, "'Rules of Purity' in Japanese Zen," pp. 139–41, 142–43, 146–47, 154–55.

53. Ibid., pp. 141–42.

54. William M. Bodiford, "Zen in the Art of Funerals: Ritual Salvation in Japanese Buddhism," *History of Religions* 32/2 (1992): 146–64.

55. William M. Bodiford, *Sōtō Zen in Medieval Japan* (Honolulu: University of Hawaii Press, 1993), p. 186.

56. Collcutt, *Five Mountains*, p. 67. The quoted passage is Collcutt's translation of *Azama kagami*, Kenchō 5 (1253)/11/25.

57. For a photograph of Tokiyori's *chinzō* see Collcutt, *Five Mountains*, p. 60 (Figure 7: "Hōjō Tokiyori in the Robes of a Zen Abbot").

58. Collcutt, *Five Mountains*, p. 73.

59. For a discussion of the use of Buddhist mortuary portraits (C. *dingxiang*, J. *chinzō*) in Song China and medieval Japan, see Foulk and Robert H. Sharf, "On the Ritual Use of Ch'an Portraiture in Medieval China," in *Cahiers d'Extrême-Asie* [Bilingual Journal of the Ecole Française d'Extrême-Orient] 7 (1993–1994): 149–219; republished in Bernard Faure, ed., *Chan Buddhism in Ritual Context* (London: Routledge Curzon, 2003), pp. 74–150.

60. Collcutt, *Five Mountains*, p. 73.

61. ZZ 2-16-5.492d.

62. Collcutt, *Five Mountains*, p. 149.

63. Stupa sites built for living abbots were known as "living stupas" or "longevity stupas" (*jutō*); they often served as residences for abbots after they retired.

64. The only sangha hall that remained standing from the medieval period was the one that still exists at Tōfukuji in Kyoto. Built in 1347, by the Edo period it had fallen into disuse and been converted into a warehouse.

65. Bodiford, *Sōtō Zen in Medieval Japan*, p. 185.

66. T 82.766a–785c.

67. See, for example, Yinyuan's statement lamenting the Japanese ignorance of precepts in his *Dharma Ceremony for Spreading the Precepts (Gukai hōgi)*, cited in James Baskind, "Ming Buddhism in Edo Japan: The Chinese Founding Masters of the Japanese Ōbaku School" (Ph.D. dissertation, Yale University, 2006).

68. T 82.778a–b.

69. T 82.778a24–27.

70. Procedures for "three platform precepts assembly" are detailed in the *Ōbaku Rules of Purity (Ōbaku shingi)*, T 82.769b–770b.

71. Fuji Masaharu and Abe Zenryō, *Furudera junrei* (Kyoto), vol. 9: *Manpukuji* (Tokyo: Tankōsha, 1977), pp. 148–51. The rite was held in: 1665, 1670, 1677, 1681, 1685, 1690, 1695, 1699, 1706, 1710, 1719, 1722, 1728, 1738, 1741, 1746, 1752, 1760,

1767, 1772, 1780, 1789, 1796, 1803, 1811, 1833, 1843, 1853, 1861, 1872, 1882, 1895, and 1922.

72. This was undertaken by the Ōbaku monk Tetsugen Dōkō (1630–1682), resulting in the 6,956 volume *Ōbakuban daizōkyō*, the printing blocks for which were completed in 1678.

73. An ambrosia hall (*kanrodō*) for this purpose was built at Manpukuji in 1665.

74. For a good summary of mortification practices in the Ōbaku school, see Baskind, "Ming Buddhism in Edo Japan," pp. 194–223.

75. For a somewhat more detailed account of this process, see Foulk, " 'Rules of Purity' in Japanese Zen," pp. 149–56.

76. Ogisu Jundō, *Myōshinji, Jisha shiriizu* 2 (Kyoto: Tōyō bunkasha, 1977), pp. 71–87. Ungo's observation of the precepts included the strict prohibition of alcohol in his monastery and a personal refusal to handle money.

77. *Sōzan kan'in kiroku*, no. 15; manuscript held at Daianzenji.

78. *Banshōzan daianzenji rokuyū*, colophon by 10th abbot, dated Kanpō 3 (1743); manuscript held at Daianzenji.

79. Daianzenji's "mountain name" (*sangō*) was *Banshōzan* or "Myriad Pine Mountain."

80. T 81.624b–687c.

81. ZZ 2-16-5. For an English translation and analysis, see Foulk, "Daily Life in the Assembly," in Donald S. Lopez, Jr., ed., *Buddhism in Practice* (Princeton: Princeton University Press, 1995), pp. 455–72.

82. Ogino Dokuen, ed., *Kinsei zenrin sōbōden* (Kyoto: Shibunkaku, 1890), s.v. *Sōgenji gisan oshō den*.

83. Philip B. Yampolsky, *The Zen Master Hakuin* (New York: Columbia University Press, 1971), p. 27.

84. Ishū Miura and Ruth Fuller Sasaki, *The Zen Koan* (New York: Harcourt, Brace & World, 1965), pp. 25–30.

85. Edo period manuscript held at Ryūkoku University library. Reprint edition: Yanagida Seizan, ed., *Chokushū hyakujō shingi sakei, Zengaku sōsho*, vol. 8A–B (Kyoto: Chūbun shuppansha, 1979).

86. Original manuscript in Mujaku's hand held at Myōshinji in Kyoto. Reprint edition: Yanagida Seizan, ed., *Zenrin shōkisen, Zengaku sōsho*, vol. 9 (Kyoto: Chūbun shuppansha, 1979). See also *Zenrin shōkisen* (Kyoto: Kaiba shoin, 1909; rpt., Tokyo: Seishin shobō, 1963).

87. T 81.688a–723c.

88. *Sōtōshū zensho: Shingi*, pp. 439–548. The full title of the text is: *Rules of Purity Handbook for Shōju Grove Daijō Nation-Protecting Zen Monastery* (*Shōjurin daijō gokoku zenji shingi shinanbo*); also known as *Shōju Grove Rules of Purity* (*Shōjurin shingi*). Gesshū's disciple, Manzan Dōhaku, assisted to such a degree in the compilation that he should be considered a co-author.

89. T 82.423c–451c.

90. For details, see Foulk, " 'Rules of Purity' in Japanese Zen," pp. 140, 143.

91. Ibid., p. 155.

92. *Sōtōshū zensho: Shingi*, 29–207. The original full title of the text is *Summary of Procedures in Rules of Purity for Sōtō Sangha Halls* (*Tōjō sōdō shingi gyōhōshō*). The colophon has the date 1741, so the text may have been completed then, but Menzan's preface to its publication is dated 1753.

93. Ibid., pp. 209–330.

94. Ibid., pp. 815–36.

95. T 82.319a–342b. For an English translation, see Taigen Daniel Leighton and Shohaku Okumura, trans., *Dōgen's Pure Standards for the Zen Community: A Translation of Eihei Shingi* (Albany: State University of New York Press, 1996).

96. *Sōtōshū zensho: Shingi*, pp. 331–416. The original full title is *Small Rules of Purity for Kichijō Mountain Eihei Monastery* (*Kichijōzan eiheiji shōshingi*).

97. For a description of the layout of those monasteries and the practical and ritual function of their various buildings, see Foulk, "Myth, Ritual, and Monastic Practice in Sung Ch'an Buddhism," pp. 167–97.

98. From *Miscellaneous Writings of Zen Master Eihei Gentō on Restoring the Old Patriarchal Rules* (*Eihei gentō zenji soki fukko zakkō*) in Zoku Sōtōshū Zensho kankōkai, ed., *Zoku Sōtōshū zensho: Shingi* (Tokyo: Sōtōshū shūmuchō, 1974–1977), p. 338b.

99. Bunkachō, ed., *Shūkyō nenkan* [Religions Almanac], 2003 edition (Tokyo: Gyōsei, 2004), p. 68.

100. For a somewhat more detailed overview of the institutions mentioned here, see T. Griffith Foulk, "The Zen Institution in Modern Japan," in Kenneth Kraft, ed., *Zen: Tradition and Transition* (New York: Grove Press, 1988), pp. 157–77.

101. Sōtōshū shūmuchō kyōkabu, ed., *Shōwa shūtei, Sōtōshū gyōji kihan* (Tokyo: Sōtōshū shūmuchō, 1988), p. 12.

102. The following account of the funeral of a lay person is based on Sōtōshū shūmuchō kyōkabu, ed., *Shōwa shūtei, Sōtōshū gyōji kihan*, pp. 348–57.

103. The full text of the *Ten Buddha Names* is given above in connection with the mealtime liturgy.

104. Sōtōshū shūmuchō kyōkabu, ed., *Shōwa shūtei, Sōtōshū gyōji kihan*, p. 361.

105. Ibid., p. 360.

106. See Stephen F. Teiser, *The Ghost Festival in Medieval China* (Princeton: Princeton University Press, 1988).

107. A more concise list of afflictions (Skt. *kleśa*, J. *bonnō*) names just three: greed, anger, and delusion.

CHAPTER 2

1. In addition to the sense used here, the term *shangtang* has a few other related meanings. Other than the conventional meaning of "going up the hall," within the Buddhist context it can also denote the monks' going to the dining hall or refectory in the monastery (or to the monks' hall, according to some texts) for a formal meal. The term is also used to refer to the upper part of the monks' hall (*sengtang*) to distinguish it from the lower part of the hall. See Komazawa Daigaku Zengaku daijiten hensanjo, ed., *Zengaku daijiten* (Tokyo: Taishūkan shoten, 1985), p. 573c.

2. For the Chan school's recasting of ritualism within the context of an antiritual stance, see Bernard Faure, *The Rhetoric of Immediacy: A Cultural Critique of Chan/Zen Buddhism* (Princeton: Princeton University Press, 1991), pp. 284–303.

3. For instance, Baizhang's biography states that after his ordination he moved to Lujiang (in present-day Anhui province), where he studied the Buddhist scriptures (see his stupa inscription, *Tang hongzhou baizhangshan gu huaihai chanshi taming*, in *Chixiu baizhang qinggui*, T 48.1156c). Similarly, Damei's biography in *Song gaoseng zhuan* states that as a child he had a prodigious memory and was able to memorize long passages from the scriptures (T 50.776a), while Wuye's biography tells us that at the early age of nine he started to study the Mahāyāna canon, including the *Diamond, Lotus, Vimalakīrti*, and *Huayan* scriptures (*Song gaoseng zhuan* 11, T 50.772b).

4. John Kieschnick, *The Eminent Monk: Buddhist Ideals in Medieval Chinese Hagiography* (Honolulu: University of Hawaii Press, 1997), pp. 120–21.

5. *Song gaoseng zhuan* 4, T 50.725c–26a; Kieschnick, *The Eminent Monk*, p. 121.

6. See Kieschnick, *The Eminent Monk*, pp. 123–30.

7. For instance, in his diary Ennin records an imperial decree issued on the ninth day of the first month in 841, which called for popular lectures (*sujiang*) to be held at seven Buddhist monasteries in the capital. Similar decrees were also issued on the first days of the fifth and ninth months of the same year. See Edwin O. Reischauer, trans., *Ennin's Diary: The Record of a Pilgrimage to China in Search of the Law* (New York: The Ronald Press Company, 1955), pp. 298–99, 307, 310 (see also p. 316 for the mention of a similar decree issued in 842).

8. Kenneth Ch'en, *The Chinese Transformation of Buddhism* (Princeton: Princeton University Press, 1973), pp. 241–42.

9. In Huijiao's (497–554) *Gaoseng zhuan* (Biographies of Eminent Monks, compiled in 519), exegetes (*yijie*) form the second of the ten main categories of eminent monks. They are allocated fascicles four through eight; the text includes 101 biographies of exegetes, the largest number among all categories of eminent monks (see T 50.346b–383b).

10. *Gaoseng zhuan* 12, T 50.406b–409a; *Gaoseng zhuan* 13, T 50.413b–415c.

11. Reischauer, *Ennin's Diary*, p. 152; and Edwin O. Reischauer, *Ennin's Travels in T'ang China* (New York: The Ronald Press Company, 1955), p. 186. See also Ch'en, *The Chinese Transformation of Buddhism*, p. 248; and Ono Katsutoshi, *Nittō guhō junrei gyōki no kenkyū*, vol. 2 (Tokyo: Hōzōkan, 1988), p. 143.

12. Reischauer, *Ennin's Diary*, pp. 152–53; Reischauer, *Ennin's Travels*, p. 186; and Ono, *Nittō guhō*, vol. 2, p. 143. Ennin also describes two additional rituals held at the same monastery, a single-day lecture and a recitation of scriptures rite. See Reischauer, *Ennin's Diary*, pp. 154–56; Ono, *Nittō guhō*, vol. 2, pp. 144–45.

13. *Gaoseng zhuan* 13, T 50.417c; cf. Ch'en, *Chinese Transformation of Buddhism*, p. 243.

14. *Gaoseng zhuan* 13, T 50.417c.

15. *Gaoseng zhuan* 13, T 50.417c; Ch'en, *Chinese Transformation of Buddhism*, pp. 243–44.

16. Neil Schmid, "Tun-huang Literature," in Victor Mair, ed., *The Columbia History of Chinese Literature* (New York: Columbia University Press, 2001), p. 984. For more on the *yuanqi* genre, see Neil Schmid, "Yuanqi: Medieval Buddhist Narratives from Dunhuang" (Ph.D. Dissertation, University of Pennsylvania, 2002); for the *bianwen* texts, see Victor H. Mair, *T'ang Transformation Texts: A Study of the Buddhist Contribution to the Rise of Vernacular Fiction and Drama in China* (Cambridge, MA: Council on East Asian Studies, Harvard University, 1989); for *jiangjing wen*, see the chapter by Hirano Genshō in Makita Tairyō and Fukui Fumimasa, eds., *Tonkō to Chūgoku Bukkyō* (Tokyo: Daitō shuppansha, 1984), pp. 321–58; and for *yazuo wen*, see the chapter by Kanaoka Shōkō, in Kanaoka Shōkō, ed., *Tonkō no bungaku bunken* (Tokyo: Daitō shuppansha, 1990), pp. 339–88.

17. Schmid, "Yuanqi," pp. 132–44.

18. The Pelliot collection of Dunhuang manuscripts, catalogue no. 3849; see also the Stein collection of Dunhuang manuscripts, catalogue no. 4417.

19. Schmid, "Yuanqi," pp. 145–47; Hirano Kenshō, *Tangdaide wenxue yu fojiao*, trans. by Zhang Tongsheng (Taipei: Yejiang chubanshe, 1987), pp. 205–6; Mair, *T'ang Transformation Texts*, pp. 148–49; and Wang Zhongmin et al., eds., *Dunhuang bianwen ji* 471.3 (Beijing: Renmin wenxue chubanshe, 1957). Schmid points out (p. 148) that besides scriptures, popular narratives could also be used as the focal texts of popular lectures.

20. Examples of early Chan texts that were written down in the form of treatises include Dazhu Huihai's (fl. 8th c.) *Dunwu rudao yaomen lun* (Treatise on the Essentials of Entering the Way via Sudden Awakening); Northern school's *Guanxin Lun* (Treatise on Mind Contemplation), probably written by Shenxiu (606?–706); and Niutou school's *Jueguan lun* (Treatise on the Transcendence of Contemplation), traditionally attributed to Niutou Farong (594–657).

21. The traditional attribution to Huineng has been extensively questioned by modern scholarship. For the Dunhuang version of the text, see T 48.337a–345b. For an English translation and study, see Philip B. Yampolsky, trans., *The Platform Sutra of the Sixth Patriarch* (New York: Columbia University Press, 1967); for a Japanese translation (which also contains the original text), see Nakagawa Taka, trans., *Rokuso dangyō* (Tokyo: Chikuma shobō, 1976).

22. *Wanling lu*, T 48.386b; Iriya Yoshitaka, trans., *Denshin hōyō, Enryō roku* (Tokyo: Chikuma shobō, 1969), pp. 134; cf. John Blofeld, *The Zen Teaching of Huang-po on the Transmission of Mind* (New York: Grove Press, 1958), p. 87.

23. *Baizhang guanglu*, Xu zangjing 118.86b; Thomas Cleary, trans., *Sayings and Doings of Pai-chang* (Los Angeles: Center Publications, 1978), p. 52. For the original passage in the *Lotus Scripture*, see *Miaofa lianhua jing* 3, T 9.22b, and Burton Watson, trans., *The Lotus Sutra* (New York: Columbia University Press, 1993), p. 119. For the same reference in Linji's record, see T 47.502a.

24. In *Linji yulu* the two terms are used as headings for the first two sections of the text, possibly indicating a distinction between the two (at least in the minds of the Song-period editors who compiled the text). Both terms are discussed in Yanagida Seizan, "Goroku no rekishi: Zen bunken no seiritsu shiteki kenkyū," *Tōhō gakuhō* 57

(1985): 513–25. There Yanagida argues that there is a significant difference between the two of them (see esp. pp. 513–14). According to him, during Mazu's time *shizhong* was used to refer to his sermons, but by the time of his disciple Baizhang, the old preaching format was replaced by the new procedure of *shangtang*, which supposedly was a central part of Baizhang's institution of a new system of Chan monastic life. Yanagida's arguments about the distinct uses of these two terms are informed by his acceptance of traditional lore regarding Baizhang's role as the patron saint of Chan monasticism, but they are not supported by any compelling historical evidence. In fact, the term *shangtang* does not appear at all in *Baizhang guanglu* (Baizhang's Extensive Record). There are numerous examples in Chan texts where the two terms are used interchangeably. A case in point is fascicle twenty-eight of *Chuandeng lu*, in which the sermons of some Chan teachers start with *shizhong* while those of other monks start with *shangtang* (see T 51.437c–49a).

25. *Chuandeng lu* 6, T 51.251a; English translation from Cheng-chien, trans., *Sun-Face Buddha*, p. 34. See also Martin Collcutt, *Five Mountains: The Rinzai Zen Monastic Institution in Medieval Japan* (Cambridge, MA: Harvard University Press, 1981), p. 140.

26. The complex issues surrounding the provenance and the authorship of the *Platforms Scripture* have been the subject of many scholarly publications. For more on the text's compilation, see Yampolsky, *The Platform Sutra*, pp. 89–110, Yanagida Seizan, *Shoki zenshū shisho no kenkyū* (Kyoto: Hōzōkan, 1967), pp. 253–78, and Yanagida, "Goroku no rekishi," pp. 404–25.

27. T 48.337a; translation adapted with minor modifications from Yampolsky, *The Platform Sutra*, pp. 125–26. It is unlikely that the text is a reliable record of the Huineng's teachings. But that is largely beside the point in this case; the text undoubtedly illuminates conceptions of preaching rituals prevalent within a Chan milieu at the time of its compilation, which is our main concern here.

28. For symbolic exegesis, see Bernard Faure, *The Will to Orthodoxy: A Critical Genealogy of Northern Chan Buddhism* (Stanford: Stanford University Press, 1997), p. 41; and John R. McRae, *The Northern School and the Formation of Early Ch'an Buddhism* (Honolulu: University of Hawaii Press, 1986), pp. 201–2.

29. T 48.339a; translation adapted with minor modifications from Yampolsky, *The Platform Sutra*, p. 141.

30. T 48.339b–c; Yampolsky, *The Platform Sutra*, pp. 143–46.

31. See Daoxuan's biography in *Song gaoseng zhuan* 14, T 50.790b–91b; *Da song sengshi lüe* 1, T 54.238b; Sato Tatsugen, *Chūgoku Bukkyō ni okeru kairitsu no kenkyū* (Tokyo: Mokujisha, 1986), pp. 113–37; John R. McRae, "Daoxuan's Vision of Jetavana: The Ordination Platform Movement in Medieval Chinese Buddhism," in William M. Bodiford, ed., *Going Forth: Visions of the Buddhist Vinaya* (Honolulu: University of Hawaii Press, 2005), pp. 68–100; and Ono, *Nittō guhō*, vol. 1, p. 241, vol. 2, p. 381, and vol. 4, pp. 468–69.

32. See John R. McRae, "Shenhui's Vocation on the Ordination Platform and our Visualization of Medieval Chinese Ch'an Buddhism," *Zen bunka kenkyūjo kiyō* 24 (1998): 43–66.

33. Yang Zengwen, ed., *Shenhui heshang chanhua lu* (Beijing: Zhonghua shuju, 1996), p. 5.

34. Yang, *Shenhui heshang chanhua lu*, pp. 34–35.

35. See Mario Poceski, *"Guishan jingce* and the Ethical Foundations of Chan Practice," in Steven Heine and Dale S. Wright, eds., *Zen Classics: Formative Texts in Zen Buddhism* (New York: Oxford University Press, 2006), pp. 15–42; and Mario Poceski, "Xuefeng's Code and the Chan School's Participation in the Development of Monastic Regulations," *Asia Major, New Series* 16/2 (2003): 33–56.

36. Mario Poceski, *"Mazu yulu* and the Creation of the Chan Records of Sayings," in Steven Heine and Dale S. Wright, eds., *The Zen Canon: Understanding the Classic Texts* (New York: Oxford University Press, 2004), pp. 53–79.

37. *Chuandeng lu* 24, T 51.398b; cf. Andy Ferguson, trans., *Zen's Chinese Heritage: The Masters and their Teachings* (Boston: Wisdom Publications, 2000), p. 317.

38. T 47.548a; translation adapted from Urs App, trans., *Master Yunmen: From the Record of the Chan Teacher "Gate of Clouds"* (New York: Kodansha International, 1994), p. 113.

39. T. Griffith Foulk, "Myth, Ritual, and Monastic Practice in Sung Ch'an Buddhism," in Patricia Buckley Ebrey and Peter N. Gregory, eds., *Religion and Society in T'ang and Sung China* (Honolulu: University of Hawaii Press, 1992), p. 149. This sweeping statement is for the most part applicable to stories that feature Tang-era monks, but it does not work equally well in the cases of tenth-century monks.

40. App, *Master Yunmen*, pp. 24–28.

41. As stated by Bernard Faure, "Just as the iconoclasm or aniconism of Chan turned out to be a mirror image of its iconism, Chan antiritualism remains essentially a ritual move." Faure, *The Rhetoric of Immediacy*, p. 297.

42. For a general survey of the organization and operation of Chan monasteries during the Southern Song period, see Foulk "Myth, Ritual, and Monastic Practice in Sung Ch'an Buddhism," pp. 167–91. Additional information about the various types of monasteries and their relationship with the imperial Song state can be found in Morten Schlütter, "Vinaya Monasteries, Public Abbacies, and State Control of Buddhism under the Song Dynasty (960–1279)," in Bodiford, ed., *Going Forth*, pp. 136–60.

43. For the Dharma hall, see Yifa, *The Origins of Buddhist Monastic Codes in China: An Annotated Translation and Study of the* Chanyuan Qinggui (Honolulu: University of Hawaii Press, 2002), p. 72; Collcutt, *Five Mountains*, pp. 194–97; and Foulk, "Myth, Ritual, and Monastic Practice in Sung Ch'an Buddhism," pp. 176–77, 180.

44. Mochizuki Shinkō, ed., *Bukkyō dai jiten*, vol. 3, rev. ed. (Kyoto: Sekai seiten kankō kyōkai, 1954–1963), pp. 2707–8.

45. Yifa, *The Origins of Buddhist Monastic Codes in China*, p. 112; Kagamishima Genryū, et al., trans., *Yakuchū: Zennen shingi* (Tokyo: Sōtōshū shūmuchō, 1972), p. 3.

46. See Yifa, *The Origins of Buddhist Monastic Codes in China*, pp. 53–98.

47. Yifa, *The Origins of Buddhist Monastic Codes in China*, p. 135, with some changes, and Kagamishima, *Zennen shingi*, pp. 71–72. The last sentence in parenthesis

is an interlinear note found in the original text; the same applies to the subsequent quotations from the same text.

48. See Robert H. Sharf, "Ritual," in Donald S. Lopez Jr., ed., *Critical Terms for the Study of Buddhism* (Chicago: The University of Chicago Press, 2005), p. 265.

49. Yifa, *The Origins of Buddhist Monastic Codes in China*, pp. 135–36, with minor changes, and Kagamishima, *Zennen shingi*, pp. 72–73.

50. Foulk "Myth, Ritual, and Monastic Practice in Sung Ch'an Buddhism," p. 177.

51. Yifa, *The Origins of Buddhist Monastic Codes in China*, p. 136, and Kagamishima, *Zennen shingi*, p. 74.

52. Yifa, *The Origins of Buddhist Monastic Codes in China*, pp. 136, with minor changes, and Kagamishima, *Zennen shingi*, p. 75.

53. The ascending the hall ceremony was the central and most formal preaching event in the Chan monasteries, but not the only one. *Chanyuan qinggui* and other monastic texts also describe other preaching events, such as "entering the (abbot's) room" (*rushi*) and the "informal sermon" (*xiaocan*, lit. "small/minor convocation"). While these were typically enacted on a smaller scale and were supposed to be less formal, they were also highly stylized and involved predetermined sets of ritual actions such as bowing and offering of incense. See Kagamishima, *Zennen shingi*, pp. 63–69, 78–85, and Yifa, *The Origins of Buddhist Monastic Codes in China*, pp. 131–34, 138–41.

54. Faure, *The Rhetoric of Immediacy*, pp. 294–301.

55. The brief account of these developments presented here is based on Jiang Wu, "Problems with Enlightenment: The Performance of Encounter Dialogue in Seventeenth-century Chinese Chan Buddhism" (paper presented at the American Academy of Religion annual conference, Philadelphia, 2005).

56. Ibid.

57. Robert E. Buswell, *The Zen Monastic Experience* (Princeton: Princeton University Press, 1992), pp. 182–83.

58. Ibid., pp. 183–87.

59. Ibid., p. 186.

60. Catherine Bell, "Performance," in Mark C. Taylor, ed., *Critical Terms for Religious Studies* (Chicago: The University of Chicago Press, 1998), p. 214.

61. While it is true that there are passages in Chan literature that point in the direction of antiritualism, especially if one takes them out of their original historical contexts, I would suggest that the popular but mostly ahistorical image of trenchant antiritualism as a central feature of Chan/Zen teachings and practices is a relatively recent development, which apparently has found profound resonance with prevalent modern sensibilities, especially in the West but also in Korea and Japan.

CHAPTER 3

1. Martin Collcutt, *Five Mountains: The Rinzai Zen Monastic Institution in Medieval Japan* (Cambridge, MA: Harvard University Press, 1981), p. 40.

2. Albert Welter, "Zen Buddhism as the Ideology of the Japanese State: Eisai and the *Kōzen gokokuron*," in Steven Heine and Dale S. Wright, eds., *Zen Classics:*

Formative Texts in the History of Buddhism (New York: Oxford University Press, 2006), pp. 65–112.

3. Sanskrit, *Karunika-raja-Sutra* (?). Because the original is no longer extant, it is widely considered to be a composition conceived in China (Kamata Shigeo, ed., *Chūgoku Bukkyōshi jiten* [Tokyo: Tokyodō shuppan, 1981], p. 307a). Two Chinese "translations" are extant, one by Kumarajiva in 401 (*Taishō-shinshū daizokyō*, hereafter abbreviated as T vol. 8, no. 245), the other by Amoghavajra (Chinese, Bukong), ca. 765 (no. 246).

4. Sanskrit, *Saddharma-pundarika-Sutra*; among several translations of the *Hokke-kyō* in Chinese, the one by Kumarajiva in A.D. 406 (T vol. 9, no. 262) is standard.

5. Sanskrit, *Suvarnaprabhasottama-Sutra*. Three Chinese translations exist (T vol. 16, nos. 663–665). It was promoted at the court of Emperor Temmu (r. 672–686) on the pretext, asserted in the *sutra*, that the Four Deva Kings (*shi-tennō*) would protect the ruler who followed its teachings. The complete version, the *Konkōmyō-saishōō-kō* (*Golden Light Sutra of the Most Victorious Kings*, no. 665), was translated by Yijing (Japanese, Gijo 635–713) in the early eighth century. Yijings's version included mystic incantations, lacking in earlier versions, important to followers of esoteric Buddhist traditions in the Tendai and Shingon schools. It was often recited at major court festivals. In Japan, major commentaries were written on it, including ones by Saichō and Kukai.

6. Numerous commentaries were written on these scriptures by Chinese and Japanese Buddhist masters. The scriptures also provided the basis for numerous court rituals in Japan. On these points, see Inoue Mitsusada, *Nihon kodai no kokka to Bukkyō* [Buddhism and the State in Ancient Japan] (Tokyo: Iwanami shoten, 1971), and M. W. de Visser, *Ancient Buddhism in Japan*, 2 vols. (Leiden, Netherlands: E. J. Brill, 1935).

7. Collcutt, *Five Mountains*, p. 25.

8. See "Regulations of the Mountain School in Six Articles I," in Ryusaku Tsunoda and Paul Groner, trans., *Sources of Japanese Tradition*, vol. 1 (New York: Columbia University Press, 2001), pp. 145–47 (*Dengyō Daishi zenshū* I, pp. 11–13 [1989 ed.]).

9. The title of section eight is given differently in the preface, *kenritsu shimoku* (Established Program of Rituals), and at the outset of section eight, *Zenshū shimoku* (Program of Rituals of the Zen School). The fact that the aim of the rituals is designed for the protection of the country is implicit from the title of the work and its contents.

10. See Robert E. Buswell, Jr., *The Zen Monastic Experience* (Princeton: Princeton University Press, 1992); T. Griffith Foulk, "Myth, Ritual, and Monastic Practice in Sung Ch'an Buddhism," in Patricia Buckley Ebrey and Peter N. Gregory, eds., *Religion and Society in T'ang and Sung China* (Honolulu: University of Hawaii Press, 1993), pp. 147–208; Yifa, *The Origins of Monastic Codes in China: An Annotated Translation and Study of the* Chanyuan Chinggui (Honolulu: University of Hawaii Press, 2002); Bernard Faure, ed., *Chan Buddhism in Ritual Context* (London: RoutledgeCurzon, 2003); and Morten Schlütter, "Vinaya Monasteries, Public Abbacies, and State Control

of Buddhism under the Song (960–1279)," in William M. Bodiford, ed., *Going Forth: Visions of Buddhist Vinaya* (Honolulu: University of Hawaii Press, 2005), pp. 136–60.

11. The *Chanyuan qinggui* was compiled by Chanlu Zongze in 1103; an edition is available in the *Xinwenfeng* edition of *Zokuzōkyō*, vol. 111. For a translation, see Yifa, *The Origins of Buddhist Monastic Codes in China*, pp. 112–220.

12. All references to the *Kōzen gokokuron* text are to Yanagida Seizan's edition and translation in *Chūsei zenka no shisō*, in *Nihon chūsei taikei* 16 (Tokyo: Iwanami shoten, 1972), hereafter abbreviated as Yanagida ed. and Yanagida tr. I have also consulted the translation of Furuta Shokin in *Eisai, Nihon no Zen goroku* 1 (Tokyo: Kodansha, 1977), and the *Taishō* edition of the text, T vol. 80, no. 2543.

In addition to the *Chanyuan qinggui*, Eisai also allegedly based his program on "current practices in great countries" (*daikoku gengyō*). Yanagida (p. 80 note) suggests *daikoku gengyō* is the name for a handbook (C. *Daguo jianxing*) relating current practice in India and China, but no reference is given. Judging from Eisai's description that follows, *daikoku gengyō* could easily be a reference to descriptions of "current" practice disclosed in a number of sources, such as vinaya texts, or Chinese sources that would have been either unknown or little known in Japan (for example, Zanning's *Dasong sengshilue* [J. *Daisō sōshiryaku*; Outline History of the Sangha Compiled in the Great Song Dynasty]), which include descriptions of a number of current institutional practices in China.

13. These are examples all drawn from fascicle one (ZZ 111.877–884); additional examples could be cited from each of the remaining five fascicles.

14. Yifa, *The Origins of Buddhist Monastic Codes in China*, p. 98, observes how important it is to recognize the influence of elements from Chinese governmental policies and traditional Chinese etiquette on the *Chanyuan qinggui*.

15. Collcutt, *Five Mountains*, p. 135 (chart 4).

16. The discussion here follows Eisai's presentation in section eight of the *Kōzen gokokuron*, Yanagida ed., pp. 117b–19a; Yanagida tr., pp. 80–86.

17. Foulk, "Myth, Ritual, and Monastic Practice in Sung Ch'an Buddhism," pp. 167–91.

18. Based on comments attributed to Baizhang Huaihai in *Jingde chuandeng lu* (T 51.251a).

19. Yifa, *The Origins of Buddhist Monastic Codes in China*, p. 112. This is not to suggest that Zongze approved of it without reservation. He is quite explicit in stating that it is appropriate only for those who are "extraordinarily pure and exalted," and that observance of vinaya regulations should not be neglected.

20. The precepts of the lesser vehicle refer, in this context, to the *Sifen lu* (Four Part Vinaya) of the Dharmaguptaka school, T 22, no. 1428. The bodhisattva precepts are drawn from the *Fanwang jing* (Brahma Net Sutra), T 24, no. 1484.

21. According to William M. Bodiford, "Bodhidharma's Precepts in Japan," in William M. Bodiford, ed., *Going Forth*, p. 188, scholars (especially Ishida Mizumaro) have recently begun to question whether the documents compiled in support of this proposition to renounce the *Four Part Vinaya* are an accurate reflection of Saichō's

teaching or are more consistent with views espoused by Saichō's disciple, Kōjō, in Saichō's name.

22. It is somewhat ironic, given the associations that modern readers have with the two denominations, that Pure Land, rather than Zen, is the movement within the Kamakura that best represents the radical nature of Buddhist developments during this period.

23. Collcutt, *Five Mountains*, pp. 215–18. Collcutt also calls attention to the fact that no such reading rooms survive in Japanese Rinzai monasteries, owing to the emphasis on kōan introspection rather than discursive understanding as the way to instigate awakening.

24. Taigen Daniel Leighton and Shohaku Okumura, trans., *Dōgen's Pure Standards for the Zen Community: A Translation of* Eihei Shingi (Albany: State University of New York Press, 1996), p.109. According to Collcutt, *Five Mountains*, p. 217, sutra stands at Jinshan si were reserved for the study of the *Avatamsaka Sutra* (*Huayan jing*) and Chan classics (*Chan dian*).

25. Yanagida ed., p. 118a; Yanagida, tr., p. 81.

26. Ibid.

27. All times have been converted to the western clock; times given follow Yanagida, *op. cit.* and Furuta, *op. cit.*, and differ slightly from the "approximate times" given by Yifa, *The Origins of Buddhist Monastic Codes in China*, p. 39 (table 3). Notes in small typeface appear in the original text.

28. The term for the "longevity of the emperor" (*hōsan*) literally refers to adding years to the treasure (of the country), i.e., the emperor.

29. Yanagida ed., p. 118a; Yanagida, tr., p. 82.

30. The Rector was one of the most senior members of the monastery, charged with, among other things, administering punishments for transgressions; see Yifa, "Chanyuan qinggui," in *The Origins of Buddhist Monastic Codes in China*, pp. 152–54.

31. Along with the large outer robe, the upper and lower garments constitute the three robes regulated in the vinaya rules.

32. Foulk, "Myth, Ritual, and Monastic Practice in Sung Ch'an Buddhism," pp. 190–91.

33. Welter, "Zen Buddhism as the Ideology of the Japanese State: Eisai and the *Kōzen gokokuron*."

34. The *Daihannya haramitta kyō* (T 5, no. 220), *Ninnō gokoku kyō* (T 8, no. 245 and 246), *Hokke kyō* (T 9, no. 262), and *Konkōmyō saishō kyō* (T 16, no. 665), collectively referred to as the four sutras for protecting the country, figure prominently in rituals promoting the welfare of the state.

35. *Nenju* (*niansong*) is an abbreviation for *nenbutsu* (*nianfo*) "buddha invocation" and *jukyō* (*songjing*) "sutra chanting."

36. The *honji suijaku* theory derives from the traditional Buddhist theory of an original prototype (*honji*) of buddha as an essentialized and absolute form, as opposed to local manifestations (*suijaku*) like Sakyamuni, who appear in the world for the benefit of sentient beings. When extended to Shinto in Japan, kami came to be

included as bodhisattva figures, local manifestations who appear in the world to rescue sentient beings.

37. See the ground plan for the Beishan Lingyin si monastery reproduced and discussed by Foulk in "Myth, Ritual, and Monastic Practice in Sung Ch'an Buddhism."

38. Collcutt, *Five Mountains*, pp. 143–44.

39. An official ceremony for commemorating the five hundred arhats.

40. A ceremony for providing offerings to the relics of the Buddha. According to Yanagida (p. 83 note), the ceremony was initiated by Ennin (a.k.a. Jikaku daishi).

41. According to Yanagida (p. 83 note), this refers to various types of Dharma assemblies which differed yearly. Furuta (p. 267 note) suggests that the purpose was to recite the *Kegon kyō* (C. *Huayan ching*).

42. According to Yanagida (p. 84 note) and Furuta (p. 267 note), the *Butsumyō kyō* (C. *Foming ching*; T 14, no. 440 or 441) is recited for the confession of sins committed in the previous year.

43. In the Buddhist canon, two sutras bear the title *Surangama Sutra* (*Shu ryōgon kyō*): a two fascicle work translated by Kumarajiva (T 15, no. 642), and a ten fascicle work translated later, in 705 (T 19, no. 945). The latter work, a discourse on the nature of mind containing some esoteric practices, was of special interest to both the Zen and Shingon schools and is the likely one intended here.

44. *Chūsei zenka no shisō*, p. 84 note.

45. See Yifa, *The Origins of Buddhist Monastic Codes in China*, pp. 159–61.

46. See the plan for the reading room of the Jinshan si, reproduced and discussed in Collcutt, *Five Mountains*, pp. 215–18.

47. According to Yanagida (p. 84 note), these ceremonies later included repentance rituals, ceremonies for feeding hungry ghosts and releasing living beings.

48. Yifa, *The Origins of Buddhist Monastic Codes in China*, p. 169. For Yifa's explanation of the rite, see Yifa's note (n. 45) on pp. 290–91. For a study of the water-land ritual, see Makita Tairyō, "Suiriku e shōkō," in Tairyō Makita, ed., *Chūgoku kinsei Bukkyōshi kenkyū* (Kyoto: Heirakuji shoten, 1957), pp. 169–93.

49. Regarding Zunshi's promotion of these rituals, see Daniel Stevenson, "Protocols of Power: Tz'u-yun Tsun-shih (964–1032) and T'ien-t'ai Lay Buddhist Ritual in the Sung," in Peter Gregory and Daniel Getz, *Buddhism in the Sung* (Honolulu: University of Hawaii Press, 1999), pp. 340–408. More broadly, on the social background of Zunshi's creation of a Pure Land patriarchy, see Daniel Getz, "T'ien-t'ai Pure Land Societies and the Creation of the Pure Land Patriarchate," in ibid., pp. 477–523.

50. T 20.34b–38a; Stevenson, "Protocols of Power," pp. 358–59.

51. *Wangsheng jingtu chanyuan yi* (T 47.490c–494c) and *Wangsheng jingtu jueyi xingyuan ermen* (T 47.144c–147c). On these, see Stevenson, "Protocols of Power," pp. 359–63, and Getz, "T'ien-t'ai Pure Land Societies and the Creation of the Pure Land Patriarchate," p. 483.

52. Yifa, *The Origins of Buddhist Monastic Codes in China*, pp. 132–34.

53. Ibid., p. 134.

54. Foulk, "Myth, Ritual, and Monastic Practice in Sung Ch'an Buddhism," p. 181.

55. Yanagida ed., p. 113b; Yanagida, tr., p. 63.

56. Ibid. Elder Fu was the dharma-heir of Xuefeng Yicun. His biography appears in *Jingde chuandeng lu* 19. He also appears in the *Blue Cliff Records*, cases 47 and 99. According to Yanagida (p. 397b), this story about Elder Fu is told by Dahui (Dai'e) in *Zhengfa yanzang* (J. *Shōbōgenzō*; ZZ 2-23-61a).

57. See *Zutang ji* 19 and *Jingde chuandeng lu* 12.

58. The biography of Leshan Daoxian is found in *Zutang ji* 9 and *Jingde chuandeng lu* 17; Shishuang Chingchu (807–888) in *Zutang ji* 6, *Jingde chuandeng lu* 15, and *Song gaoseng zhuan* 12.

59. The biography of Yantou (828–887) is found in *Zutang ji* 7, *Jingde chuandeng lu* 16, and *Song gaoseng zhuan* 23.

60. Yanagida ed., pp. 113b–114a; Yanagida tr., p. 64.

61. The twelve two-hour periods that divided the day (and night) in premodern Japanese definitions of time.

62. Yanagida ed., p. 114a; Yanagida tr., pp. 64–65. The saying is from the *Sutra on the Great Perfection of Wisdom* (T 7.939a).

63. See, for example, the *Mahasanghika vinaya* (T 22.262b).

64. The subject of ch. 14 of the *Lotus Sutra*.

65. T 29.2c.

66. In a directive to his students, Confucius bade them: "Be stimulated by the *Odes*, take your stand on the rites and be perfected by music" (*Lun yu* VIII-8: D. C. Lau, trans., *The Analects* [Middlesex, UK: Penguin, 1979], p. 93), providing a succinct formula for the integral role of poetry, ritual, and music in the development of moral character in the Confucian tradition.

67. *Xunzi*, section 2; Burton Watson, trans., *Xunzi: Basic Writings* (New York: Columbia University Press, 2003), p. 26.

68. According to Xunzi:

> Through rites Heaven and earth join in harmony, the sun and moon shine, the four seasons proceed in order, the stars and constellations march, the rivers flow and all things flourish.... Through them what is fundamental and what is peripheral are put in proper order; beginning and end are justified; the most elegant forms embody all distinctions; the most penetrating insight explains all things. In the world those who obey the dictates of ritual will achieve order; those who turn against them will suffer disorder. Those who obey them will win safety; those who turn against them will court danger. Those who obey them will be preserved; those who turn against them will be lost. (*Xunzi*, section 19; Watson, trans., p. 98, with minor changes).

69. According to Xunzi:

> If the plumb line is properly stretched, then there can be no doubt about crooked and straight; if the scales are properly hung, there can be no doubt about heavy and light; if the T square and compass are properly adjusted,

there can be no doubt about square and round; and if the gentleman is well versed in ritual, then he cannot be fooled by deceit and artifice. The line is the acme of straightness, the scale is the acme of fairness, the T square and compass are the acme of squareness and roundness, and rites arc the highest achievement of the Way of man. Therefore, people who do not follow and find satisfaction with the rites may be called people without direction, but those who follow and find satisfaction in them may be called men of direction. (*Xunzi*, section 19; Watson, trans., p. 99).

70. James Legge, trans., *Li Chi: Book of Rites*, vol. 2 (Hong Kong: Hong Kong University Press, 1960), pp. 100–1 (XIX-23); Ch'u Chai and Winberg Chai, eds., *Li Chi: Book of Rites* (New Hyde Park, NY: University Books, 1967), p. xlv.

71. Legge, trans., *Li Chi: Book of Rites*, p. 99 (XIX-19).

72. Legge, trans., *Li Chi: Book of Rites*, pp. 102–3, xliv–xlv. According to ancient Chinese speculation, the human soul derives from the two forces that permeate the universe: *yin* and *yang*. The human soul in turn possesses a dual nature: as *po* (deriving from *yin*), and as *hun* (deriving from *yang*). Simply stated, the *po* constitutes the animal or sentient life that inheres in the body, the "corporeal soul," while the *hun* constitutes the spiritual essence, the "ethereal soul." Beliefs regarding the fate of the *po* and *hun* at death had a great impact on ritual practices at Chinese sacrifices. The *po*, or animal nature, was believed to descend to earth and assume a ghostly form known as *gui*. The *hun*, or spiritual nature, was thought to ascend to heaven where it assumed a spiritual form known as *shen*. In this way, the *gui* and *shen* represented the transformed presences of the deceased and the focus of attention at Chinese sacrifices. Heaven and earth are also derivations of the same primal forces, *yin* and *yang*. Music and ritual, in turn, constitute the response or adaptation of these same forces to the model and pattern provided by heaven and earth, in terms suitable to human behavior. This is how music is said to accord with *shen* spirits and ritual is said to accord with ghost-like *gui*. In order that the whole structure is understood in terms of a Confucian perspective, the sequence of related concepts is subsumed under Confucian moral theory, the virtues of benevolence (*ren*) and righteousness (*yi*). These serve as the moral pretext for ritual behavior. The aim here is that the external manipulation of symbols in the ritual context is not merely a formal one but is matched by an internal transformation whose purpose is to improve the human character.

It should be noted here that as committed as the Confucian tradition was to rites and ceremonies, particularly those honoring the spirits of departed ancestors, a persisting ambiguity remained. This ambiguity stems from the rational tendency in Confucian thought and its reluctance to acknowledge the existence of ancestral spirits as such. The origins of this reluctance can be traced to Confucius himself. In a famous exchange, Zilu asks how the *gui* and *shen* should be served, to which Confucius replies, "You are not yet able to serve man. How can you serve the *gui* (and the *shen*)?" When Zilu asks about death, Confucius responds, "You do not yet understand life. How can you understand death?" (*Lun yu* XI-12). Elsewhere in the *Lun yu*, Confucius refuses to speak about the *shen* (and *gui*?) (VII-21). Still, this did not prevent Confucius from participating in rites honoring the spirits. When taking meals, for example, we are told that Confucius invariably offered a little in sacrifice, and always with a solemn demeanor (X–11). In one instance, Confucius openly advocates sacrificing to *shen* as if they are present (III–12). In effect, Confucius prized the attitude of reverence and respect encouraged by ritual while expressing indifference toward the spirits at which ritual services were directed. He seemed determined to uphold the memory of the departed out of honor and respect but uninterested in agreeing to their existence in some sort of afterlife. He was committed to upholding the traditional rites and ceremonies inherited from the past but not to affirming the literal symbolism that lay behind their performance. From the perspective of Confucian theory, the attitudes of reverence and solemnity (as expressions of Confucian virtue) generated by participation in ritual became the bases for ritual. This tended to displace the older legacy from which the rites themselves originally grew, the world of spirits.

73. In one respect, the use of fragrances is compatible with the Confucian view of ritual as a means of preserving social order by satisfying natural human desires (including the sense of smell). According to Xunzi, the sage kings of Chinese antiquity formulated ritual principles to provide positive outlets for natural human desires. By introducing limits and degrees to human appetites, desires could be satisfied and disorder avoided. Appetites in need of satisfaction are discussed by Xunzi in terms of the five senses, including the nose and sense of smell (*Xunzi*, section 19; Watson, trans., pp. 93–94).

74. James Legge, trans., *The Shu King or Book of Historical Documents* (Hong Kong: Hong Kong University Press, 1960), p. 539, with changes.

75. L. Weiger, *Chinese Characters: Their Origin, Etymology, History, Classification, and Signification* (New York: Dover Publications, 1965; originally published 1915), p. 185; Morohashi Tetsuji, *Dai Kanwa jiten*, vol. 12 (Tokyo: Taishūkan shoten, 1957–60), p. 445a (explanation derived from *Shuo wen*).

76. The use of incense in China predates the arrival of Buddhism. Evidence for this is suggested by the recovery of various *xiang hu*, or incense burners, from tombs of the Former Han Dynasty (206 BC–AD 8).

77. A seventh-century glossary explaining Buddhist loan words in Chinese, the *Yijiejing yingyi*, notes that the Sanskrit word for incense or fragrance, *gandha*, transliterated into Chinese as *jianta* (modern pronunciation), has the same meaning as *xiang* in Chinese when translated. Little is known of the compiler of this work, Xuanying. A brief biography of him is included in the *Xu gaoseng zhuan*, fascicle 30 (T 50.704c), appended to the biography of Zhiguo.

The association of the Chinese character *xiang* with *gandha* (or *jianta*) was a cause of confusion and resentment among Buddhists. In the sixth century, the Sui Dynasty exegete Huiyuan (523–592) lamented the inadequacy of referring to Buddhist incense with the Chinese character *xiang*, owing to its associations with Chinese sacrificial customs. See the *Dacheng yizhang* (T 44, no. 1851: 631a12–29). The biography of Huiyuan is found in *Xu gaoseng zhuan*, fascicle 8 (T 50.489c26–492b1), not to be confused with the earlier exegete of the same name who became famous in Pure Land circles.

78. T 14, no. 475, fascicle 10; see Burton Watson, trans., "Fragrance Accumulated," in *The Vimalakirti Sutra* (New York: Columbia University Press, 1997), pp. 112–20.

79. See the translation from the Pali by T. W. Rhys-Davids, *Buddhist Suttas* (Delhi: M. Banarsidass, 1965), pp. 122–26. The use of fragrances here represents a classic example in the history of religions. At a symbolic level, pleasant aromas are of the nature of the divine, as discussed previously. In ancient times, such aromas were commonly associated with human figures whose feats seemed to defy the ordinary. In Buddhist scriptures, various fragrances are associated with those thought to be majestic and distinguished (as an example, see ch. 4 of the *Lotus Sutra*; Leon Hurvitz, trans., *Scripture of the Lotus Blossom of the Fine Dharma* [New York: Columbia University Press, 1976], p. 86). According to the *Maha-parinibbana sutta*, the Buddha was cremated with rites and honors customarily reserved for a great king. In addition, the use of fragrances also had a practical significance, especially in hot climates, in masking unpleasant odors associated with the corpse between the time of death and cremation.

80. Incense rites were particularly important for the spread of Buddhism in China. Daoan (312–385) was largely responsible for promoting them as a means to block the spread of precept violations. According to Zanning, Daoan established a series of regulations to compensate for the lack of knowledge regarding the Buddhist precepts in China at that time. The regulations provided guidelines for incense-offering ceremonies, meditation sessions, public lectures, penitential rituals, and *uposatha* celebrations, etc. (see the *Dasong Seng shilue*, section 24 [T 54, 241a–b]). Nothing is known of the content of these regulations. They are also mentioned in the biography of Daoan in *Gaoseng zhuan*, ch. 5 (T 50, 353b).

81. *Digha-nikaya*, no. 5; Rhys-Davids, trans., *Dialogues of the Buddha I* (London: Luzac, 1956), p. 180. In the *Kutadanta-sutta*, a Brahmin by the name of Kutadanta seeks the Buddha's advice on matters of ritual detail. Through a parable, the Buddha advises (among other things) that no creature be harmed in the sacrifice, and that it be accomplished strictly in keeping with Buddhist vegetarian requirements. In place of the sacrifice we have a sort of community celebration representing the collective joy and good will of the members of the community. Other activities are recommended as superior to sacrifice (in ascending order): providing gifts to virtuous recluses; establishing a monastic site for members of the Buddhist order; putting one's own trust in Buddhism; obeying the five cardinal Buddhist precepts; and following the discipline of a Buddhist monk oneself, culminating in spiritual cultivation leading to enlightenment. This description, it might be noted, also reveals the tendency in Buddhism to value inner realization over public ceremony. It expresses clearly that the ultimate goal is to become a monk and realize enlightenment. In the process of achieving this goal, meditation replaces sacrifice as the ritual context.

82. The reason for this appeal was associated with the acceptance of Buddhist mythological elements in Chinese society. Particularly popular were morality tales from the Buddhist folk tradition that explained the destiny of departed souls and suggested ways in which that destiny could be influenced.

83. The most famous example of this type of tale is the *Ullambana-Sutra*, C. *Yulanpen jing* (T 16, no. 685). For an extensive study of this text and its place in the ghost festival in medieval China, see Stephen F. Teiser, *The Ghost Festival in Medieval China* (Princeton: Princeton University Press, 1988). The story tells of one, Maudgalyayana (Mulian), who is instructed by the Buddha on the means necessary to save his departed mother from her fate as a hungry ghost (*preta*): provide food offerings for the Buddha and Buddhist clergy. The spiritual merit thus received may be transferred by Maudgalyayana to his mother and her suffering alleviated. The implications of this are clear: the incense rite and vegetarian banquet may serve as expressions of filial piety. In a social context where Buddhist salvation is deemed as a filial responsibility, Buddhist rites are harmonious with Confucian principles and may serve as means to express one's Confucian virtue. The ability to help departed ancestors easily became a requirement to do so. This requirement was strengthened by Buddhist beliefs about what happened to the soul at death.

According to Buddhist belief, the soul passed into an intermediate state of existence upon death lasting between seven and forty-nine days. At the end of each seven-day period, the soul may be reborn, providing that karmic forces are sufficient. At the end of forty-nine days, the soul will be reborn in hell unless otherwise dispatched. The message is clear: it is incumbent upon the living that provision be made for the soul's future. Failure to do so would amount to a serious breach in filial obligations. On this, see Kenneth Ch'en, *The Chinese Transformation of Buddhism* (Princeton: Princeton University Press, 1973), pp. 53–55.

CHAPTER 4

1. *Dōgen zenji zenshū*, ed. Kagamishima Genryū, Kawamura Kōdō, Suzuki Kakuzen, Kosaka Kiyū, et. al., 7 vols. (Tokyo: Shunjūsha, 1988–1993) (hereafter DZZ), 1: 469.

2. From my notes taken during interviewing the abbots at Mt. T'ien-t'ung and Mt. A-yü-wang, along with local officials from the tourism and religious administrative bureaus in December 2004, there are two main points that stand out. First, the local officials, apparently hearing that there are about ten million Sōtō sect adherents in Japan, inflated the number fourfold, following the style often used in the fanciful counting of Japanese new religious movements, which figure that a follower will bring all the members of his or her nuclear family into the fold. The second point is that the T'ien-t'ung abbot eloquently explained the connection between Juching and Dōgen as being based on a simple, intimate feeling that the teacher had finally found a prize pupil who could carry forth his message and the disciple had located the ideal mentor after struggling to find a teacher. I wrote in my notebook at this point in the conversation, "Dry is why..."

3. See Steven Heine, *Did Dōgen Go to China? What He Wrote and When He Wrote It* (New York: Oxford University Press, 2006).

4. T. Griffith Foulk, "The Historical Context of Dōgen's Monastic Rules," in Daihonzan Eiheiji, ed., *Dōgen zenji kenkyū ronshū* (Tokyo: Taishūkan shoten, 2002), p. 1017.

5. *Shōsan* was one style of informal sermon used by Dōgen in *Shōbōgenzō zuimonki* and *Eihei kōroku*, vol. 8, whereas the main style used in the *Shōbōgenzō* was the *jishu* style. Both are in Japanese vernacular rather than Sino-Japanese (*kanbun*).

6. Of the early Japanese Zen temples, Kenchōji in Kamakura was probably the closest to a "pure" seven-hall style. Also, Mt. T'ien-t'ung had an exceptionally large Monks Hall, initially built by Hung-chih in 1132–1134, which was 200 feet in length and 16 zhang (160 feet) in width, with a statue of Manjusri in the center of the hall enshrined as the holy monk; see Yifa, *The Origins of Buddhist Monastic Codes in China: An Annotated Translation and Study of the Chanyuan Qinggui* (Honolulu: University of Hawaii Press, 2002) pp. 70–71.

7. See, for example, *Tenzokyōkun*, DZZ 5: 2–25.

8. Shunjō, who enjoyed support from the retired emperor Gotoba, the court aristocracy, and the third regent of the Kamakura shogunate, Hōjō Yasutoki, made the temple a center for the practice of the Precepts (Ritsu), Tendai, Zen, and Pure Land teachings. He is generally not considered a leader of Zen per se, but some of the ritual practices he learned from China and implemented in Japan are quite similar to what Eisai, Dōgen, and others brought over.

9. In *Shōbōgenzō* "Senmen"—one of two fascicles on hygiene along with "Senjō"—Dōgen says that the toothbrush was not being used in Chinese monasteries, but other evidence suggests it was in practice at the time; he also credits Ju-ching with starting a new tradition of washing during the third night watch.

10. Ishii Seijun, "Eiheiji senjutsu bunseki ni miru Dōgen zenji no sōdan un-ei," in Daihonzan Eiheiji, ed., *Dōgen zenji kenkyū ronshū* (Tokyo: Taishūkan shoten, 2002), pp. 409–40; and http://homepage1.nifty.com/seijun.

11. These figures may have been preceded by a monk named Kakua, who is said to have played a flute when asked in an imperial meeting to expound the tenets of Zen, indicating that he must have received authentic Ch'an training in China in 1171; see Martin Collcutt, *Five Mountains: The Rinzai Zen Monastic Institution in Medieval Japan* (Cambridge, MA: Harvard University Press, 1981), pp. 38–39, citing the *Genkō shakusho*.

12. The ranking of the Five Mountains temples was: 1. Mt. Ching-shan Wan-shou Ch'an ssu, of Hang-chou; 2. Mt. A-yü-wang-shan Kuang li Ch'an ssu, of Ming-chou; 3. Mt. T'ai-pai-shan T'ien-t'ung Ching-te Ch'an ssu, of Ming-chou; 4. Mt. Pei-shan Ch'ing-te ling-yin Ch'an ssu, of Hang-chou; 5. Mt. Nan-shan Ch'ing tz'u pao en kuang hsiao Ch'an ssu, of Hang-chou. The system actually consisted of some fifty temples in a three-tiered ranking. Japanese temples were influenced by a small handful of Sung Chinese temples with diagrams in the *Gozan jissatsu zu* held at Gikai's Daijōji temple in Kanazawa and in the *Kenchōji sashizū* based on Mt. T'ien-t'ung, which had an impact on both Sōtō and Rinzai sects. See Collcutt, *Five Mountains*, pp. 175–77.

13. Patricia Buckley Ebrey, *The Cambridge Illustrated History of China* (Cambridge: Cambridge University Press, 1996), p. 144.

14. It was a city advanced in printing and developing libraries and in early modern times was the place where the game of Mah jhong was developed based on traditional card and board games of chance.

15. The A-yü-wang specimen was supposedly one of 84,000 relics that King Asoka disseminated and is housed in a seven-step stupa about twenty inches high in the reliquary. The other two relics, according to temple sources that indicate that Jiang Zemin visited the A-yü-wang relic in 2002, are a tooth held in a Beijing temple and a finger joint held in Xian (formerly the T'ang capital, Chang-an). Dating the origins of the monasteries as being in the Ch'an order is more complicated than it might seem, because these are the dates that they seem to have been awarded "Public" monastery status, and the assumption is that at the time this designation meant "Ch'an," although there is some ambiguity that remains in textual and epigraphical evidence. See Morten Schlütter, "Vinaya Monasteries, Public Abbacies, and State Control of Buddhism under the Song (960–1279)," in William M. Bodiford, ed., *Going Forth: Visions of Buddhist Vinaya* (Honolulu: University of Hawaii Press, 2005), pp. 104–5. Mt. Ta-mei in the Ming-chou area also became a Public temple at this point.

16. This fascicle includes a lengthy passage in which Dōgen describes two visits to the temple, first in the summer retreat of 1223 and again two years later during the summer when he was first training under Ju-ching. The passage indicates that Dōgen was very much dissatisfied with the lack of Ch'an insight on the part of the monks, but it is also the case that he was critical of all of the temples he visited, including Mt. T'ien-t'ung until Ju-ching arrived there in 1225. Furthermore, Mt A-yü-wang did not have a seven-hall style monastic layout characteristic of Mt. T'ien-t'ung and some other Ch'an temples.

17. Heine, *Did Dōgen Go to China?*

18. DZZ 1: 31–33.

19. See Nakaseko Shōdō, "*Shōbōgenzō* 'Busshō' kan no rokushushōchi to Minamoto no Sanetomo no shari nōkotsu mondai ni tsuite," in *Dōgen zenji kenkyū ronshū* (Fukui City, Japan: Daihonzan Eiheiji, 2002). The passage in "Busshō" refers to visiting "six" sites at the temple, but it is unclear whether this is meant in a literal or metaphorical sense. A key point is that travel from the home temple during the summer retreat was strictly forbidden, as itinerancy (*tangaryō*) was limited to the nine-month period of "liberation" outside the retreat period. Nakaseko refutes a theory proferred by Sugio Gen'yū that Dōgen went to Mt. A-yü-wang during the summer retreat of 1225 (the year that Hōjō Masako died) to fulfill a memorial mission for the deceased shogun, Sanetomo, who was installed at age eleven in 1203 and assassinated on new year's day in 1219 on the steps of the Hachiman Jingu shrine in Kamakura. Already stripped of much of his power well before his death, Sanetomo fervently dedicated himself to poetry and cultural activities and apparently always had a dream of going to Mt. A-yü-wang in China to visit the relic and even tried to set sail, but the boat was defective. According to tradition, the monk Kakushin took his remains to the Chinese temple, but Sugio suggests that it was actually Dōgen who later became a teacher for a brief period and administered the bodhisattva precepts to Kakushin in

1242. See Sugio, "Minamoto Sanetomo no nyōsō kikaku to Dōgen zenji," *Shūgaku kenkyū* 8 (1976): 41–46.

20. DZZ 1: 197–98. Te-kuang was attacked by Dōgen apparently because he sanctioned the controversial rival Daruma school, which was proscribed by the government in 1193.

21. Hee-Jin Kim, *Dōgen Kigen—Mystical Realist* (Tucson: University of Arizona Press, 1975), p. 59.

22. DZZ 7: 14.

23. See Kōdō Kawamura, *Eihei kaizan Dōgen zenji gyōjō: Kenzeiki* (Tokyo: Taishūkan shoten, 1975), pp. 27–30.

24. "Without sojourning . . . in quiet serenity" echoes the admonitions by Ju-ching, for example, "You must immediately make your dwelling in steep mountains and dark valleys, and nurture the sacred embryo of the buddhas and patriarchs for a long time. You will surely reach the experience of the ancient virtuous ones." See Takeshi James Kodera, *Dōgen's Formative Years in China* (Boulder, CO: Prajna Press, 1980), p. 122.

25. DZZ 4: 82–84. See also *Dōgen's Extensive Record: A Translation of the Eihei Kōroku*, trans. Taigen Dan Leighton and Shohaku Okumura (Boston: Wisdom, 2004), pp. 445-46.

26. DZZ 7: 170.

27. Earl Miner, *An Introduction to Japanese Court Poetry* (Stanford: Stanford University Press, 1968), p. 127.

28. DZZ 4: 290.

29. DZZ 3: 206–8.

30. DZZ 3: 274.

31. DZZ 4: 120–24.

32. DZZ 3: 230. *Jōdō*, literally "ascending the hall," which are sermons collected in the first seven volumes of the *Eihei kōroku*, were the standard form of preaching in Sung China. Sermons occurred regularly in the Dharma Hall, during which the rank-and-file monks were standing while the master sat on the high seat on the altar. In the *Ch'an-yüan ch'ing-kuei* of 1103, the primary source of Chinese monastic regulations that Dōgen relied on for his *Eihei shingi* text on monastic rules, the *jōdō* were supposed to be given on special occasions, as well as six times a month, on the 1st, 5th, 10th, 15th, 20th, and 25th days of the month. Many of the recorded sayings (*goroku*) of the classical masters include *jōdō*. Although there might sometimes have been questions and discussions from the monks, in *Eihei kōroku*, usually only Dōgen's words were recorded. In this sermon, "After a pause Dōgen said: If you want to know a person from Jiang-nan, go toward where the partridges sing." This comment relates to a Ch'an saying Dōgen cites elsewhere, "I always remember Jiang-nan in the third month, when the partridges sing and a hundred blossoms open." Jiang-nan is the area south of the Yangtze River, where many Ch'an temples were located and which functioned as a symbol of spiritual renewal.

33. DZZ 3: 242.

34. DZZ 4: 30.

35. DZZ 3: 162–64.

36. This section after the pause, from "Without ceasing, one, two, three raindrops..." until the end of this sermon, is cited from the first volume of the recorded sayings of Ju-ching.

37. According to Collcutt, the seven-hall style, which was "no more than the essential minimum skeleton of the Zen monastery," may have developed in the Sung and been transferred to Kamakura Japan, but "does not seem to have been applied to Chinese monasteries"; in *Five Mountains*, p. 186.

38. Kuroda Toshio, *Nihon chūsei no shakai to shūkyō* (Tokyo: Iwanami shoten, 1990). For other interpretations in the complex issues involved in examining the changes in Buddhism during the Kamakura era, see Matsuo Kenji, *Shin Kamakura Bukkyō no tanjō* (Tokyo: Kōdansha gendai shinsho, 1995); and Kenji Matsuo, "What is Kamakura New Buddhism? Official Monks and Reclusive Monks," *Japanese Journal of Religious Studies* 14/1–2 (1997): 179–89. Matsuo tends to support Ishii's approach but also broadens the context considerably by explaining Dōgen as an example of a "reclusive monk" (*tonseisō*), along with Hōnen, Shinran, Nichiren, and others, who established orders that catered to the needs of monks and laypersons alike, although in contrast to Ishii, Matsuo also stresses the role of individual salvation in these movements.

39. It should be stressed that the laypersons that Dōgen dealt with at Eiheiji were a far different group than the literati in Sung China, where "The state had lost interest in all but the most illustrious monks and the greatest monasteries. All these factors caused elite Buddhism to focus its efforts on literati and local government officials in order to obtain needed financial and political support," in Morten Schlütter, "Silent Illumination, Kung-an Introspection, and the Competition for Lay Patronage in Sung Dynasty Ch'an," in Peter N. Gregory and Daniel A. Getz, eds., *Buddhism in the Sung* (Honolulu: University of Hawaii Press), p. 137.

Also, one area Dōgen did not attend to was funerals; as Duncan Ryūken Williams points out, Dōgen "did not include funerary procedures in his ritual repertoire, so it was not until the third-generation monk Gikai's death in 1309 that the first Sōtō Zen funeral was conducted under Chinese Chan monastic regulations. The first Japanese Sōtō Zen monastic regulations, which included a section on how to perform funerals was the *Keizan shingi*," in *The Other Side of Zen: A Social History of Sōtō Zen Buddhism in Tokugawa Japan* (Princeton: Princeton University Press, 2005), p. 40.

40. The Rinzai Rinka temples were generally based in Kyoto with a network of countryside temples, such as Daitokuji and Myōshinji, with prominent intellectual/literary abbots such as Daitō, Ikkyū, and Bassui, and the Sōtō Rinka temples were generally in rural areas with popular preachers such as Gasan Jōseki, Tsūgen Jakurei, and Gennō Shinshō.

41. Ishikawa Rikizan, "Chūsei Sōtōshū ni okeru kirigami sōjō ni tsuite," *Indogaku Bukkyōgaku kenkyū* 30/2 (1982): 742–46.

CHAPTER 5

1. See, for example, Richard Payne, ed., *Tantric Buddhism in East Asia* (Boston: Wisdom Publications, 2006).

2. Robert Thurman, "Vajra Hermeneutics," in Donald Lopez, ed., *Buddhist Hermeneutics* (Honolulu: University of Hawaii Press, 1988), p. 122.

3. Thomas Kasulis, "Truth Words: The Basis of Kūkai's Theory of Interpretation," in Lopez, ed., *Buddhist Hermeneutics*, p. 260.

4. Ibid., p. 271.

5. Shohaku Okumura and Taigen Daniel Leighton, trans., *The Wholehearted Way: A Translation of Eihei Dōgen's "Bendōwa" with Commentary by Kōsho Uchiyama Roshi* (Boston: Tuttle, 1997), pp. 26–27.

6. Foreword by Ikkō Narasaki Roshi in Taigen Daniel Leighton and Shohaku Okumura, trans., *Dōgen's Pure Standards for the Zen Community: A Translation of Eihei Shingi* (Albany: State University of New York Press, 1996), p. x.

7. For a full discussion of the textual variants of "Fukanzazengi" and its indebtedness to Chinese Chan sources, see Carl Bielefeldt, *Dōgen's Manuals of Zen Meditation* (Berkeley: University of California Press, 1988). An abbreviation of the "Fukanzazengi" essay from 1243 called "Zazengi" is included as part of *Shōbōgenzō*. It includes mostly the procedural portions of "Fukanzazengi," with only minor revisions. See Kazuaki Tanahashi, ed. and trans., *Moon in a Dewdrop: Writings of Zen Master Dōgen* (New York: North Point Press, a division of Farrar, Straus and Giroux, 1985), pp. 29–30.

8. Taigen Dan Leighton and Shohaku Okumura, trans., *Dōgen's Extensive Record: A Translation of the Eihei Kōroku* (Boston: Wisdom Publications, 2004), p. 533.

9. Ibid., p. 534.

10. Ibid.

11. Leighton and Okumura, trans., *Dōgen's Pure Standards for the Zen Community*, p. 63.

12. Ibid., pp. 63–64.

13. Bielefeldt, trans., *Dōgen's Manuals of Zen Meditation*, p. 190. See also Kazuaki Tanahashi, ed. and trans., *Beyond Thinking: Meditation Guide by Zen Master Dogen* (Boston: Shambhala, 2004), p. 38; and Gudō Wafu Nishijima and Chōdō Cross, trans., *Master Dogen's Shobogenzo*, vol. 2 (Woods Hole, MA: Windbell Publications, 1996), p. 93.

14. For this story in the 1241 *Shōbōgenzō* essay "Kokyō" ("Ancient Mirror"), see Nishijima and Cross, *Master Dogen's Shobogenzo*, vol. 1, pp. 239–59. For the version with Dōgen's verse comments in *Eihei kōroku*, see Leighton and Okumura, *Dōgen's Extensive Record*, pp. 561–62.

15. Leighton and Okumura, *Dōgen's Extensive Record*, pp. 561–62.

16. Bielefeldt, trans., *Dōgen's Manuals of Zen Meditation*, p. 193.

17. Ibid., p. 197.

18. Ibid., p. 200.

19. See Leighton and Okumura, *Dōgen's Extensive Record*, pp. 19–25.

20. Ibid., p. 292.

21. Ibid., p. 404.

22. For Dōgen's attitude toward this element of the traditional Chan practice schedule, see dharma hall discourse 193, in ibid., p. 210.

23. Ibid., p. 466.

24. Ibid., p. 472.

25. Ibid. pp. 257–58.

26. See Okumura and Leighton, *The Wholehearted Way*, pp. 14–19, 21–24, 43, 63–65, 105–6.

27. Hee-Jin Kim, *Eihei Dōgen: Mystical Realist* (Boston: Wisdom Publications, 2004), p. 55.

28. Leighton and Okumura, *Dōgen's Extensive Record*, p. 258.

29. Tanahashi, *Beyond Thinking*, p. 79.

30. Ibid.

31. Ibid., p. 80.

32. Leighton and Okumura, *Dōgen's Extensive Record*, pp. 328–29. The story also appears as case 59 in Dōgen's collection of ninety kōans with his verse comments in volume nine of *Eihei kōroku*, in ibid., pp. 575–76; and in the *Shōbōgenzō* essay, "Henzan" ("All-Inclusive Study"), Tanahashi, *Moon in a Dewdrop*, p. 198. It may be noted that the historicity of Tang dynasty Chan stories is generally suspect, as many of them were not recorded until centuries after the supposed event, and there is no means to verify the oral traditions. Nevertheless, these stories were cherished throughout the later Chan/Zen traditions.

33. Leighton and Okumura, *Dōgen's Extensive Record*, p. 328.

34. Okumura and Leighton, *The Wholehearted Way*, p. 30.

35. Ibid., p. 31.

36. Leighton and Okumura, *Dōgen's Extensive Record*, pp. 519–22.

37. Ibid., p. 521.

38. Ibid.

39. Ibid.

40. Ibid.

41. Ibid.

42. Tanahashi, *Beyond Thinking*, p. 94.

43. Ibid.

44. Leighton and Okumura, *Dōgen's Extensive Record*, p. 124. For other examples of how Dōgen uses *jōdō* or dharma hall discourses as enactment rituals, see Taigen Dan Leighton, "The *Lotus Sutra* as a Source for Dōgen's Discourse Style," in Richard Payne and Taigen Dan Leighton, eds., *Discourse and Ideology in Medieval Japanese Buddhism* (London: RoutledgeCurzon, 2006).

45. Leighton and Okumura, *Dōgen's Extensive Record*, p. 507.

46. Dōgen recounts and comments on this story in dharma hall discourses 8 and 319 and calls Mazu's teaching "most intimate." See ibid., pp. 79, 292–93. Parts of this story are included in cases 30 and 33 of the kōan anthology *Mumonkan* (*Gateless Barrier*). See Zenkei Shibayama, *The Gateless Barrier: Zen Comments on the Mumonkan* (Boston: Shambhala, 2000), pp. 214–22, 235–39.

47. This story is cited by Dōgen as case 19 in his collection of 300 kōans without any of his own commentary in his *Shinji* (or *Mana*, i.e., Chinese) *Shōbōgenzō*, not to be confused with the more noted work *Shōbōgenzō* with long essays, often commenting

at length on kōans. See Kazuaki Tanahashi and John Daido Loori, trans., *The True Dharma Eye: Zen Master Dōgen's Three Hundred Kōans*, with commentary and verse by John Daido Loori (Boston: Shambhala, 2005), pp. 26–27. The story also is included as case 19 in the kōan anthology *Mumonkan* (*Gateless Barrier*). See Shibayama, *The Gateless Barrier*, pp. 140–47.

48. See Shunryū Suzuki, *Branching Streams Flow in the Darkness: Zen Talks on the Sandokai* (Berkeley: University of California Press, 1999). See also Carl Bielefeldt, T. Griffith Foulk, Taigen Leighton, and Shohaku Okumura, trans., "Harmony of Difference and Equality," in *Cultivating the Empty Field: The Silent Illumination of Zen Master Hongzhi*, trans. Taigen Leighton and Yi Wu (Boston: Tuttle and Co., 2000), pp. 74–75.

49. Leighton and Wu, *Cultivating the Empty Field*, pp. 72–73.

50. Ibid.

51. Ibid., p. 30.

52. Ibid., p. 37.

53. Thomas Cleary, ed. and trans., *Timeless Spring: A Soto Zen Anthology* (Tokyo: Weatherhill, 1980), p. 112.

54. Ibid., pp. 118–19.

55. See Shohaku Okumura, trans. and ed., *Dōgen Zen* (Kyoto: Kyoto Sōtō Zen Center, 1988), pp. 43–135. For more on Menzan, see David Riggs, "The Rekindling of a Tradition: Menzan Zuihō and the Reform of Japanese Sōtō Zen in the Tokugawa Era," Ph.D. Dissertation, University of California, Los Angeles, 2002.

56. Okumura, *Dōgen Zen*, p. 51.

57. Ibid., p. 52.

58. Ibid., p. 53.

59. Ibid., p. 73.

CHAPTER 6

1. In this section I am providing information for the reader to understand the steps taken to ensure reliability of the data. For further discussion on criteria used to evaluate qualitative versus quantitative data, see Roland Scholz and Olaf Tietje, *Embedded Case Study Methods: Integrating Quantitative and Qualitative Knowledge* (Thousand Oaks, CA: Sage Publications, 2002). On p. 242, they assert, "Dealing with the case enactively opens the door to intuitive thinking and understanding." Doing research "enactively" resonates with my mentor Wilfred Cantwell Smith's methodological orientation, which stresses that a primary aim of a religion scholar is to strive to see the world through the eyes of the people you are studying. Applying this to an ethnographic approach ideally leads to "intuitive thinking and understanding."

2. Paula Arai, *Women Living Zen: Japanese Sōtō Buddhist Nuns* (New York: Oxford University Press, 1999). This underscores the benefits of establishing extended relationships in the field. Not only would I not have known there was even a ritual called the *Anan Kōshiki*, I would also not have had an understanding of the context in which to see and analyze the significance of this ritual for their community.

3. There are several excellent examples that illustrate the nature of self-reflexivity in ethnographic research. Three notable ones from the field of religion are: Karen McCarthy Brown, *Mama Lola: A Vodou Priestess in Brooklyn* (Berkeley: University of California Press, 1991); Ann Grodzins Gold, *Fruitful Journeys: The Ways of Rajasthani Pilgrims* (Delhi: Oxford University Press, 1989); and Barbara Tedlock, *The Woman in the Shaman's Body: Reclaiming the Feminine in Religion and Medicine* (New York: Bantam Books, 2005). For an example of a study conducted in Japan out of the field of anthropology, see Dorinne Kondo, *Crafting Selves: Power, Gender, and Discourses of Identity in a Japanese Workplace* (Chicago: University of Chicago, 1990).

4. Clinical psychology has undergone a major shift or development. According to a clinical psychologist who is a leader in this new direction, Michael Yapko, Ph.D., the focus was exclusively on pathologies but has expanded to include attention to "studying people's strengths or people's capacity to overcome problems creatively." Michael Yapko, *Breaking Patterns of Depression* (New York: Broadway Books, 1997), p. 54. My scholarly aims are resonant with this shift that occurred in the field of clinical psychology. In this work, I am not seeking negative examples of where and how rituals did not help empower or heal, but where and how they did.

5. Catherine Bell, *Ritual Perspectives and Dimensions* (New York: Oxford University Press, 1997).

6. Ibid., p. 265.

7. Ibid.

8. Ibid., p. 267.

9. "Bendōwa" in Mizuno Yaoko, trans., *Shōbōgenzō*, vol. 1 (Tokyo: Iwanami shoten, 1993), p. 28.

10. "Genjō Kōan" in Mizuno, trans., *Shōbōgenzō*, vol. 1, pp. 53–61.

11. See Dōgen's *Eihei shingi* for more examples of this type of concern/activity.

12. The women under consideration in this work include nuns at Aichi Senmon Nisōdō in Nagoya, Japan, and lay women who are affiliated with this Sōtō Zen nunnery. I did not strive to find a sample that represents the spectrum of women in terms of demographics or types of practices because there is no data available to ascertain what the spectrum includes.

13. For more detailed information on Dōgen's teachings about women and his female disciples, see chapter 2 of my volume, *Women Living Zen*.

14. This explanation and insight is from my late mentor at Harvard University, Masatoshi Nagatomi Sensei.

15. These rituals are not included in the *Sōtōshū zensho* (eighteen volumes) or the *Zoku Sōtōshū zensho* (ten volumes). There is one chapter in an edited volume published under the auspices of the Zen sect by Ebie Gimyō, "Anan Kōshiki" in Sōtō-shū jissen sōsho hensan iinkai, ed., *Sōtō-shū jissen sōsho*, vol. 8. (Kiyomizu, Japan: Dao-zōsha, 1985).

16. For an in-depth exploration of how and why fundamental concepts of self and knowledge need to be taken into consideration, especially when researching people who are not continuous with the civilizations that gave rise to the Western academy, see Linda Tuhiwai Smith, *Decolonizing Methodologies: Research and*

Indigenous Peoples (Dunedin, NZ: University of Otago Press, 1999). Pages 47–48 include discussion of how a Greek-based concept of the individual is assumed in much of current academic research. Here is an excerpt from p. 48: "What makes ideas 'real' is the system of knowledge, the formations of culture, and the relations of power in which these concepts are located. What an individual is—and the implications this has for the way researchers or teachers ... might approach their work—is based on centuries of philosophical debate ... and systems for organizing whole societies predicated on these ideas."

17. Thomas Lewis, Fari Amini, and Richard Lannon, *A General Theory of Love* (New York: Vintage Books, 2000), p. 95. Other researchers have drawn a similar conclusion that "a powerfully affective resolution arises primarily from ritual or meditation and rarely, if ever, from a cognitive unification of antinomies alone," p. 162 of Eugene d'Aquili and Charles Laughlin, "The Neurobiology of Myth and Ritual," in Eugene d'Aquili, Charles Laughlin, and John McManus, eds., *The Spectrum of Ritual: A Biogenetic Structural Analysis* (New York: Columbia University Press, 1979), pp. 152–82. Unlike Buddhist-based ritual, this theory of ritual assumes a fundamental duality: "The *ultimate* union of opposites that is the aim of all human religious ritual is the union of contingent and vulnerable man with a powerful, possibly omnipotent force." Ibid., p. 162

18. Lewis, et al., *A General Theory of Love*, pp. 51–52.

19. Ibid., p. 53. This explanation of the mechanics of emotion is the most common, but it is not accepted by all. Most notably, the research of Richard Davidson, director of the Laboratory of Affective Neuroscience at the University of Wisconsin-Madison, contends that "the frontal lobes [in the neocortex] ... are the brain's executive center and play a role in regulating emotions," in "The Neuroscience of Emotion" in Daniel Goleman, narrator, *Destructive Emotions: How Can We Overcome Them? A Scientific Dialogue with the Dalai Lama* (New York: Bantam Books, 2003), pp. 179–204 (p. 186) There is agreement that the limbic system is associated with emotions, especially negative emotions, but explicating the specific relationship and mechanics between the limbic and neocortex regions of the brain and what role they play in human experience of emotions requires further research.

20. For an interdisciplinary volume that explores ritual from scientific and social scientific lenses, see d'Aquili, Laughlin, and McManus, eds., *The Spectrum of Ritual*. Several other studies focus on meditation, consciousness, and brain activity. Most notable are the studies done in conjunction with the Dalai Lama Tenzin Gyatso's Mind and Life Conferences. See Zara Houshmand, Robert Livingston, and B. Alan Wallace, *Consciousness at the Crossroads: Conversations with the Dalai Lama on Brain Science and Buddhism* (Ithaca, NY: Snow Lion Publications, 1999); and Goleman, narr., *Destructive Emotions*. One volume in particular examines Zen meditation. James H. Austin, M.D., *Zen and the Brain: Toward an Understanding of Meditation and Consciousness* (Cambridge, MA: MIT Press, 1998).

21. Eugene d'Aquili and Charles Laughlin also come to this conclusion in their chapter, "The Neurobiology of Myth and Ritual" in d'Aquili, Laughlin, and McManus,

eds., *The Spectrum of Ritual*, p. 160: "Religious ritual is always embedded in a cognitive matrix—a web of meaning."

22. Here, too, d'Aquili and Laughlin come to a similar conclusion that "ritual behavior is one of the few mechanisms at man's [and woman's] disposal that can possibly solve the ultimate problems and paradoxes of human existence," in *The Spectrum of Ritual*, p. 179.

23. Again, the work of d'Aquili and Laughlin resonates with the findings of this study. They find that "social unity is a common theme running through the myth associated with most human rituals," in *The Spectrum of Ritual*, p. 158.

24. Other *Kōshiki* include: *Daruma Daishi Kōshiki, Nehan Kōshiki, Yakushiji Kōshiki, Daihannya Kōshiki, Fudō Kōshiki,* and *Jizō Kōshiki.* More fully developed historical contextualization, description, and analysis of the *Anan Kōshiki* ritual is located in my chapter, "An Empowerment Ritual for Nuns in Contemporary Japan," in Ellison Banks Findly, ed., *Women's Buddhism, Buddhism's Women: Tradition, Revision, Renewal* (Boston: Wisdom Publications, 2000), pp. 119-30.

25. Catherine Bell, *Ritual Theory, Ritual Practice* (New York: Oxford University Press, 1992), p. 81.

26. For a fuller explanation of the dynamics of Zen healing rituals, please see Paula Arai, *Healing Zen: Japanese Buddhist Women's Rituals of Transformation* (Honolulu: University of Hawaii Press, forthcoming).

27. It would be interesting to do an interdisciplinary study involving ritual scholars with ethologists and neuroscientists to see if the rhythmic chanting characteristic of Zen ritual ceremonies results in a similar phenomenon observed by ethologists that "rhythmic quality in and of itself produces positive limbic discharges resulting in decreased distancing and increased social cohesion," in d'Aquili, Laughlin, and McManus, eds., *The Spectrum of Ritual*, p. 159. Barbara Lex has done a study on "The Neurobiology of Ritual Trance" that indicates such a study would yield positive findings. Her chapter is included in ibid., pp. 117-51.

28. "Ikka myōju" ["One Bright Pearl"] in Terada Tōru, ed., *Dōgen*, vol. 1 (Tokyo: Iwanami shoten, 1980), p. 105.

CHAPTER 7

1. In the completely different context of Asian Christianity, it may be worth mentioning that the same Chinese characters pronounced *shukusei* in Japanese are used as the translation of the Latin *consecratio* to indicate the "consecration" of a church or the appointment of a bishop.

2. Here, I will use the word "monastery" as an equivalent for the modern Japanese *sōdō* (literally "monk's hall") or *senmon dōjō* ("specialized practice place"). One important point to keep in mind is that, especially in the Rinzai school, these training monasteries have emerged in a form similar to the present one only during the mid-Tokugawa period. Strictly speaking, it is therefore not entirely appropriate to use the word "monasteries" for the Japanese training temples before the Tokugawa. The Chinese context is different, and I will follow the current

usage of speaking of "monasteries" for the huge temples where Chan was practiced.

3. The only specific publications I am aware of are, in chronological order, Nishio 1977/1986 and Cheng 2003.

4. Takahashi 1991, p. 197.

5. This function is described in fascicle 22 of the *Seven Slips of a Cloudy Satchel* (*Yunji qiqian*). The cult of this deity under the name Taishan fujun is alive in China. See Takahashi 1991, p. 152 and Masuda 1998, pp. 132–35.

6. See in particular Stephenson 2005.

7. Payne 2004, p. 196.

8. Concerning the various implications of "opening the hall" or "opening a mountain," see Heine 2002.

9. *Zengaku daijiten*, p. 144c and 511a.

10. T 49 no. 2035, p. 456b08–b22.

11. T 49 no. 2035, p. 354a20 and p. 456b13. The year given for this event is Shiguang 2. The *Fozu tongji* adds here that this marks the origin of "monasteries for the celebration of the sage's birthday" (*shengjie daochang*).

12. See Mohr 2006.

13. T 52 no. 2102, p. 29c19–34c26. Huayan's letters are anterior to the 425 edict.

14. T 52 no. 2102, p. 76c02. Some of Huiyuan's correspondence is translated in Robinson 1967, in particular passages included in "Spirit Does Not Perish" (pp. 196–99, paraphrase pp. 102–4).

15. T 49 no. 2035, p. 456b11–b16.

16. This is Cheng's assertion 2003, p. 602, but he doesn't provide enough evidence to be convincing.

17. T 47 no. 1979, p. 438a07–08. Similarly, the role of Fazang (643–721) legitimizing the court has recently been the object of a detailed examination. See Chen 2005.

18. The longest tributary of the Yangtze River.

19. *Tiansheng guangdenglu*, fascicle 22, Z 135 p. 821b18–822a01 (old edition p. 411b–c). Note that the expression translated as "His Majesty" corresponds to the Chinese *shengming*. The character *zhu* functions here as a verb that can be rendered as "invocating" or "celebrating."

20. *Chanyuan qinggui*, fascicle 7, ZZ 111 p. 916a05 (old edition p. 458c). Compare with Yifa 2002, p. 216.

21. In the sense given to this expression by John Langshaw Austin (1911–1960), who emphasized "speech acts."

22. Yanagida 1967.

23. For example: Yangqi Fanghui (992–1049) T 47 no. 1994B, p. 641a16–a17, T 47 no. 1994B, p. 646b02; Huanglong Huinan (1002–1069) T 47 no. 1993, p. 629c11–c12; and Wuzu Fayan (1024?–1104) T 47 no. 1995, p. 649a12.

24. T 47 no. 1997, p. 727c29–728a01. The fact that this expression appears in the *Baizhang Rules of Purity* just corroborates its late redaction, since it was completed in 1343. See T 48 no. 2025 p. 1114a01.

25. A discussion of this contemporary dimension has appeared in the newspaper *Mainichi*, evening edition of September 6, 2005, p. 2. My own research indicates that one of the first occurrences in a Japanese source might be the above-mentioned chapter on Kōgyoku in the *Nihon shoki*, fascicle 24. It records that after the Buddhists had failed in their intercession for rain and the empress Kōgyoku succeeded through her Daoist ritual, relieved "peasants exclaimed 'ten thousand years!' and said 'superior virtue [belongs to] the empress!' "

26. See Nakamura 2001, p. 622a.

27. See the entry for the Chinese character *shuku* in Katō 1983, p. 445. Like most characters, it is a combination of a radical giving the meaning, here the altar, and a phonetic element. The phonetic element also carries the meaning of "bringing down" the deity through prayer. The Chinese word *zhuwu* indicates someone who recites incantations or a shaman.

28. On the specificity of these spells within the Chinese context, see McBride 2005.

29. Although his date of death is usually cited as 1744, in fact Mujaku died on the first year of the Enkyō era, twelfth month, twenty-third day, at the age of 92. This corresponds to January 25, 1745. See Ōtsuki 1988, pp. 345b–46b.

30. Mujaku 1698, p. 513a.

31. Translation by Watson 1968, pp. 130–31 (emphasis added).

32. Sharf 2001 provides a useful discussion of the "sage" and how this figure was idealized, pp. 90–93.

33. This text is included in ZZ 111 pp. 972–1012 (old edition pp. 486c–506d). See also Foulk 2004, p. 303, and the entry in the *Zengaku daijiten*, p. 286b. The CBETA Chinese Electronic Tripitaka provides it as *Xuzangjing* vol. 63, no. 1248, pp. 571b01–591c22. See http://www.cbeta.org.

34. Mujaku 1698, pp. 512b–13a.

35. *Nihon shoki*, fascicle 24, chapter on Kōgyoku. See also Takahashi 1991, p. 151, and Masuda 1998, p. 193.

36. *Zhouli* 3, description of the office of the Great Master of Sacrificial Rites (*Dazongbo*). Text of the *Zhouli* retrieved from http://chinese.pku.edu.cn/david/zhouli.html (January 30, 2006).

37. Sometimes also translated as "Rituals for Sending Petitions to the Heavens."

38. Concerning this figure, see Sharf 2002, p. 52 and ff.

39. An alternative translation for *dōjō* is the literal rendition "arena of awakening" (*bodhimaṇḍa*) proposed by Faure 1996, p. 217.

40. On this point, see also Nishio 1977, p. 3.

41. T 82 no. 2582, p. 91b09–17; Suzuki Kakuzen 1988–1993, vol. 1, pp. 340–41.

42. The compound *seika* (also pronounced *shōka*) is difficult to translate because it refers to both the emperor's rule and to the benefits derived from his teachings (*kyōke*) and his virtue (he is regarded as a sage or a bodhisattva). Alternative translations could be "noble guidance, noble presence, virtuous leadership, or enlightening guidance." The adjective "noble" refers here to the usage of the Chinese character *sheng* to translate the Sanskrit *ārya*. The *Treasure Store Treatise* includes the term

shenghua, rendered as "the transformations of the sage" Sharf 2002, p. 217; T 45 no. 1857, p. 147a08).

43. T 82 no. 2582, p. 20c02–06; Suzuki Kakuzen 1988–1993, vol. 2, p. 476. It is important to notice that the manuscript of *Bendōwa* contains a corresponding passage, but the compound *seika* is missing. Suzuki Kakuzen 1988–1993, vol. 2, p. 551.

44. See Nishio 1977, pp. 10–24, and Foulk 2006, p. 140.

45. The original place of Keizan in the Sōtō tradition is examined by Faure (1996).

46. T 82 no. 2589, p. 425c25–c26.

47. T 82 no. 2589, p. 425c12.

48. Kraft 1992, p. 23.

49. See the fascinating account of this in Amino 1986.

50. T 82 no. 2588; mentioned by Faure 1996, p. 75.

51. T 82 no. 2588, p. 423c07.

52. Rudimentary information on the Eihōji is found in the *Zengaku daijiten*, p. 89a. The complete name of this temple is Kokeizan Eihōji, but the monastery is simply called Kokei sōdō. The evidence of *Shukushin* still being performed was found on http://www.tajimi.com/eihoji/ekoumyo.html (retrieved on October 2, 2005).

53. The Shimabara and Amakusa insurrection occurred in 1637. On this period and the role of Buddhist monks in the "pacification" of the region, see Mohr 2002.

54. Preface to the Ōbaku *shingi*, T 82 no. 2607, p. 766a10–11.

55. T 82 no. 2607, p. 766a14–a15.

56. A clear reference to the *Baizhang Rules of Purity*, whose first section has the same title. T 48 no. 2025, p. 1111b09.

57. The word *guowei* (J. *kai*) indicates a rank obtained as retribution for good deeds in a previous existence, but it can suggest the ultimate fruit of Buddhahood (C. *foguowei*, J. *bukkai*). See Nakamura 2001, p. 177a.

58. T 82 no. 2607, p. 766b22–b26. Kimura's modern Japanese translation is not reliable, 2005, p. 395.

59. It is included in the sutra *Sheng wuliangshou jueding guangmingwang rulai tuoluoni jing*, T 19 no. 937. Note the use of the word *Sheng* for "holy" or "noble" at the beginning of the title.

60. T 81 no. 2579. This monastic code is still used to a certain extent in present-day Rinzai monasteries. See Foulk 2006, p. 153.

61. Baroni 2000.

62. A picture taken around 1926 shows this inscription on the Treasure Hall of the Great Hero (i.e., Śākyamuni, Daxiong baodian) at Huangboshan (Wanfusi). See the photograph at the beginning of Yamada 1926.

63. See Mohr 1994/2000 and, more specifically on Hakuin, Mohr 1999.

64. First year of the Kaei era, twelfth month, eighth day. T 81 no. 2574, p. 513a20.

65. T 81 no. 2574, p. 513a26–b03. Compare with the more concise account of the original in T 80 no. 2548, p. 94c05–08.

66. *Biography of Tōrei*, age 48. Nishimura 1982, p. 209. In this case, nominal funerary tablets (*ihai*) have been entrusted to Ryūtakuji. This usage should be

differentiated from the prescribed placing of three tablets (*sanpai*) dedicated to the present emperor and his family in front of the altar in Zen temples. On the latter usage, see the detailed description in the Mochizuki dictionary (Tsukamoto 1973, vol. 2, pp. 1633c–34a).

67. Miura 1985, p. 72. Seisetsu became teacher at the Shōzokuin monastery of Engakuji in 1781 and thoroughly reformed it.

68. See Victoria 2003, p. 232.

69. Concerning Sōgen's controversial attitude during the war, see Victoria 1997: 162–66.

70. Some discussion of it is found in Mohr 1999.

71. T 82 no. 2607, p. 766c02–c03.

72. Sharf 2002, p. 91.

CHAPTER 8

1. S-Chūkai, vol. 4.

2. My deepest gratitude to Professor Kosaka Kiyū, who read the core *Kinhinki* with me at Komazawa University. Some years later Professor Tatsuguchi Myōsei of Ryūkoku University spent long hours with me working through the maze of details of vinaya texts and travelers' reports used by Menzan in his commentary. His generous patience is as boundless as my appreciation. My thanks to the Japan Foundation and to the Numata Foundation for their financial support during various parts of this research. The electronic texts of the Chinese Buddhist Electronic Text Association were invaluable in tracking down Menzan's quotations. My appreciation to them for making this resource freely available.

3. Azuma Ryūshin, *Sōtōshū: Wagaka no shūkyō* (Tokyo: Daihōrinkaku, 1983), p. 245.

4. Gary Gach, *The Complete Idiot's Guide to Understanding Buddhism* (New York: Alpha Books, 2001), p. 175.

5. Kawamura Yasutarō, *Zengaku hōten* (Kyoto: Baiyu shoin, 1910); Kuruma Takadō, *Zenmon Sōtōshū ten* (Tokyo: Komeisha, 1930); and Ono Genmyō, *Bussho kaisetsu daijiten* (Tokyo: Daitō shuppan, 1933–36, 1974), p. 3: 391.

6. Janine Anderson Sawada, *Confucian Values and Popular Zen: Sekimon shingaku in Eighteenth-Century Japan* (Honolulu: University of Hawaii Press, 1993), p. 108.

7. See David E. Riggs, "The Life of Menzan Zuihō, Founder of Dōgen Zen," *The Japan Review* 16 (2004): 67–100. Menzan's role in the Sōtō reform is discussed in David E. Riggs, "The Rekindling of a Tradition: Menzan Zuihō and the Reform of Japanese Sōtō Zen in the Tokugawa Era." (Ph.D. diss., University of California, 2002).

8. Helen J. Baroni, *Obaku Zen: The Emergence of the Third Sect of Zen in Tokugawa Japan* (Honolulu: University of Hawaii Press, 2000).

9. Kagamishima Genryū, "Endonkai to Busso Shōden bosatsukai," in *Dōgen Zenji to sono shuhen* (Tokyo: Daitō shuppansha, 1985), p. 161.

10. William M. Bodiford, "Dharma Transmission in Sōtō Zen: Manzan Dōhaku's Reform Movement," *Monumenta Nipponica* 46/4 (1991): 423–51.

11. ZZ 63#1245. Kagamishima Genryū, Satō Tatsugen, and Kosaka Kiyū, eds., *Yakuchū Zennen shingi* (Tokyo: Sōtōshū shūmuchō, 1972); and T. Griffith Foulk, "'Rules of Purity' in Japanese Zen," in Steven Heine and Dale S. Wright, eds., *Zen Classics: Formative Texts in the History of Zen Buddhism* (Oxford: Oxford University Press, 2006), p. 140.

12. Mochizuki Shinkō, *Bukkyō daijiten* (Kyoto: Sekai seiten kankō kyōkai, 1933–1936), p. 1: 572.

13. ZZ 63#1222: 15b23–c15.

14. Kagamishima, Satō, and Kosaka, eds., *Yakuchū Zennen shingi*, pp. 81, 364.

15. ZZ 63#1246: 558a13.

16. Mujaku Dōchū, *Zenrin shōkisen* (Tokyo: Seishin shobō, 1963), p. 336.

17. D 2.

18. ZZ 2b:21: 293a–324b.

19. D 1:160.6.

20. D 2:317.

21. D 2:357.

22. Takashi James Kodera, *Dogen's Formative Years in China: A Historical Study and Annotated Translation of the Hōkyō-ki* (London: Routledge and Kegan Paul, 1980).

23. S-Shūgen 2: 427a11–13.

24. S-Chūkai-4: 623–37.

25. Menzan only uses the name *Eihei shingi*, but he is referring to the same passages from the *Bendōhō* that were discussed in the introduction.

26. There is nothing like this passage in the *Sarvāstivādavinaya*, nor anything close in the canon, as far as I can determine. One of the eighty characteristics of the Buddha is his magnificent walk, like a great white bird; see Nakamura Hajime, *Bukkyō go daijiten* (Tokyo: Tokyo shoboku, 1981), p. 245.

27. The text has "stand for a short time," just as Menzan quotes it. Perhaps the mistake he is referring to is the earlier quote about how to hold the hands, and then to sit a short while, where Menzan altered it to read stand. ZZ 63#1222: c03b.

28. The word rendered as "knees" is *po*, which usually means shoulder or shoulder blade. The phrase in parentheses is Menzan's addition, and Menzan's chosen meaning of knee is indeed found in the *Shih-ming*, a Later Han era list of definitions collected by Liu Xi. The definition is at the end of the eighth section in the second chapter, exactly as Menzan has quoted. This is, however, a meaning that is not attested in any of the other dictionaries I consulted. Furthermore, the progression of the lower body part to the upper body argues for taking the word as shoulder blades, the most straightforward reading.

29. Prajñātāra is regarded as the teacher of Bodhidharma. This stock phrase, which is inverted here from the usual order, can be found in the third case of the *Ts'ung-chung lu*, T 48#2004: 229a.

30. Menzan expresses no reservations about using the *Hsiu-ch'an yao-chüeh*, but according to Ono, the authenticity of the text is suspect. It claims to be the record of a 677 discussion with the Indian monk Buddhapālita, but the prefaces to the text

included in the *Zokuzōkyō* say it was copied in 1077 in China and compiled in 1784 in Japan; see Ono, *Bussho kaisetsu daijiten*, p. 5: 84.

31. S-Chūkai 4: 628a1–5.

32. ZZ 63#1222: 15b23–c15.

33. S-Shingi 31b11.

CHAPTER 9

1. The founding members of the SZBA are: Tenshin Reb Anderson, Chozen Jan Bayes, Bernard Tetsugen Glassman, Keido Les Kaye, Jakusho Bill Kwong, Daido John Loori, Gempo Merzel, and Sojun Mel Weltsman.

2. SZBA 2004b.

3. This essay represents a substantially revised version of an address delivered at the First National conference of the Soto Zen Buddhist Association, Great Vow Monastery, Caltskanie, Oregon. I thank the organizers of that event for providing me an opportunity to discuss this topic.

4. In this chapter the word "Soto" is spelled without macrons when used in reference to North America but with macrons (Sōtō) when used in reference to Japan.

5. DZZ 1.376.

6. DZZ 1.376–377.

7. DZZ 1.377.

8. Schlütter 2005, pp. 152–57.

9. Regarding China, see Welch 1963 and 1967. Regarding Korea, see Buswell 1992, pp. 22, 149–50. Vietnam presents an ambiguous case. Nguyen 1997, pp. 98–99, states that Vietnam lacks any identifiable Zen monasteries or Zen communities, but that nonetheless Vietnamese Buddhist leaders always have claimed a Zen identity whenever they wished to assert their own orthodoxy.

10. Wright 1992, pp. 39–40.

11. Yifa 2002, pp. 88–89.

12. Bodiford 1991.

13. Bodiford 2000.

14. Tamamura 1981a and 1981b; Welch 1963, pp. 136–40.

15. I use the term "transmission documents" as a collective designation for a variety texts, scrolls, certificates, diplomas, sheets of paper, and booklets, the possession of which would be restricted to initiates. These include (but are not limited to): succession certificates (*shisho*), blood lineages (*kechimyaku*), lineage charts (*shūhazu*), dharma scrolls (*hokkan*), certificates (*kirikami*), transcripts (*shōmono*), secret initiation registers (*hissanchō*), and so forth.

16. Ishikawa 2002.

17. Schlütter 2005.

18. Reichelt 1927, p. 271, and Welch 1963.

19. Foulk 1999, pp. 154–55.

20. *Jingde chuandeng lu*, fasc. 1, pp. 204b–205b.

21. *Genkō shakusho*, fasc. 7, p. 86a–b.

22. For examples of specific types of ritual performances, see Bodiford 2000 for medieval Japan and Welch 1963 for early twentieth-century China.

23. See Bodiford 1991.

24. Contemporary North America similarly lacks established norms or social expectations for its Zen Centers.

25. Bodiford 1993, pp. 64, 85–86.

26. Ibid., pp. 128–35.

27. Ibid., p. 133.

28. The term *zuise* seems to be unique to Japanese Sōtō. Kuriyama 1980, p. 201 explains it as a contraction of the standard Buddhist terms "auspicious" (*zui*) and "appearance in the world" (*shusse*), which allude to the manner in which Sakyamuni Buddha's appearance in our world (*shutsugen o se*) was accompanied by auspicious omens. Zen texts use the word *shusse* to refer to the debut abbotship of a priest at a teaching monastery, whose inauguration as a new Zen teacher is likened to the appearance in our world of a new Buddha. The Japanese Sōtō tradition takes this idea one step further by defining an "auspicious appearance" (*zuise*) as a symbolic inauguration as an honorary abbot at Eiheiji or Sōjiji (or both).

29. Modern Japanese Sōtō recognizes four broad classes of religious establishments: head temples (*honzan*, i.e., Sōjiji and Eiheiji); teaching monasteries (*kakuchi*), where ninety-day training retreats occur at least once a year; dharma temples (*hōchi*); and ordinary temples (*jun hōchi*). For details, see Nara and Nishimura 1979, pp. 24–26.

30. The procedure for *zuise* is not included in *Shōwa shūtei Sōtōshū gyōji kihan* (1988), the comprehensive manual of Sōtō rituals compiled by the Sōtō headquarters. It is described in detail in *Sōtōshū hōshiki sahō shashin kaisetsu* (1983), which is difficult to obtain.

31. For details, see Bodiford 2006.

32. Bodiford 1991.

33. For example, Robert Bellah 1985, pp. 151–52. Bellah specifically cites Kasulis 1981, who in turn draws on Watsuji Tetsurō's (1889–1960) notion of *nengen* (literally, the human realm) as providing an alternative view of human nature that escapes from the excessive emphasis on individuality found in European thought; see Watsuji 1996.

34. The Sōtō School is incorporated under the Religious Juridical Persons Law as an umbrella (*hōkatsu*) organization for affiliated temples and organizations, each one of which also might be independently incorporated under that same law. Under this law, the school operates in accordance with three sets of governing documents: Sōtōshū Constitution (*Sōtōshū shūken*); Regulations for the Religious Juridical Person Sōtōshū (*Shūkyō hōnin Sōtōshū kisoku*), and Sōtōshū Standard Procedures (*Sōtōshū kitei*). The first two of these are reprinted in Nara and Nishimura 1979, pp. 9–17 and 36–46. While the precise wording of these texts is subject to regular review and revision, the main outline presented in the 1979 version remains unchanged.

35. See note 9.

36. Nara and Nishimura 1979, pp. 25 and 31.

37. Ecclesiastical status reflects one's academic qualifications for providing religious instruction. The levels from bottom to top are: instructor third class (*santō kyōshi*), instructor second class (*nitō kyōshi*), instructor first class (*ittō kyōshi*), instructor proper (*sei kyōshi*), adjunct senior instructor (*gon daikyōshi*), senior instructor (*daikyōshi*), adjunct prefect (*gon daikyōsei*), and prefect (*daikyōsei*). See Nara and Nishimura 1979, pp. 23–24.

38. Dharma seniority reflects one's religious qualifications and devotion to traditional forms of Buddhist practice. The levels from bottom to top are: elder (*jōza*), chief seat (*zagen*), upādhyāya (*oshō*), and great upādhyāya (*daioshō*). See Nara and Nishimura 1979, pp. 23–24.

39. Jaffe 2001.

40. I am using the phrases "world imagined" and "world lived" in the senses coined by Geertz 1966 as the worldview taught by religion and the ethos enacted through religious rituals, respectively.

41. Different family models might well produce different Zen outcomes. The Zen teacher Victor Hori has noted (1994) that Chinese Americans who participated in one week-long Zen training retreat commented on how the practice helped them better comprehend their indebtedness to their families, while European Americans at the same retreat spoke only of their own personal spiritual progress. I thank David Chappell (2005) for drawing my attention to Hori's essay.

42. A very telling incident occurred in 1998 when the leader of one Zen Center in North America told the editorial board of the Soto Text Translation Project that members of his center would feel more comfortable if the translations of daily liturgy could omit the word "Buddha."

43. Wetzel 2002.

44. The SZBA intends for the Dharma Heritage Ceremony to be performed periodically (about once every three years) and for it to move from location to location so that it will not become identified with any one Soto faction or institution (SZBA 2004b).

45. *Harmony of Difference and Sameness* is an English translation of the *Santongqi* (*Sandōkai*), a hymn or poem attributed to the priest Shitou Xiqian (J. Sekitō Kisen, pp. 700–90).

46. This quest is by no means unique to Zen communities but is faced by all minority religions whether they are splinter sects from established denominations, based in immigrant communities, or composed largely of converts. Recent years have witnessed an explosive growth in the academic study of Asian religions, particularly Buddhism, in America. For further reading, the following works can be recommended: Heine and Prebish 2003; Morreale 1998; Numrich 1996; Prebish 1999; Prebish and Baumann 2002; Prebish and Tanaka 1998; Tweed and Prothero 1999; Williams and Queen 1999; and Yoo 1999.

Index